WARNINGS FROM THE LORD

Godsword Godswill Onu

Second Edition: 2014

ISBN: 978-1508816003

Copyright © 2014 by Godsword Godswill Onu

Many Scriptural quotations or citations were paraphrased, abridged, edited, or summarized, and a combination of the New King James Version and the King James Version of the Holy Bible were used, except where indicated otherwise.

Published by:
*Godsword Christian Publications,
Okigwe, Nigeria.*

*All Rights Reserved
Never duplicate this book/ebook for any commercial purpose, by any means (paper, electronic, digital, internet, etc), without an express permission from either Apostle Godsword or the publisher. Excerpts can be used for those doing research, preaching, teaching, writing, etc. For the ebooks, if you want to share to another person's computer/electronic system or to the public on any platform, do not share the whole/complete ebook (except to your husband or wife); but you may share/post/use or reshare/repost/reuse an excerpt or part of the ebook.*

For order, enquiry, seminar, prayer, sponsorship, comments, programmes, etc, contact:
APOSTLE GODSWORD GODSWILL ONU
WHOLE LIFE SPIRIT-WORD MINISTRIES
A.k.a. HOLY GHOST AND GODSWORD CHRISTIAN NETWORK,
OKIGWE, IMO STATE, NIGERIA.

Call or text: +234 8030917546, 8052563967, 8020648283, 8092582282.
E-mail: godswordgodswill@yahoo.com

TABLE OF CONTENTS

Dedications...5
Acknowledgments/Appreciation...6
Preface..8
Introduction..9
Do Not Love the World..11
The Law of Liberty..19
Hell...21
The Power of Sin to Bring Curses..27
The Works of the Flesh and Youthful Lusts..31
Making Your Calling and Election Sure...37
The Rapture of the Saints..43
Running the Race..47
Signs of His Coming and of the End of the Age...55
End-time Realities...59
The Judgment of the Last Day...63
Testing and Proving All Things...69
The Laws of God's Kingdom...71
God Is No Respecter of Persons..75
The Revelation of God's Judgment and Wrath...83
Living in Pleasure...87
The Great Tribulation and the Beast/Antichrist...93
The It-doesn't-matter Syndrome..99
Speaking Lies in Hypocrisy...105
Running After Prophecies and Miracles..109
Robbing God...113
Chastening the Believers...115
Punishment for Backsliding...117
Evil Company Corrupts Good Manners...123
You Must be Born Again..127
Knowing and Understanding the Word of God..131
Confronting Your Confrontations...135
The Spiritual Christian..143
Secrets to Successful Ministry..149
Abounding in the Fruit of the Spirit...153
Pleasing God...157
Being Fruitful and Productive...165
A Heaven to Gain and a Hell to Avoid...169
Being Strong in the Lord...175
Becoming a Prayer-warrior...181
Obedience, Holiness, and Righteousness..187
Being Led by God..191
Jesus Christ Comes Very Soon..197
False Ministers and Agents of Darkness...203
Indecent Dressing and Outward Appearance..209
The Believer Should Not Perish..213

Receiving, Thinking, Believing, Confession, and Possession...219
Watchfulness, Vigilance, and Sobriety..225
The Wrong Mentality..231
The Immutability of God's Word and Standard..239
Sin and Disobedience..245
Psalms About Holiness, Obedience, Goodness, and Righteousness and the Rewards..........251
Demonic and Satanic Activities Today..255
Divine Revelations and Near Death Experiences (NDE's)...259
Dressing and Outward Appearance (Special Edition)..279
Books by Apostle Godsword...312

DEDICATIONS

I dedicate this work to the Almighty God the Father, Who loves us so dearly; to His Son, the Lord Jesus Christ, Who is my Lord and Saviour; to the Holy Spirit of the Living God, Who is my Great Helper and Comforter; and to all those, who love the Lord Jesus Christ sincerely, and want to know and practice the Truth.

ACKNOWLEDGMENTS/APPRECIATION

I appreciate my Heavenly Father, Who gave me Jesus Christ – my Lord and Saviour. I thank my Lord Jesus Christ, Who gave me the Holy Spirit – the Spirit of Wisdom and of Power. Thank You, Holy Spirit, for making the writing of this book possible; when I consider the strength of the teaching anointing, and when I feel it, I marvel how awesome the Anointing of the Holy Spirit is!

I acknowledge the efforts, prayers, contributions, and encouragements, in one way or the other, of my Christian brothers and sisters, who equip and are being equipped, for the work of the ministry, for the edifying of the Body of Christ, till we all come to the unity of the faith and of the Knowledge of the Son of God, to a perfect man, to the measure of the stature of the Fulness of Christ; that we should no longer be children, tossed to and fro and carried about with every wind of doctrine, by the trickery of men, in the cunning craftiness of deceitful plotting, but, speaking the Truth in love, grow up in all things into Him Who is the Head: Christ.

I appreciate all those who contributed positively, in one way or the other, to my Christian life, my ministry, and the writing and publication of this book. As we look forward to the Rapture of the Saints and Second Coming of our Saviour, Lord, and Master: Jesus Christ the Son of the Living God, don't lose your focus. Look unto Jesus Christ, the Author and Finisher of our faith, Who for the Joy that was set before Him, endured the Cross, despising the Shame, and has sat down at the Right Hand of the Throne of God.

God did not call us to serve Him in vain, but He will reward us abundantly for the labour we have laboured in His Name. He shall also give us the Crown of Life. Remember that there is a Heaven to gain, and there is a Hell Fire to avoid. Live in total obedience to the Word of God; live in righteousness and holiness, without which no eye shall see the Lord. God bless you!

Never Say That God Said What He Did Not Say!

Jesus Christ Is Coming Very Soon: Heaven And Hell Are Real!

Let No One Deceive You: Without Holiness, No One Will See The Lord

This hymn will help keep us focused:

IT PAYS TO SERVE JESUS

1. It pays to serve Jesus; I speak from my heart,
   He'll always be with us, if we do our part,
   There is nothing in this wide-world can pleasure afford,
   There is peace and contentment in serving the Lord.

Chorus:
   I'll love Him far better than in days gone by,
   I'll serve Him more truly than ever before,
   I'll do as He bids me whatever the cost,
   I'll be a true soldier; I'll die at my post.

2. And often when I am tempted to turn from the track,
   I think of my Saviour, my mind wanders back,
   To the place where they nailed Him on Calvary's Tree,
   I hear a Voice saying, "I suffered for thee."

3. There is no one like Jesus can share me today,
   His Love and Kindness can never fade away,

Never Say That God Said What He Did Not Say!

In winter, in summer, in sunshine and rain,
His Love and Affection is always the same.
                              APOSTLE GODSWORD

PREFACE

The Bible says that the Lord reveals what He wants to do to His Servants, the prophets. God warns us ahead of time concerning His Plans and Purposes, and concerning the plans and purposes of the devil. Reading through the Bible you will see many things that the Lord warned us, ahead of time, will happen. And many of these things are happening now. He loves us so much, that He warned us ahead of time, so that when they happen, we will not be taken unawares.

One of the things that the Lord warned us of, is that there will be increase of lawlessness or iniquity in the last days, which will lead to the love of many Believers growing cold. But He has told us that he that endures to the end that shall be saved. The Lord told us that false prophets, teachers, and ministers will abound. There will be wars, rumours of wars, pestilences, and earthquakes in various places. He also let us know that we will be persecuted, and warned us to be ready for His Coming.

The Word says, "Now the Spirit expressly says that in latter times some will depart from the faith, giving heed to deceiving spirits and doctrines of demons, speaking lies in hypocrisy, having their own conscience seared with a hot iron. Preach the Word! Be ready in season and out of season. Convince, rebuke, exhort, with all longsuffering and teaching. For the time will come when they will not endure Sound Doctrine, but according to their own desires, because they have itching ears, they will heap up for themselves teachers, and they will turn their ears away from the Truth, and be turned aside to fables" (1 Tim. 4:1-2; 2 Tim. 4:2-4).

GODSWORD GODSWILL ONU,
2012.

INTRODUCTION

In God's Love, He warns us ahead of time of what He intends to do, and what the devil plans to do. Of course, there are things that happen which the Lord may not tell us about before they happen for certain reasons. The secret things belong to the Lord our God, but the things which are revealed belong to us and to our children forever... (Deut. 29:29).

Speaking through Apostle Paul, the Lord said, "Now the Spirit expressly says that in latter times some will depart from the faith, giving heed to deceiving spirits and doctrines of demons, speaking lies in hypocrisy, having their own conscience seared with a hot iron" (1 Tim. 4:1-2). This is speaking of false preaching teaching, and doctrine.

But the Lord told us another side of this pathetic situation, when the Spirit, through Paul, said, "Preach the Word! Be ready in season and out of season. Convince, rebuke, exhort, with all longsuffering and teaching. For the time will come when they will not endure Sound Doctrine, but according to their own desires, because they have itching ears, they will heap up for themselves teachers; and they will turn their ears away from the Truth, and be turned aside to fables" (2 Tim. 4:2-4).

This other one is talking about people who do not want the Truth, but want false preaching and preachers. It is a great problem to have false ministers; but it is a greater problem for the people themselves to want false ministry, ministers, and teachings. That condition will encourage the abundance of false teachings and doctrines.

In His Own Words, Jesus Christ said, "Beware of false prophets, who come to you in sheep's clothing, but inwardly they are ravenous wolves. You will know them by their fruits" (Matt. 7:15-16). Any ministry, preaching, teaching, prophecy, or minister that leads you away from God and the life of obedience, holiness, and righteousness is either from the devil or has been invaded by the devil. Forget about the signs, wonders, miracles, and prophecies!

The Lord warned us concerning the endtime, saying, "Take heed that no one deceives you. For many will come in My Name, saying, 'I am the Christ,' and will deceive many. And you will hear of wars and rumours of wars. See that you are not troubled; for all these things must come to pass, but the end is not yet.

"For nation will rise up against nation, and kingdom against kingdom. And there will be famines, pestilences, and earthquakes in various places. All these are the beginning of sorrows. Then they will deliver you up to tribulation and kill you, and you will be hated by all nations for My Name's sake.

"And then many will be offended, will betray one another, and will hate one another. Then many false prophets will rise up and deceive many. And because lawlessness will abound, the love of many will grow cold. But he who endures to the end will be saved. And this Gospel of the Kingdom will be preached in all the world as a witness to all the nations, and then the end will come" (Matt. 24:4-14).

The Lord also warns us, saying, "Watch and pray, lest you enter into temptation. The spirit indeed is willing, but the flesh is weak" (Matt. 26:41). To watch is to be sober and alert, taking note of what is happening around you. Being sensitive to the Spirit's Leading is being watchful. Also, knowing and understanding the Word of God will make you watchful. You have to understand the strategies of the devil. And prayer gets you strong to resist the devil.

Concerning, the Lord's Coming, the Word says, "And as it was in the days of Noah, so it will be also in the Days of the Son of Man: They ate, they drank, they married wives, they were given in marriage, until the day that Noah entered the ark, and the Flood came and destroyed them all.

"Likewise as it was also in the days of Lot: they ate, they drank, they bought, they sold, they planted, they built; but on the day that Lot went out of Sodom it rained fire and brimstone from heaven and destroyed them all.

"Even so it will be in the Day when the Son of Man is revealed. In that Day, he who is on the housetop, and his goods are in the house, let him not come down to take them away. And likewise the one who is in the field, let him not turn back. Remember Lot's wife.

"Whoever seeks to save his life will lose it, and whoever loses his life will preserve it. I tell you, in that night there will be two men in one bed: the one will be taken and the other will be left.

"Two women will be grinding together: the one will be taken and the other left. Two men will be in the field: the one will be taken and the other left" (Lk. 17: 26-36). ...So you also, when you see these things happening, know that the Kingdom of God is near. Assuredly, I say to you, this generation will by no means pass away till all things take place. Heaven and earth will pass away, but My Words will by no means pass away.

"But take heed to yourselves, lest your hearts be weighed down with carousing, drunkenness, and cares of this life, and that Day come on you unexpectedly.

"For it will come as a snare on all those who dwell on the face of the whole earth. Watch therefore, and pray always that you may be counted worthy to escape all these that will come to pass, and to stand before the Son of Man" (Lk. 21:33-36).

Never Say That God Said What He Did Not Say!

DO NOT LOVE THE WORLD

The Bible commands us to love not the world. If anyone loves the world, the Love of the Father is not in him. All that is in the world are the lust of flesh, the lust of the eyes, and the pride of life. These things do not come from the Father, but from the world. The world and its works will pass away, but he who does the Will of God lasts forever (1 Jn 2:15-17). The Bible says that friendship with the world is becoming an enemy of God; and he that will be a friend of the world will be an enemy of God, for God is a Jealous God (Jas 4:4).

The Word of God says that we should come out from among them and be separate, and we should touch no unclean thing (2 Cor. 6:17-18). The world will present many things that are appealing to your eyes, flesh, and ego to you. Think of money, wealth, women, power, fame, flashy cars, exotic buildings, and many other things too numerous to mention!

The Bible recorded that the devil took Jesus Christ to a high mountain, showed Him the kingdoms of the earth in a moment, and told Him to fall down and worship him so that the Lord Jesus Christ will have all those things. That is exactly what the devil will do to you.

He will tell you to pursue money with all your time, effort, and energy, and have no time for God so that you will be rich. He may even tell you to give God 5% of your effort and time, and the other 95% to yourself and the pursuit of the things of this world. He will tell you to lie so that you can make more money.

The devil will suggest that you falsify a certificate so that you may get a job, telling you that all things work together for good to them that love God. He will tell you to cheat in examinations so that you may get a good certificate.

Jesus Christ says that anyone that loves anything or anyone more than Him is not worthy of Him. Anyone that loves his own life more than the Lord Jesus Christ is not worthy of Him; and anyone that does not take up his cross and follow Him is not worthy of Him (Matt. 10:37-38).

By the way, the Lord has promised that whosoever leaves land, house, mother, brother, sister (and let me add, your job or profession), for Him and for the Gospel's sake, shall receive all those things hundred folds in this life, and in the life to come Eternal Life (Mk 10:29-30). God has a good and abundant reward for anything that you do for Him.

The world may give you money, but it will not give you peace. It may give you happiness, but it will not give you overflowing joy. It may give you security guards, but it will not ensure your protection. The world may give you food and wealth, but it will not give you life. The world cannot guarantee your health.

Woe to him that puts his trust in the arms of the flesh, on man. If you trust that the president of your country will be your help, what of if he dies or is removed tomorrow? Only the Lord can really save and guarantee your safety. One angel of the Lord killed one hundred and eighty-five thousand Assyrian soldiers in one night (Isa. 37:36).

The Lord delivered the children of Israel from the hands of the Egyptians by a Strong and Mighty Hand when He showed Himself strong to Pharaoh and his people; and they had to plead with the Israelites to leave their place.

All the money, wealth, certificates, fame, power, and whatever you may have, will end on this earth. When you die, you will carry none of them with you, for you did not bring any of them with you. What shall it profit a man if he gains the whole world and loses his own soul? Or what shall a man give in exchange for his soul? (Matt. 16:26).

Do not lay up treasures for yourself in this world, but lay up treasures for yourself in Heaven; for where your treasure is, is where your heart will be. By the way, rust and decay destroy things stored up in this world; and robbers and thieves break in and do away with things stored up in this world.

Even banks have folded and liquidated. But whatever you store in Heaven, whatever you do for God, and however you obey God, those things are things that will count for eternity.

People pursue school certificates to the detriment of their souls, when they don't have time for God and when they do evil practices to get those certificates. People run around for money to the destruction for their souls, when they don't have time for God and carry out all forms of malpractices and deceits to make money.

Many run around for women to please their flesh; but if our wife cannot satisfy you, then no other woman will satisfy you, for you will still want others. People kill their opponents to win elections and achieve their goals. People do this and that to achieve what they want to achieve and do not worry where they are heading towards. The god of this world, the devil, has blinded their eyes so that they cannot see.

Beware of worldliness. You are in the world, but you are not of the world, as a Christian (Jn 17:14). Worldliness is creeping into the Church of Jesus Christ. But the Lord Jesus Christ will come for the Church that does not have spot, wrinkle, blemish, or any such things (Eph. 5:27).

If you don't want to miss the Rapture, if you don't want to suffer in the Lake that burns with fire and brimstone, then live for God and not for yourself, the world, or for the devil. There is nothing to enjoy in this world. If your hope in Christ is only in this world, you are of all men the most miserable (1 Cor. 15:19).

The devil will not let you see the end of the evil, disobedience, and sin you may be living in. He loves no man and does not want any to get to Heaven where he was pushed down from. God is Love and does not want any soul to go to Hell Fire. But God is a Jealous, Righteous, and Just God, and He is no respecter of persons.

God has exalted His Word above all His Names, and God cannot change His Word for any man. Though God is Love, He is also a Consuming Fire (Heb. 12:29). Take heed to yourself and to the Doctrine, for in doing this, you shall save both yourself and those that hear you (1 Tim. 4:16).

In many churches, you hear people say that it doesn't matter. Believers do many things that unbelievers do and the claim that it doesn't matter. Some dress half-naked and come to church and walk along the streets, and they say that it doesn't matter. Many Believers paint themselves and make up the same way the unbelievers do. Many wear all kinds of bangles and jewels that unbelievers wear, and they claim that it doesn't matter.

Believers perm and jerry-curl their hair and wear weavons like unbelievers, and they say that those things don't matter. Brethren, the Believer's appearance must be different from the appearance of the unbeliever. This is no joke, for out of the abundance of the heart, the mouth speaks. If your outward appearance is evil, something is likely to be wrong on the inside.

The Bible does not say that God is not interested in outward appearance, but that He looks at the heart (1 Sam. 16:7). God knows that when the heart is right, then the outward appearance, the actions, and the words will be right also. We shall not be like the people of the world, for we are not of the world. Don't set your mind on things of this world but on things that are Above – in Heaven (Col. 3:1-2).

To be successful in life is to fulfill God's Purpose and Plan for your life. This is why the Lord says that life is not in the abundance of what a man possesses (Lk. 12:15).

This is why the poor members of the Church of Smyrna were told by the Lord that they were rich (Rev. 2:9), and the rich members of the Church of the Laodiceans were told that they were poor and wretched (Rev. 3:17).

God sees differently from how men see. Do you know that, even as a minister, you can have the largest church and organize the biggest crusade, and still not be following God's Plan for your life?

What people call 'success' is no success at all. If you become the wealthiest, richest, most famous, most powerful, or most educated person of all ages, and you lose your soul in Hell at last, you were very unsuccessful.

Material blessings, academic blessings, marital blessings, ministerial blessings, and many others are good and necessary; after all, without money, how can the Gospel go to the ends of the earth?

But let me tell you the truth, true success is obedience to the Word of God, and the achievement of God's Purpose for your life.

Abraham was successful in life, even though he had only one son after many years (apart from the son of the bondwoman Ishmael). Moses was successful; even though he did not make it to the land of Canaan, he made it to Heaven.

Joshua and Caleb were successful; of all the adults that left Egypt, only two of them made it to Canaan, and they fulfilled God's Purpose for their lives. Samuel, David, Isaiah, Daniel, Jesus Christ, Peter, Paul, and many others were successful. David was rich and Daniel was famous, but all of them fulfilled God's Plans for their lives.

Most of the adults that left Egypt at the exodus of the Israelites did not make it to Canaan, and to Paradise. Sampson lost his ministry and his eyes due to irresponsibility.

Solomon lost the kingdom of Israel after his death, because his heart was estranged from God, though he was very wise and rich. Judas Iscariot fell by the way. King Asa did not end well. These and many others were unsuccessful in life. They displeased God and lost their missions.

What does it mean to be successful in life? The word 'success' means the achieving of something you have been trying to do, with a good result. If you do very well in what you want to do or in what you are to do (like your Christian life, your ministry, or your job), you are a success.

However, Godly success is not always the same with human success. What humans regard as success may be seen by God as destruction. What humans may regard as foolishness may be seen by God as success.

Concerning success, I will like to speak about Apostle Paul. This holy and fiery apostle of the Almighty God had a great success in his ministry. This is not to say that he did not make mistakes; of course, he made some mistakes.

This holy apostle and prophet of Jesus Christ suffered dearly in the ministry. He traveled by foot and by ship; he was stoned and beaten with rod and whips; he suffered hunger and rejection. Nevertheless, he called all those things, and many more, light afflictions (2 Cor. 4:17).

Apostle Paul wanted and desired to succeed in the ministry and be faithful to the Lord that he despised the pains and the shame he encountered, and pressed for the prize of the High Call of God.

He did not have internet services, aircraft, cars, duplexes, cathedrals; yet he decided to preach the Gospel where Christ had not been named. He did not collect tithes and offerings to enrich himself, and keep a lot in store.

He used what he collected for the Work of God. Today, many have removed their focus from Jesus Christ, Heaven, and souls; they are interested in money.

Let me talk about other areas of success before I go back to the real success — spiritual success. But the spirit-realm controls the physical realm; therefore, spiritual success is supposed to show physically.

However, if you are not rich yet, it does not necessarily mean that you have a problem spiritually, even though you may have to check your life of obedience and faith; your unwillingness to get rich will affect God's Supply for you (Isa. 1:19). God's Divine Power has given us all things we need for life and Godliness.

Also, God's people suffer due to ignorance (Hos. 4:6). Some don't even know that it is God's Will for them to prosper materially and financially. The earth is the Lord's and the fullness of it (Psa. 24:1).

Silver and gold is God's; a thousand cattle by the hill are His (Psa. 50:10). God did not create these things for the devil and his children, but for God's people, even though Adam sold out his inheritance to the devil when he disobeyed God and sinned against Him.

Thus satan became the god of this world (2 Cor. 4:4). But Jesus Christ came to bring that inheritance back to us and we are gods and kings of the Great God and King (Psa. 82:6; Rev. 1:6).

Jesus Christ became poor so that through His poverty, we might be made rich (2 Cor. 8:9). It is God's Will for us to prosper in material things. Of course, many of the early apostles, prophets, and Disciples were not rich materially.

One reason this was so is because they were committed to winning souls: we must be committed to winning souls like them; they won souls in the face of fierce persecutions. We live more peaceably now.

Another reason is that many of them were ignorant of God's Will in this area. They didn't have the entire Bible as we have today; we can compare one part with another. Nevertheless, they pursued the substance, and today many of us seem to be pursuing the shadows — riches and material blessings.

No wonder they were more spiritual than many today. However, never set your mind on temporal things, things that perish and do not have eternal value. Riches and wealth have eternal value when used for God's Glory.

Physical prosperity or success is very necessary. I am speaking of health and healing here. No matter how much you have, if you are sick and can't work or stand, it is a very big problem. In that case, you wouldn't even enjoy your meals.

But God has provided health and healing for us. Jesus Christ carried our sicknesses and diseases, and it is God's Will for us to be healthy. If you choose to be sick, you are just giving the devil a place in your life. God is not responsible for it.

Abraham was very rich in cattle, in silver, and in gold (Gen. 13:2). He had 318 trained servants, and more than that, for he couldn't have used all for the war he fought (Gen. 14:14). The Lord blessed Abraham in all things (Gen. 24:1).

Isaac reaped a hundred-fold of what he planted. He waxed great, and went forward, and grew until he became very great (Gen. 26:12-13). Isaac had possession of flocks, and possession of herds, and great store of servants: and the Philistines envied him (Gen. 26:14).

Jacob increased exceedingly, and had much cattle, and maidservants, and menservants, and camels, and asses (Gen. 30:43). Job was blameless and upright, and one who feared God and shunned evil. He had so much that he was the greatest of all the people of the east (Job 1:1-3).

David was righteous and feared God, yet he was a king and prepared for the House of the Lord a hundred thousand talents of gold, and a thousand talents of silver, and of brass and iron without weight for it was in abundance: timber also and stone he prepared (1 Chron. 22:14).

Even in the New Testament, people of God were rich. That is why Apostle Paul told Timothy to charge the rich to do good (1 Tim. 6:17). Talking of promotion and power, Daniel and his three friends were high in positions in the Babylonian government.

They were blessed academically also, for they were ten times wiser than the others. God blessed them in appearance also. (Dan. 1:15,19-21; Dan. 3:29-30; Dan 6:1-3). Mordecai was highly promoted and honoured by God (Esth. 6:1-14). God delivered the Israelites with a strong hand (Exo. 12:29-33). Joseph was the prime minister of Egypt for God was with him (Gen. 41:38-44).

But, Brethren, do not love the world or anything in the world. The love of money is the root of all evil. He who loves silver will not be satisfied with silver. Whatever God gives you, use it for His Glory and to expand the Church on earth.

Heaven should be your main goal, and you must strive to please God. The Word of God shall not depart from your mouth, but you shall meditate on it day and night, that you may do all His Word. For then you will make your way prosperous, and then you will have good success (Josh. 1:8).

Curses and spiritual attacks can hinder somebody's progress in life. Be sensitive to the Spirit, because He will give you a signal, by any way He chooses, of the existence of any of them in your life. Then, break them in the Name of Jesus Christ.

God has given you the power to decree a thing and it will be established. Whatever you decree will come to pass; don't doubt. You may need to add fasting to your prayer.

The Power, Presence, and Favour of God bring increase and multiplication in all areas of life: spiritual, mental, physical, and otherwise. God is a Good God!

If many Christians apply half of what they know now, satan, his demons, and his human agents will be so afraid of them, that they will relate with them from afar.

But the devil operates almost freely in the lives of many Christians without much fear. God has told and taught many people many things and yet they don't apply them. It is applied knowledge that brings results.

If you know all and apply nothing, instead of gaining, you will lose, because the Servant that knows His Master's Commands and does not do them will be beaten with more stripes (Lk. 12:47-48).

There is a level of lack of knowledge, and that is a more terrible level, because you will not apply the things you don't know. Hence, the Word of God says that God's people perish for lack of knowledge (Hos. 4:6).

Ignorance of God, His Word and Ways, and the ways of the devil will lead to loss, death, and destruction.

Of course, no one knows everything about God or the devil, but you can increase your knowledge by the study and reading of the Bible and other Godly Christian materials.

Some people listen to their pastors or general-overseers only. Though that approach has a positive side of being in a better position to avoid error and intrusion of false teachings, yet it has the negative side of not receiving what God may want to pass to you through other ministers.

There are many people that the Lord has called, and they have different ministries, abilities, and areas of calling. All you need for your Christian life can never be passed to you by any one preacher.

However, as you listen to anybody or read their materials, be careful to follow God's Spirit and His Word. This is why you must be sensitive to the Anointing that teaches you all things (1 Jn 2:20,27).

And you must be full of the Word of God so that you can test and prove the teachings you hear. If you are sincere, God will lead you into the truth and lead you away from the spirit of error.

This is not to say that you must listen to everybody. Don't listen to those you are convinced (without bias) are not teaching the truth.

Remember that a little leaven leavens the whole lump. Small error can cause great havoc to your Christian faith.

I am saying this because we know that there are many false prophets and false teachers who use the Bible and the Name of Jesus Christ to extend the thoughts, plans, and works of the devil. There are many false ministers.

However, we are speaking about knowing what to do and not doing it. Whoever knows the good he should do and does not do it, to him it is sin (Jas. 4:17). God commands us to be doers of the Word, and not just hearers alone.

He tells us that if we hear and do not do what we hear, we are deceiving ourselves (Jas 1:22). But don't deceive yourself nor let another person deceive you. God can never be mocked.

God loves obedience, and doing His Word proves to Him that you love Him (Jn 14:15). Absolute complete obedience is holiness, and without holiness, no man can see the Lord.

Even when you might have not reached perfection, make up your mind that whatever you are sure God wants you to do, you will do. That state of mind is consecration and dedication to God, and it is holiness.

God will then increase your knowledge and help you do what you are to do in order to perfect holiness (2 Cor. 7:1). The grace and ability to obey Him is there; use it!

Prayer is one area people don't apply what they know. When they listen to good messages about prayer, they decide to be consistently prayerful, but many never make it, for they go back after few days.

Some go back because of discouragement, but you don't need to be discouraged; you only need to be persistent. Think about this: those that take part in games train and discipline themselves in order to succeed, and many of them make mistakes and fail along the line.

But it is persistence and consistence that produce champions. A winner or a champion had made many mistakes before.

Some principles of God's Word don't produce fruits overnight; and God doesn't always settle His Account with people every twenty-four hours.

Some principles take a very long time to mature and produce the needed fruits. Others may take a short or shorter time, but make up your mind to achieve the results.

The Word of God is a seed and you know that some seeds or trees (crops) produce within a year (annual crops); some produce within two years (biennial crops); and some produce after many years (perennial plants).

Even pregnancy among animals takes different lengths of time. Some can produce within a short period (like insects); others within nine months (like human beings); and others after more than a year (like elephants).

In building construction, the bigger and taller the building, the deeper and more solid the foundation (of course, the nature of the ground or soil matters a lot; rocky basement will require a shallower foundation than sandy or clayey soil). Some foundations can cost what you may use to finish a five-storey building, like foundations for sky-scrappers.

You must apply what you know and wait patiently to reap its results. The devil has no mercy, and ignorance is no excuse to him.

In fact, he will want you to be ignorant of him and his devices; but we are not ignorant of his devices, and he will not get an advantage over us. In battle, if you don't know of your enemy's strategy, you may be destroyed in a split-second.

How can you use a machete to attack someone coming against you with a gun? And why will you use a gun to fire someone throwing bombs on you from fighter-jets? Be wise as serpents and harmless as doves (Matt. 10:16).

Demonic works and strongholds need confrontation. You must confront demonic conditions with God's Power. It may require fasting, and you have to do it (as led by the Holy Spirit).

Only counseling will not do the work. That is why people are counseled often, and they remain in their problems. Of course, if someone submits to counseling under God's Word and Anointing, he will receive result because God's Word is anointed.

The five foolish virgins should have carried extra oil; but they didn't, either by ignorance or by carelessness, and missed the bridegroom (Matt. 25:1-13). Let this not be your portion in any area in the Name of Jesus Christ. Amen.

Renew your mind by the Word of God and think the Way God thinks, and you will do God's Will. You need more information from the Word of God to increase your faith and function more effectively.

Some don't apply what they know because of unbelief. There are two kinds of unbelief: unbelief that comes by lack of the knowledge of the Word of God, and the unbelief that exists, not because you don't know, but because you are not persuaded by the Word that you know.

The second one is what the other ten spies, apart from Joshua and Caleb, exhibited. God had told them that Jericho will fall for their sake, but because of what they saw with their physical eyes, they doubted the Word of God (Num. 13 & 14).

The secret of receiving what you want is obedience, and obedience is the application of what you know. It is the application that produces the results and not just the knowledge.

Science without technology amounts to nothing. Science is the finding and the knowledge, and technology is the application of scientific findings and knowledge to solve the existing needs. This is true in medical, biological, chemical, engineering, and agricultural fields.

The same is applicable in Christianity. God's Word is meant to solve needs. If you want people to believe in your God, then your God will have to solve their problems.

Many Christians wonder why unbelievers go to witch-doctors for this or that solution. Preach and teach the real Word of God and allow God manifest Himself through you; if you do, more souls will accept our Lord and Christ.

Abraham was told to leave his country, and he left in obedience to God's Voice. Noah was directed to build an ark, with specifications, and he did it. Moses was told to build the ark of covenant and the tabernacle exactly the way he saw them, and he did it so.

Jesus Christ followed God's Plan for His Life and succeeded in His Earthly Ministry. Follow God's Word and Leading for you, as an individual, and what you will see will blow your mind!

THE LAW OF LIBERTY

The Bible says that we have been called to liberty; however, we are not to our liberty as an occasion for the flesh, but by love serve one another (Gal. 5:13). In Christ Jesus, we are free and not bound. Of course, we are bound to the Lord Jesus Christ Himself. And He tells us that we are His Friends if we do whatever He tells or commands us (Jn 15:14).

In Christ Jesus, we are bound to nothing but the Lord Himself. We are bound to one another because He commanded us to love one another. We are not bound to sin, the world, or the devil. We have been redeemed and set free by the Blood of the Righteous and Spotless Lamb.

The Word of God commands us to speak and do as they that shall be judged by the Law of Liberty (Jas 2:12). God did not leave the Believers in Christ without Laws and Commandments, but He gave us the perfect Law of Liberty. Some people assume that because they are free in Christ, they can do what they want to do.

But the Word says, "Therefore, having been justified by faith, we have peace with God through our Lord Jesus Christ, through Whom also we have access by faith into this grace in which we stand, and rejoice in hope of the Glory of God.

"And not only that, but we also glory in tribulations, knowing that tribulation produces perseverance, and perseverance, character, and character, hope. Now hope does not disappoint, because the Love of God has been poured out in our hearts by the Holy Spirit Who was given to us.

"For when we were still without strength, in due time Christ died for the ungodly. For scarcely for a righteous man will one die; yet perhaps for a good man someone would even dare to die. But God demonstrates His Own Love towards us, in that while we were still sinners, Christ died for us.

"Much more then, having now been justified by His Blood, we shall be saved from wrath through Him. For if when we were enemies we were reconciled to God through the Death of His Son, much more, having been reconciled we shall be saved by His Life. And not only that, but we also rejoice in God through our Lord Jesus Christ, through Whom we have now received reconciliation.

"Therefore, just as through one man sin entered the world, and death through sin, and thus death spread to all men, because all sinned – (for until the Law sin was in the world, but sin is not imputed where is no law).

"Nevertheless death reigned from Adam to Moses, even over those who have not sinned according to the likeness of the transgression of Adam, who is a type of Him Who was to come. But the free gift is not like the offence. For if by one man's offence many died, much more the Grace of God and the gift by the Grace of the One Man, Jesus Christ, abounded to many.

"And the gift is not like that which came through the one who sinned. For the judgment which came from one offence resulted in condemnation, but the free gift which came from many offences resulted in justification. For if by one man's offence death reigned through the one, much more those who receive the abundance of grace and of the gift of righteousness will reign in life through the One Jesus Christ.

"Therefore, as through one man's offence judgment came to all men, resulting in condemnation, even so through One Man's Righteous Act the free gift came to all men, resulting in justification of life. For as by one man's disobedience many were made sinners, so also by One Man's Obedience many will be made righteous.

WARNINGS FROM THE LORD

"Moreover the Law entered that offence might abound. But where sin abounded, grace abounded much more, so that as sin reigned in death, even so grace might reign through righteousness to Eternal Life through Jesus Christ our Lord.

"What shall we say then? Shall we continue in sin that grace may abound? Certainly not! How shall we who died to sin live any longer in it? Or do you not know that as many of us as were baptized into Christ Jesus were baptized into His Death?

"Therefore we were buried with Him through baptism into death, that just as Christ was raised from the dead by the Glory of the Father, even so we also should walk in newness of life. For if we have been united together in the likeness of His Death, certainly we also shall be in the likeness of His Resurrection.

"Knowing this, that our old man was crucified with Him, that the body of sin might be done away with, that we should no longer be salves of sin. For he who has died has been freed from sin. Now if we died with Christ, we believe we shall also live with Him.

"Knowing that Christ, having been raised from the dead, dies no more. Death has no longer dominion over Him. For the death that He died, He died to sin once for all, but the life that He lives, He lives to God. Likewise you also, reckon yourselves to be dead indeed to sin, but alive to God in Christ Jesus our Lord.

"Therefore do not let sin reign in your mortal body, that you should obey it in its lusts. And do not present your members as instruments of unrighteousness to sin, but present yourselves to God as being alive from the dead, and your members as instruments of righteousness to God.

"For sin shall not have dominion over you, for you are not under law but under grace. What then? Shall we sin because we are not under law but under grace? Certainly not! Do you not know that to whom you present yourselves slaves to obey, you are the one's slaves whom you obey, whether of sin leading to death, or of obedience leading to righteousness?

"But God be thanked that though you were slaves of sin, yet you obeyed from the heart that form of Doctrine to which you were delivered. And having been set free from sin, you became slaves of righteousness. I speak in human terms because of the weakness of your flesh.

"For just as you presented your members as slaves of uncleanness, and of lawlessness leading to more lawlessness, so now present your members as slaves of righteousness for holiness. For when you were slaves of sin, you were free in regard to righteousness.

"What fruit did you have then in the things of which you are now ashamed? For the end of those things is death. But now having been set free from sin, and having become slaves of God, you have your fruit to holiness, and the end, Everlasting life. For the wages of sin is death, but the Gift of God is Eternal Life in Christ Jesus our Lord" (Rom. 5 & 6).

Christianity is not a life of lawlessness. No, our Lord Jesus Christ left us with Laws (though not the Law but the Law of Liberty) and Commandments. And quoting Him verbatim, He says, "If you love Me, keep My Commandments. You are My Friends if you do whatever I command you" (Jn 14:15; Jn 15:14).

So where did this 'lawless' or it-doesn't-matter form of Christianity come from? It came from the devil who wants to drag the souls of men to Hell Fire. He is not satisfied with the very large number of unbelievers that he already has: he wants Believers, Christians, preachers, and ministers. Escape for your dear life now! Run your race while there is time!

God loves us, and He doesn't want us to perish in Hell Fire. This is why He sent His Son Jesus Christ to die for our sins, shedding His Blood on the Cross of Calvary. And our Great High priest, Jesus Christ, is sitting at the Right Hand of God, making intercession for us.

However, studying the Bible reveals that God is no respecter of any person (Rom. 2:11); and He cannot change His Word, which He has magnified above all His Names, for any person. The Word says, "Then many false prophets will rise up and deceive many. And because lawlessness will abound, the love of many will grow cold. But he who endures to the end shall be saved" (Matt. 24:11-13).

HELL

Hell is the place where sinners and unbelievers go to suffer punishment when they die. Hell is beneath the earth – deep down under the surface of the earth. Whereas someone goes up to Heaven, somebody goes down to Hell. Hell is a place of Everlasting Torment. Jesus Christ spoke much about Hell when He was on the surface of the earth. The suffering of Hell cannot be understood by human beings; and the horror and torment of Hell cannot be explained by human word or experience.

Speaking of Hell, Jesus Christ said, "There was a certain rich man who was clothed in purple and fine linen and fared sumptuously every day. But there was a certain beggar named Lazarus, full of sores, who was laid at his gate, desiring to be fed with the crumbs which fell from the rich man's table. Moreover the dogs came and licked his sores.

"So it was that the beggar died, and was carried by the angels to Abraham's bosom. The rich man also died and was buried. And being in torment in Hades, he lifted up his eyes and saw Abraham afar off, and Lazarus in his bosom. Then he cried and said, 'Father Abraham, have mercy on me, and send Lazarus that he may dip the tip of his finger in water and cool my tongue; for I am tormented in this flame.'

"But Abraham said, 'Son, remember that in your lifetime you received your good things, and likewise Lazarus evil things; but now he is comforted and you are tormented. And besides all this, between us and you there is a great gulf fixed, so that those who want to pass from here to you cannot, nor can those from there pass to us.'

"Then he said, 'I beg you therefore, father, that you would send him to my father's house, for I have five brothers, that he may testify to them, lest they also come to this place of torment.' Abraham said to him, 'They have Moses and the prophets; let them hear them.' And he said, 'No, father Abraham; but if one goes to them from the dead, they will repent.' But he said to him, 'If they do not hear Moses and the prophets, neither will they be persuaded though one rise from the dead'" (Lk. 16:19-31).

The first thing I want you to notice is that the Bible did not specifically mention any particular sin (as many people know sin) of the rich man. But we can observe that he was a sinner who did not care for Lazarus who was just by his gate, and suffering to the extent of desiring to be fed with the crumbs which fell down from the rich man's table, and also having the dogs leaking his sores. So apart from the lack of love, the Bible did not mention any particular sin of the rich man.

But another sin of the rich man would have been that he lived extravagant and wasteful life. And he would have sought to be famous, recognized, praised, and regarded high – he would have been full of pride. It was not because he was rich that led him to Hell or Hades; it was that he loved riches and the world; and he lived to please and satisfy his flesh and ego, instead of worshipping, obeying, serving, and glorifying God.

Jesus Christ, based on a rich man's reaction to His Word, looked around and said to His Disciples, "How hard it is for those who have riches to enter the Kingdom of God!" And the Disciples were astonished at His Words. But He answered again and said to them, "Children, how hard it is for those who trust in riches to enter the Kingdom of God! It is easier for a camel to go through the eye of a needle than for a rich man to enter the Kingdom of God."

And they were greatly astonished, saying among themselves, "Who then can be saved?" But Jesus Christ looked at them and said, "With men it is impossible, but not with God; for with God all things are possible" (Mk 10:23-27). A rich man who loves money, riches, and wealth cannot enter the Kingdom of God. But God is able, if he will humble himself and submit to God, to remove that love of money and riches from his heart and mind. Then he can enter God's Kingdom.

Apostle Paul said, "Now Godliness with contentment is great gain. For we brought nothing into this world, and it is certain we can carry nothing out. And having food and clothing, with these we shall be content. But those who desire to be rich fall into temptation and a snare, and into many foolish and harmful lusts which drown men in destruction and perdition. For the love of money is a root of all kinds of evil; for which some have strayed from the Faith in their greediness, and pierced themselves through with many sorrows" (1 Tim. 6:6-10).

He commanded Timothy, saying, "Command those who are rich in this present age not to be haughty, nor trust in uncertain riches but in the Living God, Who gives us richly all things to enjoy. Let them do good, that they be rich in good works, ready to give, willing to share, storing up for themselves a good foundation for the time to come, that they may lay hold on Eternal Life" (1 Tim. 6:17-19).

The Word of God says, "Let the lowly brother glory in his exaltation, but the rich in his humiliation, because as a flower of the field he will pass away. For no sooner has the sun risen with a burning heat than it withers the grass, its flowers falls, and its beautiful appearance perishes. So the rich man also will fade away in his pursuits" (Jas 1:9-11). If you are lowly placed, find out what will encourage you. If you are rich, find out ways to keep yourself humble.

And notice also that no good work or righteousness of Lazarus was particularly mentioned; but what was described was his suffering and poverty. However, both Lazarus and the rich man would have been Israelites or Jews, because Abraham spoke to the rich man, telling him that his brothers have Moses and the Prophets. The Gentiles were excluded from the commonwealth of Israel.

So Lazarus, being an Israelite or a Jew, would have committed and yielded himself to God and obeyed His Laws and Commandments. Since he did not have the things of this world, he would have put his hope in God and on His Promises. But what you have to know is that Lazarus did not go to Paradise because he was poor – there are poor people who are still proud of whatever they can glory in; and many poor people are full of sin and wickedness, from their own areas of desires, lusts, and plans.

Lazarus found himself in Abraham's bosom – Paradise (Abraham's bosom is a phrase used by the Jews to describe Paradise). And the rich man found himself in Hell. Though the New King James Version used Hades, the King James Version used Hell. The Greek word used there is Hades, which means the unseen world of departed spirits or souls of sinners and the wicked. It is an equivalent of the Hebrew word – Sheol.

So, why was it possible for the rich man to see Lazarus after death? Before the Death and Resurrection of Jesus Christ, both Paradise and Hell were beneath (under) the earth. But when Jesus Christ died and resurrected, He took the righteous people who were in the Paradise of below to an Above Paradise. Therefore, Paradise is no more beneath (under) the earth; rather, it is Above now.

Speaking of this event, the Bible says, "And Jesus cried out again with a loud Voice, and yielded up His Spirit. Then, behold, the veil of the temple was torn in two from top to bottom; and the earth quaked, and the rocks were split, and the graves were opened; and many bodies of the Saints who had fallen asleep were raised; and coming out of the graves after His Resurrection, they went into the holy city and appeared to many" (Matt. 27:50-53).

Of course, you saw the level of his torment in Hell. But I want you to notice that Abraham, based on the rich man's request, told him that his brothers have Moses and the Prophets, that they should hear them. Abraham was saying that the living should obey the Word of God to avoid going to Hell. Therefore those who do not obey the Word of God, but live to please the desires of their hearts and minds, will end in Hell.

Then again, when the rich man told Abraham that his brothers would hear if someone rises from the dead to preach to them, Abraham told him that if they did not hear Moses and the Prophets (the Word of God being preached and taught), neither would they be persuaded though someone rose from the dead. First, it was Abraham, and not God or Jesus Christ, who told the rich man that. God knows better than Abraham; and if He knows that people will listen to someone that rises from the dead, He can send the person.

Abraham couldn't even cross the gulf between Paradise and Hell; how then could he send Lazarus back to the earth? He did not have that level of authority or power to send a dead person to the living; but God has the power, ability, and authority to do that. Also, notice that Abraham did not say that nobody (none) could hear the dead that rises from the dead, but that the rich man's brothers would not hear. Why? Because they had made up their minds on what they wanted.

But many people will believe the story that would be told them by someone who rises from the dead; and many people will still not believe the story told them by someone who rises from the dead, no matter what, because the devil has hardened their hearts and they have made up their minds on what they want. The Bible says, "And behold, there was a great earthquake; for an angel of the Lord descended from Heaven, and came and rolled back the stone from the door, and sat on it.

"His countenance was like lightning, and his clothing as white as snow. And the guards shook for fear of him, and became like dead men. ...Now while they were going, behold, some of the guards came into the city and reported to the chief priests all the things that had happened. When they had assembled with the elders and consulted together, they gave a large sum of money to the soldiers,

"Saying, 'Tell them, "His Disciples came at night and stole Him away while we slept." And if this comes to the governor's ears, we will appease him and make you secure.' So they took the money and did as they were instructed; and this saying is commonly reported among the Jews until this day" (Matt. 28:2-15). Can you imagine the hardness of men's (some men's) hearts and minds?

Instead of being grateful to God for saving them from death, and also giving them the opportunity to witness such a great sight, they decided to accept money and spread false story. Who will blame God when He judges and punishes sinners with Eternal Death in His Great Wrath? But His Hands are still open now for whoever will submit to His Word and Grace!

Notice also that it was some of the guards (not all of them) that went to report; some of them might have repented from that incident. Yet the religious chief priests and elders hardened their hearts. Abraham was right when he told the rich man that, because whereas some people will accept the testimony of the person who rises from the dead, many will still never believe his testimony, because their minds are made up.

Hell is a terrible place of torment. Escape Hell, and do not go there. But it is your life on earth that determines where you will spend your eternity. The Bible says, "If your hand causes you to sin, cut it off. It is better for you to enter into life maimed, rather than having two hands, to go to Hell, into the fire that shall never be quenched – where 'their worm does not die; and the fire is not quenched.'

"And if your foot causes you to sin, cut it off. It is better for you to enter life lame, rather than having two feet, to be cast into Hell, into the fire that shall never be quenched – where 'their worm does not die and the fire is not quenched.' And if your eye causes you to sin, pluck it out. It is better for you to enter the Kingdom of God with one eye, rather than having two eyes, to be cast into Hell Fire – where 'their worm does not die, and the fire is not quenched.'

"For everyone will be seasoned with fire, and every sacrifice will be seasoned with salt" (Mk 9:43-49). May God give you understanding in all things! Whatever will deprive you of Heaven and give you a ticket to Hell, get rid of that thing! The devil will use temporal, worldly, and fleshly things to blind and harden the hearts and minds of many people; and he will not allow them to see what lies ahead of them.

Matthew puts an extra thing to what Mark says. The Word says, "If your right eye causes you to sin, pluck it out and cast it from you; for it is more profitable for you that one of your members perish, than for your whole body to be cast into Hell. And if your right hand causes you to sin, cut it off and cast it from you; for it more profitable for you that one of your members perish, than for your whole body to be cast into Hell" (Matt. 6:29-30).

The Book of Matthew tells us to not only pluck it out or cut it off; but we are also to cast it off – throw it away from us. If you pluck it out or cut it off, and you are still holding it in your hand, you may put it back. Heaven is worth everything. Notice also that it says, "If your right eye causes you to sin…." The power of the devil over man is sin, disobedience, and compromise. And the strength of Hell is when anybody sins against God.

Speaking of what will happen in the end, the Bible says, "The devil, who deceived them, was cast into the Lake of Fire and Brimstone where the beast and the false prophet are. And they will be tormented day and night forever and ever. Then I saw a Great White Throne and Him Who sat on it, from Whose Face the earth and the heaven fled away. And there was found no place for them. And I saw the dead, small and great, standing before God, and books were opened. And another Book was opened, which is the Book of Life.

"And the dead were judged according to their works, by things which were written in the books. The sea gave up the dead who were in it, and Death and Hades delivered up the dead who were in them. And they were judged, each one according to his works. Then Death and Hades were cast into the Lake of Fire. This is the Second Death. And anyone not found written in the Book of Life was cast into the Lake of Fire" (Rev. 20:10-15).

Notice that Hell or Hades is a temporary place of suffering for the dead sinner. And the devil and his demons, for now, may be tormenting those who are presently suffering in Hell. But at the fulness of time, the devil and his fallen angels and demons will be cast into the Lake of Fire. And any person whose name is not found written in the Book of Life will also be cast into the Lake of Fire.

It is true that the time of fallen angels and demons has not come; but when their time comes, they will know that God has the kind of fire, that is available in the Lake of Fire and Brimstone, which will burn and torment them to wail and cry.

The Bible says, "The wicked shall be turned into Hell, and all the nations that forget God (Psa. 9:17). Now therefore, listen to Me, My children; pay attention to the words of my mouth: Do not let your heart turn aside to her [harlot's] ways, do not stray into her paths; for she has cast down many wounded, and all who were slain by her were strong men. Her house is the way to Hell, descending to the chambers of death (Prov. 7:24-27).

"The way of life winds upwards for the wise, that he may turn away from Hell below (Prov. 15:24). Hell and Destruction are before the Lord; so how much more the hearts of the sons of men (Prov. 15:11). Do not withhold correction from a child, for if you beat him with a rod, he will not die. You shall beat him with a rod, and deliver his soul from Hell (Prov. 23:13-14). Hell and Destruction are never full; so the eyes of man are never satisfied (Prov. 27:20).

"Therefore my people have gone into captivity, because they have no knowledge; their honourable men are famished, and their multitude dried up with thirst. Therefore Sheol [Hell/Hades] has enlarged itself and opened its mouth beyond measure; their glory and their multitude and their pomp, and he who is jubilant, shall descend into it" (Isa. 5:13-14). Hell from beneath is excited about you, to meet you at your coming.... Yet you shall be brought down to Sheol (Hell), to the lowest depths of the Pit (Isa. 14:9,15).

"And do not fear those who kill the body but cannot kill the soul. But rather fear Him Who is able to destroy both soul and body in Hell (Matt. 10:28). And you, Capernaum, who are exalted to heaven, will be brought down to Hades; for if the mighty works which were done in you had been done in Sodom, it would have remained until this day. But I say to you that it shall be more tolerable for the land of Sodom in the Day of Judgment than for you (Matt. 11:23-24). Serpents, brood of vipers! How can you escape the condemnation of Hell?" (Matt. 23:33).

Sinners, unbelievers, and the disobedient will have their part in Hell and in the Lake of Fire and Brimstone forever. And the passage in the Book of Proverbs tells us that the house of a harlot and prostitute is the way to Hell. Fornication, adultery, and lust will take someone to Hell. This is what the devil will hide from the fornicator, allowing him to see the few minutes' 'enjoyment' he gets. And following the way of life and of righteousness will take you to Heaven, and you will not go to Hell.

Also, the Word tells us that Hell and Destruction are never full. Think about the millions of people who have gone to Hell! And Hell will still take in more people, as many as reject Jesus Christ or live in sin. The Bible authorizes you to punish and chastise your child, so that he may learn to do the right thing; because if you don't, he will get spoilt and end up in Hell. Instruction and teaching goes along with punishment; therefore do not stop at telling him to do the right thing; punish him for disobedience.

We also saw that Hell has enlarged itself. It enlarged itself to accommodate more sinners. And people even go there being joyful and jubilant. But when they end up there, their joy and jubilation goes immediately, and there will be no second chance. Sin seems to be enjoyable; but it leads to Hell. Yet God tells us to fear Him alone; because He is the Only One Who can destroy both soul and body in Hell. Do not deny Jesus Christ or sin against God, because of fear of persecution or physical death. If you die a righteous man, you will wake up in Heaven!

Jesus Christ says, "Do not be afraid; I am the First and the Last. I am He Who lives, and was dead, and behold, I am alive forevermore. Amen. And I have the keys of Hades and of Death" (Rev. 1:17-18). Jesus Christ holds the key of Hell and of Death. He holds the key of both the death of now and of the Second Death. Nobody can die without the Permission of God. And it is God that sends people to Hell to punish them for loving the devil. Even if a demon drags you to Hell, it is because God released you to him, because of sin.

In the Bible, Hell also refers to the kingdom of satan and of darkness. To this end, the Word says, "Woe to you, scribes and Pharisees, hypocrites! For you travel land and sea to win one proselyte, and when he is won, you make him twice as much a son of Hell as yourselves" (Matt. 23:15). Even in this present age, many people who call themselves apostles, prophets, evangelists, pastors, teachers, preachers, and ministers, are nothing but workers of iniquity and agents of satan, who bind souls of men for satan and for Hell!

And speaking to Peter, Jesus Christ said, "Blessed are you, Simon Bar-Jonah, for flesh and blood has not revealed this to you, but My Father Who is in Heaven. And I also say to you that you are Peter, and on this rock I will build My Church, and the gates of Hades (Hell) shall not prevail against it. And I will give you the keys of the Kingdom of Heaven, and whatever you bind on earth will be bound in Heaven, and whatever you loose on earth will be loosed in Heaven" (Matt. 16:17-19). Here, the gates of Hell or Hades refer to the forces and powers of darkness.

Never Say That God Said What He Did Not Say!

THE POWER OF SIN TO BRING CURSES

The story of Achan tells us how sin and disobedience can bring about curses. The Bible says, "And the seventh time it happened, when the priests blew the trumpets, that Joshua said to the people: 'Shout, for the Lord has given you the city!

'Now the city shall be doomed by the Lord to destruction, it and all who are in it. Only Rahab the harlot shall live, she and all who are with her in the house, because she hid the messengers that we sent.

'And you, by all means abstain from the accursed things, lest you become accursed when you take of the accursed things, and make the camp of Israel a curse, and trouble it.

'But all the silver and gold, and vessels of bronze and iron, are consecrated to the Lord; they shall come into the treasury of the Lord' (Josh. 6:16-19).

"But the children of Israel committed a trespass regarding the accursed things, for Achan the son of Carmi, the son of Zabdi, the son of Zerah, of the tribe of Judah, took of the accursed things; so the Anger of the Lord burned against the children of Israel.

"Now Joshua sent men from Jericho to Ai, which is beside Beth Aven, on the east side of Bethel, and spoke to them, saying, 'Go up and spy out the country.' So the men went up and spied out Ai.

"And they returned to Joshua and said to him, 'Do not let all the people go up, but let about two or three thousand men go up and attack Ai. Do not weary all the people there, for the people of Ai are few.' So about three thousand men went up there from the people, but they fled before the men of Ai.

"And the men of Ai struck down about thirty-six men, for they chased them from before the gate as far as Shebarim, and struck them down on the descent; therefore the hearts of the people melted and became like water.

"Then Joshua tore his clothes, and fell to the earth on his face before the ark of the Lord until evening, he and the elders of Israel; and they put dust on their heads.

"And Joshua said, 'Alas, Lord God, why have You brought this people over the Jordan at all – to deliver us into the hand of the Amorites, to destroy us? Oh, that we had been content, and dwelt on the other side of the Jordan!

'O Lord, what shall I say when Israel turns its back before its enemies? For the Canaanites and all the inhabitants of the land will hear it, and surround us, and cut off our name from the earth. Then what will You do for Your Great Name?'

"So the Lord said to Joshua: 'Get up! Why do you lie thus on your face? Israel has sinned, and they have also transgressed My Covenant which I commanded them. For they have even taken some of the accursed things, and have both stolen and deceived; and they have also put it among their own stuff.

'Therefore the children of Israel could not stand before their enemies, but turned their backs before their enemies, because they have become doomed to destruction. Neither will I be with you anymore, unless you destroy the accursed from among you.

'Get up, sanctify the people, and say, "Sanctify yourselves for tomorrow, because thus says the Lord God of Israel: 'There is an accursed thing in your midst, O Israel; you cannot stand before your enemies until you take away the accursed thing from among you.'

"In the morning therefore you shall be brought according to your tribes. And it shall be that the tribe which the Lord takes shall come according to families; and the family which the Lord takes shall come by households; and the household which the Lord takes shall come man by man.

"Then it shall be that he who is taken with the accursed thing shall be burned with fire, he and all that he has, because he has transgressed the Covenant of the Lord, and because he has done a disgraceful thing in Israel.'"

"So Joshua rose early in the morning and brought Israel by their tribes, and the tribe of Judah was taken. He brought the clan of Judah, and he took the family of the Zarhites; and he brought the family of the Zarhites man by man, and Zabdi was taken.

"Then he brought his household man by man, and Achan the son of Carmi, the son of Zabdi, the son of Zerah, of the tribe of Judah, was taken. Now Joshua said to Achan, 'My son, I beg you, give glory to the Lord God of Israel, and make confession to Him, and tell me now what you have done; do not hide it from me.'

"And Achan answered Joshua and said, 'Indeed I have sinned against the Lord God of Israel, and this is what I have done: When I saw among the spoils a beautiful Babylonian garment, two hundred shekels of silver, and a wedge of gold weighing fifty shekels, I coveted them and took them. And there they are, hidden in the earth in the midst of my tent, with the silver under it.'

"So Joshua sent messengers, and they ran to the tent; and there it was, hidden in his tent, with the silver under it. And they took them from the midst of the tent, brought them to Joshua and to all the children of Israel, and laid them out before the Lord.

"Then Joshua, and all Israel with him, took Achan the son of Zerah, the silver, the garment, the wedge of gold, his sons, his daughters, his oxen, his donkeys, his sheep, his tent, and all that he had, and they brought them to the Valley of Achor.

"And Joshua said, 'Why have you troubled us? The Lord will trouble you this day.' So all Israel stoned him with stones; and they burned them with fire after they had stoned them with stones.

"Then they raised over him a great heap of stones, still there to this day. So the Lord turned from the fierceness of His Anger. Therefore the name of that place has been called the Valley of Achor to this day" (Josh. 7).

Yes, sin, disobedience, and unrighteousness bring curses, losses, and destruction. See how the Israelites fell to the small Ai, because of sin and disobedience! Many of the things which many of us suffer are because of sin, unrighteousness, and disobedience, both in our lives and in our ministries. But this is not the Will of God for us.

The Word of God says, "Do not envy the oppressor, and choose none of his ways; for the perverse person is an abomination to the Lord, but His Secret Counsel is with the upright.

"The Curse of the Lord is on the house of the wicked, but He blesses the home of the just. Surely He scorns the scornful, but gives grace to the humble. The wise shall inherit glory, but shame shall be the legacy of fools" (Prov. 3:31-35).

"There is one who scatters, yet increases more; and there is one who withholds more than is right, but it leads to poverty. The generous soul will be made rich, and he who waters will also be watered himself.

"The people will curse him who withholds grain, but blessing will be on the head of him who sells it. He who earnestly seeks good finds favour, but trouble will come to him who seeks evil (Prov. 11:24-27).

"These things also belong to the wise: It is not good to show partiality in judgment. He who says to the wicked, 'You are righteous,' him the people will curse; nations will abhor him. But those who rebuke the wicked will have delight, and a good blessing will come upon them" (Prov. 24:23-25).

The prophet Zachariah said, "Then I turned and raised my eyes, and saw there a flying scroll. And he said to me, 'What do you see?' So I answered, 'I see a flying scroll. Its length is twenty cubits and its width ten cubits.'

"Then he said to me, 'This is the curse that goes out over the face of the whole earth: "Every thief shall be expelled," according to this side of the scroll; and, "Every perjurer shall be expelled," according to that side of it.'

"'I will send out the curse,' says the Lord of Hosts; 'It shall enter the house of the thief and the house of the one who swears falsely by My Name. It shall remain in the midst of his house and consume it, with its timber and stones'" (Zech. 5:1-4).

Speaking to the priests who ministered to God's people, God said, "And now, O priests, this Commandment is for you.

"If you will not hear, and if you will not take it to heart, to give glory to My Name," says the Lord of Hosts, "I will send a curse upon you, and I will curse your blessings. Yes, I have cursed them already, because you do not take it to heart.

"Behold, I will rebuke your descendants and spread refuse on your faces, the refuse of your solemn feasts; and one will take you away with it. Then you shall know that I have sent this Commandment to you, that My Covenant with Levi may continue," says the Lord of Hosts.

"My Covenant was with him, one of life and peace, and I gave them to him that he might fear Me; so he feared Me and was reverent before My Name. The Law of Truth was in his mouth, and injustice was not found on his lips. He walked with Me in peace and equity, and turned many away from iniquity.

"For the lips of a priest should keep knowledge, and people should seek the Law from his mouth; for he is the messenger of the Lord of Hosts. But you have departed from the way; you have caused many to stumble at the Law. You have corrupted the covenant of Levi," says the Lord of Hosts.

"Therefore I also have made you contemptible and base before all the people, because you have not kept My Ways but have shown partiality in the Law" (Mal. 2:1-9).

Stealing from God, in tithes and offerings, brings curses, lack, poverty, and failure. To this end, the Bible says, "Will a man rob God? Yet you have robbed Me! But you say, 'In what way have we robbed You?' In tithes and offerings.

"You are cursed with a curse, for you have robbed Me, even this whole nation. Bring all the tithes into the storehouse, that there may be food in My House, and try Me now in this," says the Lord of Hosts,

"If I will not open for you the windows of Heaven and pour out for you such blessing that there will not be room enough to receive it. And I will rebuke the devourer for your sakes, so that he will not destroy the fruit of your ground, nor shall the vine fail to bear fruit for you in the field," says the Lord of Hosts;

"And all nations will call you blessed, for you will be a delightful land," says the Lord of Hosts" (Mal. 3:8-12).

THE WORKS OF THE FLESH AND YOUTHFUL LUSTS

The works of the flesh are what the flesh desires and produces, and they are contrary to what the Spirit of God or the recreated, sincere, and tender human spirit desires and produces. We have been called to liberty, but we must not use liberty as an opportunity for the flesh. Walk in the Spirit, and you shall not fulfil the lust of the flesh.

Now the works of the flesh are evident, which are: adultery, fornication, uncleanness, lewdness, idolatry, sorcery, hatred, contentions, jealousies, outbursts of wrath, selfish ambitions, dissensions, heresies, envy, murders, drunkenness, revelries, and the like. Those who practice such things will not inherit the Kingdom of God. All things that we think, say, or do, that are contrary to the Spirit of God and the recreated human spirit are works of the flesh.

The Fruit of the Spirit is love, joy, peace, longsuffering, kindness, goodness, faithfulness, greatness, self-control. Against such there is no law. And those who are Christ's have crucified the flesh with its passions and desires. Let us walk in the Spirit. Let us not become conceited, provoking one another, envying another (Gal. 5:13-26).

There is no condemnation to those who are in Christ Jesus, who do not walk according to the flesh, but walk according to the Spirit. For those who live according to the flesh set their minds on the things of the flesh, but those who live according to the Spirit, the Things of the Spirit. For to be carnally minded is death, but to be spiritually minded is life and peace.

Because the carnal mind is enmity against God; for it is not subject to the Law of God, nor indeed can be. So then those who are in the flesh cannot please God. But you are not in the flesh but in the Spirit, if indeed the Spirit of God dwells in you. Now if anyone does not have the Spirit of Christ, he is not His.

And if Christ is in you, the body is dead because of sin, but the Spirit is life because of righteousness. But if the Spirit of Him Who raised Jesus Christ from the dead dwells in you, He Who raised Christ Jesus from the dead will also give life to your mortal bodies through His Spirit Who dwells in you.

Therefore, brethren, we are debtors – not to the flesh, to live according to the flesh. For if you live according to the flesh, you will die; but if by the Spirit you put to death the deeds of the flesh, you will live. For as many as are led by the Spirit of God, these are the sons of God (Rom. 8:1-14).

Let love be without hypocrisy. Abhor what is evil. Cling to what is good. Be kindly affectionate to one another with brotherly love. Be of the same mind towards one another. Repay no one evil for evil. Do not be overcome by evil, but overcome evil with good.

Present your bodies a living sacrifice, holy, acceptable to God, which is your reasonable service. And be not conformed to this world, but be transformed by the renewing of your mind, that you may prove what is that Good and Acceptable and Perfect Will of God (Rom. 12).

Concerning men (unbelievers and sinners), the Bible says that the Wrath of God is revealed from Heaven against all ungodliness and unrighteousness of men, who suppress the Truth in unrighteousness. Although they knew God, they did not glorify Him as God, nor were thankful, but became futile in their thoughts, and their foolish hearts were darkened.

Professing to be wise, they became fools, and changed the glory of Incorruptible God into an image made like a corruptible man – and birds and four-footed animals and creeping things. Therefore God also gave them up to uncleanness, in the lusts of their hearts, to dishonour their bodies among themselves, who exchanged the Truth of the Lord for the lie, and worshipped and served the creature rather than the Creator, Who is blessed forever. Amen.

For this reason, God gave them up to vile passions. For even their women exchanged the natural use for what is against nature. Likewise also the men, leaving the natural use of the woman, burned in their lust for one another, men with men committing what is shameful, and receiving in themselves the penalty of their error which was due.

And even as they did not want to retain God in their knowledge, God gave them over to a debased mind, to do those things which are not fitting, being filled will all unrighteousness, sexual immorality, wickedness, covetousness, maliciousness; full of envy, murder, strife, deceit, evil-mindedness;

They are whisperers, backbiters, haters of God, violent, proud, boaster, inventors of evil things, disobedient to parents, undiscerning, untrustworthy, unloving, unforgiving, unmerciful, who, knowing the Righteous Judgment of God, that those who practice such things are deserving of death, not only do the same but also approve of those who practice them (Rom. 1:18-32).

Brethren, do you not know that the unrighteous will not inherit the Kingdom of God? Do not be deceived. Neither fornicators, nor idolaters, nor adulterers, nor homosexuals, nor sodomites, nor thieves, nor covetous, nor drunkards, nor revilers, nor extortioners will inherit the Kingdom of God.

And such were some of you. But you were washed, but you were sanctified, but you were justified in the Name of Lord Jesus Christ and by the Holy Spirit of our God (1 Cor. 6:9-11).

Moreover, brethren, I do not want you to be unaware that all the fathers of Israel were under the cloud, all passed through the sea, all were baptized into Moses in the cloud and in the sea, all ate the same spiritual food, and all drank the same spiritual drink. But with most of them God was not well pleased, for their bodies were scattered in the wilderness.

Now these things became our examples, to the intent that we should not lust after evil things as they also lusted. And do not become idolaters as were some of them. Nor let us commit sexual immorality, as some of them did, and in one day twenty-three thousand fell, nor let us tempt Christ, as some of them also tempted, and were destroyed by serpents; nor complain, as some of them also complained, and were destroyed by the destroyer.

Now all these things happened to them as examples, and they were written for our admonition, upon whom the ends of the ages have come. Therefore, let him who thinks he stands take heed lest he fall. No temptation has overtaken you except such as is common to man; but God is faithful, Who will not allow you to be tempted beyond what you are able, but with the temptation will also make the way of escape, that you may be able to bear it (1 Cor. 10:1-13).

Do not touch what is unclean and the Lord will receive you. "Come out from among the sinners and be separate," says the Lord. Brethren, let us cleanse ourselves from all filthiness of the flesh and Spirit, perfecting holiness in the Fear of God.

Walk worthy of the calling with which you were called, with all lowliness and gentleness, with longsuffering, bearing with one another in love, endeavouring to keep the Unity of the Spirit in the bond of peace (Eph. 4:1-3).

Do not walk any longer as the rest of the Gentiles walk, in the futility of their mind, having their understanding darkened, being alienated from the Life of God, because of the ignorance that is in them, because of the blindness of their heart; who being past feeling, have given themselves over to lewdness, to work all uncleanness with greediness.

But you have not so learned Christ, if indeed you have heard Him and have been taught by Him, as the Truth is in Jesus Christ: that you put off, concerning your former conduct, the old man which grows corrupt according to the deceitful lusts, and be renewed in the spirit of your mind, and that you put on the new man which was created according to God, in true righteousness and holiness.

Let no corrupt word proceed out of your mouth, but what is good for necessary edification, that it may impart grace the hearers. And do not grieve the Holy Spirit of God, by Whom you were sealed for the Day of Redemption.

Let all bitterness, wrath, anger, clamour, and evil speaking be put away from you, with all malice. And be kind to one another, tenderhearted, forgiving one another, even as God in Christ forgave you (Eph. 4:17-32). Be imitators of God as dear children. Let not fornication and all uncleanness or covetousness be named among you, as is fitting for Saints; neither filthiness, nor foolish talking, nor coarse jesting, which are not fitting, but rather giving of thanks.

For this you know, that no fornicator, unclean person, nor covetous man, who is an idolater, has any inheritance in the Kingdom of Christ and God. Let no one deceive you with empty words, for because of these things the Wrath of God comes upon the sons of disobedience.

Therefore do not be partakers with them. For you were once darkness, but now you are light in the Lord. Walk as children of light (for the Fruit of the Spirit is in all goodness, righteousness, and Truth), finding out what is acceptable to the Lord. And have no fellowship with the unfruitful works of darkness, but rather expose them.

For it is shameful, even to speak of those things which are done by them in secret. See that you walk circumspectly, not as fools but as wise, redeeming the time, because the days are evil. Therefore do not be unwise, but understand what the Will of the Lord is (Eph. 5:1-17).

A true Christian has been crucified with Christ; he should no longer be the one living, but Christ living in him, and the life which he now lives in the flesh, he ought to live by faith in the Son of God, Who loved him and gave Himself for him (Gal. 2:20).

Work out your own salvation with fear and trembling; for it is God Who works in you both to will and to do for His Good Pleasure. Do all things without complaining and disputing, that you God without fault in the midst of a crooked and perverse generation, among whom you shine as light in the world, holding fast the Word of Life (Phil. 2:12-16).

Walk worthy of the Lord, fully pleasing Him, being fruitful in every good work and increasing in the Knowledge of God. You ought to be holy, and blameless, and above reproach in God's Sight (Col. 1:10,22). If you were raised with Christ, seek those things which are above, where Christ is, sitting at the Right Hand of God.

Set your mind on things above, not on things on the earth. For you died, and your life is hidden with Christ in God. When Christ Jesus Who is our Life appears, then you also will appear with Him in glory. Therefore put to death your members which are on the earth: fornication, uncleanness, passion, evil desire, and covetousness, which is idolatry.

Because of these things the Wrath of God is coming upon the sons of disobedience, in which you yourselves once walked when you lived in them. But now you yourselves are to put off all these: anger, wrath, malice, blasphemy, filthy language, out of your mouth.

Do not lie to one another, since you have put off the old man with his deeds, and have put on the new man who is renewed in knowledge according to the Image of Him Who created him.

Therefore, as the Elect of God, holy and beloved, put on tender mercies, kindness, humility, meekness, longsuffering; bearing with one another, and forgiving one another, if anyone has any complaint against another; even as Christ forgave you, so you also must do.

But above all these things put on love, which is the bond of perfection. And let the Peace of God rule in your hearts. Let the Word of Christ dwell in you richly in all wisdom (Col. 3:1-16). Walk in such a way as to please God.

WARNINGS FROM THE LORD

Your sanctification is the Will of God: that you should abstain from sexual immorality. God did not call us to uncleanness, but in holiness. Anyone who rejects this does not reject man, but God, Who has also given us His Holy Spirit. Brethren, stand fast and hold the traditions which you were taught, whether by word or by letter (2 Thes. 2:15).

These later times, some will depart from the faith, giving heed to deceiving spirits and doctrines of demons, speaking lies in hypocrisy, having their own conscience seared with a hot iron (1 Tim. 4:1-2).

Take heed to yourself and to the Doctrine. Continue in them, for in doing this you will save both yourself and those who hear you (1 Tim. 4:16). He or she who lives in pleasure is dead while he or she lives (1 Tim. 5:6).

In the last days (which days we are in), perilous times have come: for men have become lovers of themselves, lovers of money, boasters, proud, blasphemers, disobedient to parents, unthankful, unholy, unloving, unforgiving, slanderers, without self-control, brutal, despisers of good, traitors, headstrong, haughty, lovers of pleasure rather than Lovers of God, having a form of Godliness but denying its power. And from such people turn away (2 Timothy 3:1-5).

The time has come that people do not endure Sound Doctrine, but according to their own desires, because they have itching ears, they will heap up for themselves teachers; and they will turn their ears away from the Truth, and be turned aside to fables (2 Tim. 4:3,4).

Today, if you hear His Voice, do not harden your heart. There is no creature that is hidden from God's sight, but all things are naked and open to the eyes of Him to Whom we must give account (Heb. 4:13).

Therefore, do not cast away your confidence, which has great reward. For you have need of endurance, so that after you have done the Will of God, you may receive the promise. The just shall live by faith, but if anyone draws back, God's Soul has no pleasure in him. But we are not of those who draw back to perdition, but of those who believe to the saving of the soul (Heb. 10:35-39).

Look carefully, lest anyone fall short of the Grace of God; lest any root of bitterness springing up cause trouble, and by this many become defiled, lest there be any fornicator or profane person like Esau, who for one morsel of food sold his birthright.

For you know that afterwards, when he wanted to inherit the blessing, he was rejected; for he found no place for repentance, though he sought it diligently with tears (Heb. 12:15-17). Our God is a Consuming Fire (Heb. 12:29).

Blessed is the man who endures temptation, for when he has been approved, he will receive the Crown of Life which the Lord has promised to those who love Him (Jas 1:12). Each of us is tempted when he is drawn away by his own desires and enticed. Then, when desire has conceived, it gives birth to sin; and sin, when it is full-grown, brings forth death (Jas 1:14,15).

Lay aside all filthiness and overflow of wickedness, and receive with meekness the implanted Word, which is able to save your souls. But be doers of the Word, and not hearers only, deceiving yourselves (Jas 1:21,22).

For whoever shall keep the whole Law, and yet stumble in one point, he is guilty of all. For He Who said, "Do not commit adultery," also said, "Do not murder." Now if you do not commit adultery, but you do murder, you have become a transgressor of the Law (Jas 2:10,11). Therefore, brother, don't chose which things to obey and which ones to ignore. If anyone does not stumble in word, he is a perfect man, able also to bridle the whole body. (Jas 3:2).

Adulterers and adulteress! Do you not know that friendship with the world is enmity God? Whoever therefore wants to be a friend of the world makes himself an enemy of God. Draw near to God and He will draw near to you. Cleanse your hands, you sinners; and purify your hearts, you double minded. Lament and mourn and weep! Let your laughter be turned to mourning, and your joy to gloom. He who knows to do good and does not do it, the same sins (Jas 4:4,8,9,17).

As obedient children, do not conform yourselves to the former lusts, as in your ignorance, but as He Who called you is holy, you also be holy in all your conduct. And if you call on the Father, Who without partiality judges according to each one's work, conduct yourself throughout the time of your stay here in fear (1 Pet. 1:14-17).

Giving all diligence, add to your faith virtue, to virtue knowledge, to knowledge self-control, to self-control perseverance, to perseverance Godliness, to Godliness brotherly kindness, and to brotherly kindness love. For if these thing are yours and abound, you will be neither barren nor unfruitful in the Knowledge of our Lord Jesus Christ.

For he who lacks these things is short-sighted, even to blindness, and has forgotten that he was cleansed from his old sins. Therefore, brethren, be even more diligent to make your call and election sure, for if you do these things you will never stumble; for so an entrance will be supplied to you abundantly into the Everlasting Kingdom of our Lord and Saviour Jesus Christ (2 Pet. 1:5-11).

Do not love the world or anything in the world. If anyone loves the world, the Love of the Father is not in him. For all that is in the world – the lust of the flesh, the lust of the eyes, and the pride of life – is not of the Father, but is of the world. And the world is passing away, and the lust of it, but he who does the Will of God abides forever (1 Jn 2:15-17).

We know that when the Lord shall appear, we shall be like Him for we shall see Him as He is. And everyone who has this hope in Him purifies himself, just as He is pure. Whoever commits sin also commits lawlessness, and sin is lawlessness. And you that He was manifested to take away our sins, and in Him there is no sin. Whoever abides in Him does not sin. Whoever sins has neither seen Him nor known Him.

Let no one deceive you. He who practices righteousness is righteous, just as He is righteous. He who sins is of the devil, for the devil has sinned from the beginning. For this purpose the Son of God was manifested, that He might destroy the works of the devil.

Whoever has been Born of God does not sin, for His Seed remains in him; and he cannot sin, because he has been Born of God. In this the children of God and the children of the devil are manifest. Whoever does not practice righteousness is not of God, nor is he who does not love his brother (1 Jn 3:2-10).

But I want to remind you, though you should know this, that the Lord, having saved the people of Israel out of the land of Egypt, afterwards destroyed those who did not believe. And the angels who did not keep their proper domain, but left their own abode, He has reserved in everlasting chains under darkness for the judgment of the Great Day.

Sodom and Gomorrah, and the cities around them in a similar manner to these, having given themselves over to sexual immortality and gone after strange flesh, are set forth as an example, suffering the vengeance of Eternal Fire (Jude 1:5-7).

Jesus Christ testified that the Ephesian Christians had left their first love (Rev. 2:4). The Laodicean Christians were neither hot nor cold, and the Lord said He was going to spew them out of His Mouth. They thought they were rich and had need of nothing without knowing that they were wretched, miserable, poor, blind, and naked (Rev. 3:14-17).

And anyone not found written in the Book of Life was cast into the Lake of Fire (Rev. 20:15). Remember that Jesus Christ said that He will not cancel the name of anyone who overcomes from the Book of Life (Rev. 3:5).

This means that the name of him who does not overcome or who does not endure to the end, will be blotted out of the Book of Life. The Lord said that he who overcomes shall inherit all things and He shall be his God and he shall be His son.

But the cowardly, unbelieving, abominable, murderers, sexually immoral, sorcerers, idolaters, and all liars shall have their part in the Lake which burns with fire and brimstone, which is the Second Death (Rev. 21:7,8). He who is unjust, let him be unjust still; he who is filthy, let him be filthy still; he who is righteous, let him righteous still; he who is holy, let him be holy still.

Behold the Lord Jesus Christ is coming quickly, and His Reward is with Him, to give to every one according to his work. Blessed are those who do His Commandments, that they may have right to the Tree of Life, and may enter through the gates into the City (Rev. 22:11-14).

These days, many youths have strong negative lusts, desires, and passions. Many young people desire to get rich by any means; many of them are ready to sell their souls to the devil in exchange for money. And many of them are involved in armed robbery, stealing, prostitution, cultism, and many other things. But we have the responsibility to preach to them, and to pray for them.

Writing to Timothy, Apostle Paul said, "Let no one despise your youth, but be an example to the Believers in word, in conduct, in love, in spirit, in faith, in purity. The love of money is a root of all kinds of evil.... But you, O man of God, flee these things and pursue righteousness, Godliness, faith, love, patience, gentleness.

"Fight the good fight of faith, lay hold on Eternal Life, to which you were also called and have confessed the good confession in the presence of many witnesses. Flee also youthful lusts; but pursue righteousness, faith, love, peace with those who call on the Lord out of a pure heart" (1 Tim. 4:12; 6:10-12; 2 Tim. 2:22).

Whether you call them works of the flesh or youthful lusts, they represent sin and disobedience towards God. They also represent the life that leads to Hell Fire. Now is the time for repentance and change; tomorrow may be too late. There is no forgiveness in Hell. Repent now!

Never Say That God Said What He Did Not Say!

MAKING YOUR CALLING AND ELECTION SURE

The Lord, through Apostle Peter, tells us to give diligence to making your calling and election sure. He says that if we do this, we will not fall; rather, we will make Heaven (2 Pet. 2:10-11). God has called us and elected us for His Kingdom. He called us out of the kingdom of darkness into the Kingdom of His Dear Son.

The Lord has elected and appointed us to His Kingdom. When we were yet sinners, He elected and appointed us to be His Own people, who will obey Him and live to please Him in this world, so that after this life, we will live with Him forever in His Kingdom. However, there is need to make this election and appointment sure.

When God says that we should make our election sure, it means that it is possible for us (or some of us) not to attain or make our election or appointment. How? By living a careless life. The life of sin and disobedience is a life of carelessness. It also means that if we follow the steps and rules given us, we shall attain (make) our election or appointment.

God did not leave us without direction. He has given us His Word, the Bible, so that we can run the race set before us the way we should run it. The Bible contains the dos and don'ts of the Christian race, our calling and election. If you live your life according to the Word of God, you will not fall, but you will be ushered into Heaven. Read, study, and meditate on the Word of God so that you may know the Mind of God.

The Lord has given us His Holy Spirit, the Spirit of Truth, Who teaches us all Truth. The Spirit of God will use the Word of God to lead us. He will make us understand the Word of God in our hearts. He will give us the ability to please God, and we should depend on Him, for without Him, we can do nothing. The Spirit of God leads us through many means; however, in all things, He doesn't go contrary to the Bible, because He inspired the Bible (2 Tim. 3:16; 2 Pet. 1:21).

Apostle Peter gives us insights on how we can make our calling and election sure. He tells us to add to our faith virtue, to virtue knowledge, to knowledge self-control, to self-control perseverance, to perseverance Godliness, to Godliness brotherly kindness, and to brotherly kindness love. He tells us to do those things with all diligence. If we do it abundantly, we will be neither barren nor unfruitful in the Knowledge of our Lord Jesus Christ (2 Pet. 1:5-8).

Give diligence to prayer, for the spirit is willing but the flesh is weak. Be watchful always, for if you don't, you may not even be aware that the enemy is around. Live the life of holiness, obedience, and consecration. Learn to discipline your body and bring it under subjection. The Grace of the Lord is abundantly available to us. We shall stand for the Lord, now and forever. Amen.

The Word lets us know that some who are first will be the last, and the last first. May it not be so with us! It is not he who calls Jesus Christ, "Lord," that will enter the Kingdom of Heaven, but he who does the Will of God. No matter what you may be doing for the Lord, always remember that without holiness no man shall see the Lord (Heb. 12:14).

Jesus Christ tells us that if we keep His Commandments, we will abide in His Love, as He kept the Father's Commandment and abide in the Father's Love.

Jesus Christ is the True Vine and we are the branches. The Father, Who is the Vine-dresser, takes away every branch that does not bear fruit.

However, He prunes the branches that bear fruit, that they may bear more fruit. We are in Jesus Christ, and just as Jesus Christ bore Fruit by getting Followers and pleasing the Father, we too ought to win souls and please God.

Abide in Jesus Christ, and let Him abide in you. As the branch cannot bear fruit of itself, unless it abides in the vine, neither can you, unless you abide in the Lord. He who abides in Him, and He in him, bears much fruit; for without Him, you can do nothing.

Anyone who does not abide in Him is cast out as a branch and is withered and burnt. The Father is glorified when we bear much fruit, so as to confirm that we are Jesus Christ's Disciples.

If we abide in Him and His Words abide in us, we will ask what we desire, and it shall be done for us. If we keep His Commandment, we will abide and remain in His Love, just as He kept His Father's Commandments and abides in His Love.

We are His Friends if we do whatever He commands us. We did not choose Him, but He chose us and appointed us that we should go and bear fruit, and that our fruit should remain, that whatever we ask the Father in His Name He may give us (Jn 15).

When Moses was instructed by God to build the tabernacle, God told him to make it according to all that He showed him, after the pattern of the tabernacle, and the pattern of all the instruments thereof.

God emphasized this when He said, "See to it that you make them after their pattern, which was shown you on the mountain" (Exo. 25:9,40).

Apostle Paul stressed the importance of this when he referred to this interaction between God and Moses in the Book of Hebrews and used it to compare to Jesus Christ's Ministry (Heb. 8:4-6).

God has a pattern for whatever He tells us to do. The Bible speaks of a pattern of good works (Tit. 2:7). We are not to seek the praise of men but that of God. We are ambassadors of Christ, and we should represent Him well.

Even, when we say that this or that person is a man of God, we are saying that the person is sent by God and represents God. Apostle Paul emphasized the importance of doing things the right way when he said that if anyone competes in athletics, he is not crowned unless he competes according to the rules (2 Tim. 2:5).

No wonder he instructed us to run in such a way that we may obtain the prize. Everyone who competes for the prize is temperate in all things. Now they do it to obtain a perishable crown, but we an imperishable crown.

This made him to run thus: not with uncertainty. Thus he fought: not as one who beats the air: but he disciplined his body, and brought it into subjection, lest, when he had preached to others, he himself should become disqualified (1 Cor. 9:24-27).

Paul says, "But what things were gain to me, these I have counted loss for Christ. Yet indeed I also count all things loss for the excellence of the knowledge of Christ Jesus my Lord, for Whom I have suffered the loss of all things, and count them as rubbish, that I may gain Christ,

"And be found in Him, not having my own righteousness which is from the Law, but that which is through faith in Christ, the righteousness which is from God by faith;

"That I may know Him and the power of His Resurrection and the fellowship of His Sufferings, being conformed to His Death, if by any means, I may attain to the Resurrection from the dead.

"Not that I have already attained, or am already perfected; but I press on, that I may lay hold of that for which Christ Jesus has also laid hold on me. Brethren, I do not count myself to have apprehended;

"But one thing I do, forgetting those things which are behind and reaching forward to those things which are ahead, I press towards the goal for the prize of the Upward Call of God in Christ Jesus.

"Therefore, let us as many as are mature, have this in mind, and if in anything you think otherwise, God will reveal even this to you" (Phil. 3:7-15).

God wants faithfulness in whatever He calls you to do. We are pilgrims, sojourners, and strangers in this world, and we must live our lives with that consciousness.

The questions are, "Do you know what He has called you to do? Are you doing it? If so, are you doing it God's Way or Pattern?" God called us to become His children by the acceptance of the Gospel. Have you become born again? If so, are you living the Christian life?

Then how is your Christian life? Also, God calls each of us to do specific thing(s) for Him. Do you know that (those) thing(s)? Are you doing it (them)? How are you doing it (them)?

It is possible to live your whole life on earth without knowing what God has called you to do. This is why many have lived and died without even hearing that there is a Jesus Christ.

Many have heard about Him, but have hardened their hearts to the Gospel; but many have not heard about Him, even now.

We have the responsibility to preach the Gospel and teach the Word of God to the ends of the world. This is what we call 'the Great Commission.' How are you committed to the Great Commission, individually and collectively?

You must preach the Gospel (the Good News of the Kingdom of God). You must preach by yourself because, in a sense, everybody is a preacher and an evangelist. No wonder Apostle Paul told Pastor Timothy, "Do the work of an evangelist" (2 Tim. 4:5).

The Bible tells us that some are called, specifically, as evangelists. But you must preach, starting from your home, office, or school. You can sponsor others financially to help them preach where you may not go.

Then many who have been born again live their Christian lives the way they want to. Many have chosen (consciously or unconsciously) what they will obey and what they will not obey.

People do many different things which are ungodly, unbiblical, and satanic in churches and say, "It does not matter." But what will they do on the Day of Judgment when they find out that they actually matter? But then, it will be too late, and there will be no second chance. God is no respecter of persons, for He created all.

Then they will cry and say, "Had I known, I..." and their cries will not be heard. These will go into everlasting punishment in Hell Fire. They will have their appointment with the hypocrites and compromisers.

The angels told Lot, saying, "Escape for your life, do not look behind you nor stay anywhere in the plain. Escape to the mountains, lest you be destroyed" (Gen. 19:17). My brethren, let us amend our ways while there is still time.

God did not call us to destroy us along the way; but if anyone destroys himself, let him not blame God. Work out your own salvation with fear and trembling. If you live in pleasure, living to gratify your flesh, you are heading to Hell Fire. Live a holy life, and get perfected in holiness.

There is no agreement between light and darkness; do not do evil or exaggerate, thinking you want to help God. Live in righteousness and it will be well with your soul. God's Grace is available to us always.

It is the Will of God that you are sanctified. God wants you to be consecrated to doing His Word and Will, no matter the cost. There are things you must sacrifice for the Cause of Jesus Christ.

You must carry your cross daily and follow Him. We must obey the Commandments of our Lord and Master. We must serve God, our Maker; He is worthy of our service.

Make every effort to make your calling and election sure, because if you do this, you will be with God and the Lord Jesus Christ forever. Take heed to yourself and the doctrine that you preach, teach, and enforce. In doing this, you will save both yourself and the people that hear and follow you.

We are to walk in the light and truth. To walk in the light is to act and do according to the Word of God, which is a lamp to our feet, and a light to our path.

To walk in the truth is to live, act, and speak according to the Word of God, which is truth. Also, to walk in truth is also to be honest, transparent, and truthful.

We are the light and the salt of the world. We are a source of direction to the people of the world; God uses us to show them the right way, and to lead them out of darkness.

As the salt of the world, we are to add flavour and taste to people's lives, and we should cause them to be preserved by the Power of God.

Jesus Christ is our Focus, and the Word of God (the Bible) our standard. Apostle Paul's life and ministry is worthy of emulation, even though he did make some mistakes.

Moreover, brethren, I do not want you to be unaware that all the fathers of Israel were under the cloud, all passed through the sea, all were baptized into Moses in the cloud and in the sea, all ate the same spiritual food, and drank of that spiritual rock that followed them, and that Rock was Christ.

But with most of them God was not well pleased, for their bodies were scattered in the wilderness. Now these things became our examples, to the intent that we should not lust after evil things as they also lusted.

And do not become idolaters as were some of them. As it is written, "The people sat down to eat and drink, and rose up to play." Nor let us commit sexual immorality, as some of them did, and in one day twenty-three thousand fell.

Don't say, "That was in the Old Testament," because God struck Ananias and Saphirah in the New Testament. Let us not tempt Christ, as some of them also tempted, and were destroyed by serpents; nor complain, as some of them also complained, and were destroyed by the destroyer.

Now all these things happened to them as examples, and they were written for our admonition, upon whom the ends of the ages have come. Therefore, let him who thinks he stands take heed lest he fall.

No temptation has overtaken you except such as is common to man, but God is faithful, Who will not allow you to be tempted beyond what you are able, but with the temptation will also make the way of escape, that you may be able to bear it (1 Cor. 10:1-13).

People backslide and fall away from the faith, from Jesus Christ and His Word. Even people who had been used mightily by God have gone away from God and became separated from the Life of God. My brethren, this ought not to be so.

He that has entered God's Rest has himself also ceased from his work as God did from His. Let us, therefore, be diligent to enter that rest, lest anyone fall according to the same example of disobedience.

For the Word of God is living and powerful, and sharper than any two-edged sword, piercing even to the division of soul and spirit, and of joints and marrow, and is a discerner of the thoughts and intents of the heart.

And there is no creature hidden from His Sight, but all things are naked and open to the Eyes of Him to Whom we must give account (Heb. 4:10-13).

The covenant we have in Jesus Christ is a better covenant than the one the Israelites had with God, and it is based on better promises. The punishment for rejecting Jesus Christ and His Word is worse than the punishment the Israelites received for disobeying the Law, though we may not see it now.

Beware of the little leaven that leavens the whole lump; beware of the little foxes that destroy the vine. Beware of the little 'it-doesn't-matter' that spoils things in the House of God. Beware of the false prophets and the false teachers.

Concerning the specific assignment(s) God has for each one of us, let us take time, in prayer, fasting, and waiting on Him, to know what He wants us to do. And whatever the cost and sacrifice, let us not love our lives even to death.

Let us not do what we want to do. Remember that it is to God that you will render account to. Don't love the praise of men.

If God called you to be an evangelist, don't remain a pastor; if He called you to be a pastor, don't remain an evangelist. If God doesn't want you to open a church, don't open one.

Do you know that you can have one of the largest churches in the world, and organize one of the largest crusades in the world, and still not follow God's Plan for your life? God will help you fulfil His Task for you.

God has a pattern for success; follow that pattern to be successful in life. Learn to call what God calls 'success,' 'success,' and what He calls 'failure,' 'failure.' If you follow the pattern of the world, you can't be successful in God's Sight. Remember that life is not in the abundance of what you possess.

Strike the shepherd, and the sheep will be scattered. You have to know that if you don't follow the pattern of Godliness, others will follow you do the same things, as a minister.

Never Say That God Said What He Did Not Say!

THE RAPTURE OF THE SAINTS

Speaking about the Rapture (catching away) of the Saints, Apostle Paul wrote: "But I do not want you to be ignorant, brethren, concerning those who have fallen asleep, lest you sorrow as others who have no hope. For if we believe that Jesus died and rose again, even so God will bring with Him those who sleep in Jesus. For this we say to you by the Word of the Lord, that we who are alive and remain until the Coming of the Lord will by no means precede those who are asleep.

"For the Lord Himself will descend from Heaven with a shout, with the voice of an archangel, and with the Trumpet of God. And the dead in Christ will rise first. Then we who are alive and remain shall be caught up together with them in the clouds to meet the Lord in the air. And thus we shall always be with the Lord. Therefore comfort one another with these Words.

"But concerning the times and the seasons, brethren, you have no need that I should write to you. For you yourselves know perfectly that the Day of the Lord so comes as a thief in the night. For when they say, 'Peace and safety!' then sudden destruction comes upon them, as labour pains upon a pregnant woman. And they shall not escape.

"But you, brethren, are not in darkness, so that this Day should overtake you as a thief. You are all sons of light and sons of the day. We are not of the night nor of darkness. Therefore let us not sleep, as others do, but let us watch and be sober. For those who sleep, sleep at night, and those who get drunk are drunk at night.

"But let us who are of the day be sober, putting on the breastplate of faith and love, and as a helmet the hope of salvation. For God did not appoint us to wrath, but to obtain salvation through our Lord Jesus Christ, Who died for us, that whether we wake or sleep, we should live together with Him. Therefore comfort each other and edify one another, just as you also are doing" (1 Thes. 4:13 to 5:11). Notice that we will continue to be free from God's Wrath if we continue in the light. We are to watch and be sober.

The word – rapture – means great excitement and happiness. Being rapturous is expressing great happiness or admiration. The Rapture of the Saints is an event which Believers and Christians look forward to expectantly – an event which will bring great excitement and happiness to them when they see their Lord and Master in the cloud, having escaped the devil, the world, and eternal damnation. Therefore the Rapture is the catching away of the Saints to be with their Lord forever – an event which will bring great excitement and happiness to them.

The Word of God says, "Heaven and earth will pass away, but My Words will by no means pass away. But of that Day and Hour no one knows, not even the angels of Heaven, but My Father only. But as the days of Noah were, so also will the Coming of the Son of Man be. For as in the days before the Flood, they were eating and drinking, marrying and giving in marriage, until the day that Noah entered the ark,

"And did not know until the Flood came and took them all away, so also will the Coming of the Son of Man be. Then two men will be in the field: one will be taken and the other left. Two women will be grinding at the mill: one will be taken and the other left. Watch therefore, for you do not know what hour your Lord is coming.

"But know this, that if the master of the house had known what hour the thief would come, he would have watched and not allowed his house to be broken into. Therefore you also be ready, for the Son of Man is coming at an hour you do not expect. Who then is a faithful and wise servant, whom his master made ruler over his household, to give them food in due season?

"Blessed is that servant whom his master, when he comes, will find so doing. Assuredly, I say to you that he will make him ruler over all his goods. But if that evil servant says in his heart,

'My master is delaying his coming,' and begins to beat his fellow servants, and to eat and drink with the drunkards, the master of that servant will come on a day when he is not looking for him and at an hour he is not aware of,

"And will cut him into two and appoint him his portion with the hypocrites. There shall be weeping and gnashing of teeth" (Matt. 24:35-51). Notice that the Word says, "Heaven and earth will pass away…" (Matt. 24:35). This is consistent with what Apostle Peter said, when he wrote: "But the Day of the Lord will come as a thief in the night, in which the heavens will pass away with a great noise, and the elements will melt with fervent heat;

"Both the earth and the works that are in it will be burned up. Nevertheless we, according to His Promise, look for New Heavens and a New Earth in which righteousness dwells" (2 Pet. 3:10,13). Therefore, know that everything in this world will be destroyed by fire. Notice also that people will be doing normal things when the Rapture will take place without any previous warning, other than the signs of the last days.

Concerning what Jesus Christ said, Mark put it this way: "But of that Day and Hour no one knows, not even the angels in Heaven, nor the Son, but only the Father. Take heed, watch and pray; for you do not know when the Time is. It is like a man going to a far country, who left his house and gave authority to his servants, and to each his work, and commanded the doorkeeper to watch.

"Watch therefore, for you do not know when the Master of the House is coming – in the evening, at midnight, at the crowing of the rooster, or in the morning – lest coming suddenly, He finds you sleeping. And what I say to you, I say to all: Watch!" (Mk 13:32-37). Mark adds that not even Jesus Christ Himself (at least, as at the time He was here on earth) knows (knew) the Time of His Coming. And He tells us to take heed, watch, and pray.

According to Luke's Account, "Heaven and earth will pass away, but My Words will by no means pass away. But take heed to yourselves, least your hearts be weighed down with carousing, drunkenness, and cares of this life, and that Day come on you unexpectedly. For it will come as a snare on all those who dwell on the face of the whole earth.

"Watch therefore, and pray always that you may be counted worthy to escape all these that will come to pass, and to stand before the Son of Man" (Lk. 21:33-36). The Rapture is going to happen to take away the faithful Believers and Saints, so that they will escape the Great Tribulation that will come upon the earth at the coming of the beast. But we need to watch and pray always to be counted worthy to escape the Great Tribulation.

Speaking to the church in Philadelphia, Jesus Christ said, "Because you have kept My Command to persevere, I also will keep you from the hour of trial which shall come upon the whole world, to test those who dwell on the earth. Behold, I am coming quickly! Hold fast what you have, that no one may take your crown" (Rev. 3:10-11). If you are faithful and you persevere, God will keep you away from the sufferings of the Great Tribulation by the Rapture.

Luke also states: "And as it was in the days of Noah, so it will be also in the Days of the Son of the Man: They ate, they drank, they married wives, they were given in marriage, until the day that Noah entered the ark, and the Flood came and destroyed them all. Likewise as it was also in the days of Lot: They ate, they drank, they bought, they sold, they planted, they built;

"But on the day that Lot went out of Sodom it rained fire and brimstone from heaven and destroyed them all. Even so will it be in the Day when the Son of Man is revealed. In that Day, he who is on house top, and his goods are in the house, let him not come down to take them away. And likewise the one who is in the field, let him not turn back. Remember Lot's wife.

"Whoever seeks to save his life will lose it, and whoever loses his life will preserve it. I tell you, in that night there will be two men in one bed: the one will be taken and the other will be left. Two women will be grinding together: the one will be taken and the other left. Two men will be in the field; the one will be taken and the other left" (Lk. 17:26-36). Remember Lot's wife who looked back in disobedience, maybe because of loving material things, and turned to a pillar of salt.

And John wrote: "Behold what manner of love the Father has bestowed on us, that we should be called children of God! Therefore the world does not know us, because it did not know Him. Beloved, now we are children of God; and it has not yet been revealed what we shall be, but we know that when He is revealed, we shall be like Him, for we shall see Him as He is. And everyone who has this hope in Him purifies himself, just as He is pure" (1 Jn 3:1-3).

After the Rapture, that is, during the period of the Great Tribulation, there shall be the Marriage of the Lamb in Heaven. Concerning this, the Bible says, "Then a voice came from the Throne, saying, 'Praise our God, all you His Servants and those who fear Him, both small and great!' And I heard, as it were, the voice of a great multitude, as the sound of many waters and as the sound of mighty thunderings, saying, 'Alleluia! For the Lord God Omnipotent reigns.

'Let us be glad and rejoice and give Him glory, for the Marriage of the Lamb has come, and His wife has made herself ready.' And to her it was granted to be arrayed in fine linen, clean and bright, for the fine linen is the righteous acts of the Saints. Then he said to me, 'Write: "Blessed are those who are called to the Marriage Supper of the Lamb!"' And he said to me, 'These are the True Sayings of God'" (Rev. 19:5-9).

Apostle Paul encouraged us, no matter what we may be going through, with these words: "For to me, to live is Christ, and to die is gain. But if I live on in the flesh, this will mean fruit from my labour; yet what I shall choose I cannot tell. For I am hard pressed between the two, having a desire to depart and be with Christ, which is far better. Nevertheless to remain in the flesh is more needful for you.

"Knowing that He Who raised up the Lord Jesus will also raise us up with Jesus, and will present us with you. For all things are for your sakes, that grace, having spread through many, may cause thanksgiving to abound to the Glory of God. Therefore we do not lose heart. Even though our outward man is perishing, yet the inward man is being renewed day by day.

"For our Light affliction, which is but for a moment, is working for us a far more exceeding and eternal weight of glory, while we do not look at the things which are seen, but at the things which are not seen. For the things which are seen are temporary, but the things which are not seen are eternal. For we know that if our earthly house, this tent, is destroyed, we have a building from God, a house not made with hands, eternal in the Heavens.

"For in this we groan, earnestly desiring to be clothed with our habitation which is from Heaven, if indeed, having been clothed, we shall not be found naked. For we who are in this tent groan, being burdened, not because we want to be unclothed, but further clothed, that mortality may be swallowed up by life.

"Now He Who has prepared us for this very thing is God, Who also has given us the Spirit as a Guarantee. So we are always confident, knowing that while we are at home in the body we are absent from the Lord. For we walk by faith, not by sight. We are confident, yes, well pleased rather to be absent from the body and to be present with the Lord. Therefore we make it our aim, whether present or absent, to be well pleasing to Him" (Phil. 1:21-24; 2 Cor. 4:14 to 5:9).

Never Say That God Said What He Did Not Say!

RUNNING THE RACE

There is a race that we have to run. That race is to please God and do His Will, so that we will make Heaven and God's Kingdom with great reward at last. In some areas, the race is the same for every Christian; and in some areas, the race is different for different people.

For instance, the race we are running to abide with God forever is the same for every Christian. The call to live a holy life is the same for all Christians; the call to pray is the same also. But someone may be called to be a prophet and the other called to be a pastor. Even within the office of the prophet, for instance, there different areas and methods of operation.

And Apostle Paul encouraged us to run the race in a manner that we may obtain (1 Cor. 9:24). Apostle Paul said that he didn't fight or beat aimlessly; he fought purposefully. When running your race, when doing what the Lord has assigned for you, do it in the way God wants you to do it; do what God wants you to do diligently, consistently, and faithfully.

The race we are running to Heaven is the highest race of this life. What shall it profit a man if he gains the whole world and loses his own soul? (Matt. 16:26). Nothing! The Lord said that it is better to enter life maimed than to be complete and be cast into Hell Fire (Matt. 5:29). No matter the cost, we should live to please God, and to be at peace with Him. As we all know, God is no respecter of persons.

In First Corinthians, chapter three, we see that one can build on the Foundation, which is Jesus Christ, using: hay, stubble, wood, costly stones, silver, or gold. What material are you building with? What is your motive for doing what you are doing? Is it for your belly or to be seen by men? You may have a trailer-load of work; but how will you gain if the trailer-load is of stubble, hay, or wood? You will experience loss!

As you run the race, concentrate on the race that God has set before you; don't run another man's race. Run your race as God expects you to do, and not as another one is running his. Remember that you will not be crowned except you run lawfully.

The soldier is not supposed to entangle himself with the affairs of this life. The hard-working farmer will rejoice at the harvest time. Those that compete in sports discipline themselves and train well in order to win. The Lord Jesus Christ is coming very soon, and He will reward everyone according to his work (Rev. 22:12).

The Word says, "Therefore we also, since we are surrounded by so great a cloud of witnesses, let us lay aside every weight, and the sin which so easily ensures us, and let us run with endurance the race that is set before us, looking unto Jesus, the Author and Finisher of our faith, Who for the Joy that was set before Him endured the Cross, despising the Shame, and has sat down at the right hand of the Throne of God" (Heb. 12:1-2).

Having been promised great and precious things by God, let us cleanse ourselves from all filthiness of the flesh and spirit, perfecting holiness in the Fear of God. And if you call on the Father, Who without partiality judges according to each one's work, conduct yourselves throughout the time of your stay here in fear.

And giving all diligence, add to your faith virtue, to virtue knowledge, to knowledge self-control, to self-control perseverance, to perseverance Godliness, to Godliness brotherly kindness, and to brotherly kindness love. For if these things are yours and abound, you will neither be barren nor unfruitful in the Knowledge of our Lord Jesus Christ.

For he who lacks these things is shortsighted, even to blindness, and has forgotten that he was cleansed from his old sins. Therefore, brethren, be even more diligent to make your call and election sure, for if you do these things you will never stumble; for so an entrance will be supplied to you abundantly into the Everlasting Kingdom of our Lord and Saviour Jesus Christ (2 Pet. 1:5-11).

The race we are running will certainly cost you some things. If you love anything, anyone, or even yourself more than the Lord Jesus Christ, then you are not worthy of Him. But remember that it is he who endures to the end that shall be saved, for God's Soul will have no pleasure in the one that draws back!

The Lord warned the apostles not to leave Jerusalem until they were filled with the Holy Spirit.

When the apostles needed deacons, who were to help them in taking care of the Disciples, they required that the people to be appointed had certain qualifications. They were to be people of good reputation, full of the Holy Spirit, and wisdom.

However, in many churches, many people are appointed deacons and elders, and they do not have these qualifications. Many are appointed to positions of authority in churches based on their fame, financial power, contributions to the church, age, and other human judgments.

Christians have a Wonderful Inheritance Who is the Holy Spirit. The Lord Jesus Christ did not leave us helpless, He sent the Holy Spirit to us (Jn 16:7). The Lord Jesus Christ baptizes with the Holy Spirit and fire.

The Holy Spirit of God is the Manifester of God's Power. In the beginning, when darkness covered the surface of the deep (water), the Spirit of God moved upon the face of the water, and when God declared that anything be on earth, His Spirit brought it to pass.

Some say that the Holy Spirit is the Power of God. That is true and untrue, depending on what you mean. The Holy Spirit is a Personality; He is the Third Person in the Holy Trinity, the Three in One.

Many don't believe in the Trinity, but the Bible teaches so. Jesus Christ told the apostles to baptize the Believers in the Name of the Father and of the Son and of the Holy Spirit (Matt. 28:19).

Apostle Paul prayed that the Grace of the Lord Jesus Christ, the Love of God, and the Communion of the Holy Spirit be with the Corinthian Christians (2 Cor. 13:14). For through Him (Jesus Christ), we both have access by one Spirit (the Holy Spirit) to the Father (Eph. 2:18).

The Lord (Jesus Christ) began the Message of Salvation which God (the Father) bears witness to with signs and wonders, and the Gifts of the Holy Spirit (Heb. 2:3-4).

There are Three that bear witness in Heaven: the Father, the Word (Jesus Christ), and the Holy Spirit; and these Three are One. (1 Jn 5:7). These Scriptures and others speak of the Trinity.

Believers receive power when the Holy Spirit comes upon them, so as to be witnesses to the Lord in their area and to the ends of the earth (Acts 1:8). This is why the Lord Jesus Christ told His apostles not to leave Jerusalem until they are endued with power from on High (Lk. 24:49).

But many try to do the Lord's Work without being filled with the Holy Spirit, and the powerlessness in their lives and ministries is the testimony they may not even be aware of. Will a policeman, who either carries no gun or have a mark 4 gun, put fear to well-armed robbers?

When you are baptized with the Holy Spirit and filled with Him, you have all the potential power that you will ever need, and He will release His Power in your life more and more as you obey Him, control yourself, and please God.

There are levels of anointing, and the Holy Spirit will anoint you with greater anointing as you follow His Leading and increase in your knowledge of the Lord God Almighty. Fasting will be useful.

Baptism in the Holy Spirit will be evidenced by speaking in tongues as in the Early Church. Many, instead of taking up the responsibility, instead of finding out why they have not been baptized and spoken in tongues, settle for a lower Christian life and say that everybody must not speak in tongues.

I could have settled for that also after seeking the baptism for a very long time and not receiving; but thanks to God for His Grace.

You can preach Jesus Christ, but to prove Him with the required signs and wonders, you must be filled with the Holy Spirit.

Note that the apostles and the Disciples had done marvelous things (signs and wonders) when the Lord imparted His Own Anointing on them, and yet, they were to wait for the Promise of the Father (Lk. 10:1-20).

Even though the Name of Jesus Christ in your mouth, as a Believer, can work miracles and wonders, there is a great difference when the anointing is resident on you.

Peter received the revelation of Whom Jesus Christ was when he was not yet filled with the Holy Spirit (Matt. 16:13-20). That you received a revelation, a vision, or that you prayed and God answered the prayer does not mean that you have been filled with the Holy Ghost.

You can only be full of the Power of the Holy Spirit after you must have been filled with the Person of the Holy Spirit (Acts 10:38; 1 Cor. 2:4; 1 Thes. 1:5). There is no other way, your title or position notwithstanding.

Being full of the Holy Spirit is the door to the Spiritual Gifts of the Holy Spirit (1 Cor. 12:1-11). After being baptized with the Holy Spirit, you must maintain the full measure of the Holy Spirit to keep on operating in His Power the way you should.

The Ephesian Christians were told to be filled (literally, be being filled) with the Holy Spirit (Eph. 5:18). The Roman Christians were told to be fervent in spirit (be on fire in the Spirit, maintain the Glow of the Holy Spirit) (Rom. 12:11).

When you are filled with the Holy Spirit, you will speak in tongues and to maintain the fullness of the Spirit, you will continue to speak.... This is a Biblical way, and any other way is not Biblical and cannot work.

This does not mean that God cannot use you if you are not filled with the Holy Spirit. The Disciples were filled with the Holy Spirit on the day of Pentecost and they spoke in other tongues as the Spirit gave them utterance (Acts 2:4).

Apostle Peter said that the Gift of the Holy Spirit is for every Believer (Acts 2:38-39). The Ephesian Believers that Apostle Paul found, even though they were Disciples, had not been filled with the Holy Spirit.

Thanks to God that they were filled with the Holy Spirit when hands were laid on them. Note that they spoke in tongues and prophesied (Acts 19:1-7).

Cornelius and his household only listened and believed Apostle Peter's message, and they were filled with the Holy Spirit and spoke in other tongues (Acts 10:44-48; Acts 11:13-15).

Saul (later known as Paul) was saved when he met Jesus Christ on his way to Damascus. Apostle Paul was filled with the Holy Spirit when Ananias laid hands on him (Acts 9:1-22), and he spoke in tongues (1 Cor. 14:18).

Apostle Paul encouraged Christians to speak with tongues in their individual prayers (1 Cor. 14:4,14; Jude 1:20). Speaking in tongues helps you pray for what you and others may not know about (Rom. 8:26). Speaking in tongues will help you tame the tongue (Jas 3:8).

Don't be afraid of receiving the wrong spirit, if you are born again and God is your Father. If our earthly parents will not give us fake or dangerous things, how much more will the Good, Loving, and Faithful Almighty God give us all good things? (Lk. 11:9-13).

Speaking in tongues is not the evidence of being born again, but of being baptized and filled with the Holy Spirit. The qualification for going to Heaven is being born again, and not speaking in tongues.

When you are born again, you receive a measure of the Holy Spirit to keep you going on in your Christian life, but when you are baptized and filled with the Holy Spirit, you are filled with the Holy Spirit to overflowing and this leads to power for witnessing for Jesus Christ.

The purpose of being filled with the Holy Spirit is to be a witness for Jesus Christ. It is to produce proofs and evidence that Jesus Christ is the Son of God, and He is alive. No wonder the Lord says that Believers will do the works that He did, even greater works than them (Jn 14:12).

The Holy Spirit will lead you into all truth and show you things to come. He will remind you of what you had heard and read (Jn 16:13; Jn 14:26).

There is no substitute for the Holy Spirit. He is in-charge of the world today, and as the Christians co-operate with Him, in obedience and prayer, He will bring the Will of God to pass on the earth.

Personality, learning, certificate, title, position, fame, and money cannot substitute the Holy Spirit, because it is not by power, nor by might, but by the Spirit of the Living God (Zech. 4:6). We must live and walk in the Spirit.

There is a Pentecostal mentality. Some assume that because they go to churches that are called Pentecostal churches, they have more power or gifts in them than others, but that is not the yardstick of measurement of the Power and Gifts of the Spirit.

Some assume that because they speak in tongues, they have arrived in the Things of the Spirit, but there is so much more to the Things of the Spirit. Then some others may assume that if you are not baptized in the Holy Spirit you will not go to Heaven, but this is far from the truth.

When you are full of the Holy Spirit, and you are obedient to Him, you will be full of the Mighty Power of God. Then you will affect your generation in a mighty way and bring much glory and praise to the Almighty God. Amen.

If you must walk in God's Miracle-working Power, you must have an intimate relationship with Him. I am speaking of walking in that power consistently. An intimate relationship with God will necessitate your knowing and understanding His Word.

His Word will tell you His Character and His Ability. From His Word, you will get to know your rights and privileges as a child of God; you will develop your faith, for faith comes by hearing the Word of God.

Let the Word of God dwell in you richly in all wisdom (Col. 3:16), and study to show yourself approved to God, a workman that needs not to be ashamed, rightly dividing the Word of Truth (2 Tim. 2:15).

When you study the Word well, and compare Scripture with Scripture, you will understand it clearly and put the Word of God where it belongs: you will not misapply the Word. The devil wanted Jesus Christ to misapply the Scripture when he quoted Scripture for the wrong purpose.

To walk in God's Miracle-working Power consistently requires that you maintain a consistent prayer-life. The Lord Jesus Christ communed with the Father daily and always when He was on this earth as a Man.

He rose up very early in the morning and prayed till daybreak. He spent whole nights or almost the whole praying sometimes. He prayed from daylight into the night. He prayed in the public, and he prayed in private.

Prayer is the master-key, and you can't do without it. The more consistent your prayer-life is, the more consistent will be the manifestation of the Power of God through you to people.

The early apostles and Disciples prayed. They prayed in group, and they prayed privately. Even buildings shook when they prayed and sang. Don't get too busy working for God that you do not have time to commune with Him daily.

Another thing that will activate the Power of God in your life is fasting. Fasting helps you put the body under subjection to your spirit so that you can obey God and do His Will better.

You know that the spirit-man desires to do the Will of God, while the flesh (because it is weak) will want its desires to be met. Some of those desires are not sinful and some are.

For instance, the desires for food and sleep are not sinful, but you can eat too much or at the improper times that the fulfilled desire can hinder the Free-flow of the Spirit of God through you.

Also, if you love sleep, it will affect your prayer-life adversely, because you will sleep more than is necessary. Too much sleep will bring weakness and laziness into your life, and these will make you ineffective in your walk with God.

Therefore, you must learn to limit those desires that are not necessarily sinful; and do not yield to the sinful desires of the body at all. There are: absolute fasting, total fasting, partial fasting, fruit or juice fasting, etc. You can even fast from newspapers and televisions, and use the extra time to pray and study the Word.

Then you must walk in love towards God, your brethren, and the rest of the people. Faith works by love, and without love, you are nothing.

Even if you have all faith so that you can remove mountains, if you have the gift of prophecy, and you receive the Revelations and Visions of God, without love, you amount to nothing and God will not allow you into His Kingdom.

Love will enable you to obey God and do the right things to your neighbours. You will need to have compassion for the people you are ministering to; be patient with them and forbear their weaknesses and immature behaviours.

Many of the miracles Jesus Christ performed were done because He had compassion on the people. Compassion will activate the Power and the Gift of God in you. The Spirit of God works with the meek in spirit. You must be gentle and not be ruled by harshness.

Humility is very necessary also. God resists the proud but gives grace to the humble (Jas 4:6). God will not share His Glory with anyone (Isa. 48:11).

Whatever God uses you to do, give all the glory and praise to Him. It is not because you ran or because you willed. No, it is because God showed you mercy. The power that wrought the miracle is His, and you are only a vessel and an instrument.

He that plants and he that waters are nothing; it is God that makes the seed grow and produce that worths all; and we must recognize that God is a Good God.

To walk in signs, wonders, and miracles require total and unreserved obedience. Obedience is better than sacrifice. Don't go by feelings: if God leads you to go and preach when you don't feel high spiritually, obey Him and go. That may be the day you will see the greatest miracle in your life.

We walk by faith and not by sight. You will be able to punish every act of disobedience when your obedience is complete (2 Cor. 10:6). Don't be a hearer of the Word, deceiving yourself; but be a doer of the Word.

God is of Purer Eyes than to behold iniquity (Habk. 1:13). If you hide iniquity in your heart, the Lord will not hear you. Therefore, you must live the life of holiness if you want to see mighty miracles through you. Let no sin or weight remain in your life: sin entangles, and weight hinders.

Get rid of them; let righteousness rule in your life. Above all, know that whatever you may accomplish for God, if you miss Heaven, if you go to Hell, you achieved nothing. Without holiness, no man can see the Lord.

Then you must be perfect as your Heavenly Father is perfect (Matt. 5:48). God cannot tell us to do what we cannot do: God is just. In every area of your life, be perfect.

In words, be perfect; in actions, be perfect; in character, be perfect; in spirit, faith, love, and purity, be perfect; whatever you do, be perfect. Even your thoughts are to be perfect. Perfection has to do with maturity. Even holiness should be perfected (2 Cor. 7:1).

You must not allow any idle word out of your mouth. Let no corrupt word proceed out of your mouth. Fresh water and bitter water do not flow from the same source. Curses and blessings ought not to flow from the same mouth of the child of God.

Be careful how you think because your thoughts will affect your words. Let your words be seasoned with grace, so that your hearers will benefit. In preaching, do not preach wrong things. Teach the Right Doctrines.

If you are going to walk in God's Supernatural Power, you will have to expect persecutions, tests, and trials. Jesus Christ passed through them, and you cannot expect the opposite.

Satan will entice people to persecute you as he did towards Apostle Paul. But don't be discouraged; neither be dismayed. Allow no fear into your heart. Do not fear him who can touch the body but has no power over the soul in Hell. Fear Him who can destroy both the body and the soul in Hell.

Remember to deal with any wrong foundation in your life, for if the foundation is destroyed, what can even the righteous do? For instance, if you live in sin, you have a wrong foundation. Don't think that, by exaggeration, you will glorify God.

No, God hates lies, and you don't help God by lying. If you supplanted your friend, by deceit, to marry her fiancé, go and ask for her forgiveness. Don't waste your life working for God, when you are heading to Hell. Give no place to the devil.

When the apostles and Disciples went out and preached everywhere, the Lord worked with them confirming their Gospel with signs and wonders. If you want to see mighty healings and miracles in your life, you must go out and preach the Gospel.

Preach in buses, preach in markets, preach in streets, preach in houses; go out for early-morning cries, preach in season and out of season, preach everywhere.

If you preach the Gospel of the Kingdom, then God will confirm the Gospel you preach, because God confirms His Word. Don't sit back and wait to preach in your church's pulpit.

There are so many things you can learn from the Bible that will help you manifest God's Power. Among them are: self-discipline, self-denial, wisdom, watchfulness, diligence, honesty, and perseverance.

Don't worry yourself if it seems as though you failed or did not accomplish much at your first outing. Worrying, instead of adding, will remove from you.

Be confident in your God and His Word, and soon, everybody will be looking for you to be prayed for. Elisha persisted and received the double-portion of Elijah's anointing!

Forget the past and mind the future. Beware of bad and evil company; evil association corrupts good manners. Get rid of ignorance, mistakes, and foolishness. Preach and teach the Word of God, in season and out of season. Never walk against God and His Plans, Purposes, and Will.

Godliness with contentment is of great gain, for we brought nothing into the world and it is certain that we can carry nothing with us at our death. Greed and covetousness will hamper the manifestation of the Power of God through you.

David was described by God as a man after His Heart, and Abraham was described as a Friend of God. What will you be described as? You must have the fear of God in your heart; without the fear of God, you can't please God.

Touch not, taste not, and handle not anything that offends God and that is contrary to Godliness and our faith. Give diligence to pressing toward the mark, the prize of the High Call of God in Christ Jesus.

SIGNS OF HIS COMING AND OF THE END OF THE AGE

As Jesus Christ went out and departed from the temple, His Disciples came up to show Him the buildings of the temple. And He said to them, "Do you not see all these things? Assuredly, I say to you, not one stone shall be left here upon another, that shall not be thrown down." Now as He sat on the Mount of Olives, the Disciples came to Him privately, saying, "Tell us, when will these things be? And what will be sign of Your Coming, and of the end of the age?"

And the Lord Jesus Christ answered and said to them: "Take heed that no one deceives you. For many will come in My Name, saying 'I am the Christ,' and will deceive many. And you will hear of wars and rumours of wars. See that you are not troubled; for all these things must come to pass, but the end is not yet.

"For nation will rise against nation, and kingdom against kingdom. And there will be famines, pestilences, and earthquakes in various places. All these are the beginning of sorrows. Then they will deliver you up to tribulation and kill you, and you will be hated by all nations for My Name's sake. And then many will be offended, will betray one another, and will hate one another.

"Then many false prophets will rise up and deceive many. And because lawlessness will abound, the love of many will grow cold. But he who endures to the end shall be saved. And this Gospel of the Kingdom will preached in all the world as a witness to all the nations, and then the end will come.

"Therefore when you see the 'abomination of desolation,' spoken of by Daniel the prophet standing in the holy place" (whoever reads, let him understand), "then let those who are in Judea flee to the mountains. Let him who is on the housetop not go down to take anything out of his house. And let him who is in the field not go back to get his clothes.

"But woe to those who are pregnant and to those who are nursing babies in those days! And pray that your flight may not be in winter or on the Sabbath. For then there will be great tribulation, such as has not been since the beginning of the world until this time, no, nor ever shall be. And unless those days were shortened, no flesh would be saved; but for the Elect's sake those days will be shortened.

"Then if anyone says to you, 'Look, here is the Christ!' or 'There!' do not believe it. For false christs and false prophets will rise and show great signs and wonders to deceive, if possible, even the Elect. See I have told you beforehand. Therefore if they say to you, 'Look, He is in the desert!' do not go out; or, 'Look, He is in the inner rooms!' do not believe it.

"For as the lightning comes from the east and flashes to the west, so also will the Coming of the Son of Man be. For wherever the carcass is, there the eagles will be gathered together. Immediately after the tribulation of those days the sun will be darkened, and the moon will not give its light; the stars will fall from heaven, and the powers of the heavens will be shaken.

"Then the Sign of the Son of Man will appear in heaven, and then all the tribes of the earth will mourn, and they will see the Son of Man coming on the clouds of heaven with power and great glory. And He will send His angels with a great sound of a trumpet, and they will gather together His Elect from the four winds, from one end of heaven to the other.

"Now learn this parable from the fig tree: When its branch has already become tender and puts forth leaves, you know that summer is near. So you also, when you see all these things, know that it is near – at the doors! Assuredly, I say to you, this generation will by no means pass away till all these things take place. Heaven and earth will pass away, but My Words will by no means pass away" (Matt. 24:1-35).

WARNINGS FROM THE LORD

According to Mark, "Take heed that no one deceives you. For many will come in My Name, saying, 'I am He,' and will deceive many. But when you hear of wars and rumours of wars, do not be troubled; for such things must happen, but the end is not yet. For nation will rise against nation, and kingdom against kingdom. And there will be earthquakes in various places, and there will be famines and troubles. These are the beginning of sorrows.

"But watch out for yourselves, for they will deliver you up to councils, and you will be beaten in the synagogues. You will be brought before rulers and kings for My Sake, for a testimony to them. And the Gospel must first be preached to all nations. But when they arrest you and deliver you up, do not worry beforehand, or premeditate what you will speak. But whatever is given you in that hour, speak that; for it is not you who speak but the Holy Spirit.

"Now brother will betray brother to death, and a father his child; and children will rise up against parents and cause them to be put to death. And you will be hated by all for My Name's sake. But he who endures to the end shall be saved" (Mk 13:5-13).

Luke says, "And there will be great earthquakes, in various places, and famines and pestilences; and there will be fearful sights and great signs from heaven. But before all these things, they will lay their hands on you and persecute you, delivering you up to the synagogues and prisons. You will be brought before kings and rulers for My Name's sake. But it will turn out for you as an occasion for testimony.

"Therefore settled it in your hearts not to meditate beforehand on what you will answer; for I will give you mouth and wisdom which all your adversaries will not be able to contradict or resist. You will be betrayed even by parents and brothers, relatives and friends; and they will put some of you to death. And you will be hated by all for My Name's sake. But not a hair of you shall be lost. By your patience possess your souls.

"But when you see Jerusalem surrounded by armies, then know that its desolation is near. Then let those who are in Judea flee to the mountains, let those who are in the midst of her depart, and let not those who are in the country enter her. For these are the days of vengeance, that all things which are written may be fulfilled. But woe to those who are pregnant and to those who are nursing babies in those days!

"For there will be great distress in the land and wrath upon this people. And they will fall by the edge of the sword, and be led away captive into all nations. And Jerusalem will be trampled by Gentiles until the times of the Gentiles are fulfilled. And there will be signs in the sun, in the moon, and in the stars; and on the earth distress of nations, with perplexity, the sea and the waves roaring;

"Men's hearts failing them from fear and the expectations of those things which are coming on the earth, for the powers of the heavens will be shaken. Then they will see the Son of Man coming in a cloud with power and great glory. Now when these things begin to happen, look up and lift up your heads, because your redemption draws near" (Lk. 21:11-28).

Apostle Paul, by the Holy Spirit, let us to know how evil the last days will be. He wrote: "But know this, that in the last days perilous times will come: For men will be lovers of themselves, lovers of money, boasters, proud, blasphemers, disobedient to parents, unthankful, unholy, unloving, unforgiving, slanderous, without self-control, brutal, despisers of good,

"Traitors, headstrong, haughty, lovers of pleasure rather than Lovers of God, having a form of Godliness but denying its power. And from such people turn away! For of this sort are those who creep into households and make captives of gullible women loaded down with sins, led away by various lusts, always learning and never able to come to the knowledge of the Truth.

"Now as James and Jambres resisted Moses, so do these also resist the Truth: men of corrupt minds, disapproved concerning the Faith; but they will progress no further, for their folly will be manifest to all, as theirs also was. But you have carefully followed my Doctrine, manner of life, purpose, faith, longsuffering, love, perseverance, afflictions. ...Out of them all the Lord delivered me.

"Yes, and all who desire to live Godly in Christ Jesus will suffer persecution. But evil men and impostors will grow worse and worse, deceiving and being deceived. But you must continue in the things which you have learned and been assured of, knowing from whom you have learned them....

"All Scripture is given by Inspiration of God, and is profitable for Doctrine, for reproof, for correction, for instruction is righteousness, that the man of God may be complete, thoroughly equipped for every good work" (2 Tim. 3).

These many false teachings, doctrines, ministries, and ministers that are in existence in the church-world today are signs of the end times. Of course, over the ages, even in the time of the early apostles, there have been false teachings, doctrines, and ministers. Yet it is more observable these days than during their days; and these things are happening because the devil knows that his time is short, and wants to take to Hell even those who want God and Jesus Christ.

And because human beings want what satisfies their flesh, many people, both ministers and followers, have joined the bandwagon of the devil; but they are headed for destruction, except they turn back to the Truth of the Word of God, and follow the pathway of righteousness, obedience, holiness, and Truth.

Even among unbelievers and sinners, evil abound; and many of them love satan and his activities. Let men arise, who will go and warn all sinners, whether in the church or outside the church!

These cases and rumours of wars, insurgency, terrorism, cultism, covetousness, and sexual immorality are signs of the last days. The Judgment and Wrath of God upon men and the earth has already begun in different forms. Earthquakes, famines, pestilences, and adverse natural changes, are part of the signs of the last days.

But instead of men to recognize these things as signs to warn them, they think that they are normal things to expect; and they use science and human intelligence to soothe their fears. But greater terror is coming.

God loves us, and He does not want us to be taken unawares. This is why He is warning both Christians and unbelievers to get ready, because the end is at hand. Let the Christians straighten and correct anything that will stop them from making Heaven; and let the unbelievers receive the Gospel!

END-TIME REALITIES

These are the last days and the end-time. And there are many things that the Lord told us in the Bible that will happen in this present age we are in. God loves us so much, and this is one of the reasons why He forewarned us, so that we will not be taken unawares, and disappoint Him. God knows the future.

One thing that will mark these last days is the rise of many false ministers and false teachings. The Word of God says, "Now the Spirit expressly says that in latter times some will depart from the faith, giving heed to deceiving spirits and doctrines of demons, speaking lies in hypocrisy, having their own conscience seared with a hot iron" (1 Tim. 4:1-2).

Apostle Peter put it this way: "But there were also false prophets among the people, even as there will be false teachers among you, who will secretly bring in destructive heresies, even denying the Lord Who bought them, and bring on themselves swift destruction.

"And many will follow their destructive ways, because of whom the Way of Truth will be blasphemed. By covetousness they will exploit you with deceptive words; for a long time their judgment does not slumber.

"Having eyes full of adultery and that cannot cease from sin, enticing unstable souls. They have a heart trained in covetous practices, and are accursed children. They have forsaken the right way and gone astray, following the way of Balaam the son of Beor, who loved the ways of unrighteousness.

"These are wells without water, clouds carried by a tempest, for whom is reserved the blackness of darkness forever. For when they speak great swelling words of emptiness, they allure through the lusts of the flesh, through lewdness, the ones who have actually escaped from those who live in error.

"While they promise them liberty, they themselves are slaves of corruption; for by whom a person is overcome, by him also he is brought into bondage. For if, after they have escaped the pollutions of the world through the Knowledge of the Lord and Saviour Jesus Christ, they are again entangled in them and overcome, the latter end is worse for them than the beginning.

"For it would have been better for them not to have known the way of righteousness, than having known it, to turn from the Holy Commandment delivered to them. But it has happened to them according to the true proverb: 'A dog returns to his own vomit,' and, 'a sow, having washed, to her wallowing in the mire'" (2 Pet. 2).

Jesus Christ puts it this way: "Beware of false prophets, who come to you in sheep's clothing, but inwardly they are ravenous wolves. You will know them by their fruits. Do men gather grapes from thornbushes or figs from thistles? Even so, every good tree bears good fruit; but a bad tree bears bad fruit.

"A good tree cannot bear bad fruit, nor can a bad tree bear good fruit. Every tree that does not bear good fruit is cut down and thrown into the fire. Therefore by their fruits you will know them.

"Not everyone who says to Me, 'Lord Lord,' shall enter the Kingdom of Heaven, but he who does the Will of My Father in Heaven. Many will say to Me in that Day, 'Lord, Lord, have we not prophesied in Your Name, cast out demons in Your Name, and done many wonders in Your Name?'

"And then I will declare to them, 'I never knew you; depart from Me, you who practice lawlessness!'" (Matt. 7:15-23). He also adds: "For false christs and false prophets will rise and show great signs and wonders to deceive, if possible, even the Elect. See, I have told you beforehand" (Matt. 24:24-25).

Apostle Paul himself said, "For such are false apostles, deceitful workers, transforming themselves into apostles of Christ. And no wonder! For satan himself transforms himself into an angel of light. Therefore it is no great thing if his ministers also transform themselves into ministers of righteousness, whose end will be according to their works" (2 Cor. 11:13-15).

Inspired by the Holy Ghost, Jude wrote: "Beloved, while I was very diligent to write to you concerning our common salvation, I found it necessary to write to you exhorting you to contend earnestly for the faith which was once for all delivered to the Saints. For certain men have crept in unnoticed, who long ago were marked out for this condemnation, ungodly men, who turn the Grace of our God into lewdness and deny the only Lord God and our Lord Jesus Christ.

"These are grumblers, complainers, walking according to their own lusts; and they mouth great swelling words, flattering people to gain advantage. But you, beloved, remember the Words which were spoken before by the apostles of our Lord Jesus Christ; how they told you that there would be mockers in the last time who would walk according to their own ungodly lusts. These are sensual persons, who cause divisions, not having the Spirit.

"But you, beloved, building yourselves up on your most holy faith, praying in the Holy Spirit, keep yourselves in the Love of God, looking for the Mercy of our Lord Jesus Christ unto Eternal Life" (Jude 1).

Apostle Paul said, "And this occurred because of false brethren secretly brought in (who came in by stealth to spy out our liberty which we have in Christ Jesus, that they might bring us into bondage), to whom we did not yield submission even for an hour, that the Truth of the Gospel might continue with you" (Gal. 2:4-5).

And Apostle John wrote: "Beloved, do not believe every spirit, but test the spirits, whether they are of God; because many false prophets have gone out into the world. And this is the spirit of the antichrist, which you have heard was coming, and is now already in the world" (1 Jn 4:1,3).

Other things that will characterize the end-time are deception, lukewarmness, and backsliding. These things are connected to false apostles, prophets, evangelists, pastors, and teachers. But apart from the false ministers, people will be deceived because their love has waxed or grown cold, and they want what the flesh likes.

To this end the Word of God says, "I charge you therefore before God and the Lord Jesus Christ, Who will judge the living and the dead at His Appearing and His Kingdom: Preach the Word! Be ready in season and out of season. Convince, rebuke, exhort, with all longsuffering and teaching.

"For the time will come when they will not endure Sound Doctrine, but according to their own desires, because they have itching ears, they will heap up for themselves teachers; and they will turn their ears away from the Truth, and be turned aside to fables. But you be watchful in all things, endure afflictions, do the work of an evangelist, fulfil your ministry" (2 Tim. 4:1-5).

Apostle Paul wrote; "For I am jealous over you with Godly jealousy. For I have betrothed you to one Husband, that I may present you as a chaste virgin to Christ. But I fear, lest somehow, as the serpent deceived Eve by his craftiness, so your minds may be corrupted from the simplicity that is in Christ.

"For if he who comes preaches another Jesus whom we have not preached, or if you receive a different spirit which you have not received or a different gospel which you have not accepted – you may well put up with it!" (2 Cor. 11:2-4).

Writing to the Galatians, he said, "I marvel that you are turning away so soon from Him Who called you in the Grace of Christ to a different gospel, which is not another; but there are some who trouble you and want to pervert the Gospel of Christ.

"But even if we, or an angel from Heaven, preach any other gospel to you than what we have preached to you, let him be accursed. As we have said before, so now I say again, if anyone preaches any other gospel to you than what you have received, let him be accursed" (Gal. 1:6-9).

Jesus Christ Himself said, "And then many will be offended, will betray one another, and will hate one another. Then many false prophets will rise up and deceive many. And because lawlessness will abound, the love of many will grow cold. But he who endures to the end shall be saved" (Matt. 24:10-13).

Another thing that characterizes these last days and end-time is increased sin and wickedness. This is why the Word of God says, "But know this, that in the last days perilous times will come: for men will be lovers of themselves, lovers of money, boasters, proud, blasphemers,

"Disobedient to parents, unthankful, unholy, unloving, unforgiving, slanderers, without self-control, brutal, despisers of good, traitors, headstrong, haughty, lovers of pleasure rather than Lovers of God, having a form of Godliness, but denying its power. And from such people turn away!" (2 Tim. 3:1-5).

Another thing that will happen (and is happening) in the last days is that scoffers and mockers will ask whether Jesus Christ will still come again. This is why the Bible says, "Knowing this first: that scoffers will come in the last days, walking according to their own lusts,

"And saying, 'Where is the promise of His Coming? For since the fathers fell asleep, all things continue as they were from the beginning of creation.' For this they wilfully forget: that by the Word of God the heavens were of old, and the earth standing out of the water and in the water, by which the world that then existed perished, being flooded with water.

"But the heavens and the earth which are now preserved by the same Word, are reserved for fire until the Day of Judgment and perdition of ungodly men. But, beloved, do not forget this one thing, that with the Lord one day is as a thousand years, and a thousand years as one day.

"The Lord is not slack concerning His Promise, as some count slackness, but is longsuffering towards us, not willing that any soul should perish but that all should come to repentance. But the Day of the Lord will come as a thief in the night" (2 Pet. 3:3-10).

Another thing to the end-time is that many people will come in the Lord's Name, saying, "I am Christ," and will deceive many. And you will hear of wars and rumours of wars. Nation will rise against nation and kingdom against kingdom. And there will be famines, pestilences, and earthquakes in various places (Matt. 24:5-7).

In these last days, the devil is fighting tooth and nail, because he knows that the end is near. However, many Christians don't understand the time we are in, not to talk of what they should be doing in this end-time. Jesus Christ is coming very soon; and the devil is very much aware of this Truth.

The Coming of the Lord will be like the days of Noah were. For in the days before the Flood, they were eating and drinking, marrying and giving in marriage, until the day that Noah entered the ark, and did not know until the Flood came and took them all away, so also will the Coming of the Son of Man be (Matt. 24:37-39).

Likewise as it was also in the days of Lot: they ate, they drank, they bought, they sold, they planted, they built; but on the day that Lot went out of Sodom, it rained fire and brimstone from Heaven and destroyed them all. Even so it will be in the day when the Son of Man is revealed.

In that Day, he who is on housetop, and his goods are in the house, let him not come down to take them away. And likewise the one who is in the field, let him not turn back. Remember Lot's wife. Whoever seeks to save his life will lose it, and whoever loses his life will preserve it.

In that Night there will be two men in one bed: the one will be taken and the other will be left. Two women will be grinding together: the one will be taken and the other left. Two men will be in the field: the one will be taken and the other left (Lk. 17:28-36).

Apostle Paul said, "For when they say, 'Peace and safety!' then sudden destruction comes upon them, as labours pains upon a pregnant women. And they shall not escape. But you, brethren, are not in darkness, so that this Day should overtake you as a thief" (1 Thes. 5:3-4).

Never Say That God Said What He Did Not Say!

THE JUDGMENT OF THE LAST DAY

The Bible, speaking of the Judgment of the Last Day, says, "Then I saw a great White Throne and Him Who sat on it, from Whose Face the earth and the heaven fled away. And there was found no place for them. And I saw the dead, small and great, standing before God, and books were opened. And another book was opened, which is the Book of Life.

And the dead were judged according to their works, by the things which were written in the books. The sea gave up the dead who were in it, and Death and Hades delivered up the dead who were in them. And they were judged, each one according to his works. Then Death and Hades were cast into the Lake of Fire. This is the Second Death. And anyone not found written in the Book of Life was cast into the Lake of Fire" (Rev. 20:11-15).

When the Son of Man comes in His Glory, and all the holy angels with Him, then He will sit on the Throne of His Glory. All the nations will be gathered before Him, and He will separate them one from another, as a shepherd divides his sheep from the goats. And He will set the sheep on His Right Hand, but the goats on the Left.

Then the King will say to those on His Right Hand, "Come, you blessed of My Father, inherit the Kingdom prepared for you from the foundation of the world: for I was hungry and you gave Me food; I was thirsty and you gave Me drink; I was a stranger and you took Me in; I was naked and you clothed Me; I was sick and you visited Me; I was in prison and you came to Me."

Then the righteous will answer Him, saying "Lord, when did we see You and feed You or thirsty and give You drink? When did we see You a stranger and take You in, or naked and clothe You? Or when did we see You sick or in prison, and come to You?" And the King will answer and say to them, "Assuredly, I say to you, inasmuch as you did it to one of the least of these My brethren, you did it to Me."

Then He will also say to those on the Left Hand, "Depart from Me, you cursed, into the Everlasting Fire prepared for the devil and his angels; for I was hungry and you gave Me no food; I was thirsty and you gave Me no drink; I was a stranger and you did not take Me in, naked and you did not clothe Me, sick and in prison and you did not visit Me."

Then they also will answer Him, saying, "Lord, when did we see You hungry or thirsty or a stranger or naked or sick or in prison, and did not minister to You?" Then He will answer them, saying, "Assuredly, I say to you, inasmuch as you did not do it to one of the least of these, you did not do it to Me." And these will go away into Everlasting Punishment, but the righteous into Eternal Life (Matt. 25:31-46). Therefore, the Lord Jesus Christ will judge men based on the works that they have done – good or bad.

Apostle Peter wrote: "Beloved, I now write to you this Second Epistle (in both of which I stir up your pure minds by way of reminder), that you may be mindful of the Words which were spoken before by the holy prophets, and of Commandments of us, the apostles of the Lord and Saviour, knowing this first: that scoffers will come in the last days, walking according to their own lusts,

"And saying, 'Where is the promise of His Coming? For since the fathers fell asleep, all things continue as they were from the beginning of creation.' For this they wilfully forget: that by the Word of God the heavens were of old, and the earth standing out of water and in the water, by which the world that then existed perished, being flooded with water.

"But the heavens and the earth which are now preserved by the same Word, are reserved for fire until the Day of Judgment and perdition of ungodly men. But beloved, do not forget this one thing, that with the Lord one day is as a thousand years, and a thousand years as one day.

The Lord is not slack concerning His Promise, as some count slackness, but is longsuffering towards us, not willing that any should perish but that all should come to repentance.

"But the Day of the Lord will come as a thief in the night, in which the heavens will pass away with a great noise, and the elements will melt with fervent heat; both the earth and the works that are in it will be burned up. Therefore, since all these things will be dissolved, what manner of persons ought you to be in holy conduct and Godliness?

"Looking for and hastening the coming of the Day of God, because of which the heavens will be dissolved, being on fire, and the elements will melt with fervent heat? Nevertheless we, according to His Promise, look for New Heavens and a New Earth in which righteousness dwells.

"Therefore, beloved, looking forward to these things, be diligent to be found by Him in peace, without spot and blameless; and consider that the Longsuffering of our Lord is salvation – as also our beloved brother Paul, according to the wisdom given to him, has written to you, as also in all his Epistles, speaking in them of these things,

"In which are some things hard to understand, which untaught and unstable people twist to their own destruction, as they do also the rest of the Scriptures. You therefore, beloved since you know this beforehand, beware lest you also fall from your own steadfastness, being led away with the error of the wicked; but grow in the Grace and Knowledge of our Lord and Saviour Jesus Christ. To Him be the glory both now and forever. Amen" (2 Pet. 3).

Apostle Paul said, "Therefore we make it our aim, whether present or absent, to be well pleasing to Him. For we must all appear before the Judgment Seat of Christ, that each one may receive the things done in the body, according to what he has done, whether good or bad. Knowing therefore the Terror of the Lord, we persuade men; but we are well known to God, and I also trust are well known in your consciences" (2 Cor. 5:9-11).

Speaking of God's Judgment and Wrath, and the reaping (harvesting) of the earth, the Bible says, "Then I saw another angel flying in the midst of heaven, have the Everlasting Gospel to preach to those who dwell on the earth – to every nation, tribe, tongue, and people – saying with a loud voice, 'Fear God and give glory to Him, for the hour of His Judgment has come; and worship Him Who made Heaven and earth, the sea and springs of water.'

"And another angel followed, saying, 'Babylon is fallen, is fallen, that great city, because she has made all nations drink of the wine of the wrath of her fornication.' Then a third angel followed them, saying with a loud voice, 'If anyone worships the beast and his image, and receives his mark on his forehead or on his hand, he himself shall also drink of the wine of the Wrath of God,

'Which is poured out full strength into the cup of His Indignation. He shall be tormented with fire and brimstone in the presence of the holy angels and in the Presence of the Lamb. And the smoke of their torment ascends forever and ever; and they have no rest day or night, who worship the beast and his image, and whoever receives the mark of his name.'

"Here is the patience of the Saints; here are those who keep the Commandments of God and the Faith of Jesus. Then I heard a voice from Heaven saying to me, 'Write: "Blessed are the dead who die in the Lord from now on"' 'Yes', says the Spirit, 'that they may rest from their labours, and their works follow them.'

"Then I looked, and behold, a white cloud and on the cloud sat One like the Son of Man, and in His Hand a sharp sickle. And another angel came out of the temple, crying with a loud voice to Him Who sat on the cloud, 'Thrust in Your Sickle and reap, for the time has come for You to reap, for the harvest of the earth is ripe.'

"So He Who sat on the cloud thrust in His Sickle on the earth, and the earth was reaped. Then another angel came out of the temple which is in Heaven, he also having a sharp sickle. And another angel came out from the altar, who had power over fire, and he cried with a loud cry to him who had the sharp sickle, saying, 'Thrust in your sharp sickle and gather the clusters of the vine of the earth, for her grapes are fully ripe.'

"So the angel thrust his sickle into the earth and gathered the vine of the earth, and threw it into the great winepress of the Wrath of God. And the winepress was trampled outside the city, and blood came out of the winepress, up to the horses' bridles, for one thousand six hundred furlongs.

"Then I saw another sign in Heaven, great and marvelous: seven angels having the seven last plagues, for in them the Wrath of God is complete. And I saw something like a sea of glass mingled with fire, and those who have the victory over the beast, over his image, and over his mark and over the number of his name, standing on the sea of glass, having Harps of God.

"They sing the song of Moses, the Servant of God, and the Song of the Lamb, saying: "Great and marvelous are Your Works, Lord God Almighty! Just and true are Your Ways, O King of the Saints! Who shall not fear You, O Lord, and glorify Your Name? For You alone are holy. For all nations shall come and worship before You, for Your Judgments have been manifested.'

"After these things, I looked, and behold, the temple of the tabernacle of the testimony in Heaven was opened. And out of the temple came the seven angels having the seven plagues, clothed in pure bright linen, and having their chests girded by golden bands. Then one of the four living creatures gave to the seven angels seven golden bowls full of the Wrath of God Who lives forever and ever.

"The temple was filled with smoke from the Glory of God and from His Power, and no one was able to enter the temple till the seven plagues of the seven angels were completed. Then I heard a loud voice from the temple saying to the seven angels, 'Go and pour out the bowls of the Wrath of God on earth.' So the first went and poured out his bowl upon the earth, and a foul and loathsome sore came upon the men who had the mark of the beast and those who worshipped his image.

"Then the second angel poured out his bowl on the sea, and it became blood as of a dead man; and every living creature in the sea died. Then the third angel poured out his bowl on the rivers and springs of water, and they became blood. And I heard the angel of the waters saying: 'You are righteous, O Lord, the One Who is and Who was and Who is to be, because You have judged these things.

'For they have shed the blood of Saints and prophets, and You have given them blood to drink. For it is their just due.' And I heard another from the altar saying, 'Even so, Lord God Almighty, true and righteous are Your Judgments.' Then the fourth angel poured out his bowl on the sun, and power was given him to scorch men with fire. And men were scorched with great heat, and they blasphemed the Name of God Who has power over these plagues; and they did not repent and give Him glory.

"Then the fifth angel poured out his bowl on the throne of the beast, and his kingdom became full of darkness; and they gnawed their tongues because of the pain. They blasphemed the God of Heaven because of their pains and their sores, and did not repent of their deeds. Then the sixth angel poured out his bowl on the great river Euphrates, and its water was dried up, so that the way of the kings from the east might be prepared.

"And I saw three unclean spirits like frogs coming out of the mouth of the dragon, out of the mouth of the beast, and out of the mouth of the false prophet. For they are spirits of demons, performing signs, which go out to the kings of the earth and of the whole world, to gather them to the battle of that Great Day of God Almighty.

"'Behold, I am coming as a thief. Blessed is he who watches, and keeps his garments, lest he walk naked and they see his shame.' And they gathered them together to the place called in Hebrew, Armageddon. Then the seventh angel poured out his bowl into the air, and a loud voice came out of the temple of Heaven, from the Throne, saying, 'It is done!'

"And there were noises and thunderings and lightings; and there was a great earthquake, such a mighty and great earthquake as had not occurred since men were on the earth. Now the great city was divided into three parts, and the cities of the nations fell. And great Babylon was remembered before God, to give her the cup of the wine of the fierceness of His Wrath.

"Then every island fled away; and the mountains were not found. And great hail from heaven fell upon men, each hailstone about the weight of a talent. Men blasphemed God because of the plague of the hail, since that plague was exceedingly great" (Rev. 14:6-20; 15; and 16).

Speaking of the judgment of Babylon the great, the Bible says, "After these things I saw another angel coming down from heaven, having great authority, and the earth was illuminated with his glory. And he cried mightily with a loud voice, saying, 'Babylon the great is fallen, is fallen, and has become a dwelling place of demons, a prison for every foul spirit, and a cage for every unclean and hated bird!

'For all the nations have drunk of the wine of the wrath of her fornication, the kings of the earth have committed fornication with her, and the merchants of the earth have become rich through the abundance of her luxury.' And I heard another voice from heaven saying, 'Come out of her, my people, lest you share in her sins, and lest you receive of her plagues.

'For her sins have reached to Heaven, and God has remembered her iniquities. Render to her just as she rendered to you, and repay her double according to her works; in the cup which she has mixed, mix double for her. In the measure that she glorified herself and lived luxuriously, in the same measure give her torment and sorrow; for she says in her heart, "I sit as queen, and am no widow, and will not see sorrow."

'Therefore her plagues will come in one day – death and mourning and famine. And she will be utterly burned with fire, for strong is the Lord God Who judges her. The kings of the earth who committed fornication and lived luxuriously with her will weep and lament for her, when they see the smoke of her burning, standing at a distance for fear of her torment, saying, "Alas, alas, that great city Babylon, that mighty city! For in one hour your judgment has come."

'And the merchants of the earth will weep and mourn over her, for no one buys their merchandise anymore: merchandise of gold and silver, precious stones and pearls, fine linen and purple, silk and scarlet, every kind of citron wood, every kind of object of ivory, every kind of object of most precious wood, bronze, iron, and marble;

'And cinnamon and incense, fragrant oil and frankincense, wine and oil, fine flour and wheat, cattle and sheep, horses and chariots, and bodies and souls of men. The fruit that your soul longed for has gone from you, and all the things which are rich and splendid have gone from you, and you shall find them no more at all.

'The merchants of these things, who became rich by her, will stand at a distance for fear of her torment, weeping and wailing, and saying, "Alas, alas, that great city that was clothed in fine linen, purple, and scarlet, and adorned with gold and precious stones and pearls! For in one hour such great riches came to nothing." Every shipmaster, all who travel by ship, sailors, and as many as trade on the sea, stood at a distance and cried out when they saw the smoke of her burning, saying, "What is like this great city?"

'They threw dust on their heads and cried out, weeping and wailing, and saying, "Alas, alas, that great city, in which all who had ships on the sea became rich by her wealth! For in one hour she is made desolate." Rejoice over her, O Heaven, and you holy apostles and prophets, for God has avenged you on her!'

"Then a mighty angel took up a stone like a great millstone and threw it into the sea, saying, 'Thus with violence the great city Babylon shall be thrown down, and shall not be found anymore. The sound of harpists, musicians, flutists, and trumpeters shall not be heard in you anymore. No craftsman of any craft shall be found in you anymore, and the sound of a millstone shall not be heard in you anymore.

'The light of a lamp shall not shine in you anymore, and the voice of bridegroom and bride shall not be heard in you anymore. For your merchants were the great men of the earth, for by your sorcery all the nations were deceived. And in her was found the blood of prophets and Saints, and of all who were slain on the earth' (Rev. 18).

"After these things I heard a loud voice of a great multitude in Heaven, saying, 'Alleluia! Salvation and glory and honour and power belong to the Lord our God! For true and righteous are His Judgments; because He has judged the great harlot who corrupted the earth with her fornication; and He has avenged on her the blood of His Servants shed by her.'

"Again they said, 'Alleluia! Her smoke rises up forever and ever!' And the twenty-four elders and the four living creatures fell down and worshipped God Who sat on the Throne, saying, 'Amen! Alleluia!'" (Rev. 19:1-4).

Never Say That God Said What He Did Not Say!

TESTING AND PROVING ALL THINGS

All that glitters is not gold. You will be deceiving yourself by believing that something is gold just because it appears like gold, without examining it closely and the right way. In the spirit-realm, the same is applicable. The spirit-realm or the supernatural realm consists of positive and negative forces; it consists of good and evil spirits. The realm of the spirit comprises God's Side and the devil's side.

The Side of God consists of God the Father, God the Son, Jesus Christ, God the Holy Spirit, the angels, and all the host of the Kingdom of God. The side of the devil consists of satan, his fallen angles, demons, witches, and all the host of the kingdom of the devil.

However, the original kingdom is that of God. The devil rebelled against God and against His Judgment, and when he was pushed down, out of Heaven, he organized his kingdom as a kingdom that is opposed to God and what God does.

Because the devil knows that God's Kingdom and His Ways are the real ones, he tries to imitate and fake some things the Lord does in order to deceive people and side-track the Elect of God, the Christians. The devil even comes as an angel of light and his servants come, camouflaging as ministers of Christ (2 Cor. 11:13-15). But God did not leave us helpless, because He has given us adequate resources by which we will be able to differentiate the things of God from the things of the devil.

The Lord tells us to prove all things, and to hold on to that which is good and true (1 Thes. 5:21). The Lord commands us to test every spirit, because He is aware that every spirit is not from Him (1 Jn 4:1). Even, the Bible tells us to judge what prophets have uttered (1 Cor. 14:29).

We have to prove all things, because there are doctrines of devils and lies of seducing spirits, which they work out night and day to deceive us. The devil and his devils love no man; they don't want anyone to be obedient to God and His Word. They don't want anyone to make Heaven, from where they were pushed down.

God and His Word agree. The Word of God is a representative of God. Therefore, you have to use the Word of God, the Bible, to prove all things and test ever spirit. This is one of the reasons why you should make good effort and meditate on the Word of God.

If you don't know the Word of God, the devil will deceive you and you will perish because of ignorance (Hos. 4:6). Let the Word of God dwell in you richly in all wisdom (Col. 3:16). Study the Word of God to be an approved minister of God, so that you can interpret God's Word God's Way (2 Tim. 2:15).

If the Word of God dwells in you poorly, that is a big problem. If it dwells in you richly without wisdom, you are in a problem also. If you, as a minister, feels you know too much of the Word of God, so that you stop reading and studying it privately, you will mess things up.

If you interpret the Bible the way you like, and you use the Bible to support your own ideas, you have been defeated by the devil, and you have trapped by him. Be open to God and His Word and don't harden your heart towards God and His Word. That attitude leads to using the Bible to support yourself, instead of allowing the Bible to support you.

The Bible says it is good to compare spiritual things with spiritual things. We should compare Scripture with Scripture (1 Cor. 2:13). Don't just take a word, a statement or a verse out of context and use it to propagate what you want. Wrong doctrines are spread when people don't interpret the Bible aright. The Word of God, interpreted the right way, is an authoritative way of proving all things and testing every spirits.

No matter how anointed a man is, always compare what he says with the Word of God. The Bible says that the Bereans were of a more noble character, because when Apostle Paul taught them, they went back to check whether he taught them aright (Acts 17:11). Whether you received the message by vision, audible voice, or prophecy, judge it by the Scriptures. Even if you were on a long fast when you received the revelation, compare it with the Word of God, the Bible.

God has also given us His Spirit so that we may know the Things of God. Your spirit is born again, is a new creature, and the Spirit of God lives inside of you. Maintain a tender conscience towards God and His Word. Don't harden your heart with doubt, unbelief, sin, or disobedience.

Develop your spirit by reading, mediating on, and confessing the Word of God. Also, obey God's Word instantly; and learn to pray in the Spirit often (speak in tongues often). Learn to be quiet before God, and the Holy Spirit will lead you.

Your spirit is a safe guide, if it is tender and sincere and has not been hardened. Fasting can help you to be more sensitive to the Holy Spirit and to bring your body under subjection to your spirit. Whatever you hear, see, or receive, whether by audible voice, vision, prophecy, or what, listen to your heart (your spirit), to know whether it is troubled or it is at peace. Peace on your inside is a go-ahead signal, while uneasiness is a red or stop signal.

God loves you and He doesn't want you to be deceived. He wants you to follow the right way so that it may be well with your soul. Know that there is a way that seems good to a man, but the way leads to destruction (Prov. 14:12).

Submit yourself to God and His Word (Jas 4:7). Trust in the Lord with all your heart, and lean not on your own understanding (Prov. 3:5). May the Lord bless you and be with you as you follow Him!

Never Say That God Said What He Did Not Say!

THE LAWS OF GOD'S KINGDOM

A law is a rule that people in a particular country, city, or local area must obey. A rule is an official instruction that says how things must be done or what is allowed, like in an organization or a job.

When we talk of the Laws of God's Kingdom, we are speaking of Rules which people who are in the Kingdom of God must obey or follow. The Rules instruct and command us on how things must be done, or the things that are allowed in it.

The Laws of God's Kingdom also refer to how things happen in the Kingdom of God. In other words, the Laws of God's Kingdom describe the outcomes or resultant effects of doing this and that, or not doing this and that.

Some things may happen in your life, which you did not expect or which you may not explain; but it may just be that an existing Law in the Kingdom of God has worked.

One Law of the Kingdom of God says, "But what does it say? 'The Word is near you, in your mouth and in your heart' (that is, the Word of Faith which we preach):

"That if you confess with your mouth the Lord Jesus and believe in your heart that God has raised Him from the dead, you will be saved. For with the heart one believes unto righteousness, and with the mouth confession is made unto salvation" (Rom.10:8-10).

If you believe and confess Jesus Christ, you will be saved. A related Statement/Law is, "Unless one is born again, he cannot see the Kingdom of God" (Jn 3:3).

The expanded form of this Law is, "Unless one is born of water and the Spirit, he cannot enter the Kingdom of God" (Jn 3:5). Unless you live according to the Word of God (the water) and in obedience to Spirit of God, even though you can see the Kingdom of God, yet you cannot enter it.

Another Law of the Kingdom of God is, "Give, and it will be given to you: good measure, pressed down, shaken together, and running over will be put into your bosom. For with the same measure that you use, it will be measured back to you" (Lk. 6:38).

When you give to God or to men in the Name of God, God will give back to you through different means, in good measure and above the measure which you used.

This is also seen in the Book of Malachi, where the Bible says, "Bring all the tithes into the storehouse, that there may be food in My House, and try Me now in this," says the Lord of Hosts, "if I will not open for you the windows of Heaven and pour out for you such blessing that there will not be room enough to receive it.

"And I will rebuke the devourer for your sakes, so that he will not destroy the fruit of your ground, nor shall the vine fail to bear fruit for you in the field," says the Lord of Hosts; and all nations will call you blessed, for you will be a delightful land," says the Lord of Hosts (Mal. 3:10-12).

The Bible also declares that without holiness no one will see the Lord (Heb. 12:14). This Law is consistent with the teaching of the Bible. Apostle Peter stated this Law this way: "As obedient children, not conforming yourselves to the former lusts, as in your ignorance;

"But as He Who called you is holy, you also be holy in all your conduct, because it is written, 'Be holy, for I am holy.'

"And if you call on the Father, Who without partiality judges according to each one's work, conduct yourselves throughout the time of your stay here in fear" (1 Pet. 1:14-17).

Another Law of the Kingdom of God is that you reap what you sow. To this end, the Bible says, "Do not be deceived, God is not mocked; for whatever a man sows, that he will also reap.

"For he who sows to his flesh will of the flesh reap corruption, but he who sows to the Spirit will of the Spirit reap Everlasting Life" (Gal. 6:7-8).

Another Law of God's Kingdom is that carnal mindedness leads to death, while spiritual mindedness leads to life. The Bible says, "For those who live according to the flesh set their minds on the things of the flesh, but those who live according to the Spirit, the Things of the Spirit.

"For to be carnally minded is death, but to be spiritually minded is life and peace. Because the carnal mind is enmity against God; for it is not subject to the Law of God, nor indeed can be. So then, those who are in the flesh cannot please God.

"But you are not in the flesh but in the Spirit, if indeed the Spirit of God dwells in you. Now if anyone does not have the Spirit of Christ, he is not His. And if Christ is in you, the body is dead because of sin, but the Spirit is Life because of righteousness" (Rom. 8:5-10).

Another Law of the Kingdom of God is that the proof that you love Jesus Christ is that you keep His Commandments. This is why the Word of God says, "If you love Me, keep My Commandments (Jn 14:15).

"He who has My Commandments and keeps them, it is he who loves Me. And he who loves Me will be loved by My Father, and I will love him and manifest Myself to him.

"If anyone loves Me, he will keep My Word; and My Father will love him, and We will come to him and make Our Home with him. He who does not love Me does not keep My Words; and the Word which you hear is not Mine but the Father's Who sent Me" (Jn 12:21,23,24).

"If you love Me, keep My Commandments." Similar to this Law is the Law that you abide in God's Love by keeping His Commandments. This is why the Bible says, "As the Father loved Me, I also have loved you; abide in My Love.

"If you keep My Commandments, you will abide in My Love, just as I have kept My Father's Commandments and abide in His Love" (Jn 15:9-10).

The Word of God is forever settled in Heaven – it cannot change. It is not men who decide on what they are to do and what they are to avoid; rather, it is God, Who is the Head of His Kingdom, Who decides on how those in His Kingdom have to live their lives – whether they are spirits or humans.

The Word of God says, "I will praise You with my whole heart; before the gods I will sing praises to You. I will worship towards Your holy temple, and praise Your Name for Your Lovingkindness and Your Truth; for You have magnified Your Word above all Your Name" (Psa. 138:1-2).

God has magnified and exalted His Word above all His Name. Therefore, be careful not to go against the Laws of the Kingdom of God.

Speaking to the Israelites, Moses said, "Now it shall come to pass, if you diligently obey the Voice of the Lord your God, to observe carefully all His Commandments which I command you today, that the Lord your God will set you high above all nations of the earth.

"And all these blessings shall come upon you and overtake you, because you obey the Voice of the Lord your God: Blessed shall you be in the city, and blessed shall you be in the country.

"Blessed shall be the fruit of your body, the produce of your ground and the increase of your herds, the increase of your cattle and the offspring of your flocks. Blessed shall be your basket and your kneading bowl.

"Blessed shall you be when you come in, and blessed shall you be when you go out. The Lord will cause your enemies who rise against you to be defeated before your face; they shall come out against you one way and flee before you seven ways.

"The Lord will command the blessing on you in your storehouses and in all to which you set your hand, and He will bless you in the land which the Lord your God is giving you. The Lord will establish you as a holy people to Himself, just as He has sworn to you, if you keep the Commandments of the Lord your God and walk in His Ways.

"Then all peoples of the earth shall see that you are called by the Name of the Lord, and they shall be afraid of you. And the Lord will grant you plenty of goods, in the fruit of your body, in the increase of your livestock, and in the produce of your ground, in the land of which the Lord swore to your fathers to give you.

"The Lord will open to you His Good Treasure, the heavens, to give the rain to your land in its season, and to bless all the work of your hand. You shall lend to many nations, but you shall not borrow.

"And the Lord will make you the head and not the tail; you shall be above only, and not be beneath, if you heed the Commandments of the Lord your God, which I command you today, and are careful to observe them.

"So you shall not turn aside from any of the Words which I command you this day, to the right or the left, to go after other gods to serve them.

"But it shall come to pass, if you do not obey the Voice of the Lord your God, to observe carefully all His Commandments and His Statutes which I command you today, that all these curses will come upon you and overtake you…" (Deut. 28:1-15).

You decide whether you want blessings or curses. Of course, Jesus Christ has delivered us from the curse of the Law. However, we still operate by the Perfect Law of Liberty, which states: "For you, brethren, have been called to liberty; only do not use liberty as an opportunity for the flesh, but through love serve one another (Gal. 5:13).

"My little children, let us not love in word or in tongue, but in deed and in truth. And by this we know that we are of the Truth, and shall assure our hearts before Him.

"For if our heart condemns us, God is greater than our heart, and knows all things. Beloved, if our heart does not condemn us, we have confidence towards God.

"And whatever we ask we receive from Him, because we keep His Commandments and do those things that are pleasing in His Sight.

"And this is His Commandment: that we should believe on the Name of His Son Jesus Christ and love one another, as He gave us Commandment.

"Now he who keeps His Commandments abides in Him, and He in him. And by this we know that He abides in us, by the Spirit Whom He has given us" (1 Jn 3:18-24).

In this Kingdom of God, mercy triumphs over judgment; and He will have mercy and compassion on whom He chooses to have mercy and compassion.

The Bible says, "So speak and so do as those who will be judged by the Law of Liberty. For judgment is without mercy to the one who has shown no mercy. Mercy triumphs over judgment (Jas 2:12-13).

"And not only this, but when Rebecca also had conceived by one man, even by our father Isaac (for the children not yet being born, nor having done any good or evil, that the Purpose of God according to election might stand, not of works but of Him Who calls),

"It was said to her, 'The older shall serve the younger.' As it is written, 'Jacob I have loved, but Esau I have hated.'

WARNINGS FROM THE LORD

"What shall we say then? Is there unrighteousness with God? Certainly not! For He says to Moses, 'I will have mercy on whomever I will have mercy, and I will have compassion on whomever I will have compassion.'

"So then it is not of him who wills, nor of him who runs, but of God Who shows mercy. For the Scripture says to the Pharaoh, 'For this very purpose I have raised you up, that I may show My Power in you, and that My Name may be declared in all the earth.'

"Therefore He has mercy on whom He wills, and whom He wills He hardens. You will say to me then, 'Why does He still find fault? For who has resisted His Will?' But indeed, O man, who are you to reply against God? Will the thing formed say to him who formed it, 'Why have you made me like this?'

"Does not the potter have power over the clay, from the same lump to make one vessel for honour and another for dishonour? What if God, wanting to show His Wrath and to make His Power known, endured with much longsuffering the vessels of wrath prepared for destruction,

"And that He might make known the riches of His Glory on the vessels of mercy, which He had prepared beforehand for glory, even us whom He called, not of the Jews only, but also of the Gentiles? (Rom. 9:10-24).

Never Say That God Said What He Did Not Say!

GOD IS NO RESPECTER OF PERSONS

The Bible says that God is no respecter of persons (Acts 10:34). God created all men, and every man is His Handiwork. God is not responsible to any man; and He is not committed to any man. The covenants God makes with men are made out of His Grace and Love for mankind.

When God makes covenants with man, He abides by the covenants; and He is always faithful, because God respects and honours His Word. God cannot go contrary to His Word, whether written or unwritten. He is a Trustworthy God, and you can be sure that whatever comes out of His Mouth shall be performed by Him.

God honours His Word – the Bible. The Word of God is the basis His Dealings with men. When God acts, He acts according to His Word; when God judges, He judges according to His Word; and when He takes decisions, He decides according to His Word. The Word of God represents God; and if you have heard His Word (including the Bible), you have heard God.

When you preach the Word of God as God gave it to you, God will accompany and confirm the Word with signs and wonders; not because He is honouring you, but because He is honouring His Word. That is why all the glory for whatever God does in your life and ministry should go to God, and God alone! Don't share in Gods Glory, for He is a Jealous God (Isa. 42:8; Exo. 34:14).

If the preaching and teaching that you undertake have not been producing results, if they have not been confirmed with signs and wonders, then check what you have been preaching and teaching. Have you been preaching or teaching half-truth? Have you been preaching and teaching unbelief? Psychology and philosophy will not get the job done. Only the Word of God works. It will work in your life and in the life of any man.

The Word of God is spirit; it is life (Jn 6:63). When you speak the Word of God, the Spirit of God makes it alive, and it can give life. The Word of God is fire also (Jer. 23:29). It can burn off anything that offends. It is a purifier. Jesus Christ said that the Word He spoke to His apostles had cleansed them (Jn 15:3). One of the reasons why the Word of God is spiritually understood or discerned is because it is spirit itself; it is spiritual.

When God gives His Gifts of the Spirit, it is as He wills. When God calls people into different callings, offices, and ministries, it is according to His Grace and Will. When God gives you a greater responsibility in any calling or gift, it s not necessarily because you are better than others, though faithfulness in one area can lead to your being committed with another responsibility.

When God judges the Church, He will not say that because you are an apostle, a prophet, an evangelist, a pastor, a teacher, an intercessor, a musician, or a giver, He will bend His Word for you. He judges according to His Word, though He will have mercy on whom He wills and have compassion on whom He wills. And the mercy He has on you is to lead you back to His Word.

God is not interested that you are a president, a governor, a professor, a millionaire, or a consultant. You cannot bribe God. God created everything and everybody; no matter what you become in this world, God gave you the life and the health to become it.

Prepare yourself to meet your God. Will God call you a good and faithful Servant when you stand before Him? Make sure you are occupying your position; make sure you are doing what the Lord wants you to do. Do that thing diligently and as God wants you to do it; do it Gods Way and Method.

If God could deliver His Adam over to death because of disobedience, if He could overthrow His Lucifer because of pride and rebellion, if God could insist that His Moses would not enter the land of promise (Canaan) because of misbehavior, if God could turn His Face away from Jesus Christ because He was carrying the sins of the world on the Cross of Calvary, then take heed to yourself!

"But there were also false prophets among the people, even as there will be false teachers among you, who will secretly bring in destructive heresies, even denying the Lord Who bought them, and bring on themselves swift destruction.

"And many will follow their destructive ways, because of whom the Way of Truth will be blasphemed. By covetousness they will exploit you with deceptive words; for a long time their judgment has not been idle, and their destruction does not slumber.

"For if God did not spare the angels who sinned, but cast them down to Hell and delivered them into chains of darkness, to be reserved for judgment; And did not spare the ancient world, but saved Noah, one of eight people, a preacher of righteousness, bringing in the Flood on the world of the ungodly; and turning the cities of Sodom and Gomorrah into ashes, condemned them to destruction, making them an example to those who afterwards would live ungodly;

"And delivered righteous Lot, who was oppressed by the filthy conduct of the wicked (for that righteous man, dwelling among them, tormented his righteous soul from day to day by seeing and hearing their lawless deeds) –

"Then the Lord knows how to deliver the Godly out of temptations and to reserve the unjust under punishment for the Day of Judgment, and especially those who walk according to the flesh in the lust of uncleanness and despise authority. They are presumptuous, self-willed. They are not afraid to speak evil of dignitaries, whereas angels, who are greater in power and might, do not bring a reviling accusation against them before the Lord.

"But these, like natural brute beasts made to be caught and destroyed, speak evil of the things they do not understand, and will utterly perish in their own corruption, and will receive the wages of unrighteousness, as those who count it pleasure to carouse in the daytime.

"They are spots and blemishes, carousing in their own deceptions while they feast with you, having eyes full of adultery and that cannot cease from sin, enticing unstable souls. They have a heart trained in covetous practices, and are accursed children. They have forsaken the right way and gone astray, following the way of Balaam the son of Beor, who loved the wages of unrighteousness" (2 Pet. 2:1-15).

Think of how God wasted all the people who lived at the time of Noah, because of sin and iniquity! Think of how God destroyed Sodom and Gomorrah with fire, because of evil and immorality! Think of how God wasted and destroyed the Israelites, because of sin and unbelief!

There are different levels of relationships. Some relationships are loose, while others are strong. Some are casual, while others are intimate.

In our relationship with God, we should develop a strong and an intimate relationship with Him. This is evident because the first Commandment in the Ten Commandments is that we shall have no other gods before the Living God (Exo. 20:3).

Also, when Jesus Christ was asked about the greatest Commandment, He said that the first and Great Commandment is to love the Lord your God with all your heart, with all your soul, and with all your mind (Matt. 22:36-38).

Hear, O people of God, the Lord our God, the Lord is One. And you shall love the Lord your God with all your heart, with all your soul, with all your mind, and with all your strength. This is the first Commandment (Mk 12:29-30).

Man is tripartite in nature, comprising spirit (or heart), soul (or mind), and body. All these components or natures of man must be fully dedicated to God. No wonder Apostle Paul prayed that the whole spirit, soul, and body be preserved blameless at the Coming of our Lord Jesus Christ (1 Thes. 5:23).

You dedicate your spirit to God by first being born again, so that your spirit is regenerated and made a new creature in Christ Jesus. You then desire the sincere milk of the Word of God so that you can grow thereby.

Also, your spirit should be filled with the Holy Spirit, the Spirit of Power, and you get edified by praying in the Holy Spirit. You build up your most holy faith by praying in the Holy Ghost (Jude 1:20).

Many in the Church need revival. By prayer (sometimes, added with fasting), you get more sensitive to the Holy Spirit, and it will be easier for Him to lead you.

You also renew your mind with the Word of God so that you think as God thinks and make decisions according to His Will and Mind (Rom. 12:1-2).

You are to present your body, which is the Temple of God, a living sacrifice, holy, acceptable to God, which is your reasonable service.

Shall we continue in sin that grace may abound? Certainly not! How shall we who died to sin live any longer in it? Just as Christ was raised from the dead by the Glory of the Father, even so we also should walk in newness of life.

Our old man was crucified with Him, that the body of sin might be done away with, that we should no longer be slaves of sin. Reckon yourselves to be dead, indeed, to sin, but alive to God in Christ Jesus our Lord. Therefore, do not let sin reign in your mortal body, that you should obey it in its lusts.

And do not present your members as instruments of unrighteousness to sin; but present yourselves to God as being alive from the dead, and your members as instruments of righteousness to God.

Sin shall not have dominion over you, for you are not under Law but under grace. Do you not know that to whom you present yourselves slaves to obey, you are the one's slaves whom you obey, whether of sin leading to death, or of obedience leading to righteousness?

But God be thanked that though you were slaves of sin, yet you obeyed from the heart that form of Doctrine to which you were delivered. And having been set free from sin, you became slaves of righteousness.

Just as you presented your members as slaves of uncleanness, and of lawlessness leading to more lawlessness, so now present your members as slaves of righteousness for holiness.

Having been set free from sin, and having become the Slaves of God, you have your fruit to holiness, and the end, Everlasting Life. For the wages of sin is death, but the Gift of God is Eternal Life through Christ Jesus our Lord (Rom. 6).

Without prayer, your relationship with God cannot be strong. Every Christian should pray for at least two hours everyday. Take enough time to worship God. Pray in tongues, so that you can speak mysteries to God and pray for things you may not know about.

Be consistent in your prayer-life. Watch and pray so that you do not fall into temptation. Watchfulness and vigilance should be part of you so that you can know the enemy's plans and stop them.

Having a strong relationship with God requires that you live the life of faith. The righteous is to walk by faith, and not by sight. Without faith, you cannot please God, because he who comes to God must believe that He is and that He rewards those who diligently seek Him. By faith, God called forth the whole creation into existence.

Faith is the substance of things hoped for, the evidence of things not yet seen. Whatever God has promised you, He will give it to you, even though you may not be seeing it physically now. In no distant time, it will be yours. Pray and believe.

The Word of God contains the Mind and Will of God. This is one reason you have to study the Word of God with commitment. Let the Word of Christ dwell in you richly in all wisdom. Faith comes by hearing, and hearing by the Word of God.

It is by the Word of God that you can prove all things so that you can hold on to that which is good. The Word of God is the source of the Blessings of God. One Word from God can change your life forever. The Spirit of God inspired the Word, and two of Them agree.

All Scripture is given by the Inspiration of God, and is profitable for Doctrine, for reproof, for correction, for instruction in righteousness; that the man of God may be complete, thoroughly equipped for every good work (2 Tim. 3:16-17).

No prophecy of the Scripture is of any private interpretation, for prophecy never came by the will of man, but holy men of God spoke as they were moved by the Holy Spirit (2 Pet. 1:20-21). Desire the sincere Word of God so that you may grow and mature.

But be a doer of the Word, and not just a hearer. If you hear the Word without doing it, you deceive yourself. It is not the hearer that is commended, but the doer.

If anything, the more you hear the Word without doing it, the more your punishment will be, also. Obedience is better than sacrifice. Rebellion is like the sin of witchcraft. If you don't mix the Word with faith, it will not avail anything to you, because you will not do it.

As obedient people of God, don't fashion yourselves after the former lust, but as He Who called you is holy, so be holy in all manner of conduct.

If you desire a strong relationship with God, then you must win souls for the Lord Jesus Christ. Jesus Christ came to save sinners. You must preach the Gospel always, even against your time table or schedule.

If you are ashamed of Christ Jesus before men, He also will be ashamed of you before God and the holy angels. He that wins souls is wise.

The wise shall shine like the brightness of firmament, and those who turn many to righteousness like the stars forever and ever (Dan. 12:3). Let God be proud of you.

Giving to God and to men will help you maintain a strong relationship with God. The Bible says that where your treasure is, is where your heart will be also.

As you give to God, you have the confidence that when you get to Heaven, the Lord will reward you abundantly; and it will help you prepare for Heaven. Of course, God will reward you in this world also.

When you give to the people of God in the Name of Jesus Christ, you give to God. When you give to God's Servants, you will be blessed. As you give to the poor, you lend to God and He will repay you abundantly.

Having a strong relationship with God will require self-discipline and self-denial. You don't get taken up by the things of this world; rather, you set your mind on things Above, where Jesus Christ is.

Limit the time you spend on television and films, even for Christian programmes and films. Don't be gluttonous in your feeding. Also, do not sleep too much; sleep to get rest, and when sleep has cleared your eyes, give yourself to profitable and Godly things. The lazy man shall not excel in his endeavour.

To maintain a strong relationship with God, you must be led by the Spirit of God. The Spirit of God is the Spirit of Truth, and He will lead you into all truth. The Holy Spirit will reveal secrets to you, and tell you God's Plan and Purpose for your life.

No man can excel by the strength of the flesh. It is not by might, nor by power, but by the Holy Spirit of the Living God (Zech. 4:6). He is your Comforter, Helper, Advocate, Strengthener, Counselor, Intercessor, and Standby.

He will help you accomplish God's Assignment for your life. But He is a Gentle Spirit; therefore, you must give Him room to lead you.

Make every effort to be more like Jesus Christ our Lord. Jesus Christ had a strong relationship with God, the best any can have; therefore, put God first and every other thing second.

You can't expect to drink from the Lord's Cup and the devil's cup at the same time. You can't eat at the Lord's Table and the devil's table at the same time.

God does not do anything without revealing it to His Servants, the prophets. God seeks for a man who will stand in the gap between God and others, so that the people can receive God's Blessings and Provisions, and also escape God's Judgment.

God is a Jealous God; He will not share His Glory with another. The Spirit of God that dwells in us lusts to envy. God does not want us to be worldly as the people of the world.

He expects that your whole spirit, soul, and body be kept for Him. Your body is the Temple of the Holy Spirit. You can't serve God and satan at the same time.

You need to have a strong hunger and thirst for God and the Things of God. He who thirsts shall be filled, and his thirst shall be quenched. If you hunger and thirst for righteousness, God will satisfy that hunger and thirst. As you hunger and thirst for God, your relationship with Him will be more intimate.

Draw close to God, and the devil will not be your problem. Satan couldn't touch Job of Old Testament or anything that belonged to him without God's Permission. But the problem is that many spend so much time thinking about the devil and fearing him.

People spend a lot of time praying against the devil, his demons, and their works, while they spend smaller time praising, worshipping, seeking, and asking God. Many fear the created being – satan – more than they fear God, the Creator. These are very improper.

Depend on God for whatever thing you may be doing. This is why it is necessary to find out what the Will of God is for your life, because God is committed to whatever He starts.

Except the Lord builds the house, the builders build in vain; except the Lord watches over the city, the watchman stays awake in vain. Commit your ways to the Lord; trust also in Him, and He will bring it to pass.

All the things of this world are vanity. They worth something, when used for the Glory and Will of God, and for the furtherance of His Kingdom.

Don't spend your time pursuing the things of this world, while you have no time for what God wants you to do. It shall profit you nothing to gain the whole world and lose your own soul.

The Whole Duty of man is to fear God and keep His Commandments; and His Commandments are not burdensome. It is when you fear God and keep His Commandments that you can say, with certainty, that you have a close relationship with God. Dare to be a Godly man, woman, youth, boy, or girl!

The Bible says that in a great house, there are not only vessels of gold and silver, but also of wood and clay; some for honour and some for dishonour. It goes on to tell us what makes you a vessel of honour   sanctification and cleansing of oneself.

Therefore, if anyone cleanses himself from being a vessel of dishonour, he will be a vessel for honour, sanctified and useful for the Master, prepared for every good work (2 Tim. 2:20-21).

Interestingly, going through the second chapter of the second Book of Timothy, you will discover about eleven different things you are. You are God's son (verse 1). You are a soldier of Christ (verse 3).

You are an athlete (verse 5). You are a farmer (verse 6). You are an Elect of God (verse 10). You are a worker or a workman (verse 15). You are God's Own Property (verse 19). You name the Name of Jesus Christ (verse 19).

You are a vessel (verse 21). You are an instrument or a tool of the Master (verse 21). And you are a Servant of the Lord (verse 24).

When you were born again, you became a child of God. You belong to God, and if an earthly father gives good gifts and things to his child, how much more will our Heavenly Father give good things to us when we ask Him?

And you are a soldier of Christ, who is empowered by the Holy Spirit to wage war against the powers of darkness and destroy their works. This is why the Word says that you should give no place to the devil.

Some say that Jesus Christ has won the battle for us and we are to enjoy the victory now. Well, if you apply that correctly, you are right. Jesus Christ defeated the devil, and having spoiled principalities and powers, He made a show of them publicly, triumphing over them in it (Col. 2:15).

Yet the Word says that we wrestle with principalities and powers (Eph. 6:12), and that the weapons of our warfare are not carnal, but mighty through God to the pulling down of strongholds (2 Cor. 10:4). Don't these places tell you that we are to enforce the Victory of Jesus Christ?

Jesus Christ triumphed over the devil and collected the power and authority he had over man (because of Adam's disobedience) from him.

Jesus Christ came up and said, (and I paraphrase) "I have got all authority in Heaven and on earth, and I give you the power and authority to go and teach all nations because I am with you to the end of the age" (Matt. 28:18-20).

Paul said, "Give no place to the devil" (Eph. 4:27). James said, "Resist the devil and he will flee from you" (Jas 4:7). And Apostle Peter said, "Resist the devil steadfastly in faith" (1 Pet. 5:9).

God wants to use the Church to frustrate the plans of the kingdom of darkness; but the Church is not meeting up with God's Expectations.

God wants to make known His Manifold Wisdom by the Church to the principalities and powers in the heavenly places (Eph. 3:10). Even though God told Joshua that He had given him Jericho, Joshua and the people, still had to surround Jericho seven times and blow the trumpets at the seventh time.

When the walls of Jericho crumbled, they still had to go inside and enforce the victory. If the Church doesn't do her work, many more people will spend eternity in Hell Fire.

And you are an athlete. The Word says that if any man competes in athletics, he is not crowned unless he competes according to the rules (2 Tim. 2:5). Even if you come first in a sprint race (100m or 200m race), if you run another person's lane, you will be disqualified.

The same is applicable in the Christian race and in the ministry. Do you not know that they which run in a race all run, but one receives the prize? Run in such a way that you may obtain.

And everyone who competes for the prize is temperate in all things. Now they do it to obtain a perishable crown, but we for an imperishable crown. Therefore run thus: not with uncertainty.

Thus fight: not as one who beats the air. But discipline your body, and bring it into subjection; lest, when you have preached to others, you yourself should become disqualified (1 Cor. 9:24-27).

God told Moses to make sure that he built the tabernacle according to the pattern shown him on the mountain. God has Rules, Commandments, and Standards; they are forever settled in Heaven, and cannot change.

You are a farmer. You may sow and water, or you may sow while another waters. However, when the work is done, God gives the growth and the increase. And each one will receive his own reward according to his own labour.

We are God's fellow workers. The Church is God's Field; she is God's Building. The world is God's Harvest-field.

If a good master-builder has laid the foundation, and another builds on it, let each one take heed how he builds on it. For no other foundation can anyone lay than that which is laid, which is Jesus Christ.

Now if anyone builds on this foundation with gold, silver, precious stones, wood, hay, straw, each one's work will become clear; for the Day will declare it, because it will be revealed by fire; and the fire will test each one's work, of what sort it is.

If anyone's work which he has built on it endures, he will receive a reward. If any one's work is burned, he will suffer loss; but he himself will be saved, yet so as through fire (1 Cor. 3:6-15). You can see from here that you are God's fellow worker.

The hardworking farmer must be first to partake of the crops (2 Tim. 2:6). Therefore, be patient, brethren, until the Coming of the Lord. See how the farmer waits for the precious fruit of the earth, waiting patiently for it until it receives the early and later rain.

You also be patient. Establish your hearts, for the Coming of the Lord is at hand (Jas 5:7-8). As an Elect of God, brethren, be even more diligent to make your call and election sure always. If you do this, you will never stumble.

If you do, an entrance will be supplied to you abundantly into the Everlasting Kingdom of our Lord and Saviour Jesus Christ.

But also for this very reason, giving all diligence, add to your faith virtue, to virtue knowledge, to knowledge self-control, to self-control perseverance, to perseverance Godliness, to Godliness brotherly kindness, and to brotherly kindness love.

If these things are yours and abound, you will be neither barren nor unfruitful in the knowledge of our Lord Jesus Christ. For he who lacks those things is shortsighted, even to blindness, and has forgotten that he was cleansed from his old sins (2 Pet. 1:5-11).

As a workman, be diligent to show yourself approved to God, a worker who does not need to be ashamed, rightly dividing the Word of Truth (2 Tim. 2:15).

You are God's Own Property and the Lord knows those who are His. He watches over His Own Property and children to keep them from any evil.

Let anyone who names the Name of Christ Jesus depart from evil. This is the test for vessels and instruments of honour and dishonour. God is of Purer Eyes than to behold iniquity.

Sin, disobedience, unrighteousness, hypocrisy, and the life of compromise and carelessness, will make you dishonourable. Therefore, cleanse your vessel and your instrument from sin and contamination, and God will use you to an extent you will never expect.

As a vessel, what do you contain? Are you filled with holiness, righteousness, faithfulness, diligence, watchfulness, and integrity? Vessels are containers, and they contain something, even if it is air.

It is either you contain God or you contain the devil: you can't be a vacuum. You are either honourable or dishonourable. You are either cleansed or dirty and impure.

You will not love using a dirty plate to eat your food. Why will you think so with God? Don't be deceived, God cannot be mocked: you reap what you sow!

You are an instrument, a tool for the Master's Use. Machines are supposed to give out high output or work with low input or effort. Don't be rigid and stubborn that the Lord will work and work on you, without your being fruitful and productive in God's Sight.

Finally, you are the Lord's Servant. You are His Bondservant, and your will must be surrendered to His Own Will. God is worthy of our service, praise, honour, glory, and worship.

Beware of exaggeration, flattering, and lying. Man's wisdom does not work out the Righteousness of God. You wouldn't be helping God by saying what does not exist. There is no unrighteousness in God and with God.

The things that God expects in His vessels should abound in you. God expects uprightness, sincerity, trustworthiness, honesty, and faithfulness from His vessels. God expects obedience, righteousness, and holiness from His vessels.

THE REVELATION OF GOD'S JUDGMENT AND WRATH

God will judge this world and pour out His Great Wrath on those who despised Him and did not regard His Word and Mercy. In fact, the manifestations of God's Judgment and Wrath have already started in signs of the last days. Many more are coming. Describing the Judgment and Wrath of God, the Bible says, "Now I saw when the Lamb opened one of the seals; and I heard one of the four living creatures saying with a voice like thunder, 'Come and see.'

"And I looked, and behold, a white horse. He who sat on it had a bow; and a crown was given to him, and he went about conquering and to conquer. When He opened the second seal, I heard the second living creature saying, 'Come and see.' Another horse, fiery red, went out. And it was granted to the one who sat on it to take peace from the earth, and that people should kill one another; and there was given to him a great sword.

"When He opened the third seal, I heard the third living creature say, 'Come and see.' So I looked, and behold, a black horse, and he who sat on it had a pair of scales in his hand. And I heard a voice in the midst of the four living creatures saying, 'A quart of wheat for a denarius, and three quarts of barley for a denarius; and do not harm the oil and the wine.'

"When He opened the fourth seal, I heard the voice of the fourth living creature say, 'Come and see.' So I looked and behold, a pale horse. And the name of him who sat on it was Death, and Hades followed with him. And power was given to them over a fourth of the earth, to kill with sword, with hunger, with death, and by the beasts of the earth.

"When He opened the fifth seal, I saw under the altar the souls of those who had been slain for the Word of God and for the testimony which they held. And they cried with a loud voice, saying, 'How long, O Lord, holy and true, until You judge and avenge our blood on those who dwell on the earth?'"

"Then a white robe was given to each of them; and it was said to them that they should rest a little while longer, until both the number of their fellow Servants and their brethren, who would be killed as they were, was completed. I looked when He opened the sixth seal, and behold, there was a great earthquake; and the sun became black as sackcloth of hair, and the moon became like blood.

"And the stars of heaven fell to the earth, as a fig tree drops its late figs when it is shaken by a mighty wind. Then the sky receded as a scroll when it is rolled up, and every mountain and island was moved out of its place. And the kings of the earth, great men, the rich men, the commanders, the mighty men, every slave and every free man, hid themselves in the caves and in the rocks of the mountains,

"And said to the mountains and rocks, 'Fall on us and hide us from the Face of Him Who sits on the Throne and from the Wrath of the Lamb! For the Great Day of His Wrath has come, and who is able to stand?' After these things I saw four angels standing at the four corners of the earth, holding the four winds of the earth, that the wind should not blow on the earth, on the sea, or on any tree.

"Then I saw another angel ascending from the east, having the seal of the Living God. And he cried with a loud voice to the four angels to whom it was granted to harm the earth and the sea, saying, 'Do not harm the earth, the sea, or the trees till we have sealed the Servants of our God on their foreheads.' And I heard the number of those who were sealed. One hundred and forty-four thousand of all the tribes of the children of Israel were sealed.

"...When He opened the seventh seal, there was silence in Heaven for about half an hour. And I saw the seven angels who stand before God, and to them were given seven trumpets. Then another angel, having a golden censer, came and stood at the altar. He was given much incense, that he should offer it with the prayers of all the Saints upon the golden altar which was before the Throne.

"And the smoke of the incense, with the prayers of the Saints, ascended before God from the angel's hand. Then the angel took the censer, filled it with fire from the altar, and threw it to the earth. And there were noises, thunderings, lightings, and an earthquake. So the seven angels who have the seven trumpets prepared themselves to sound.

"The first angel sounded: And hail and fire followed, mingled with blood, and they were thrown to the earth. And a third of the trees were burned up, and all green grass was burned up. Then the second angel sounded: And something like a great mountain burning with fire was thrown into the sea, and a third of the sea became blood. And a third of the living creatures in the sea died, and a third of the ships were destroyed.

"Then the third angel sounded: And a great star fell from heaven, burning like a torch, and it fell on a third of the rivers and on the springs of water. The name of the star is wormwood, and many men died from the water, because it was made bitter.

"Then the fourth angel sounded: And a third of the sun was struck, a third of the moon, and a third of the stars, so that a third of them were darkened. A third of the day did not shine, and likewise the night. And I looked, and I heard an angel flying through the midst of Heaven, saying with a loud voice, 'Woe, woe, woe to the inhabitants of the earth, because of the remaining blasts of the trumpet of the three angels who are about to sound

"The fifth angel sounded: And I saw a star fallen from heaven to the earth. To him was given the key to the Bottomless Pit. And he opened the Bottomless Pit, and smoke arose out of the pit like the smoke of a great furnace. So the sun and the air were darkened because of the smoke of the pit. Then out of the smoke locusts came upon the earth. And to them was given power, as the scorpions of the earth have power.

"They were commanded not to harm the grass of the earth, or any green thing, or any tree, but only those men who do not have the Seal of God on their foreheads. And they were not given authority to kill them, but to torment them for five months. Their torment was like the torment of a scorpion when it strikes a man. In those days men will seek death and will not find it; they will desire to die, and death will flee from them.

The shape of the locusts was like horses prepared for battle. On their heads were crowns of something like gold, and their faces were like the faces of men. They had their hair like women's hair, and their teeth were like lions' teeth. And they had breastplates like breastplates of iron, and the sound of their wings was like the sound of chariots with many horses running into battle.

"They had tails like scorpions, and there were stings in their tails. Their power was to hurt men five months. And they had as king over them the angel of the Bottomless Pit, whose name in Hebrew is Abaddon, but in Greek he has the name Apollyon. One woe is past. Behold, still two more woes are coming after these things.

"Then the sixth angel sounded. And I heard a voice from the horns of the golden altar which is before God, saying to the sixth angel who had the trumpet, 'Release the four angels who are bound at the great river Euphrates. So the four angels, who had been prepared for the hour and day and month and year, were released to kill a third of mankind. Now the number of the horsemen was two hundred million; I heard the number of them.

"And thus I saw the horses in the vision: those who sat on them had breastplates of fiery red, hyacinth blue, and sulfur yellow; and the heads of the horses were like the heads of lions, and out of their mouths came fire, smoke, and brimstone. By these three plagues a third of mankind was killed – by the fire and the smoke and the brimstone which came out of their mouths.

"For their power is in their mouth and in their tails; for their tails are like serpents, having heads; and with them they do harm. But the rest of mankind, who were not killed by these plagues, did not repent of the works of their hands, that they should not worship demons, and idols of gold, silver, brass, stone, and wood, which can neither see nor hear nor walk. And they did not repent of their murders or their sorceries or their sexual immorality or their thefts.

"…Then I was given a reed like a measuring rod. And the angel stood, saying, 'Rise and measure the Temple of God, the altar, and those who worship there. But leave out the court which is outside the temple, and do not measure it, for it has been given to the Gentiles. And they will tread the holy city underfoot for forty-two months.

'And I will give power to my two witnesses, and they will prophesy one thousand two hundred and sixty days, clothed in sackcloth.' These are the two olives trees and two lampstands standing before the God of the Earth. And if anyone wants to harm them, fire proceeds from their mouth and devours their enemies. And if anyone wants to harm them, he must be killed in this manner.

"These have power to shut heaven, so that no rain falls in the days of their prophecy; and they have power over waters to turn them to blood, and to strike the earth with all plaques, as often as they desire. When they finish their testimony, the beast that ascends out of the bottomless pit will make war against them, overcome them, and kill them.

"And their dead bodies will lie in the street of the great city which spiritually is called Sodom and Egypt, where also our Lord was crucified. Then those from the peoples, tribes, tongues, and nations will see their dead bodies three-and-a-half days, and not allow their dead bodies to be put into graves.

"And those who dwell on the earth will rejoice over them, making merry, and send gifts to one another, because these two prophets tormented those who dwell on the earth. Now after the three-and-a-half days the breath of life from God entered them, and they stood on their feet, and great fear fell on those who saw them.

"And they heard a loud voice from Heaven saying to them, 'Come up here'. And they ascended to Heaven in a cloud, and their enemies saw them. In the same hour there was a great earthquake, and a tent of the city fell. In the earthquake seven thousand people were killed, and the rest were afraid and gave glory to the God of Heaven. The second woe is past. Behold, the third woe is coming quickly.

"Then the seventh angel sounded. And there were loud voices in Heaven, saying, 'The kingdoms of this world have become the Kingdom of our Lord and of His Christ, and He shall reign forever and ever!' And the twenty-four elders who sat before God on their thrones fell on their faces and worshipped God, saying: 'We give You thanks, O Lord God Almighty, the One Who is and Who was and Who is to come,

'Because You have taken Your Great Power and reigned. The nations were angry, and Your Wrath has come, and the time of the dead, that they should be judged, and that You should reward Your Servants the prophets and the Saints, and those who fear Your Name, small and great, and should destroy those who destroy the earth'. Then the Temple of God was opened in Heaven, and the ark of His Covenant was seen in His Temple. And there were lightings, noises, thunderings, an earthquake, and a great hail" (Rev. 6, 7, 8, 9, & 11).

If men know what is coming upon them, they will run for their dear lives to escape from the Great Wrath of God. These things are preliminaries which will culminate to everlasting suffering, torment, and punishment the Lake of Fire which burns with fire and brimstone, where Death and Hell will be cast into, including all those whose names are not in the Book of Life.

Never Say That God Said What He Did Not Say!

LIVING IN PLEASURE

To live in pleasure is to live according to the devil, the world, and the flesh. These three are contrary to God and His Word. The devil wants you to live contrary to how God wants you to live. The world will try to lure you into its provisions and pleasures. The flesh will encourage you to live according to its passions.

The devil rebelled against God, and he was thrown down from Heaven. He came and deceived our first parents, Adam and Eve, and they were separated from God. The devil, since then, has been doing all he can to thwart God's Purposes and Plans. He so much lured the first world into sin and disobedience, that God regretted He made man; and He wiped out that generation, saving only Noah and seven others (his family).

Even after the flood, the devil has kept on working on the minds of men to keep them in sin and disobedience. The devil, satan, is pleased when you go contrary to the Word of God. He comes to steal, to kill, and to destroy (Jn 10:10). Satan has made himself an enemy of God, and he wants man to be like him (a rebel).

But even though the devil works evil, Jesus Christ came to give life (and more abundant life) to men. Accept Him now, and abide in Him and in His Word; and it will be well with you, both in this life and in the life to come.

The world shows you many deceptive things to draw away your soul from God. All that is in the world are the lust of the eyes, the lust of the flesh, and the pride of life. We have been commanded not to love the world. The world and all in it will pass away; only the one who does the Will of the Father shall abide forever. If you love the world, then you hate God and do not love Him.

Forget about the money, the power, the wealth, and all the 'good' things you see. They will pass away; the buildings, the cars, the certificates, etc will be burnt with fire on the Last Day. What will count are the things you did for the Lord Jesus Christ. He who loves his life will lose it; but he who gives his life for the Lord, His Church, and His Work will save it on the Day that Jesus Christ will reward the faithful and punish the faithless.

The flesh is the strongest enemy of the Christian. Satan is not God's match at all. The authority and power we have cannot be equated with that of satan. Your greatest enemy is within you; and you must bring it under subjection always if you want to prosper and be successful in your Christian life. Paul did it and told us to do it (1 Cor. 9:27; Rom. 6:19). There is no other way out.

The thing that tells you that are too weak to pray is your flesh. The thing that tells you that reading and studying the Bible is boring is the flesh. The flesh tells you to procrastinate the evangelism till tomorrow. The flesh is in enmity with God. It is not subject to the Word of God, and can't be. It is opposed to the Ways of the Spirit of God; and if you are in the flesh, if you live according to the flesh, you cannot please God. It is as simple as that.

The flesh will tell you that that lady is more beautiful than your wife, that your wife cannot satisfy you, that you should go for other women. To be carnally minded is death (Rom. 8:6). The flesh will tell you to eat and eat and eat till you overfeed and become insensitive spiritually. It will tell you to sleep and sleep and sleep, and you won't do the necessary things you should do, both in your Christian life and in everyday life.

The Word of God says that if you live in pleasure, you are dead while you are living (1 Tim. 5:6). Only God can tell you what is good and what is bad. God is Truth, and in Him is neither darkness nor lie. Trust in God's Wisdom, and abide by His Word. He will richly reward you when He comes.

WARNINGS FROM THE LORD

The people that ran the race of the Kingdom of God suffered for this Heavenly race; they denied themselves of so many pleasures of life in order to please God. They overcame, and God was faithful in helping them till they left this world. Just as they pleased God, we must make up our minds to please God and shame the devil.

Enter by the narrow gate; for wide is the gate and broad is the way that leads to destruction, and there are many who go in by it. Because narrow is the gate and difficult is the way which leads to life, and there are few who find it.

Every good tree bears good fruit, but a bad tree bears bad fruit. A good tree cannot bear bad fruit, nor can a bad tree bear good fruit. Every tree that does not bear good fruit is cut down and thrown into the Fire.

Not everyone who says to the Lord Jesus Christ, 'Lord, Lord,' shall enter the Kingdom of Heaven, but he who does the Will of His Father, Who also is our Father in Heaven.

Many will say to Him on that Day, "Lord, Lord, have we not prophesied in Your Name, cast out demons in Your Name, and done many wonders in Your Name?" He will then declare to them, "I never knew you, depart from Me, you who practice lawlessness" (Matt. 7:13-23).

A good man out of the good treasure of his heart brings forth good, and an evil man out of the evil treasure of his heart brings forth evil. For out of the abundance of the heart his mouth speaks.

But why do you call Him 'Lord, Lord,' and do not do the things which He says? (Lk. 6:45-46). Some people, after giving their lives to the Lord Jesus Christ, turn back to be the lords of their own lives. Many worship the Lord with their lips, but their hearts are far from Him.

Many will not do evil things when fellow Christians are around, but they will do those things when no one is watching. What about God Who sees in secret, whose Eyes run to and fro the earth?

Many Christians live the life of 'it-doesn't-matter'. They choose what they will give up and what they wouldn't give up. No wonder someone said, "Not just decisions, but Disciples."

People go to the altar-calls, and yet their hearts are far from God. Do you know that, even agents of the kingdom of darkness go out for altar-calls in pretence, just to deceive?

People stay in churches for years, and even rise up to hold positions of authority in the churches, and yet are either not born again or live in iniquity.

No matter how corrupt a generation may be, anyone who sincerely wants to please God will please Him. Take, for instance, the time before the Flood: Enoch walked with God and pleased Him that God had to take him away to Heaven, and he did not see death (Gen. 5:24).

Though the earth was very corrupt in the days of Noah, yet Noah found favour in the Eyes of God, because he was a just man and blameless in his generation (Gen. 6:9).

Abraham followed God in his generation. Though Lot lived in Sodom, yet, he was a righteous man (2 Pet. 2:6-9). They followed the narrow road!

You are the salt of the earth; but if the salt loses its flavour, how shall it be seasoned? You are the light of the world. A city that is set on a hill cannot be hidden.

Nor do they light a lamp and put it under a basket, but on a lampstand, and it gives light to all who are in the house. Let your light so shine before men, that they may see your good works and glorify your Father in Heaven.

Whoever breaks one of the least of God's Commandments, and teaches men so, shall be called least in the Kingdom of Heaven; but whoever does and teaches them, he shall be called great in the Kingdom of Heaven.

For unless your righteousness exceeds the righteousness of the hypocrites, who show outward righteousness, but are corrupt inside, you will by no means enter the Kingdom of Heaven.

Whoever looks at a woman to lust for her has already committed adultery with her in his heart. If your right eye causes you to sin, pluck it out and cast it from you; for it is more profitable for you that one of your members perish than for your whole body to be cast into Hell.

Whoever divorces his wife for any reason, except sexual immorality, causes her to commit adultery; and whoever marries a woman that is divorced commits adultery. Let your 'Yes' be 'Yes' and your 'No,' 'No.'

Give to him who asks you, and from him who wants to borrow from you do not turn away. Love your enemies, bless those who curse you.

Do good to those who hate you, and pray for those who spiteful use you and persecute you: that you may be sons of your Father in Heaven; for He makes His sun rise on the evil and on the good, and sends rain on the just and on the unjust.

For if you love those who love you, what reward have you? Do not even sinners do the same? You shall be perfect, just as your Father in Heaven is perfect (Matt. 5).

When you do a charitable deed, do it in secret; and your Father Who sees in secret will Himself reward you openly.

When you pray, go into your room, and when you have shut your door, pray to your Father Who is in the secret place, and your Father Who sees in secret will reward you openly.

Also, when you fast, anoint your head and wash your face, so that you do not appear to men to be fasting, but to your Father Who is in the secret place, and your Father Who sees in secret will reward you openly.

Do not lay up for yourselves treasures on earth, where moth and rust destroy and where thieves break in and steal.

But lay up for yourselves treasures in Heaven, where neither moth nor rust destroys, and where thieves do not break in and steal. For where your treasure is, there your heart will be also.

No one can serve two masters. For either he will hate the one and love the other, or else he will be loyal to the one and despise the other. You cannot serve God and mammon.

Do not worry about your life, what you will eat or what you will drink; or about your body, what you will put on. Is not life more than food, and the body more than clothing?

But seek first the Kingdom of God and His Righteousness, and all these things shall be added to you. Do not worry about tomorrow, for tomorrow will worry about its own things. Sufficient for the day is its own trouble (Matt. 6).

If you hear the Word of God and do it, you are like a wise man who built his house on the rock, and the rain descended, the floods came, and the winds blew and beat on that house, and it did not fall, for it was founded on the rock.

But if you don't do what you hear, you are a foolish man, and when those things come on your house, which is built on the sand, it will crash. Be doers of the Word, and not just hearers, deceiving yourselves.

Pursue peace with all people, and holiness, without which no one will see the Lord (Heb. 12:14). Do not love the world or anything in the world (1 Jn 2:15).

All the fathers of the people of Israel were under the cloud, all passed through the sea, all ate the same spiritual food, and all drank the same spiritual drink. But with most of them, God was not well-pleased; for their bodies were scattered in the wilderness.

Now these things became our examples, to the intent that we should not lust after evil things as they also lusted.

And do not become idolaters as were some of them. Nor let us commit sexually immorality, as some of them did, and in one day twenty-three thousand fell.

Nor let us tempt Christ, as some of them also tempted, and were destroyed by serpents, nor complain, as some of them also complained, and were destroyed by the destroyer.

Now all these things happened to them as examples, and they were written for our admonition, upon whom the ends of the ages have come.

Therefore, let him who thinks he stands take head, lest he fall. No temptation has overtaken you, except such as is common to man; but God is faithful, Who will not allow you to be tempted beyond what you are able, but with the temptation will also make the way of escape, that you may be able to bear it (1 Cor. 10).

They are ways that seem good and right to men, but the ends of them all are Eternal Destruction, loss, and shouts of 'Had I known!'

There is a highway we must all follow, and that is the highway of holiness. The highway of holiness and the narrow gate that leads to life are friends. We must be holy in all our conduct. Instead of guiding our lives, we should allow the Word of God and His Spirit guide and lead us!

The words spoken by people, their conduct and actions, their character and habits, come from their inside. What fills the inside of a man is what he will bring forth, in words or in actions.

This is one reason that when people misbehave, you may have to look beyond that singular misbehaviour. If you can do some evil things, you can do many others, because they come from the same heart.

If you can do some good things, you don't need to fear to do many others, because they also come from the same heart. I am not talking of words and actions brought about by pretence.

The Lord Jesus Christ tells us this when He stated that you will know false prophets by their fruits. Every good tree bears good fruit, but a bad tree bears bad fruit. A good tree cannot bear bad fruit, nor can a bad tree bear good fruit (Matt. 7:5-18).

A good man out of the good treasure of his heart brings forth good, and an evil man out of the evil treasure of his heart brings forth evil. For out of the abundance of the heart his mouth speaks (Lk. 6:45).

Either make the tree good and its fruit good, or else make the tree bad and its fruit bad; for a tree is known by its fruit. How can you, being good, speak evil things? How can you, being evil speak good things? For out of the abundance of the heart, the mouth speaks (Matt. 12:33-34).

The Bible says that we should guard our hearts with all diligence, for out of it are the issues of life (Prov. 4:23). The things you see in this life are what you speak or what others speak concerning you. But you have power with God!

The Word says that you are to do the guarding. It is not God the Holy Spirit that will do it for you. He is your Helper, and He will help you do all things; but you must give Him free access.

Guard your heart by being careful of what enters your mind, because your mind is the doorway to your heart. Fill your heart with the Word of God; let the Holy Spirit fill you continually. Don't give space for the devil to occupy.

Some people feed their hearts and minds with sensual things. Some watch anything they see on television. They spend so much time on cables and videos, and spend little time with God. Some so-called Christians enjoy listening to worldly music, and say that it is not a problem.

Many have even produced music having Biblical quotations, and the Name of Jesus Christ in them, but even an unbeliever will notice that something is wrong with the music. They call them Christian reggae, Christian blues, Christian makosa, and Christian disco.

Cursed is the man who trusts in man and makes flesh his strength, whose heart departs from the Lord. Blessed is the man who trusts in the Lord, and whose Hope is the Lord. The former shall be like a shrub in the desert, and shall not see when good comes.

The later shall be like a tree planted by the water which spreads out its root by the river, and will not fear when heat comes, but its leaves will be green, and will not be anxious in the year of drought, nor will cease from yielding fruit (Jer. 17:5-8).

The Bible says that the heart is deceitful above all things and desperately wicked, who can know it? The Lord searches the heart, and tests the mind, even to give every man according to his ways, according to the fruit of his doings (Jer. 17:9-10).

Man works against God; this is because man fell when Adam (the first man) disobeyed the Word of God. Man went into more sin and disobedience that the Lord saw that the wickedness of man was great in the earth, and that every intent of the thoughts of his heart was only evil continually.

This state of man, made the Lord to become sorry that He had made man on the earth, and He was grieved in His Heart. And the Lord said, "I will destroy man whom I have created from the face of the earth." However, Noah found favour in the Eyes of the Lord (Gen. 6:6-8).

But what is the state of the unregenerated man these days? They despise and scorn God. Even many people who had been born again have backslidden in their hearts, and live for themselves.

The Lord knows the secrets of the heart (Psa. 44:21). The Bible speaks of secrets of a man's heart (1 Cor. 14:25). All things that are hidden will be revealed and made manifest at the Coming of the Lord Jesus Christ.

What is it that you are hiding in your heart? If you hide lies, hypocrisy, sin, and lust in your heart, it will be exposed at last, and you will find yourself in the Lake which burns with fire and brimstone. You can receive forgiveness now by repenting, confessing your sins, and making the right restitutions.

Let the Word of Christ dwell in you richly all wisdom (Col. 3:16). The Word of God shall not depart from your mouth, but you shall meditate in it day and night, that you may observe to do according to all that is written in it. For then you will make your way prosperous, and then you will have good success (Josh.1:8).

Meditate on the Word of God; give yourself entirely to the Word, that your progress and profiting may be evident to all (1 Tim. 4:15). You have got to be so full of the Word that the fire of the Word will pursue devilish things out of you.

It is very necessary to be filled with the Holy Spirit, and to maintain the fullness of the Spirit always. The men that were to serve as deacons were to be full of the Holy Spirit (Acts 6:3).

Do not be unwise, but understand what the Will of the Lord is. And do not be drunk with wine, in which is dissipation, but be filled with the Holy Spirit, singing and making melody in your heart to the Lord.

Give thanks always for all things to God the Father in the Name of our Lord Jesus Christ, submitting to one another in the fear of God (Eph. 5:17-21).

Blessed are the pure in heart, for they shall see God (Matt. 5:8). As a Christian, you must purify your heart and keep it pure. Pursue peace with all people, and holiness, without which no one will see the Lord.

Look carefully lest anyone fall short of the Grace of God; lest any root of bitterness springing up cause trouble, and by this many become defiled, lest there be any fornicator or profane person like Esau, who for one morsel of food sold his birthright (Heb. 12:14-16).

Blessed are the poor in spirit, for theirs is the Kingdom of Heaven. Blessed are the meek, for they shall inherit the earth. Blessed are those who hunger and thirst for righteousness, for they shall be filled.

Blessed are the merciful, for they shall obtain mercy. Blessed are the peacemakers, for they shall be called sons of God. Blessed are those who are persecuted for righteousness' sake, for theirs is the Kingdom of Heaven.

Blessed are you when they revile and persecute you, and say all kinds of evil against you falsely for the Sake of Jesus Christ (Matt. 5:3-11).

It is necessary that your whole spirit, soul, and body be preserved blameless at the Coming of our Lord Jesus Christ. He Who called us is faithful, and He will do it (1 Thes. 5:23-24).

Your spirit is your heart; don't pollute it with the love of the world or the pleasures of the flesh. Renew your mind with the Word of God so that your way of thinking will change, and instead of thinking like the natural man, you start thinking the Way God thinks.

His Thoughts are higher than our thoughts, and His Ways than men's ways. Don't pollute your body, but use the members of your body to serve God effectively.

Above all, love God fervently with your whole heart. This will make it easy for you to obey Him. The proof of your love for God is your obedience to His Word and Commandment.

Also, you must love your neighbour as yourself. This will help you to do to them as you would desire that they do to you. Love is the end of the Law. There is no fear in love, but perfect love drives away fear (1 Jn. 4:18).

The Lord pleads that you give Him your heart. When you give Him your heart, you have given Him everything, because all other things spring forth from the heart. Give God your heart (Prov. 23:26)

If anyone is born again, he is a new creature, old things have passed away, behold all things have become new (2 Cor. 5:17).

Men shall give account of every idle word they speak on the Day of Judgment. By your words you will either be condemned or justified (Matt. 12:36-37). And words proceed from the heart.

THE GREAT TRIBULATION AND THE BEAST/ANTICHRIST

Apostle John, writing what was revealed to him, said, "Then I stood on the sand of the sea. And I saw a beast rising up out of the sea, having seven heads and ten horns, and on his horns ten crowns, and on his heads a blasphemous name. Now the beast which I saw was like a leopard, his feet were like the feet of a bear, and his mouth like the mouth of a lion. The dragon gave him his power, his throne, and great authority.

"And I saw one of his heads as if it had been mortally wounded, and his deadly wound was healed. And all the world marveled and followed the beast. So they worshipped the dragon who gave authority to the beast; and they worshipped the beast, saying, 'Who is like the beast? Who is able to make war with him?'

"And he was given a mouth speaking great things and blasphemies, and he was given authority to continue for forty-two months. Then he opened his mouth in blasphemy against God, to blaspheme His Name, His Tabernacle, and those who dwell in Heaven. It was granted to him to make war with the Saints and to overcome them. And authority was given him over every tribe, tongue, and nation.

"All who dwell on the earth will worship him, whose names have not been written in the Book of Life of the Lamb slain from the foundation of the world. If anyone has ear, let him hear. He who leads into captivity shall go into captivity; he who kills with the sword must be killed with the sword. Here is the patience and the faith of the Saints.

"Then I saw another beast coming up out of the earth, and he had two horns like a lamb and spoke like a dragon. And he exercises all the authority of the first beast in his presence, and causes the earth and those who dwell in it to worship the first beast, whose deadly wound was healed. He performs great signs, so that he even makes fire come down from heaven on the earth in the sight of men.

"And he deceives those who dwell on the earth by those signs which he was granted to do in the sight of the beast, telling those who dwell on the earth to make an image to the beast who was wounded by the sword and lived. He was granted power to give breath to the image of the beast, that the image of the beast should both speak and cause as many as would not worship the image of the beast to be killed.

"He causes all, both small and great, rich and poor, free and slave, to receive a mark on their right hand or on their foreheads, and that no one may buy or sell except one who has the mark of the beast, or the number of his name. Here is wisdom. Let him who has understanding calculate the number of the beast, for it is the number of a man: His number is 666" (Rev. 13). The second beast is the false prophet who will work signs and wonders in the presence of the first beast – the antichrist.

The Great Tribulation is the forcing of every person on the face of the earth to receive a mark on their right hands or on their foreheads; and no one will either buy or sell without the mark, the name of the beast, or the number of his name. The beast will cause all, both small and great, rich and poor, free and slave, to receive it. And whoever does not worship the beast or receive the mark will be killed. And many peopled will be greatly tortured before they are finally killed.

The Bible says, "For then there will be great tribulation, such as has not been since the beginning of the world until this time, no, nor ever shall be. And unless those days were shortened, no flesh would be saved; but for the Elect's sake those days will be shortened: (Matt. 24:21-22). The Great Tribulation will be characterized by terrible, harsh, and great tribulation, suffering, pain, and death. This is the period and rulership of the antichrist.

But John lets us know that there are many antichrists, who are already in the world now, as the world waits for the antichrist. They don't necessarily have to know about him to wait for him; if they remain in sin and rejection of Jesus Christ, surely, they are waiting for the antichrist. He wrote: "Little children, it is the last hour; and as you have heard that the antichrist is coming, even now many antichrists have come, by which we know that it is the last hour.

"They went out from us, but they were not of us; for if they had been of us, they would have continued with us; but they went out that they might be made manifest, that none of them were of us. But you have an anointing from the Holy One, and you know all things. I have not written to you because you do not know the Truth, but because you know it, and that no lie is of the Truth.

"Who is a liar but he who denies that Jesus is the Christ? He is antichrist who denies the Father and the Son. Whoever denies the Son does not have the Father either; he who acknowledges the Son has the Father also. Therefore let that abide in you which you heard from the beginning. If what you heard from the beginning abides in you, you also will abide in the Son and in the Father.

"And this is the promise that He has promised us – Eternal Life. These things I have written to you concerning those who try to deceive you. But the anointing which you have received from Him abides in you, and you do not need that anyone teach you; but as the same anointing teaches you concerning all things, and is true, and is not lie, and just as it has taught you, you will abide in Him.

"And now little children, abide in Him, that when He appears, we may have confidence and not be ashamed before Him at His Coming. If you know that He is righteous, you know that everyone who practices righteousness is Born of Him" (1 Jn 2:18-29). Know for sure that there are already many antichrists in the world today. Many of them are within the circle of the church-world; and they try to deceive us by pretending that they are working and standing for God.

John added: "Beloved, do not believe every spirit, but test the spirits, whether they are of God; because many false prophets have gone out into the world. By this you know the Spirit of God: Every spirit that confesses that Jesus Christ has come in the flesh is of God, and every spirit that does not confess that Jesus Christ has come in the flesh is not of God.

"And this is the spirit of the antichrist, which you have heard was coming, and is now already in the world. You are of God, little children, and have overcome them, because He Who is in you is greater than he who is in the world" (1 Jn 4:1-4). The spirit and power of the antichrist is already at work now on the face of the earth. This spirit, wisdom, and power works against the Cause of Jesus Christ.

Writing the Thessalonian Believers, Paul said, "Now, brethren, concerning the Coming of our Lord Jesus Christ and our gathering together to Him, we ask you, not to be soon shaken in mind or troubled, either by spirit or by word or by letter, as if from us, as though the Day of Christ had come.

"Let no one deceive you by any means; for that Day will not come unless the falling away comes first, and the man of sin is revealed, the son of perdition, who opposes and exalts himself above all that is called God or that is worshipped, so that he sits as God in the temple of God, showing himself that he is God. Do you not remember that when I was still with you I told you these things?

"And now you know what is restraining, that he may be revealed in his own time. For the mystery of lawlessness is already at work; only He Who now restrains will do so until He is taken out of the way. And then the lawless one will be revealed, whom the Lord will consume with the breath of His Mouth and destroy with the brightness of His Coming.

"The coming of the lawless one is according to the working of satan, with all power, signs, and lying wonders, and with all unrighteous deception among those who perish, because they did not receive the love of the Truth, that they might be saved. And for this reason God will send them strong delusion, that they should believe the lie, that they all may be condemned who did not believe the Truth but had pleasure in unrighteousness.

"But we are bound to give thanks to God always for you, brethren beloved by the Lord, because God from the beginning chose you for salvation through sanctification by the Spirit and belief in the Truth, to which He called you by our Gospel, for the obtaining of the Glory of our Lord Jesus Christ. Therefore, brethren, stand fast and hold the traditions which you were taught, whether by word or our Epistle" (2 Thes. 2:1-15).

The Bible says that the mystery of lawlessness is already at work – the spirit of the antichrist is already at work on the face of this earth. This is why you can see and hear things that you wouldn't have seen and heard if it was not already working. This spirit is even at work among people who go to churches and ministries – those who are Believers, or say that they are Believers. The spirit of the antichrist opposes Jesus Christ and the Word of God.

But even though the spirit of the antichrist is already at work, the antichrist cannot come now, because the Holy Spirit is still on the face of the earth; and He restrains the antichrist from coming. Until after the Rapture, when the Holy Spirit will leave the earth to Heaven, the antichrist cannot come; but when He is taken out of the way, then the antichrist will come and manifest.

Yes, the powers of darkness are putting things in place (as God may allow them) in preparation for the antichrist. But the main antichrist cannot come until the Rapture occurs, when the Holy Spirit will leave this earth.

The occurrence of the Rapture is what Jesus Christ says in writing to the church in Philadelphia, "Because you have kept My Command to persevere, I also will keep you from the hour of trial which shall come upon the whole world, to test those who dwell on the earth" (Rev. 3:10). The Rapture will keep the Believers who are holy and faithful from the period of the Great Tribulation. But the unbelievers and the Believers who are left behind (because of sin and disobedience) will face the Great Tribulation.

Apostle Paul also said that the coming of the lawless one is according to the working of satan, with all power, signs, and lying wonders. This is consistent with what was revealed to Apostle John, when he wrote, "…The dragon gave him his power, his throne, and great authority. And I saw one of his heads as if it had been mortally wounded, and his deadly wound was healed. And all the world marveled and followed the beast. So they worshipped the dragon who gave authority to the beast; and they worshipped the beast….

"And he exercises all the authority of the first beast in his presence, and causes the earth and those who dwell in it to worship the first beast, whose deadly wound was healed. He performs great signs, so that he even makes fire come down from heaven on earth in the sight of men. And he deceives those who dwell on the earth by those signs…" (Rev. 13:2-4,12-14). The dragon is satan, the devil; and he empowers the beast.

But Jesus Christ will destroy the beast at His Coming. Apostle Paul, speaking of the destruction of the beast, said, "And then the lawless one will be revealed, whom the Lord will consume with the breath of His Mouth and destroy with the brightness of His Coming" (2 Thes. 2:8). Apostle John gave us a clearer picture of how the beast will be destroyed when he wrote:

"Now I saw heaven opened, and behold, a white horse. And He Who sat on him was called Faithful and True, and in righteousness He judges and makes war.

"His Eyes were like a flame of fire, and on His Head were many crowns. He had a Name written that no one knows except Himself. He was clothed with a robe dipped in blood, and His Name is called The Word of God. And the armies in Heaven, clothed in fine linen, white and clean, followed Him on white horses. Now out of His Mouth goes a sharp sword, that with it He should strike the nations.

"And He Himself will rule them with a rod of iron. He Himself treads the winepress of the Fierceness and Wrath of Almighty God. And He has on His Robe and on His Thigh a Name written: KING OF KINGS AND LORD OF LORDS. Then I saw an angel standing in the sun; and he cried with a loud voice, saying to all the birds that fly in the midst of heaven, 'Come and gather together for the Supper of the Great God, that you may eat the flesh of kings, the flesh of captains, the flesh of mighty men, the flesh of horses and of those who sit on them, and the flesh of all people, free and slave, both small and great.'

"And I saw the beast, the kings of the earth, and their armies, gathered together to make war against Him Who sat on the horse and against His army. Then the beast was captured, and with him the false prophet who worked signs in his presence, by which he deceived those who received the mark of the beast and those who worshiped his image. These two were cast alive into the lake of fire burning with brimstone. And the rest were killed with the sword which proceeded from the Mouth of Him Who sat on the horse. And all the birds were filled with their flesh" (Rev. 19:11-21).

The Rapture will take place before the Great Tribulation; but the First Resurrection will be after the Great Tribulation. Prophet Daniel said, "At that time Michael shall stand up, the great prince who stands watch over the sons of your people; and there shall be a time of trouble, such as never was since there was a nation, even to that time. And at that time your people shall be delivered, every one who is found written in the Book" (Dan. 12:1).

Concerning the beast, Prophet Daniel said, "I saw in my vision by night, and behold, the four winds of heaven were stirring up the Great Sea. And four great beasts came up from the sea, each different from the other. The first was like a lion, and had eagle's wings. I watched till its wings were plucked off; and it was lifted up from the earth and made to stand on two feet like a man, and a man's heart was given it.

"And suddenly another beast, a second, like a bear. It was raised up on one side, and had three ribs in its mouth between its teeth. And they said thus to it: 'Arise, devour much flesh!' After this I looked, and there was another, like a leopard, which had on its back four wings of a bird. The beast also had four heads, and dominion was given to it.

"After this I saw in the night visions, and behold, a fourth feast, dreadful and terrible, exceedingly strong. It had huge iron teeth; it was devouring, breaking in pieces, and trampling the residue with its feet. It was different from all the beasts that were before it, and it had ten horns. I was considering the horns, and there was another horn, a little one, coming up among them, before whom three of the first horns were plucked out by the roots.

"And there, in this horn, were eyes like the eyes of a man, and mouth speaking pompous words. I watched till thrones were put in place, and the Ancient of Days was seated; His Garment was white as snow, and the hair of His Head was like pure wool. His Throne was a fiery flame, its wheels a burning fire; a fiery stream issued and came forth from before Him.

"A thousand thousands ministered to Him; ten thousand times ten thousand stood before Him. The court was seated, and the books were opened. I watched then because of the sound of the pompous words which the horn was speaking; I watched till the beast was slain, and its body destroyed and given to the burning flame. As for the rest of the beasts, they had their dominion taken away, yet their lives were prolonged for a season and a time.

"I was watching in the night visions, and behold, One like the Son of Man, coming with the clouds of heaven! He came to the Ancient of Days, and they brought Him near before Him. Then to Him was given dominion and glory and a Kingdom, that all peoples, nations, and languages should serve Him. His Dominion is an everlasting dominion, which shall not pass away, and His Kingdom the one which shall not be destroyed" (Dan. 7:2-14).

Comparing: Rev. 12:3, "And another sign appeared in heaven: behold, a great, fiery red dragon having seven heads and ten horns, and seven diadems on his heads"; Rev. 13:1, "Then I stood on the sand of the sea. And I saw a beast rising up out of the sea, having seven heads and ten horns, and on his horns ten crowns, and on his heads a blasphemous name";

Rev 13:11-12, "Then I saw another beast coming up out of the earth, and he had two horns like a lamb and spoke like a dragon. And he exercises all the authority of the first beast in his presence, and causes the earth and those who dwell in it to worship the first beast, whose deadly wound was healed";

And Dan. 7:7, "After this I saw in the night visions, and behold, a fourth beast, dreadful and terrible, exceedingly strong. It had huge iron teeth; it was devouring, breaking in pieces, and trampling the residue with its feet. It was different from all the beasts that were before it, and it had ten horns," we see that these places describe the antichrist.

The red dragon (satan) (Rev. 12:3) will give authority to the antichrist (the beast) (Rev. 13:1 and Dan. 7:7); and the false prophet (Rev. 13:11-12) will work signs, with which he deceives the whole world, in the presence of the antichrist.

Apostle John wrote: "Then one of the seven angels who had the seven bowls came and talked with me, saying to me, 'Come, I will show you the judgment of the great harlot who sits on many waters, with whom the kings of the earth committed fornication, and the inhabitants of the earth were made drunk with the wine of her fornication.'

"So he carried me away in the Spirit into the wilderness. And I saw a woman sitting on a scarlet beast which was full of names of blasphemy, having seven heads and ten horns. The woman was arrayed in purple and scarlet, and adorned with gold and precious stones and pearls, having in her hand a golden cup full of abominations and the filthiness of her fornication.

"And on her forehead a name was written: MYSTERY, BABYLON THE GREAT, THE MOTHER OF HARLOTS AND OF THE ABOMINATIONS OF THE EARTH. I saw the woman, drunk with the blood of the Saints and with the blood of the Martyrs of Jesus. And when I saw her, I marveled with great amazement.

"But the angel said to me, 'Why did you marvel? I will tell you the mystery of the woman and of the beast that carries her, which has the seven heads and the ten horns. The beast that you saw was, and is not, and will ascend out of the Bottomless Pit and go to perdition.

'And those who dwell on the earth will marvel, whose names are not written in the Book of Life from the foundation of the world, when they see the beast that was, and is not, and yet is. Here is the mind which has wisdom: The seven heads are seven mountains on which the woman sits. There are also seven kings. Five have fallen, one is, and the other has not yet come.

'And when he comes, he must continue a short time. The beast that was, and is not, is himself also the eighth, and is of the seven, and is going to perdition. The ten horns which you saw are ten kings who have received no kingdom as yet, but they receive authority for one hour as kings with the beast.

WARNINGS FROM THE LORD

'These are of one mind, and they will give their power and authority to the beast. These will make war with the Lamb, and the Lamb will overcome them, for He is Lord of lords and King of kings; and those who are with Him are called, chosen, and faithful.'

"Then he said to me, 'The waters which you saw, where the harlot sits, are peoples, multitudes, nations, and tongues. And the ten horns which you saw on the beast, these will hate the harlot, make her desolate and naked, eat her flesh and burn her with fire. For God has put it into their hearts to fulfil His Purpose, to be of one mind, and to give their kingdom to the beast, until the Words of God are fulfilled. And the woman whom you saw is that great city which reigns over the kings of the earth'" (Rev. 17).

Never Say That God Said What He Did Not Say!

THE IT-DOESN'T-MATTER SYNDROME

"It doesn't matter." This statement is often made by Christians, either with their minds or with their tongues. Who or what does it not matter to? Is it to God or to them? Some say this or that doesn't matter 'sincerely', having been deceived; and some say it hypocritically with seared conscience, knowing what they are doing.

A Christian must keep a tender conscience. He must not harden his heart to the Promptings of the Holy Spirit. A broken and contrite heart, God will not overlook. A tender conscience is of great value to the Christian. It is a safe check and guide to him. But if his conscience is hardened, then he has fallen into a big problem.

When an unbeliever is born-again by receiving the Lord Jesus Christ as his Lord and personal Saviour, his heart or spirit is made alive spiritually to God. That is to say that his spirit, which was dead through sin, is now regenerated or recreated; and he becomes a new creation. When he does the wrong thing, his spirit will not feel well; and his conscience hurts him. But a Christian can keep on hardening his heart until his conscience becomes seared or dulled.

In this situation of seared conscience, the Christian may not care about many things which are wrong, because they appeal to his fleshly desires and soulish thoughts. He begins to live by his flesh and mind, instead of living by his spirit. He may still think that all is well, but all is not well.

Remember, the Word of God is forever settled in Heaven (Pas. 119:89). God does not change for any generation or person. Do not add to God's Word or take away from it. If you do, you will have endangered yourself. It may not matter now; but what will you do when you find out that it matters when Jesus Christ comes, and there is no second chance?

Run your race to obtain (1 Cor. 9:24). Strip off any weight or sin that may prevent you from being effective as God desires. Many doctrines of devils are being taught and practiced among Christians today. But God does not intend that it be so. There are even satanists in some churches, teaching wrong things to unsuspecting people of God to prevent them from entering Heaven.

Any revelation, vision, or voice that is contrary to the Word of God is not from God, because the Holy Spirit of the Living God inspired the Bible (2 Tim. 3:16). The Bible says that the righteous will scarcely be saved (1 Pet. 4:18). Why? Because many it-doesn't-matter's will matter on the Last Day. God is no respecter of persons (Rom. 2:11). Many Christians will cry on the Last Day, saying, "Had I known, I would have done this or that, and wouldn't have done this or that."

Don't wait till the Last Day before you think of making amendments; by then, it will be too late. God will punish disobedience. He will reward obedience. Don't live to please yourself or any man. Be ready to suffer shame for Christ Jesus as He suffered for you. Abstain from all appearance of evil (1 Thes. 5:22). The people of old had their minds set on obeying God.

Learn from Jesus Christ and follow the ancient path. Remember that though God saved all the children of Israel from Egypt, yet He destroyed many of them, because of unbelief and disobedience. Those people who 'believe' that your going to Heaven is not because of what you did or what you didn't do, but because of Jesus Christ and your faith in Him, distort some portions of the Bible to suit themselves.

For instance, when someone quotes, "Therefore, if you died with Christ from the basic principles of the world, why, as though living in the world, do you subject yourself to regulations – 'Do not touch, do not taste, do not handle,' which all concern things which perish with the using according to the commandments and doctrines of men?

Jesus Christ Is Coming Very Soon: Heaven And Hell Are Real!

"These things indeed have an appearance of wisdom in self-imposed religion, false humility, and neglect of the body, but are of no value against the indulgence of the flesh" (Col. 2:20-23). The person quoting this may fail to know that from verses 11, 16, & 17, Paul was talking of those old testament ordinances of the Sabbath, new moon, festivals, and clean and unclean foods and drinks, comparing it with physical and spiritual circumcision.

Or how can you explain "Do not be unequally yoked together with unbelievers. For what fellowship has righteousness with lawlessness? And what communion has light with darkness? And what accord has Christ with Belial? Or what part has a Believer with an unbeliever? And what agreement has the Temple of God with idols?

"For you are the Temple of the Living God. As God has said: 'I will dwell in them and walk among them. I will be their God, and they shall be My people.' Therefore 'Come out from among them and be separate, says the Lord. Do not touch what is unclean, and I will receive you. I will be a Father to you, and you shall be My sons and daughters, says the LORD Almighty'" (2 Cor. 6:14-18), where Paul tells Believers (from the Scriptures) not to even touch that which is unclean, for God to receive them as His sons and daughters?

Similarly, someone may quote: "For by grace you have been saved through faith, and that not of yourselves; it is the Gift of God, not of works, lest anyone should boast" (Eph. 2:8-9). The person who quotes here may distort the application, without recognizing that the Bible also said, "What shall we say then? Shall we continue in sin that grace may abound? Certainly not! How shall we who died to sin live any longer in it?" (Rom. 6:1-2).

Apostle Paul, in the fifth chapter of the Book of Romans, explained faith and grace which are the basis of our salvation. And fearing that he would be misunderstood and misinterpreted, he was quick to add, in the sixth chapter, that we have died to sin, and we shouldn't live any longer in it because of faith and grace.

He said, "Therefore, having been justified by faith, we have peace with God through our Lord Jesus Christ" (Rom. 5:1). He added to this by saying, "But God demonstrates His Own Love towards us, in that while we were still sinners, Christ died for us. Much more then, having now been justified by His Blood, we shall be saved from the Wrath through Him.

"For when we were enemies we were reconciled to God through the Death of His Son, much more, having been reconciled we shall be saved by His Life" (Rom. 5:8-10). Continuing, he said, "For if by the one man's offence death reigned through the one, much more those who receive abundance of grace and of the gift of righteousness will reign in life through the One, Jesus Christ" (verse 17).

After saying these things (and more), he said, "God forbid that we shall continue in sin because of the grace that is given to us, expecting the grace to abound!" He continued by saying, "For if we have been united together in the likeness of His Death, certainly we also shall be in the likeness of His Resurrection.

"Knowing this, that our old man was crucified with Him, that the body of sin might be done away with, that we should no longer be slaves of sin. For he who has died has been freed from sin (Rom. 6:5-7). Likewise you also, reckon yourselves to be dead indeed to sin, but alive to God in Christ Jesus our Lord.

"Therefore do not let sin reign in your mortal body, that you should obey it in its lusts. And do not present your members as instruments of unrighteousness to sin, but present yourself to God as being alive from the dead, and your members as instruments of righteousness to God. For sin shall not have dominion over you, for you are not under law but under grace (verses 11-14).

"Do you not know that to whom you present yourselves slaves to obey, you are that one's slaves whom you obey, whether of sin leading to death, or of obedience leading to righteousness? But now having been set free from sin, and having become Slaves of God, you have your fruit to holiness, and the end, Everlasting Life" (verses 16 & 22).

Another person may say, "But the Bible says that all our righteousness is like filthy rags (Isa. 64:6), therefore, our righteousness is of Jesus Christ." Yes, our righteousness is of Jesus Christ, because it is by His Sacrifice that we were made righteous before God. No matter what we may do or deny ourselves of, without Jesus Christ we will still remain sinners.

But have you ever seen it in the Bible where it states, "For I say to you, that unless your righteousness exceeds the righteousness of the scribes and Pharisees, you will by no means enter the Kingdom of Heaven?" (Matt. 5:20). In the beginning, it reads, "And seeing the multitudes, He went up on a mountain, and when He was seated, His Disciples came to Him. Then He opened His Mouth and taught them saying…" (Matt. 5:1-2).

You can see that He was speaking to His Disciples, which we may call the Believers. If you doubt this, read the fifth, sixth, and seventh chapters of the Book of Matthew; and you will see that they are applicable to Believers and Christians, and not unbelievers.

In case you are still doubting, after Jesus Christ had died, resurrected, and gone, the Word says, "Beloved, now we are children of God; and it has not yet been revealed what we shall be, but we know that when He is revealed, we shall be like Him, for we shall see Him as He is. And everyone who has this Hope in Him purifies himself, just as He is pure.

"Whoever commits sin also commits lawlessness, and sin is lawlessness. And you know that He was manifested to take away our sins, and in Him there is no sin. Whoever abides in Him does not sin. Whoever sins has neither seen Him nor known Him. Little children, let no one deceive you. He who practices righteousness is righteous, just as He is righteous.

"He who sins is of the devil, for the devil has sinned from the beginning. For this purpose the Son of God was manifested, that He might destroy the works of the devil. Whoever has been Born of God does not sin, for His Seed remains in him; and he cannot sin, because he has been Born of God. In this the children of God and the children of the devil are manifest: Whoever does not practice righteousness is not of God, nor is he who does not love his brother" (1 Jn 3:2-10).

This place says that the Believer who wants to be like Jesus Christ at His Appearing must purify himself, just as Jesus Christ is pure. Whoever abides in Him does not sin. He who practices righteousness is righteous, just as Jesus Christ is righteous. He who sins is of the devil. Whoever does not practice righteousness is not of God.

The Word says, "For the Grace of God that brings salvation has appeared to all men, teaching us that denying ungodliness and worldly lusts, we should live soberly, righteously, and Godly in the present age, looking for the blessed hope and glorious Appearing of our Great God and Saviour Jesus Christ" (Tit. 2:11-13). You can see that we are not to live carelessly and anyhow, but soberly, righteously, and Godly.

Someone else may say, "But Jesus Christ said that it is not what enters a man that defiles the man, but what comes out of the man" (Matt. 15:11). But if what goes into a man doesn't defile a man, why did Jesus Christ rebuke the church in Thyatira for allowing Jezebel to teach His Servants to eat things sacrificed to idols? (Rev. 2:20). And when there was a debate/argument on what the Gentile Christians should keep, why did the counsel at Jerusalem tell them to abstain from things polluted by idols, from strangled meat/animals, and from blood? (Acts 15:20).

Somebody may say that Apostle Paul said that idol is nothing, but fail to see that he said that if your brother will be offended because you ate the meat sacrificed to idol, you are to avoid it (1 Cor. 8; Rom. 14). When somebody says that Jesus Christ said that not what enters a man defiles a man, but what comes out of the man, he doesn't even know that they were discussing about washing of the hands before eating.

By the way, does vomiting defile you before God, since it came out of you? And those who want to destroy themselves have used that excuse to drink alcohol and smoke cigarettes, destroying their bodies, which is for God and should be kept holy for our God. Think of it! If the Believers were already drinking alcohol by little measure, why will Apostle Paul tell Timothy to use little wine for his stomach's sake (as a kind of soothing medicine, in that their ancient and unrefined medical practice)?

A WORD IS ENOUGH FOR THE WISE! Shall we continue to sin that grace may increase? (Rom. 6:1) Is faith without works not dead? (Jas 2:17) What will make Jesus Christ to tell those that had prophesied, cast out demons, and done mighty works in His Name, that He never knew them? (Matt. 7:21-23). Surely, they had known Christ before. I am not reducing righteousness and holiness to physical things, physical appearance, and dress code alone? Why did the Word of God put the sin of the flesh first before sin of spirit in Second Corinthians 7:1?

Some people say that we are laying unnecessary burdens on people. Which burden (if it were even to be a burden, as you think) is greater than sacrificing small things for Jesus Christ and Heaven? If you can't deny yourself of small things, because of Heaven, can you lay down your life for Jesus Christ? He who loves his life more than Christ Jesus is not worthy of Him.

By the way, have you ever seen it in the Bible that Apostle Paul gave ordinances to New Testament Believers? He wrote, saying, "Now I praise you, brethren, that you remember me in all things and keep the traditions (ordinances, the King James Version) just as I delivered them to you" (1 Cor. 11:2). Was he putting burdens on them? Certainly the Corinthian church was a 'Gentile' church.

Apostle Paul wrote, "But beware lest somehow this liberty of yours become a stumbling block to those who are weak. And because of your knowledge shall the weak brother perish, for whom Christ died? But when you thus sin against the brethren, and wound their weak conscience, you sin against Christ. Therefore, if food makes my brother stumble, I will never again eat meat, lest I make my brother stumble" (1 Cor. 8:9-13).

Writing to the Galatians, he said, "For you, brethren, have been called to liberty; only do not use liberty as an opportunity for the flesh, but through love serve one another. And those that are Christ's have crucified the flesh with its passions and desires. If we live in the Spirit, let us also walk in the Spirit" (Gal. 5:13,24,25).

Jesus Christ rebuked the scribes and the Pharisees, not because they paid tithes (because God commanded them to pay tithes), but because they neglected justice, mercy, and faith while paying tithes (Matt. 23:23). Will you cancel tithe (for example) because they neglected justice, mercy, and faith? Certainly, no, or you will still be disobeying God.

In order words, because somebody can dress virtuously and Godly like a Christian and still be evil, immoral, and wicked on the inside, will not cancel the Truth that a Christian is to dress and appear like a Christian. By that, I mean that Christians and Believers are to dress decently, Godly, and Biblically. Inside and outside, you are to be like Christ – Christian.

Let us know that we have not arrived in Heaven yet; therefore we are to be careful of how we live our lives and of the utterances we make, including how we think and reason. Let us always be open to the Holy Spirit to direct and lead us all the days of our lives till we see the Face of Jesus Christ in Heaven.

The Word says, "Moreover, brethren, I do not want you to be unaware that all our fathers were under the cloud, all passed through the sea, all were baptized into Moses in the cloud and in the sea, all ate the same spiritual food, and all drank the same spiritual drink. For they drank of that spiritual Rock that followed them, and that Rock was Christ.

"But with most of them God was not well-pleased, for their bodies were scattered in the wilderness. Now these things became our examples, to the intent that we should not lust after evil things as they also lusted. And do not become idolaters as were some of them. As it is written, 'The people sat down to eat and drink, and rose up to play.'

"Nor let us commit sexual immorality, as some of them did, and in one day twenty-three thousand fell; nor let us tempt Christ, as some of them also tempted, and were destroyed by serpents; nor complain, as some of them also complained, and were destroyed by the destroyer. Now all these things happened to them as examples, and they were written for our admonition, upon whom the ends of the ages have come.

"Therefore let him who thinks he stands take heed lest he fall. No temptation has overtaken you except such as is common to man; but God is faithful, Who will not allow you to be tempted beyond what you are able, but with the temptation will also make the way of escape, that you may be able to bear it. Therefore, my beloved, flee from idolatry" (1 Cor. 10:1-14).

Another person may say that the Bible says that God looks at the heart, but man looks at the outward appearance (1 Sam. 16:7). Could it be that God is blind of outward appearance? The One that made the physical realm, how can't He see physical appearance? Yet, your physical appearance is the reflection of what is in your heart – how your heart appears; for "out of the abundance of the heart the mouth speaks" (Matt. 12:34).

People misapply the fact that God looks at the heart. When as an African (for example), you use artificial relaxer to relax your natural hair, because you have accepted inferiority complex, which tells you that your hair is inferior to that of the Europeans, and you call God an imperfect Creator by that, do you think that God sees a perfect heart in you?

When you dress indecently and seductively, and say that you didn't dress that way to seduce anybody, but to look attractive (demonic attraction, indeed!), do you think that God sees a good heart in you, when you are openly rejecting His Word by causing your brother to fall into lust, evil thought, and fornication?

So someone can steal, because God sees in his heart that he wants to use the stolen money to help the poor? Or, rather, another person can have sexual intercourse with the other person, because he/she wants to show her/him that he/she loves her/him? Repent now and change your evil, anti-Christ, and anti-God ways, before it becomes too late!

Also, notice that Paul, who is the 'champion' of grace never encouraged worldliness, nor disregarded the importance of Godly appearance to the Believer. On the contrary, he even discouraged Christians from setting their minds on 'looking attractive', as seen in First Timothy 2:9-10, being supported by Peter in First Peter 3:3.

He even classified revelries (that is, wild noisy form of dancing) as the work of the flesh in Galatians 5:21, being supported by Peter in First Peter 4:3-4. Peter even went on to add drinking parties (not to talk of drunkenness and gluttony). If you study your Bible well, when Apostle Paul spoke of bringing people under bondage, he was speaking of commanding the Gentiles to live like the Jews.

He himself was not even given to discouraging the Jews from observing their ordinances; and you can see that he both circumcised Timothy (because of his being or travelling with him) (Acts 16:3) and shaved his own head (to show the Jews that he was not teaching against their ordinances) (Acts 21:20-26).

Never Say That God Said What He Did Not Say!

SPEAKING LIES IN HYPOCRISY

The Word of God says that someone can speak lies in hypocrisy (1 Tim. 4:2). A Believer in Christ who has departed from the faith by listening to seducing spirits and doctrines of devils will speak lies in hypocrisy. They will do this for different reasons. Some will do this to draw followers to themselves. Others will do it for their belly. Still, others will do this to be regarded as being on the right track.

What are lies, and what is hypocrisy? Lies are perversion of the Truth. Anything that is contrary to the Word of God is a lie. The devil, satan, is a liar and the father of all lies. We, the children of God, are a people of light and of the Truth. We live in the light; we live by the Word of God. Anything that is evil fears the light. We are not evil; therefore, we do not fear the light. Rather, we come to the light; because we do the right things.

Hypocrisy is saying one thing and doing another thing. Hypocrisy is saying something in pretence. It is saying something and hiding what we should say. God hates hypocrisy. When the devil comes as an angel of light, that is hypocrisy. When his workers parade themselves as workers of Christ, that is hypocrisy. We are not hypocrites, but a people of Truth.

These days, there are many occult ministers pretending to be preachers of righteousness and of the Gospel. However, their end is destruction. Jesus Christ died for them; and He will forgive them, and change them, if they repent and come to Him. People of God, don't follow miracles, voices, and revelations. Allow them to follow you rather. Follow God, His Holy Spirit, and His Word.

Even these days, there are agents of darkness even inside churches. They try to cause havoc in churches; they try to cause immorality among preachers and the people of God. They want to cause pains, barrenness, miscarriages, failure, sicknesses, diseases, poverty, frustrations, and other things. The devil, satan, takes delight in seeing man, made in the Image and Likeness of God, suffering.

A lot of false teachings abound among Christians. These teachings are of demonic origin. Many were brought in subtly by the devil. People preach half-truths; some take away from the Word, and some add to the Word. Anything that is contrary to the Word of God is not of God, and cannot be from God. I don't care how many days you fasted before you received it. I don't care whether it came by vision, audible voice, prophecy, tongues and interpretation, or by dreams.

The Holy Ghost inspired the Word of God (2 Tim. 3:16). Holy men of God spoke and wrote as they were moved by the Holy Spirit (2 Pet. 1:21). God is not an author of confusion. Also, the Almighty remains the Same and does not change (Mal 3:6). Jesus Christ is the Same yesterday, today, and forever.

But the end of evil workers, evil teachers, and their followers is destruction. Those who have itching ears and heap teachers to teach them what they want to hear will end in Hell. Hell Fire does not respect your church, your position, or your title. Whether you are a reverend, an apostle, a prophet, an evangelist, a pastor, a bishop, a professor, a governor, and whatever you may be, carry it to yourself; for God is no respecter of persons (Rom. 2:11).

The Bible says that they will speak lies in hypocrisy, because they have their own conscience seared with a hot iron. Their hearts have been hardened, and they refuse the Truth of the Word of God, following and listening to deceiving spirits and doctrines of devils. Such deceptions and doctrines are against God, anti-Christ, and unbiblical. And those who follow them will end up at the place where their originator dwells – Hell.

WARNINGS FROM THE LORD

The Word says, "Little children, it is the last hour, and as you have heard that the antichrist is coming, even now many antichrists have come; by which we know that it is the last hour. They went out from us, but they were not of us; for if they had been of us, they would have continued with us; but they went out that they might be made manifest that none of them were of us. But you have an anointing from the Holy One, and you know all things.

"…the anointing which you have received from Him abides in you, and you do not need that anyone teach you; but as the same anointing teaches you concerning all things, and is true, and is not a lie, and just as it has taught you, you will abide in Him. And now, little children, abide in Him, that when He appears, we may have confidence and not be ashamed before Him at His Coming. If you know that He is righteous, you know that everyone who practices righteousness is Born of Him" (1 Jn 2:18-20, 27-29).

Ignorance is a disease. Ignorance means lack of knowledge. Whatever area or thing you don't know of, you are ignorant of it. God said that His people perish because of lack of knowledge – ignorance (Hos. 4:6). Notice that this place is not talking about unbelievers but people of God. Ignorance is no excuse.

God does not want us to be ignorant of His Things and Ways; that is why He gave us His Word, the Bible. Apart from the Bible, God leads us today through different ways to keep us knowledgeable and not ignorant. But we have the responsibility to be ignorant or to be knowledgeable.

If you don't study your Bible, if you don't read or meditate on God's Word, you will be ignorant of many things you shouldn't be ignorant of. Also, if you don't listen to the Holy Spirit, and you are not sensitive to His Guidance, you will be ignorant of many things. Therefore, learn to be led and guided by God.

Whether in the physical or in the spiritual, ignorance is not good; and it is a kind of poverty. Ignorance will make you lose a lot of things. It will make you fall into unnecessary dangers, whether in the physical or in the spiritual. If you don't know your enemy's strategy, you may be in a great problem.

However, even when we know of certain things, sometimes we still make mistakes. Some of the mistakes we make in life is because we are ignorant of the situation or the operations of the thing. Mistakes can be costly; it can make you lose a lot. It can even destroy your life.

Being led by the Holy Spirit can save us from many mistakes, because He knows more than and better than us. Rely on His Help, and He will make you avoid mistakes. Also, study to learn, because knowledge can save you from a lot of mistakes.

Foolishness comes in various forms. When you keep on making the same mistakes, that is foolishness. When you say there is no God, you are a fool (Psa. 14:1). When you think that God is not aware of what you are doing, that is foolishness. Even choosing to be ignorant of what you should know is foolishness. Foolishness is the opposite of wisdom. Do you want to be wise? Then shun foolishness, and it will be well with you.

Ignorance, as I said before, is lack of knowledge. It is lack of knowledge or information about something or some beings. Not knowing God and understanding His Word and Ways can make you go contrary to His Will, Plan, and Purpose, even without your knowledge; and you may think that you have pleased Him, while you are disappointing Him.

Ignorance of human character, habits, motives, weaknesses, reasoning, and mentality, can affect your relationship with people. Also, not knowing and understanding the devil, his fallen angels, his demons, his human agents, and his works, can lead to loss, death, and destruction.

Of course, I am not saying that you must know everything about the devil and his hosts, but you have to know his goals, which are to kill, to steal, and to destroy. And you have to know his tactics, like: deceptions, tricks, manipulations, oppressions, obsessions, etc.

Mistake, in the other hand, refers to something unwise or stupid that someone does, which they regret doing afterwards. Unfortunately, by the time you regret the action, the deed has already been done, and the effects and results might have been experienced and noticed in someone's lifetime. Therefore, be careful, avoid mistakes as much as possible.

Foolishness refers to action, remark, etc that is stupid and shows that someone is not thinking sensibly. Stupidity refers to behaviour or actions that show a lack of good sense or good judgment. God does not want us to be ignorant; He does not want us to make mistakes; and He doesn't want His children to behave or act foolishly.

Apostle Paul wrote: "Lest Satan should take advantage of us; for we are not ignorant of his devices" (2 Cor. 2:11). Thinking, speaking, and acting out of ignorance makes the devil to gain advantage over us. If we make mistakes, he rejoices, for it is to his advantage. Acting and behaving foolishly, as Believers, will make the devil to gain.

RUNNING AFTER PROPHECIES AND MIRACLES

Prophecies and miracles are good; but we are not to run after them. God gives us prophecies and works miracles among us, because He loves us; and He wants to give us direction and solve our needs and problems. But to tell you the Truth, the end (purpose) of prophecies and miracles is to draw us to (and keep us in) the Word of God, which is the Will of God.

See what the Bible says: "Though I speak with the tongues of men and of angels, but have not love, I have become a sounding brass or a clanging cymbal. And though I have the gift of prophecy, and understand all mysteries and all knowledge, and though I have all faith, so that I could remove mountains, but have not love, I am nothing" (1 Cor. 13:1-2).

Continuing, it says, "Not everyone who says to Me, 'Lord, Lord,' shall enter the Kingdom of Heaven, but he who does the Will of My Father in Heaven. Many will say to Me in that Day, 'Lord, Lord, have we not prophesied in Your Name, cast out demons in Your Name, and done many wonders in Your Name?' And then I will declare to them, 'I never knew you; depart from Me, you who practice lawlessness!'" (Matt. 7:21-23).

What I want you to know is that inasmuch as God wants to give you prophecies and miracles, He is more interested in your obeying His Word, so that you will make His Kingdom; because you can have all the prophecies and miracles that you want, and still end in Hell Fire. Don't deceive yourself; and let no one deceive you.

The Bible says, "When the people therefore saw that Jesus was not there, nor His Disciples, they also got into boats and came to Capernaum, seeking Jesus. And when they found Him on the other side of the sea, they said to Him, 'Rabbi, when did You come here?' Jesus answered them, and said, 'Most assuredly, I say to you, you seek Me, not because you saw the signs, but because you ate of the loaves and were filled.

'Do not labour for the food which perishes, but for the food which endures to Everlasting Life, which the Son of man will give you, because God the Father has set His Seal on Him'" (Jn 6:24-27). He had fed them (about five thousand men, besides women and children) with five loaves of bread and two small fishes, which He multiplied. And instead of that level of miracle to catch their attention, so that they will pay close attention to His Teachings and do them, they wanted more miracles and miraculous feeding.

But Jesus Christ told them not to seek or run after miracles ("Do not labour for the food which perishes"), but to labour for that which endures to Everlasting Life (knowing the Word, Will, and Mind of God, and obeying it). And it is in Jesus Christ that you will get it, as you abide in Him by loving Him with your all and more than all, and obeying His Word and Commandments.

How come that the Israelites did not trust, obey, and serve God faithfully after seeing all the mighty signs and wonders that God performed in the land of Egypt and in dividing the Red Sea for them? They still rebelled against God and murmured against His Servants. Even though God gave them manna to eat, they still complained and murmured, that God's Wrath burst on them!

Where is your heart? Why do you come to church? Why are you a Believer? Do you want to know the Mind and Will of God, and do it? Or, is your concern for Him to solve your problems, needs, and wants? What is the main thing that attracts you to God? Do you honour God with your lips, while your heart is far from Him? Check yourself for what is in your mind!

When the multitude heard of what John the Baptist was doing, they came to also take part in what others were receiving from John. When John the Baptist saw them, he said, "Brood of vipers! Who warned you to flee from the wrath to come? Therefore bear fruits worthy of repentance, and do not begin to say to yourselves, 'We have Abraham as our father.' For I say to you that God is able to raise up children to Abraham from these stones.

"And even now the ax is laid to the root of the trees. Therefore every tree which does not bear good fruit is cut down and thrown into the fire." So the people asked him, saying, "What shall we do then?" He answered and said to them, "He who has two tunics, let him give to him who has none; and he who has food, let him do likewise."

Then tax collectors also came to be baptized, and said to him, "Teacher, what shall we do? And he said to them, "Collect no more than what is appointed for you." Likewise the soldiers asked him, saying, "And what shall we do?" So he said to them, "Do not intimidate anyone or accuse falsely, and be content with your wages" (Lk. 3:7-14).

Notice that they called him teacher and not preacher! Whether you are a teacher or a preacher, teach and/or preach repentance from sin and faith towards God. If all you preach and teach is faith towards God, then you have missed the mark.

Notice how the soldiers put their question in stronger form than the first two groups! And notice that John the Baptist did not fear them; for whereas he gave two instructions to the people, and one instruction to the tax collectors, he went ahead to give three instructions to the soldiers.

The Lord says, "And you will seek Me and find Me, when you search for Me with all your heart" (Jer. 29:13). To seek is to look for, to try to get, to ask for, and to move towards something. To search is to spend time looking for someone or something; it is to examine something very carefully in order to find something out. To seek for something is to go after the thing; it is to search for something. Seeking and searching God with all your heart will lead to your finding Him.

God does not desire casual relationship between Himself and His people. He wants close and heart-felt relationship. He wants His people to long after Him with all their heart. God wants you to be passionately consumed with Him and the things that concern Him. But how many of us are actually consumed by our longing for and thinking about God?

The Bible says, "Ask, and it will be given to you; seek and you will find; knock, and it will be opened to you. For everyone who asks receives, and he who seeks finds, and to him who knocks it will be opened" (Matt. 7:7-8). Notice particularly that you will find what you seek, for everyone who seeks finds. You will find what you spend time, energy, and effort to seek and search for; and if you spend time and effort to seek God, you will find Him.

The Word says, "But let him ask in faith, with no doubting, for he who doubts is like a wave of the sea driven and tossed by the wind. For let not that man suppose that he will receive anything from the Lord; he is a double-minded man, unstable in all his ways" (Jas 1:6-8).

You have to seek God in faith. Without faith, it is impossible to please God; for he who comes to God must believe that He is, and that He is a Rewarder of those who diligently seek Him (Heb. 11:6). God rewards, honours, and answers those who diligently seek Him. He will not turn a deaf Ear to your cries!

Behold, the Lord's Hand is not shortened, that it cannot save, nor His Ear heavy, that it cannot hear. But it is iniquity that separates God's people from God; it is their sins that hide His Face from them, so that He will not hear (Isa. 59:1-2). If you live in sin, you make yourself God's enemy.

Therefore, in seeking God, keep yourself far from sin and iniquity. Yes, temptations will come; but you have the power to overcome them. And God will always make a way of escape for you, even as He has also promised that He will not allow any temptation that is greater than you to come your way. You are God's child, and not the devil's child!

The Word says, "Beloved, now we are children of God; and it has not yet been revealed what we shall be, but we know that when He is revealed, we shall be like Him, for we shall see Him as He is. And everyone who has this hope in Him purifies himself, just as He is pure. Whoever commits sin also commits lawlessness, and sin is lawlessness. And you know that He was manifested to take away our sins, and in Him there is no sin.

"Whoever abides in Him does not sin. Whoever sins has neither seen Him nor known Him. Little children, let no one deceive you. He who practices righteousness is righteous, just as He is righteous. He who sins is of the devil, for the devil has sinned from the beginning. For this purpose the Son of God was manifested, that He might destroy the works of the devil.

"Whoever has been Born of God does not sin, for His Seed remains in him; and he cannot sin, because he has been Born of God. In this the children of God and the children of the devil are manifest: Whoever does not practice righteousness is not of God, nor is he who does not love his brother" (1 Jn 3:2-10).

In seeking God, you are to seek Him in faith and holiness, trusting God, having full confidence in Him, and cleansing yourself of all filthiness and sin of the flesh and spirit. God loves us; and He does not want us to be associated with the devil or the world. Have it in your innermost being that God cares for you; and He wills to manifest Himself to you more than you want to know Him.

The Bible says, "I beseech you therefore, brethren, by the Mercies of God, that you present your bodies a living sacrifice, holy, acceptable to God, which is your reasonable service. And do not be conformed to this world, but be transformed by the renewing of your mind, that you may prove what is that Good and Acceptable and Perfect Will of God" (Rom. 12:1-2).

When you present your body as a living sacrifice to God, you will serve and obey Him with the members of your body; and you will not present any part of your body as an instrument of unrighteousness to sin, but present them as instruments of righteousness to God and holiness. When you renew your mind with the Word of God, you will think and reason as God thinks and reasons.

But do you know that God also seeks for men? Yes, God seeks for men who will cooperate with Him, in order that His Will, Plan, and Purpose may come to pass on this earth. This earth has been given to men by God; and man has authority over this earth (though under the Authority of God). If we don't cooperate with God, the Purpose of God can be thwarted by the devil.

The Bible says, "So I sought for a man among them who would make a wall, and stand in the gap before Me on behalf of the land, that I should not destroy it; but I found no one. Therefore I have poured out My Indignation on them, I have consumed them with the fire of My Wrath, and I have recompensed their deeds on their own heads, says the Lord God" (Ezek. 22:30-31).

Even though the land was full of evil and wickedness, yet the Lord had wanted a man who would have stood between Him and the people of the land, so that He might have relented from pouring out His Wrath upon the people. However, God did not find a man; therefore, He poured out His Wrath and Indignation upon the people, and consumed them with the fire of His Wrath.

ROBBING GOD

Can a man really rob God? But God declared that the sons of men can rob Him. To rob someone is to take something from somebody by force without his consent, especially using violence. Robbery is done openly; but can anyone hide something from God? God is omniscient, and knows everything; and He knows of everything you have taken away from Him, whether or not you are aware of it.

God has ministers who attend to His ministries and churches in this world. Those ministers, ministries, and churches need money to carry out God's Work on earth. When the money meant for them does not reach them, or is taken away from them by way of stealing, God is being robbed. God does not need the money in Heaven, but His Works on earth need it.

Whether it is money, property, time, or opportunity needed or owned by God, depriving God of it is robbing God; and that act displeases God. Whether it is the unbeliever, who do not know God, that does it, it is robbing God; whether it is Believers, who already know God, that do it, it is robbing God. Even when ministers and preachers commit this act, it is still robbing God.

It is not as if God does not regard the acts of robbing Him: God says that he who is unholy can go ahead being unholy; he that is unrighteous can go on being unrighteous; he that is holy should go on being holy; and he that is righteous should go ahead being righteous. Why? Because the Lord Jesus Christ comes very soon to reward each man according as his work shall be (Rev. 22:12).

God is a Loving God; and He gives everyone time to repent, because He does not want anyone to perish. However, when that time expires, God judges all according to their works without showing favouritism or partiality.

All things that we have came from God; and without God, where would we have been? Without God, you wouldn't have come into this world in the first place. It is by the Mercies of God that you are alive today. The devil would have desired that you died in your mother's womb. But God has given you life and health. He has also given you the power to get or acquire something.

The Word of God says, "Beware that you do not forget the Lord your God by not keeping His Commandments, His Judgments, and His Statutes…lest – when you have eaten and are full, and have built beautiful houses and dwell in them, and when your herds and your flocks multiply, and your silver and your gold are multiplied, and all that you have is multiplied.

"When your heart is lifted up, and you forget the Lord your God Who brought you out of the land of Egypt, from the house of bondage; Who led you through that great and terrible wilderness, in which were fiery serpents and scorpions and thirsty land where there was no water; Who brought water for you out of the flinty rock.

"Who fed you in the wilderness with manna, which your fathers did not know, that He might humble you and that He might test you, to do you good in the end – then you say in your heart, 'My power and the might of my hand have gained me this wealth.' And you shall remember the Lord your God, for it is He Who gives you power to get wealth, that He may establish His Covenant….

"Then it shall be, if you by any means forget the Lord your God, and follow other gods, and serve and worship them, I testify against you this day that you shall surely perish. As the nations which the Lord destroys before you, so you shall perish, because you would not be obedient to the Voice of the Lord your God" (Deut. 8:11-20).

Notice that you don't necessarily say it with your mouth, that it is by your power, might, wisdom, intelligence, or ingenuity that you got the money or wealth you have. Your saying it with your heart or mind is pride; and it is enough for you to start disregarding the Word of God, even to the extent of robbing God – not only in tithes, but in tithes and offerings.

The Bible states: "Will a man rob God? Yet you have robbed Me! But you say, 'In what way have we robbed You?' In tithes and offerings. You are cursed with a curse, for you have robbed Me, even this whole nation. Bring all the tithes into the storehouse, that there may be food in My House, and try Me in this," says the Lord of Hosts, "if I will not open for you the windows of Heaven, and pour out for you such blessing that there would not be room enough to receive it.

"And I will rebuke the devourer for your sakes, so that he will not destroy the fruit of your ground, nor shall the vine fail to bear fruit for you in the field," says the Lord of Hosts; "and all nations will call you blessed, for you will be a delightful land," says the Lord of Hosts (Mal. 3:8-12).

Never Say That God Said What He Did Not Say!

CHASTENING THE BELIEVERS

God chastises and disciplines His children to make them live better lives for Him. The Bible discourages withholding chastisement and discipline from a son when it says, "He who spares his rod hates his son, but he who loves him disciplines him promptly" (Prov. 13:24).

You chastise and discipline your son to correct him, because you love him. And the Word says, "Correct your son, and he will give you rest, yes, he will give delight to your soul" (Prov. 29:17). Why? Because when you correct your son by discipline and chastisement, he will do the right things and the things you want him to do.

But if you say that you want to do good to your son by not beating, chastising, and disciplining him with something that will pain him, when he does (or keeps on doing) the wrong thing(s), then whether or not you know it, God sees you as someone who hates his son.

Chastisement may be mild (soft), moderate, or harsh. If someone doesn't listen to mild or moderate chastisement, then make it harsh. However, our chastisement must be done out of love, in order to correct someone, and never out of bitterness or hatred.

Also, notice that it is not only the child that may be beaten: the son (grown up one) is to be chastised and disciplined also. According to the Bible, "Foolishness is bound up in the heart of a child; the rod of correction will drive it far from him" (Prov. 22:15).

And knowing that God loves us and cares for us more than any earthly father, we have to know that He will show His Love for us by beating, disciplining, chastising, and correcting us by any means He deems appropriate. And none of us must get annoyed with the Owner of all of us when He corrects us in His Wisdom.

The Word says, "...My son, do not despise the Chastening of the Lord, nor be discouraged when you are corrected by Him. For whom the Lord loves He chastens, and scourges every son whom He receives." If you endure chastening, God deals with you as with sons; for what son is there whom a father does not chasten?

"But if you are without chastening, of which all have become partakers, then you are illegitimate and not sons. Furthermore, we have had human fathers who corrected us, and we paid them respect. Shall we not much more readily be in subjection to the Father of spirits and live?

"For they indeed for a few days chastened us as seemed best to them, but He for our profit, that we may be partakers of His Holiness. Now no chastening seems to be joyful for the present, but painful; nevertheless, afterwards it yields the peaceable fruit of righteousness to those who have been trained by it" (Heb. 12:5-11).

I want you to notice that the Bible says that God scourges every son whom He receives. To scourge someone is to hit someone with a whip as punishment. How many of us will take it that the person who whipped or scourged us did it out of love for us? If we actually believe that God scourges those that He loves, then we must also believe that even our fellow human beings can scourge or discipline us out of love.

Of course, someone can also scourge another person out of hatred or bitterness; but it doesn't do away with that fact that we can be scourged and disciplined by someone out of love. But many people, instead of correcting themselves when they are scourged by someone, feel that the person who scourged, disciplined, or corrected them hates them; and they pick offence. By the way, who would scourge you without great or persistent offence?

Concerning the Israelites, the Bible says "Every Commandment which I command you today you must be careful to observe, that you may live and multiply, and go in and possess the land of which the Lord swore to your fathers. And you shall remember that the Lord your God led you all the way these forty years in the wilderness, to humble you and test you; to know what was in your heart, whether you would keep His Commandments or not.

"So He humbled you, allowed you to hunger, and fed you with manna which you did not know nor did your fathers know, that He might make you know that man shall not live by bread alone; but man lives by every Word that proceeds from the Mouth of the Lord. Your garments did not wear out on you, nor did your foot swell these forty years.

"You should know in your heart that as a man chastens his son, so the Lord your God chastens you. Therefore you shall keep the Commandments of the Lord your God, to walk in His Ways and to fear Him. For the Lord your God is bringing you into a good land…" (Deut. 8:1-7).

God humbled them for a period of forty years. Was it because He hated them? No; rather, He loved them. And He allowed them to go hungry in order to teach them. He allowed them to pass through harsh conditions in the wilderness to test them. He chastened them to know what was in their heart.

And He still does so with us today. But what will you do if your fellow human being humbled, tried, tested, and chastened you for one complete day? Wouldn't you reason that the person hates you? But did God hate the Israelites whom He humbled for a whole forty years?

PUNISHMENT FOR BACKSLIDING

Backsliding has punishment, both in this world and in that which is to come. This is why God calls backsliders to repentance, because He does not want any soul to perish. The Word of God says, "Therefore we must give the more earnest heed to the things we have heard, lest we drift away.

"For if the Word spoken through angels proved steadfast, and every transgression and disobedience received a just reward, how shall we escape if we neglect so great a salvation, which at the first began to be spoken by the Lord,

"And was confirmed to us by those who heard Him, God also bearing witness both with signs and wonders, with various miracles, and Gifts of the Holy Spirit, according to His Own Will?" (Heb. 2:1-4). We are to give the more earnest heed to the Word of God, lest we drift away.

Speaking of sinners among the brethren (in the church), the Bible says, "It is actually reported that there is sexual immorality among you, and such sexual immorality as is not even named among the Gentiles – that a man has his father's wife!

"And you are puffed up, and have not rather mourned, that he who has done this deed might be taken away from among you. For I indeed, as absent in body but present in spirit, have already judged (as though I were present) him who has so done this deed.

"In the Name of our Lord Jesus Christ, when you are gathered together, along with my spirit, with the Power of our Lord Jesus Christ, deliver such a one to satan for the destruction of the flesh, that his spirit may be saved in the Day of the Lord Jesus.

"Your glorying is not good. Do you not know that a little leaven leavens the whole lump? Therefore purge out the old leaven, that you may be a new lump, since you truly are unleavened. For indeed Christ, our Passover, was sacrificed for us.

"Therefore let us keep the feast, not with old leaven, nor with the leaven of malice and wickedness, but with the unleavened bread of sincerity and truth. I wrote to you in my Epistle not to keep company with sexually immoral people.

"Yet I certainly did not mean with the sexually immoral people of this world, or with the covetous, or extortioners, or idolaters, since then you would need to go out of the world. But now I have written to you not to keep company with anyone named a brother, who is sexually immoral, or covetous, or an idolater, or a reviler, or a drunkard, or an extortioner –

"Not even to eat with such a person. For what have I to do with judging those also who are outside? Do you not judge those who are inside? But those who are outside God judges. Therefore 'put away from yourselves the evil person'" (1 Cor. 5:1-13).

"But I determined this within myself, that I would not come again to you in sorrow. For if I make you sorrowful, then who is he who makes me glad but the one who is made sorrowful by me? And I wrote this very thing to you, lest, when I came, I should have sorrow over those from whom I ought to have joy, having confidence in you all that my joy is the joy of you all.

"For out of much affliction and anguish of heart I wrote to you, with many tears, not that you should be grieved, but that you might know the love which I have so abundantly for you. But if anyone has caused grief, he has not grieved me, but all of you to some extent – not to be too severe.

"This punishment which was inflicted by the majority is sufficient for such a man, so that, on the contrary, you ought rather to forgive and comfort him, lest perhaps such a one be swallowed up with too much sorrow. Therefore I urge you to reaffirm your love to him.

"For to this end I also wrote, that I might put you to the test, whether you are obedient in all things. Now whom you forgive anything, I also forgive. For if indeed I have forgiven anything, I have forgiven that one for your sakes in the Presence of Christ, lest satan should take advantage of us; for we are not ignorant of his devices" (2 Cor. 2:1-11).

Writing to Timothy, Paul said, "This charge I commit to you, son Timothy, according to the prophecies previously made concerning you, that by them you may wage the good warfare, having faith and a good conscience, which some having rejected, concerning the Faith have suffered shipwreck,

"Of whom are Hymenaeus and Alexander, whom I delivered to satan that they may learn not to blaspheme" (1 Tim. 1:18-20). He delivered Hymenaeus and Alexander to satan in order that they may learn not to blaspheme.

Speaking of doing the right thing and avoiding wrath and judgment in the society, the Word of God says, "Let every soul be subject to the governing authorities. For there is no authority except from God, and the authorities that exist are appointed by God.

"Therefore whoever resists the authority resists the Ordinance of God, and those who resist will bring judgment on themselves. For rulers are not a terror to good works, but to evil. Do you want to be unafraid of the authority? Do what is good, and you will have praise from the same.

"For he is God's minister to you for good. But if you do evil, be afraid; for he does not bear the sword in vain; for he is God's minister, an avenger to execute wrath on him who practices evil. Therefore you must be subject, not only because of wrath but also for conscience' sake.

"For because of this you also pay taxes, for they are God's ministers attending continually to this very thing. Render therefore to all their due: taxes to whom taxes are due, customs to whom customs, fear to whom fear, honour to whom honour. Owe no one anything except to love one another, for he who loves another has fulfilled the Law" (Rom. 13:1-8).

And Peter added: "Beloved, I beg you as sojourners and pilgrims, abstain from fleshly lusts which war against the soul, having your conduct honourable among the Gentiles, that when they speak against you as evildoers, they may, by your good works which they observe, glorify God in the day of visitation.

"Therefore submit yourselves to every ordinance of man for the Lord's Sake, whether to the king as supreme, or to governors, as to those who are sent by him for the punishment of evildoers and for the praise of those who do good.

"For this is the Will of God, that by doing good you may put to silence the ignorance of foolish men – as free, yet not using liberty as a cloak for vice, but as Bondservants of God. Honour all people. Love the Brotherhood. Fear God. Honour the king.

"Servants, be submissive to your masters with all fear, not only to the good and gentle, but also to the harsh. For this is commendable, if because of conscience towards God one endures grief, suffering wrongfully.

"For what credit is it if, when you are beaten for your faults, you take it patiently? But when you do good and suffer, if you take it patiently, this is commendable before God. For to this you were called, because Christ also suffered for us, leaving us an Example,

"That you should follow His Steps: 'Who committed no sin, nor was deceit found in His Mouth'; who, when He was reviled, did not revile in return; when He suffered, He did not threaten, but committed Himself to Him Who judges righteously (1 Pet. 2:11-23).

"Beloved, do not think it strange concerning the fiery trial which is to try you, as though some strange thing happened to you; but rejoice to the extent that you partake of Christ's Sufferings, that when His Glory is revealed, you may also be glad with exceeding joy.

"If you are reproached for the Name of Christ, blessed are you, for the Spirit of Glory and of God rests upon you. On their part He is blasphemed, but on your part He is glorified. But let none of you suffer as a murderer, a thief, an evildoer, or as a busybody in other people's matters. Yet if anyone suffers as a Christian, let him not be ashamed, but let him glorify God in this matter" (1 Pet. 4:12-16).

Speaking to King Asa, Azariah said, "Hear me, Asa, and all Judah and Benjamin. The Lord is with you while you are with Him. If you seek Him, He will be found by you; but if you forsake Him, He will forsake you. For a long time Israel has been without the True God, without a teaching priest, and without Law;

"But when in their trouble they turned to the Lord God of Israel, and sought Him, He was found by them. And in those times there was no peace to the one who went out, nor to the one who came in, but great turmoil was on all the inhabitants of the lands.

"So nation was destroyed by nation, and city by city, for God troubled them with every adversity. But you, be strong and do not let your hands be weak, for your work shall be rewarded!" (2 Chron. 15:2-7).

But though God punishes you, there is hope if you repent before the time of your death. The Bible says, "Now go, write it before them on a tablet, and note it on a scroll, that it may be for time to come, forever and ever: That this is a rebellious people, lying children, children who will not hear the Law of the Lord;

"Who say to the seers, 'Do not see,' And to the prophets, 'Do not prophesy to us right things; speak to us smooth things, prophesy deceits. Get out of the way, turn aside from the path, cause the Holy One of Israel to cease from before us.'

"Therefore thus says the Holy One of Israel: 'Because you despise this Word, and trust in oppression and perversity, and rely on them, therefore this iniquity shall be to you like a breach ready to fall, a bulge in a high wall, whose breaking comes suddenly, in an instant.

'And He shall break it like the breaking of the potter's vessel, which is broken in pieces; He shall not spare. So there shall not be found among its fragments a shard to take fire from the hearth, or to take water from the cistern.'

"For thus says the Lord God, the Holy One of Israel: 'In returning and rest you shall be saved; in quietness and confidence shall be your strength.' But you would not, and you said, 'No, for we will flee on horses' – therefore you shall flee! And, 'We will ride on swift horses' – therefore those who pursue you shall be swift!

"One thousand shall flee at the threat of one, at the threat of five you shall flee, till you are left as a pole on top of a mountain and as a banner on a hill. Therefore the Lord will wait, that He may be gracious to you; and therefore He will be exalted, that He may have mercy on you. For the Lord is a God of Justice; blessed are all those who wait for Him" (Isa. 30:8-18).

The Word of God also teaches that there is punishment for the person who causes a Believer in Christ Jesus to backslide. To this end, the Bible says, "Whoever causes the upright to go astray in an evil way, he himself will fall into his own pit; but the blameless will inherit good (Prov. 28:10).

"Whoever causes one of these little ones who believe in Me to sin, it would be better for him if a millstone were hung around his neck, and he were drowned in the depth of the sea. Woe to the world because of offences! For offences must come, but woe to that man by whom the offence comes!" (Matt. 18:6-7).

Warning the Israelites, Moses said, "And there you will serve gods, the work of men's hands, wood and stone, which neither see nor hear nor eat nor smell. But from there you will seek the Lord your God, and you will find Him if you seek Him with all your heart and with all your soul.

"When you are in distress, and all these things come upon you in the latter days, when you turn to the Lord your God and obey His Voice (for the Lord your God is a Merciful God), He will not forsake you nor destroy you, nor forget the covenant of your fathers which He swore to them.

"For ask now concerning the days that are past, which were before you, since the day that God created man on the earth, and ask from one end of heaven to the other, whether any great thing like this has happened, or anything like it has been heard. Did any people ever hear the Voice of God speaking out of the midst of the fire, as you have heard, and live?

"Or did God ever try to go and take for Himself a nation from the midst of another nation, by trials, by signs, by wonders, by war, by a mighty Hand and an outstretched Arm, and by great terrors, according to all that the Lord your God did for you in Egypt before your eyes?

"To you it was shown, that you might know that the Lord Himself is God; there is none other besides Him. Out of heaven He let you hear His Voice, that He might instruct you; on earth He showed you His great fire, and you heard His Words out of the midst of the fire.

"And because He loved your fathers, therefore He chose their descendants after them; and He brought you out of Egypt with His Presence, with His Mighty Power, driving out from before you nations greater and mightier than you, to bring you in, to give you their land as an inheritance, as it is this day.

"Therefore know this day, and consider it in your heart, that the Lord Himself is God in Heaven Above and on the earth beneath; there is no other. You shall therefore keep His Statutes and His Commandments which I command you today, that it may go well with you and with your children after you, and that you may prolong your days in the land which the Lord your God is giving you for all time" (Deut. 4:28-40).

Speaking to the Jews, God said, "For who will have pity on you, O Jerusalem? Or who will bemoan you? Or who will turn aside to ask how you are doing? You have forsaken Me," says the Lord, "You have gone backwards. Therefore I will stretch out My Hand against you and destroy you; I am weary of relenting! And I will winnow them with a winnowing fan in the gates of the land;

"I will bereave them of children; I will destroy My people, since they do not return from their ways. Their widows will be increased to Me more than the sand of the seas; I will bring against them, against the mother of the young men, a plunderer at noonday; I will cause anguish and terror to fall on them suddenly" (Jer. 15:5-8).

Mourning for His people, God said, "Hear, O heavens, and give ear, O earth! For the Lord has spoken: 'I have nourished and brought up children, and they have rebelled against Me; the ox knows its owner and the donkey its master's crib; but Israel does not know, My people do not consider.'

"Alas, sinful nation, a people laden with iniquity, a brood of evildoers, children who are corrupters! They have forsaken the Lord, they have provoked to anger the Holy One of Israel, they have turned away backwards.

"Why should you be stricken again? You will revolt more and more. The whole head is sick, and the whole heart faints. From the sole of the foot even to the head, there is no soundness in it, but wounds and bruises and putrefying sores; they have not been closed or bound up, or soothed with ointment (Isa. 1:2-6).

"I have forsaken My House, I have left My Heritage; I have given the dearly beloved of My Soul into the hand of her enemies. My Heritage is to Me like a lion in the forest; it cries out against Me; therefore I have hated it.

"My Heritage is to Me like a speckled vulture; the vultures all around are against her. Come, assemble all the beasts of the field, bring them to devour! Many rulers have destroyed My Vineyard, they have trodden My Portion underfoot; they have made My Pleasant Portion a desolate wilderness. They have made it desolate; desolate, it mourns to Me; the whole land is made desolate, because no one takes it to heart.

"The plunderers have come on all the desolate heights in the wilderness, for the sword of the Lord shall devour from one end of the land to the other end of the land; no flesh shall have peace. They have sown wheat but reaped thorns; they have put themselves to pain but do not profit. But be ashamed of your harvest because of the Fierce Anger of the Lord" (Jer. 12:7-13).

EVIL COMPANY CORRUPTS GOOD MANNERS

The Bible says that evil company corrupts good manners. This means that following the wrong people will change you for bad. Relating with evil people or things will corrupt you. This is also true on the good or positive side. Following or relating with the right people or things will change you for good.

Do you know that a child of God today can become a child of satan tomorrow? How can this be? By following or relating with the wrong people or things. Somebody who has been living a holy life can change to living an immoral, corrupt, and hypocritical life tomorrow by following and relating with the wrong people or things.

It is possible for someone who had been hardworking to become lazy, because of following lazy companions. A Christian who had been zealous for God and committed to Things of God can become lukewarm and cold by relating with the wrong company. When you are prayerful today, be careful because your carelessness in relationship can make you not to be a prayerful Christian tomorrow.

Beware of the relationships you keep! Beware of the things you are interested in, and the things you are attracted to. The devil is a master-deceiver: He will tell you that it doesn't matter. But by the time you realize that it does matter, it may be too late. Beware of your environment!

A case of evil company corrupting good manners is seen in what happened between the Israelites and the Moabites. Before what happened, the king of Moab had hired Balaam to curse the children of Israel, because he was afraid of them. But no matter the point that Balaam (with the king of Moab) saw them from, God would not allow him to curse them. Why? Because they were His people, and they were precious in His Sight. Balaam knew that as far as the Glory of the Lord was with them, as far as God was not angry with them (because of sin), nobody could curse them.

Balaam then gave the king of Moab a wicked counsel, to put a stumbling block on their path by making them to sin against God. For the people whom Balaam could not curse for the king of Moab so that he could kill and defeat them, the Bible says, "Now Israel remained in Acacia Grove, and the people began to commit harlotry with the women of Moab. They invited the people to the sacrifices of their gods, and the people ate and bowed down to their gods.

"So Israel was joined to baal of Peor and the Anger of the Lord was aroused against Israel. Then the Lord said to Moses, 'Take all the leaders of the people and hang the offenders before the Lord, out in the sun, that the Fierce Anger of the Lord may turn away from Israel.' So Moses said to the judges of Israel, 'Every one of you kill his men who were joined to baal of Peor.'...so the plague was stopped among the children of Israel. And those who died in the plague were twenty-four thousand" (Num. 25:1-9).

The king of Moab and his people were afraid of the people of Israel; and they had wanted Balaam to curse Israel so that they could defeat them; but Balaam couldn't curse them. First, Balaam's association with Balak who wanted to reward him with big reward corrupted his mind, so that he (who had been saying that he would only do what God tells him to do) gave Balak, the king of Moab, evil counsel to cause the Israelites to sin against God.

Secondly, when the Israelites kept company with the women of Moab, they led them astray and caused them to bow down to the baal of Peor. Their being close to the Moabites made them to be attracted to their women; and they lusted after the Moabite women, and committed fornication with them. From committing fornication, they proceeded to idolatry by bowing down to their gods. The idolatry they committed got God very angry.

And because God was very angry with them, twenty-four thousand people of Israel died by plague. The plague would have continued to kill them if not because Phinehas used spear to thrust through a man of Israel and a woman of Moab who were committing fornication. God hates harlotry; and their relating sexually with the women of the heathen nation provoked God to anger.

Coupled with their idolatry, the same people that God was protecting were destroyed by God through the plague (twenty-four thousand of them), plus the ones who were killed by hanging. But these things happened, firstly because they were within their territory (close to them), and secondly because they allowed themselves to be attracted by the Moabite women. It is true that you cannot leave the world; but be careful of where you go. And don't be unequally yoked together with unbelievers.

Another example of the power and capability of evil or wrong association is King Solomon. At least, before the New Testament Gospels, he can be regarded as the wisest man that ever lived. Go through the Books of Proverbs and Ecclesiastics, and observe that he had wisdom on things concerning God and how to deal wisely in the affairs of this life.

Actually, it cannot be said that Solomon had deeper understanding about spiritual things than Moses, who knew God Face to face and also received great Commandments, Laws, Ordnances, Statutes, and Precepts from God. In terms of dealing wisely with the affairs of this life, Solomon was the wisest. But he didn't have deep spiritual experiences with God, though he knew and understood a lot about the Things and Word of God. Yes, God appeared to him in a dream; but yet he didn't have 'that kind of deep spiritual experiences' with God.

Yet, with the level of revelation about God, His Word, human beings, and the course of nature that God gave him, one would expect that Solomon would have been very committed to God until the end of his life. But this is far from what the Bible reveals; for even when he was still near God, Solomon openly despised and rejected the Word of God where God told the Israelites not to marry foreign women.

When Ezra heard that the priests, the Levites, and the Jews had taken of the daughters of the Canaanites, the Hittites, the Perizzites, the Jebusites, the Ammonites, the Moabites, the Egyptians, and the Amorites, and hence did according to their abominations, he rent his garment and his mantle, and plucked off the hair of his beard, and sat down astonished (Ezra 9:1-3).

King Cyrus of the Persian kingdom (which ruled the world at that time) declared that God had commanded him to build Him a house at Jerusalem, which is in Judah; and he decreed that any of God's people who remained in any place where he was living, the people of that place should help him with silver, and with gold, and with goods, and with beasts. Many of them returned to Jerusalem.

At Jerusalem, they wept very sore. They acknowledged that they had sinned against God by taking strange wives from the places that they had live in. Many of them were guilty of this trespass. Shechaniah said to Ezra, "Now therefore, let us make a covenant with our God to put away all the wives, and such as are born of them, according to the counsel of my lord, and of those that tremble at the Commandment of our God, and let it be done according to the Law" (Ezra 10:1-4).

Marrying a foreign wife was so grievous to God that the prophet Malachi said, "Judah has dealt treacherously, and an abomination has been committed in Israel and in Jerusalem, for Judah has profaned the Holiness of the Lord which He loves, and has married the daughter of a strange god. The Lord will cut off the man who does this, the master and the scholar out of the tabernacles of Jacob, and him that offers an offering to the Lord of Hosts" (Mal. 2:11-12).

The NKJV reads: "...the man who does this, being awake and aware, yet who brings an offering to the Lord of Hosts." The prophet was so annoyed that he said that God should kill whoever consciously married a foreign woman, whether the master or the scholar (clergy or laity, minister or non-minister), and brings an offering to God.

Anyway, God Himself, through Moses, said, "When the Lord your God brings you into the land which you go to possess, and has cast out many nations before you, the Hittites and the Girgashites and the Amorites and the Canaanites and the Perizzites and the Hivites and the Jebusites, seven nations greater and mightier than you, and when the Lord your God delivers them over to you, you shall conquer them and utterly destroy them.

"You shall make no covenant with them nor show mercy to them. Nor shall you make marriages with them. You shall not give your daughter to their son, not take their daughter for your son. For they will turn your sons away from following Me, to serve other gods, so the Anger of the Lord will be aroused against you and destroy you suddenly. But thus you shall deal with them, you shall destroy.... For you are a holy people to the Lord your God, the Lord your God has chosen you to be a people for Himself, a special treasure above all the peoples of the earth" (Deut. 7:1-6).

Being an Israelite, and knowing that Israelites were told not to marry foreign wives, Solomon felt that he had arrived (because of his riches, fame, and wisdom); and he married foreign wives. What was the result? The Bible says, "But King Solomon loved many foreign women, as well as daughter of Pharaoh, women of the Moabites, Ammonites, Edomites, Sidonians, and Hittites –

"From the nations of whom the Lord had said to the children of Israel, 'You shall not intermarry with them, nor they with you. Surely they will turn away your hearts after their gods.' Solomon clung to theses in love. And he had seven hundred wives, princesses, and three hundred concubines; and his wives turned away his heart.

"For it was so, when Solomon was old, that his wives turned his heart after other gods; and his heart was not loyal to the Lord his God, as was the heart of his father David. For Solomon went after ashtoreth the goddess of the Sidonians, and after milcom the abomination of the Ammonites. Solomon did evil in the Sight of the Lord, and he did not fully follow the Lord, as did his father David.

"Then Solomon built a high place for chemosh the abomination of Moab, on the hill that is east of Jerusalem, and for molech the abomination of the people of Ammon. And he did likewise for all his foreign wives, who burned incense and sacrificed to their gods. So the Lord became angry with Solomon, because his heart had turned from the Lord God of Israel, Who had appeared to him twice, and had commanded him concerning this thing, that he should not go after other gods; but he did not keep what the Lord had commanded" (1 Kgs 11:1-10).

Apostle Paul wrote "Do not be deceived: 'Evil company corrupts good habits.' Awake to righteousness, and do not sin; for some do not have the Knowledge of God. I speak this to your shame" (1 Cor. 15:33-34). Evil communication corrupts good manners. He wrote this to Believers in Corinth. And if you go through that whole chapter, you will find out that he was trying to convince them that there is the Resurrection from the dead.

He spent time to convince and persuade them, by teaching and explanation, that the Resurrection from the dead was real and true. But how did the Corinthian Christians get to the point of doubting the reality of the Resurrection from the dead? It may be by wrong teaching or/and association. Maybe some false teachers had led some of them to believe that the

Resurrection from the dead is not true. Or maybe, they started doubting about it by relating and associating with the unbelievers.

In the course of his teaching them about the Resurrection from the dead, he added: "Do not be deceived: 'Evil company corrupts good manners.' Awake to righteousness, and do not sin; for some do not have the Knowledge of God. I speak this to your shame." And then he continued with his sermon on the Resurrection from the dead. This suggests (or tells you) that he had the conviction or thinking that they didn't wake up from sleep to start doubting the Resurrection from the dead – some people must have corrupted their minds from the Truth of the Word of God. This is why you need to be careful of the people you relate with, or the preaching and teaching you listen to.

I am not just talking about unbelievers here; but be careful of your relationship with certain kinds of Believers, preachers, teachers, prophets, and ministers. When you tell a woman that her dressing and appearance is immoral and worldly, and she asks you whether you are her husband, you have got to know that she did not wake up from sleep to start saying that – she could have learnt that from wrong association, preaching, teaching, prophets, or ministers. Let us see whether her husband will replace God on the Judgment Throne when it gets to her turn on the Judgment Day!

Wrong teaching and association have the capability to make you start being and living like the people of the world. It has the ability to make you start doubting the Truth of the Word of God. It can put doubt, unbelief, disobedience, and compromise, in you, consciously or unconsciously. This is why you have to read, study, and meditate on the Word of God diligently by yourself.

When you hear the Bible saying, "Your glorying is not good. Do you not know that a little leaven leavens the whole lump?" you have got to know that even a small corruption within Christians and Believers can rise to infect and affect the entire body of Believers. This is similar to what happens when a computer is infected by virus or viruses. Within a short period of time, you can end up formatting the whole computer.

The Word says, "Catch us the foxes, the little foxes that spoil the vine, for our vines have tender grapes" (Song 2:15). The little foxes may be little in size and appearance; but they have the ability to spoil the vine. When the vine is spoilt, then its fruitfulness and productivity will be affected. Beware of the agents of the kingdom of darkness, and also of those who do not want to believe and obey the Word of God! They can spoil the body or congregation of Believers.

Another side to evil company corrupting good manners is what the Bible talks about when it says, "Dead flies putrefy the perfumer's ointment, and cause it to give off a foul odour; so does a little folly to one respected for wisdom and honour" (Eccl. 10:1). This is similar to saying that the bad or evil action, deed, or behaviour, of one person in a group can make people to change their minds towards the whole members of the group.

This is neither a joke nor an idle word! What you have spent a lot of time, effort, energy, and wisdom, to build and form, can be destroyed by a deed or behaviour that is offensive. And you know that the devil will make the efforts he can make in order to destroy what God is doing. However, know that the Spirit of God Who is in you is wiser than the devil; and the Almighty God Who is for you and with you is greater than the devil! Those that are with us are more and mightier than those what are against us!

Concerning what we are discussing, the New International Version's rendering of what Apostle Paul told the Corinthian Believers reads, "Do not be misled: 'Bad company corrupts good character.' Come back to your senses as you ought, and stop sinning; for there are some who are ignorant of God – I say this to your shame." Can you meditate and think on these two verses?

Never Say That God Said What He Did Not Say!

YOU MUST BE BORN AGAIN

You must be born again; you must be born of water and of the Spirit. The Lord told Nicodemus that if a man must see the Kingdom of God, he must be born again.

The Lord emphasized that for a man to enter the Kingdom of Heaven, he must be born of water and of the Spirit. There is a great difference between being born again and being born of water and of the Spirit, even though they are related.

To be born again is compulsory to the one who would see the Kingdom of God, and if the person wants to pass the stage of seeing to the stage of entering, he must be born of water and of the Spirit.

This is 'a must' for anyone and does not depend on whom you are. God is no respecter of persons (Acts 10:34). Whether you are the president of your country, the ambassador, or whatever you may be, makes no difference.

Whether you are a millionaire in any currency, it does not move God. You may be a university-professor or an outstanding scientist or engineer; you must be born again. Whether you are old or young, great or small, rich or poor, male or female, you must be born again.

Whether you have been baptized and confirmed in your church, it makes no difference. As a matter of fact, some have been baptized and made full members of their churches, and yet are not born again.

Do you know that you can be referred to as a pastor and yet not be born again? This reminds me of a story a minister told me of a sectional leader of one Pentecostal church who admitted that he was not born again even though he was referred to as a reverend, after God told a man of God to confront him. He said he entered the ministry to help his family members.

You may be referred to as a deacon, an elder, a bishop, an apostle, a church-leader, and not be born again. To be born again is to be regenerated or made a new creature by the Holy Spirit when you receive the Lord Jesus Christ as your Lord and personal Saviour (though some accept Christ as the Saviour of their souls but not the Lord of their lives).

That is what the Bible means when it says that if any man or woman be in Christ Jesus, he or she is a new creature, old things have passed away and all things have become new (2 Cor. 5:17).

When Adam sinned, he died spiritually and became separated from the Life of God. Man became God's enemy by disobeying God and lost the authority God gave him over all things.

But God sent His Son Jesus Christ to die for the sins of the world, and to pay the Sacrifice for the salvation of men from all bondages of the devil. Jesus Christ shed His Blood for the remission of our sins.

When someone acknowledges that he is a sinner who cannot help himself, and receives the Lord Jesus Christ, he is born again. With the heart, man believes to righteousness, and with the mouth he confesses that he believes on the Lord Jesus Christ to salvation (Rom. 10:10).

As many as received Him, to them gave He power to become children of God, even to them that believe on His Name, Jesus Christ the Son of the Living God (Jn 1:12).

The Lord Jesus Christ has made it known that He will not cast away anyone that comes to Him. No matter how sinful, dirty, immoral, or wicked you may be, once you repent and accept the Lord Jesus Christ, He will cleanse you to the extent that your sins will no longer be remembered (Isa. 43:25).

Consider how wicked Saul, who later became Paul, was: but when he submitted to Jesus Christ, he became one of the most faithful early apostles.

WARNINGS FROM THE LORD

To be born of water is to be changed by the Word of God. The Spirit of God uses the Word of God, which is the Sword of the Spirit to change you. Christ Jesus sanctifies and cleanses the Church with the washing of the water through the Word (Eph. 5:25).

We were born again, not of corruptible seed but incorruptible through the Word of God which lives and abides forever (1 Pet. 1:23). The Gospel that you heard and received is the Word of God, and you believed it, which made it possible for you to be born again by the Action of the Holy Spirit.

The Spirit and the Word agree, and they work together. Since you were born again by means of the Gospel, you will need to continue to live your life according to the Word of God. We must neither resist God nor His Word. You will be fulfilled in life if you obey the Spirit of God and His Word.

God will not force the sinner to receive the Gospel; in the same vein, He will not force you to live according His Word. Some people, after being born again, live lives contrary to God's Word; don't expect to enter the Kingdom of God that way. And you will need to grow in your knowledge of the Word of God.

To be Born of the Spirit is to be led by the Holy Spirit. It is to follow the voice (the conscience) of your recreated human spirit. The Spirit Himself witnesses with our spirit that this or that is right or wrong.

Following God's Spirit will help you overcome evil. The born-again experience, the regeneration of your spirit is the Work of the Holy Spirit. After being born again, you will still have to listen to His Voice if you want to enter the Kingdom of Heaven.

If you are tempted to lie, for instance, the Holy Spirit will speak to you through your spirit, your heart, and make it known to you that lying is sinful; if you go ahead to lie, He will not stop your voice or speech; and you would have sinned against God.

If you live your life contrary to the Spirit of God, you are heading to somewhere else, apart from the Kingdom of Heaven and of God. And it is either you spend eternity with God, or you spend it with the devil; and there is no partiality with God (Acts 10:34).

Whether you speak in tongues and prophesy, it makes no difference. No sinner will inherit the Kingdom of Christ and of God (Eph. 5:5).

Knowing the Terror of God, we persuade men everywhere to change their lifestyles, to change the way they live (2 Cor. 5:11). Because it is a fearful thing to fall into the Hands of the Living God (Heb. 10:31); for our God is a Consuming Fire (Heb. 12:29).

I don't know what they might have told you in the church, ministry, or fellowship that you go; take the Bible and study these things for yourself, and I know you will come to agree with what the Lord has said through me.

Is it not written in the Bible that because iniquity shall abound, the love of many shall wax cold? But those who endure to the end shall be saved (Matt. 24:12). That means that some will not endure to the end.

The Word of God says that Jesus Christ is coming for the Church that has no spot, wrinkle, blemish, or any such thing, but a holy, righteous, and sanctified Church (Eph. 5:27; 1 Thes. 5:23).

Even Apostle Paul, after being in the ministry for many years, and having done many mighty signs, wonders, and miracles, he said that he still brought his body to subjection so that after preaching to others, he himself will not be a castaway (1 Cor. 9:27).

The Lord Jesus Christ asked why some will call Him, Lord, Lord, and not do what He says (Lk. 6:46). Many will say to Him on that Day, "Lord, Lord, have we not done this or that in Your

Name?" But He will tell them to depart from Him because He never knew them, as they were workers of iniquity (Matt. 7:20-23).

I believe they had been born again, because they prophesied and did mighty works in the Name of Jesus Christ. However, they will be rejected because they were not born of water and of the Spirit.

You cannot please God if you continue to live in sin, if you continue to live according to the dictates of your flesh, by the lust of the flesh, the lust of the eyes, and the pride of life.

All men shall give account of their lives to God; and all good and evil things shall be brought to light, including all hidden things.

What do you think of God and His Christ? Remember now your God and Creator, and obey what He tells you to do. To believe in the Lord Jesus Christ is to do the Work of God; that is the very first real step to obeying Him.

Never Say That God Said What He Did Not Say!

KNOWING AND UNDERSTANDING THE WORD OF GOD

The Word of God is God. The Word of God reveals the Mind of God to us. God works through and by His Word. The Word and the Spirit agree (1 Jn 5:8), for the holy men of God who wrote the Scriptures were moved by the Holy Ghost (2 Pet. 1:21).

All Scripture is God-breathed, is inspired by God; and is profitable for Doctrine, for reproof, for correction, for instruction in righteousness, that the man of God may be complete, thoroughly equipped for every good work (2 Tim. 3:16-17).

We are to fight the good fight of faith. The fight of faith is to contend earnestly for the faith once delivered to the Saints; the fight of faith is to strive to see that the Word and Will of God comes to pass in our lives, and in the lives of others, for faith comes by hearing the Word of God.

We must also grow from faith to faith. The Bible commands us to let the Word of God, of Christ, dwell in us richly in all wisdom (Col. 3:16). That means that we are to get soaked in the Word of God. When a sponge is soaked in water and brought out, any side of the sponge you touch, water sticks on you.

The same thing applies when we are full of the Word of God. Whatever trial, temptation, or situation we may find ourselves in, we have solution in the Word available to us, and we will overcome and succeed.

Search the Scriptures as you would search for hidden treasures, for they are costlier than gold, silver, and diamond. The place we read says that the Word of God should dwell in us, not just in any measure, but in a rich measure, in a full measure, preferably. Also, in the rich measure, it must be in all wisdom.

This is why the Bible speaks of rightly dividing the Word of Truth (2 Tim. 2:15). To divide the Word of God aright is to apply it wisely and to interpret it the right way. This is why you have to compare Scripture with Scripture (you have to compare spiritual things with spiritual things) (1 Cor. 2:13).

You must study the Word of God to show yourself approved to God, a workman who does not need to be ashamed, rightly dividing the Word of Truth. Be diligent to present yourself approved to God (2 Tim. 2:15).

It is the Word of God in your heart and mouth that will help you succeed in life and Godliness, and overcome temptations. Make every effort to hear, read, study, meditate on, believe, and confess the Word of God.

When the devil tempted Jesus Christ, he used the Scripture, by quoting it to Jesus Christ. But he misapplied the Word, and Jesus Christ, being full of the Word of God, quoted the appropriate Word, and the devil was put to shame.

If you don't know the Word of God, the devil will deceive you, misapplying it to you; and you will fall into temptations. The devil has no mercy. If you don't know and apply your rights and authority in Christ, he will keep you miserable.

The Word of God is spirit and life. It will quicken your human spirit and wage your spiritual wars; it will also give life to your body and soul. The Word that you hear is spirit and it is life (Jn 6:63).

The Word of God cleanses you: spirit, soul, and body (Jn 15:3). It will build your spirit and get it to be strong spiritually. The Word is the food of the human spirit that gets him grow and matured. Desire the Word of God (1 Pet. 2:2).

The Word of God is fire that burns all things that are ungodly and satanic; it is the hammer that breaks to pieces all obstacles and hindrances (Jer. 23:29). It is the water that purifies you

WARNINGS FROM THE LORD

daily. It is truth, and God's Truth sanctifies you to holiness, blamelessness, and spotlessness (Jn 17:17).

Go for the Word of God, because all things that you ever need in your life are in it. The source of God's Blessings is the Word and the Manifester of the Blessings of God is the Holy Spirit.

When the deacons were to be appointed, the apostles declared that anyone to be appointed must be full of wisdom, and the Wisdom of God is in His Word. That was why Stephen, who was full of faith and the Holy Spirit, was selected (Acts 6:5).

To be full of faith is to be full of the Word, because faith comes by hearing and studying the Word of God (Rom. 10:17). If you have problem with faith, just take enough time to fill yourself with the Word, and you will see faith spring up from within you with great force, frequency, and magnitude.

The Word says that the Word that goes out of the Mouth of God will not go back to Him without accomplishing the purpose for which He sent it (Isa. 55:11). Instead of His Word to fail, heaven and earth shall pass away (Matt. 24:35).

God is not a man to lie, and He cannot change His Mind (Num. 23:19). Except the condition under which He said something is changed by men, He cannot change what He said for that circumstance.

God's Thoughts are higher than our thoughts and His Ways than our ways (Isa. 55:9). Don't be wise in your own eyes, trust in the Lord, and do the right (Prov. 3:7).

If what God told you has not come to pass, don't doubt Him, but be patient in believing, for the vision is yet for an appointment time: it will come to pass and will not tarry (Habk. 2:3).

If God delays His Judgment, it is because He is full of mercy and does not want anyone to perish. However, when He casts His Judgment, He does not respect anybody.

The Word of God says that we are to prove all things, and hold on to that which is true and good (1 Thes. 5:21). Do not believe every spirit, but test the spirits whether they are of God, for many false teachings, ministries, and ministers are in the world today (1 Jn 4:1).

The litmus paper is an indicator that you can easily use to distinguish an acid from an alkali. In the same vein, judging by the Word of God is a good litmus-test for the good and the evil, the Godly and the ungodly. Don't be wise in your own eyes and mind. Even prophecies are to be judged (1 Cor. 14:29).

The people of God perish and suffer because of ignorance or lack of the knowledge of the Word of God (Hos. 4:6). Even though God will want to protect you, know that the devil that is fighting against you has no mercy.

God even said that He will reject some people from being His Original Intention or Plan for them, because they rejected knowledge (Hos. 4:6). If you reject Divine Knowledge, you are heading to disaster.

Don't leave the Word to serve tables (Acts 6:2). The apostles refused to do that. But preach and teach the Word of God, in season and out of season. Convince, rebuke, exhort with all longsuffering and teaching.

For the time has come when they do not endure Sound Doctrine, but according to their own desires, because they have itching ears, they have heaped up for themselves teachers, and they turn their ears away from the truth, and are turned aside to heresies (2 Tim. 4:1-5).

Martha was worried with too much serving when Jesus Christ visited her, but Mary was at the Feet of Jesus Christ listening to Him. When Martha wanted Mary to leave listening to Jesus

Christ in order to help in the serving, Jesus Christ told Martha that Mary had taken that one thing which is needful, and it will not be taken away from her.

Receiving the Word of God and keeping it is more important than sacrifices. Also, half-obedience is disobedience in the Sight of God. Don't be hearers only, but be doers of the Word you hear.

Wisdom refers to good sense and judgment. Wisdom is knowledge gained over a period of time through learning and experience. Wisdom comes from God; the Word of God is the source of wisdom.

The Spirit of God Who is the Spirit of Excellence gives us the wisdom that we need for Godliness, and to deal with the things of this life. The Lord created the whole universe by His Wisdom, and He saw that they were good. The fear of God is the beginning of wisdom (Psa. 111:10).

Knowledge has to do with the facts, skills, and understanding that you have gained through learning or experience. Knowledge refers to the information that you have about a particular situation, event; etc.

The fear of the Lord is the beginning of knowledge (Prov. 1:7). God's people are destroyed for lack of knowledge (Hos. 4:6).

The Bible is the Book of knowledge: knowledge of God and His Ways, knowledge of the devil and his ways, knowledge of the universe and the things in it, knowledge of yourself and your inheritance in Christ Jesus. Study it to increase your knowledge.

Understanding refers to knowledge about something based on learning or experience. It is the way in which you judge the meaning of something. Understanding is the ability to know and learn. Lean not on your own understanding, but apply your heart to understanding in God's Way.

Do not be children in understanding, but in malice be children (1 Cor. 14:20). You need to have a clear understanding of the Scripture and Way of God in order to apply it aright, so that you can please God.

If anyone lacks wisdom, let him ask of God, Who gives to all liberally and without reproach, and it will be given to him. But let him ask in faith, with no doubting, for he who doubts is like a wave of the sea driven and tossed by the wind.

For let not that man suppose that he will receive anything from the Lord; he is a double-minded man; unstable in all his ways (Jas 1:5-8). Whatever it is that you need from God, ask in faith, believing that you receive, and you shall have it.

Who is wise and understanding among you? Let him show by good conduct that his works are done in the meekness of wisdom. But if you have bitter envy and seeking in your hearts, do not boast and lie against the truth.

This wisdom does not descend from Above, but is earthly, sensual, and demonic. For where envying and self-seeking exist, confusion and every evil thing are there.

But the wisdom that is from Above is first pure, then peaceable, gentle, willing to yield, full of mercy and good fruits, without partiality and without hypocrisy (Jas 3:13-17).

The Spirit of God is the Spirit of Wisdom, Knowledge, and Understanding. This is why, concerning Bezalel, the son of Uri, God said, "...and I have filled him with the Spirit of God, in wisdom, in understanding, in knowledge, and in all manner of workmanship."

No matter the work God has for you or the area that you find yourself (that is good and acceptable), if you have the Spirit of God, if you are filled with the Spirit of God, then you have access to wisdom, knowledge, and understanding (Exo. 31:3).

The lives of Daniel, Shadrach, Meshach, and Abed-Nego tell us the impact of having the Spirit of God in you. The Word of God says that Daniel distinguished himself above the governors and satraps, because an Excellent Spirit was in him; and the king gave thought to setting him over the whole realm (Dan. 6:3).

How come? First, they were Jews, God's people. In our case or dispensation we will say that they were born again. That made them candidates for the Spirit's Presence.

Daniel purposed in his heart that he would not defile himself with anything (Dan. 1:8). If you want to excel in Christianity, Godliness, and ministry, then make up your mind that whatever it takes you, you will not defile and pollute yourself with the desires of the flesh and worldliness.

Though we are in the world, yet we are not of this world. Do not love the world or anything in the world. If anyone loves the world, the Love of the Father is not in him.

For all that is in the world the lust of the flesh, the lust of the eyes, and the pride of life is not of the Father but is of the world. And the world is passing away, and the lust of it, but he who does the Will of God endures forever (1 Jn 2:15-17).

Even when the king had apportioned special delicacies: food and drink, for them, because they knew that they will be defiled by them (according to the Law God gave them), they refused eating or drinking them.

Faithfulness, holiness, and obedience produce power and God's Presence by God's Spirit. Because they refused to be defiled, when they were tested for ten days and given vegetables to eat and water to drink, they appeared better and fatter in flesh than all the young men who ate the portion of the king's delicacies.

As for these young men, God gave them knowledge and skill in all literature and wisdom, and Daniel had understanding in all visions and dreams.

When their training was over, the king interviewed them, and among all those that were trained, none was found like those four; therefore, they served before the king.

And in all matters of wisdom and understanding about which the king examined them, he found them ten times better than all the magicians and astrologers who were in all his realm (Dan. 1).

Going through the Book of Daniel tells us that they continued with the Lord their God even after their appointments. Many backslide when God puts them in high positions.

Some will not have extra-marital affairs now that they are still average in wealth and riches; but when God gives them abundant wealth, they start going after women and drinking alcohol.

Many will be dedicated to the Lord and His Work when God has not blessed their businesses. Some will even sleep in the church, doing tarry-nights and night-vigils; but when their businesses grow, they will not have time for God, His Word, and prayer again.

Riches have wings and they do fly away. If God removes His Protection from you, the devil can reduce you from a millionaire to a beggar in just few days. But Daniel, instead of abandoning God, kept on being obedient to Him and God lifted him to higher levels.

David and Solomon prayed for understanding (Psa. 119:34,73,125,144,169; 1 Kgs 3:9-12) and the Lord gave it to them.

God leads us in the ways of wisdom, knowledge, and understanding, in Godliness, in things of this life, and concerning the life which is to come.

Sometimes, Christians behave in ways that do not depict wisdom and understanding. However, God did and does all things by His Wisdom and Understanding and we are the children of God and are to be like God (Godly).

Never Say That God Said What He Did Not Say!

CONFRONTING YOUR CONFRONTATIONS

The Word of God tells us to give no place to the devil. All things are possible to the Believer. Christians are Offsprings of God Himself. Since the days of John the Baptist, the Kingdom of God suffers violence, and the violent take it by force (Matt. 11:12).

Turn your conditions around for good, and obtain your rights, privileges, and inheritances in Christ by confronting your confrontations. The righteousness which is of faith speaks in this way, "Do not say in your heart, 'Who will ascend into Heaven?' (that is, to bring Christ down from Above) or, 'Who will descend into the deep?' (that is, to bring Christ up from the dead)."

But what does it say? "The Word is near you, in your mouth and in your heart" (that is the Word of Faith which we preach). That if you shall confess with your mouth…and shall believe in your heart…you shall be saved.

For with the heart man believes…and with the mouth confession is made…. Whoever believes on Him shall not be put to shame (Rom. 10:6-11).

We, having the same spirit of faith, according as it is written, "I believed, and therefore have I spoken"; we also believe, and therefore speak (2 Cor. 4:13). You have to confront your confrontations to receive your victory.

It is not God that will do the confrontation for us. If we wait for God, we may die waiting for Him. This is why the Scripture tells us to resist the devil so that he will flee from us (Jas 4:7).

You have to resist him steadfastly in faith (1 Pet. 5:9). Don't give any place to the devil (Eph. 4:27). The devil will have the place you give him, he will occupy that place.

But the mistake many people make is to sit back and wait for God to remove the obstacles the devil has brought along their ways. Your word of faith can break that barrier. This is why God gave us the responsibility to pray.

The Word of God is the Sword of the Spirit; use the Word actively, and see the Spirit of God change your circumstances for good, better, and best. Contend, earnestly, for the faith and the Word; the Promises of God are 'Yes', and 'Amen.'

No matter how long you might have been oppressed and confronted, you can still confront your confrontations and get free. Even generational curses and covenants will crumble if you confront them.

Believe the Word of God more than any person's story or idea. The Anointing of the Holy Spirit of the Living God destroys the yokes and lifts the burdens the enemy puts on people. Jesus Christ gives peace, abundant peace.

The Philistines gathered their armies together to battle with Israel. And a champion went out from the camp of the Philistines, named Goliath, from Gath, whose height was six cubits and a span (that is, 13 feet, 4 inches).

He had a bronze helmet on his head, and he was armed with a coat of mail, and the weight of the coat was five thousand shekels of bronze (about 194 1/2 ibs in weight). And he had bronze armour on his legs and bronze javelin between his shoulders.

Now the staff of his spear was like a weaver's beam, and his iron spearhead weighed six hundred shekels (about 23 1/2 ibs, counting 224 grains to the shekel); and a shield-bearer went before him.

Can you imagine this type of a devil? He was armoured very well. He had offensive weapons of javelin and spear. Bronze is an alloy metal which is very hard. Brass is a mixture of zinc and copper, while bronze is a mixture of zinc, copper, and tin. He had both well-made defensive and offensive weapons.

Added to that is that a shield-bearer went before him. If you were to fight with Goliath naturally, his shield-bearer (who could be taller than you: Goliath himself was a giant) would stop your arrow, spear, and sword, while Goliath will thrust you through with his spear or javelin.

But I don't care about the barrier, opposition, stronghold, or attack the enemy and his demons have brought along your way, to stop you from enjoying the full benefit of the inheritance you have in Jesus Christ; if you will withstand him, he will flee.

It may not take a minute, an hour, a day or a week to break that barrier and stop the attack, but if you withstand him steadfastly in faith and pray, he will bow.

There are cases and situations that you will have to add fasting to prayer for the devil's handiwork to be destroyed. The Word says that some demonic works will be broken only by prayer and fasting (Matt. 17:21).

This does not mean that you can't cast out a demon unless you are fasting, but if the anointing in your life (gained by former prayer and fasting) is not strong enough for confronting that demonic attack, then you must fast until you have a breakthrough.

However, demons bow to the Name of Jesus Christ. Sometimes, the fasting may have to take a long time of about three, seven or more days. Imagine what would have happened if Prophet Daniel had stopped praying and fasting the twentieth day.

The answer to his prayers, which was released the first day, might have not reached him. An angel who was not a high-ranking warring angel was sent to deliver the answer, but a stronger satanic spiritual wickedness in high places withstood him.

But thanks to God that Daniel did not give up, and on the twenty-first day, another angel was sent to help the other angel. This made it possible for him to deliver the answer to Daniel (Dan. 10).

Some say that fasting is not that important; well, can you explain what you mean? Jesus Christ fasted; Apostle Paul fasted; and (I don't want to go the Old Testament now) the early Disciples and Believers fasted.

The truth is that there is a level of anointing the Holy Spirit will not anoint you with if you don't fast. Whether partial fasting, fruit-fasting, juice-fasting, the fasted life, water-fasting, or dry fasting, you will fast. Of course, dry fasting or water-fasting may, sometimes, not take as long as partial fasting.

Goliath of Gath, the Philistine, intimidated Israel many days, and said, "I defy the armies of Israel this day, give me a man that we may fight together." When King Saul and all Israel heard these words of the Philistine, they were dismayed and greatly afraid. By this time, God had rejected Saul as a king, and the anointing that was upon him had lifted.

Maybe, it was the same anointing that lifted from Saul that came upon David, because Saul was rejected by God in chapter fifteen, David was anointed king in chapter sixteen, and here comes Goliath in chapter seventeen.

But one thing we know is that the anointing had lifted from Saul, and God had anointed David as king, even though, physically, he had not become one. But what has been settled in the spiritual realm will certainly come to pass physically, because the spiritual realm is very real.

After Goliath had terrorized Israel for forty days, the youngest son of Jesse, who had been anointed with the Power and Boldness of the Spirit of God, came to the camp of Israel and heard that thrash from the mouth of Goliath. All the men of Israel, when they saw the man, fled from him, and were dreadfully afraid.

And David said, "Who is this uncircumcised Philistine, that he should defy the armies of the Living God?" Eliab, his oldest brother, heard him and was very annoyed with him. He would have thought in his mind, saying, "What can this proud small boy do?"

Do you know that people can judge you, and take you to be proud when you say what you can do by the Power of God through the Name of Jesus Christ? Apostle Peter said, "I give you what I have, and in the Name of Jesus Christ, rise up and walk" (Acts 3:1-11).

David told Saul that their hearts should not fail because of Goliath, and that he will go and fight him. Saul said, "You are not able to go against this Philistine to fight with him; for you are a youth, and he a man of war from his youth." David told Saul that he had killed a lion and a bear, and he will kill Goliath also.

You see why you shouldn't be afraid. The anointing that removed malaria can also open the eyes of the blind. Just be dedicated to making God's Anointing stronger and stronger in your life. All you need are the anointing and the real faith.

David declared that the Lord will deliver him. The anointing emboldened him and moved him. Saul armoured David with his armour and gave him a sword, but David could not use them. Some think that it must be done the same old way, but this is not true.

Find out the direction and the strategy God has for you, and you will conquer when you obey God. David used stones and a sling. The Philistine looked at David and disdained him. He cursed David by his gods. But David was not moved; he knew the outcome.

David said, "You come to me with a sword, with a spear, and with a javelin. But I come to you in the Name of the Lord of Hosts…the Lord will deliver you into my hand, and I will strike you and take your head from you….

"That all the earth may know that there is a God in Israel…the Lord does not save with sword and spear; for the battle is the Lord's…."

David hurried, took out a stone, and slung it and struck the Philistine in his forehead. The Philistine died and the others fled. David and Israel overcame by their God (1 Sam. 17).

The spiritual controls the physical. Stand upon the Word of God without doubting, and act: you will overcome always! No devil, demon, witch, or thing should stop you, as a Christian and a minister. Don't make yourself stoppable.

If you are confronting your confrontations and it seems that you are not achieving your purpose, you may have to change your strategy or battle plan. That God worked a certain way to solve a problem does not mean He will always work that way. Find out from God always how you have to approach your difficult situations.

All power in Heaven, on the earth, and in the whole universe belongs to God. God is omnipotent, He is all-powerful. The power of satan and his cohorts is nothing, and is powerless before God.

The Psalmist said that God has spoken once, and twice he has heard it, that power belongs to God (Psa. 62:11). Power belongs to God indeed.

Do you know that God did not fight satan and his fallen angels directly when they rebelled against God? God sent Archangel Michael and His warring angels to fight the devil and send him out of Heaven.

Even when the devil will be put into the bottomless pit, it will still be an angel that will do it; and angels will banish satan and his host from this universe into their eternal abode and place of torment.

WARNINGS FROM THE LORD

However, it is the Spirit of God, Who is the Holy Spirit or Holy Ghost, that empowers the angels of God to do God's Assignments for them. Even in this present age, God has empowered the Church to deal with the devil and his cohorts, and to destroy their works.

God is too much to fight the devil directly. How will a Creator fight His creature? Stop fearing the devil or man, for they can do you nothing without God's Permission. The devil is powerless before God, and God has given you power over all devils.

The Power of God is infinite. Not even the chiefest of the angels knows all about the Power of God, though they know some things about His Power.

This is one reason satan rebelled against God: at that time, the angels had not seen God deal with anyone as He dealt with satan and the fallen angels later.

The same is applicable to His Wisdom and Knowledge. The Presence of God fills the whole universe; God is everywhere and He knows all that are happening in the whole of the universe.

There are Three Persons in One God: God the Father, God the Son (Jesus Christ), and God the Holy Spirit. The Bible says that these Three are One (1 Jn. 5:7). This is a mystery.

Many times, we try to explain things based on our thinking or the small revelation we had; but there are so many things we will not understand fully now; but we will understand more, later.

It is true that the Holy Spirit reveals many things to us, but He can't reveal everything to us, but the things that God has chosen that we know. There are many things in the Bible we haven't understood yet.

When God moves to the ends of the universe, He moves By His Spirit. No wonder the prophet prophesied that the Glory of God (the Spirit of God) will fill (fills) the whole earth as the waters cover the sea (Habk. 2:14; Isa. 11:9).

God the Father sits on His Throne in Heaven, and Jesus Christ sits at His Right Hand. The Spirit of God manifests in different Forms in the Throne-room. He manifests as a River of Water.

It is the Spirit of God that carries God's Presence and Power to everywhere. If God's Spirit comes upon you, power has come upon you.

You receive power when the Holy Spirit comes upon you, and you are empowered to witness for the Lord Jesus Christ, from where you are to the ends of the earth (Acts 1:8).

This is why the Lord told His apostles to tarry in the city of Jerusalem until they are endued with power from on High (Lk. 24:49). Human power and knowledge cannot do God's Work effectively.

The Lord gives His people power and authority over the devil and all his demons. They are empowered to destroy their works, and nothing shall by any means hurt them (Lk. 10:19).

We are commanded to go into all the world and preach the Gospel to every creature. He who believes and is baptized will be saved, but he that believes not will be condemned.

And these signs shall follow those who believe: in the Name of Jesus Christ, they will cast out devils; they will speak with new tongues; they will take up serpents; if they drink anything deadly, it will by no means hurt them; and they will lay hands on the sick, and they will recover (Mk 16:15-20).

After the Lord had left, the Disciples went out and preached everywhere, the Lord working with them and confirming the Word through the accompanying signs.

The Kingdom of God is not eating and drinking, but righteousness, peace, and joy in the Holy Spirit. He, who serves Christ in these things, is acceptable to God and approved by men (Rom. 4:17-18).

The Kingdom of God is not in word but in power (1 Cor. 4:20). Apostle Paul spoke and preached in the demonstration of the Spirit and of power, that the faith of his hearers should be in the Power of God, instead of the wisdom of men (1 Cor. 2:1-5).

The burden of the enemy will be taken away from your shoulder, and his yoke from your neck, and the yoke will be destroyed because of the Anointing of God's Spirit (Isa. 10:27).

God anointed Jesus Christ of Nazareth with the Holy Spirit and with power, Who went about doing good and healing all who were oppressed by the devil, for God was with Him (Acts 10:38).

It is the devil that brings sicknesses, diseases, pains, sorrow, sufferings, poverty, disappointments and death; but the anointing will drive them and any other works of his out of men's lives.

The Spirit of God comes upon Believers to anoint them to preach the Gospel to the poor. He anoints them to heal the broken-hearted, to proclaim liberty to the captives and recovery of sight to the blind, to set at liberty those who are oppressed, to proclaim the Acceptable Year of the Lord (Lk. 4:18-19).

When the Holy Spirit fills you, He produces the flow of rivers of living water out of your heart (Jn 7:38). Nothing is impossible with God; there is nothing that cannot be done when the anointing comes.

The Anointing of the Holy Spirit teaches us the truth about God. The Holy Spirit teaches us all truth. He leads us in the way of righteousness, and shows us things to come.

The Spirit of God brings to our remembrance the things that God has taught us. The sons of God are led by the Spirit of God. The anointing in us is greater than the devil that is in the world (1 Jn 4:4).

Don't grieve the Holy Spirit; don't quench His Fire, either. The Holy Spirit will tell you the things that are freely given to us by God (1 Cor. 2:12). He is your Comforter and Helper.

The Holy Ghost is your Comforter, Counselor, Helper, Intercessor, Advocate, Strengthener, and Standby. What can you do without Him? The Holy Spirit helps your weaknesses and infirmities, and He makes intercession for us with groanings which cannot be uttered (Rom. 8:26).

Pray in the Holy Spirit; pray in tongues to build yourself up spiritually. Whether you turn to the left or the right, your ear will hear a Voice behind you, saying, "This is the way; walk in it" (Isa. 30:21). This is the Voice of the Spirit of God as He leads you.

The Holy Spirit is the Angel of God's Presence, the Carrier of God's Presence (Isa. 63:9-10). Moses knew the importance of God's Presence that he did not want to go without it (Exo. 33:15).

The Holy Spirit will lead you into all truth for He speaks what He hears God speak (Jn 16:13). The Spirit of God upon you will make you prophesy, see visions and dream dreams (Acts 2:17).

The Holy Spirit reproves the world of sin, and of righteousness, and of judgment (Jn 16:18). The Holy Spirit will refresh you and give you rest.

The Holy Spirit, when poured upon us, from on High, turns the wilderness into a fruitful field and the fruitful field into a forest (Isa. 32:15). The Holy Spirit will bring excellence into your life (Dan. 6:3).

The Holy Spirit makes you bring forth your fruit in your season, your leaves will not wither, and whatever you do shall prosper (Psa. 1:3). He will give you understanding (Job 32:8).

The Holy Spirit teaches us to profit (Isa. 48:17). The Holy Spirit will cause you to do God's Word (Ezek. 36:27). The Holy Spirit will give life to your whole being (Rom. 8:11).

Jesus Christ, Moses, Joshua, Elijah, Elisha, Daniel, the prophets, Apostles Peter and Paul, and the early apostles, prophets, and Disciples walked in the Power and Anointing of the Holy Spirit, and that was why they could turn the city upside down and the people that were against them feared them.

Even these days, we are to walk in the Power and Anointing of the Holy Spirit of the Living God. We live in the dispensation of power and authority, and the glory of the latter house shall be greater than that of the former (Hag. 2:9).

God promised to send the Later Rain and the Former Rain together in our day (Joel 2:23). The Rain is a type of the Holy Spirit. We are to walk in greater power and anointing than the early apostles and Disciples, because we are the generation that will prepare the world for the Coming of the Lord.

But you must pray, consistently and daily. You can't make it without being prayerful. Increase your knowledge of God and His Word, for God doesn't give big responsibilities to novices.

You will need to fast consistently and regularly, as the Spirit leads you. You will not, necessarily, need to fast for forty days and nights; but even if you are led to do it, you will not die doing it. Christ has already won the battle for us.

The anointing and power in the Life of Jesus Christ drew great multitude of people to Him, and even today, when the anointing in your life is strong enough, great multitudes of people will be drawn to you.

As a Christian who is filled with the Holy Spirit, the Seven Spirits of God or layers of anointing should be seen in you. These are the Spirit of the Lord, the Spirit of Wisdom, the Spirit of Understanding, the Spirit of Counsel, the Spirit of Might, the Spirit of Knowledge, and the Spirit of the Fear of the Lord.

Many have not realized the power of the tongue. This is why many of them speak the way they do. If people realize the importance, the value, or the power of the tongue, they will be careful and weigh their words before they speak.

Unfortunately, even those who have been taught along this line have offended in words, at one time or the other, and have reaped the negative impacts of their negative words.

The Bible says that life and death are in the power of the tongue (Prov. 18:21). Words, even words spoken by them, have killed many, more than we have realized.

When someone feels some symptoms of sickness or disease, and speaks with his own mouth, saying, "I am sick," that person is accepting the sickness or disease that the devil wants to bring upon him.

The spiritual controls the physical. But someone may ask, "What of when I already have the sickness?" Or, "What of when I have the symptoms?"

When you are tempted to steal, have you stolen simply because the thought came to your mind? No, you steal when you take that thing or when you have made up your mind to take it, and you are waiting for an opportunity or when you will not be caught.

In the later case, even when you have not touched that thing, God sees you as a thief; but the simple thought or temptation does not make you a thief.

The same is applicable to sickness, even though you may not see it that way. The devil will throw an arrow of sickness at you; you must reject that sickness, and confess health in the Name of Jesus Christ.

By the Stripes of Jesus Christ we were healed (not that we shall be healed) (1 Pet. 2:24). He carried our sicknesses and diseases (Matt. 8:17). Learn to speak according to the Word of God: this is faith.

But the problem is that many people want sympathizers. Those people that sympathize with you are not God, and if you want sympathy, it will destroy your faith.

In fact, the devil will use the words of those sympathizers to keep your eyes off Jesus Christ, the Author and Finisher of our faith, and keep you looking at the problems.

And if you look at the problems and you look away from your God, you will sink as did Peter. When he saw the wind boisterous, he began to sink (Matt. 14:30), and if not because he cried for help, he might have sunk, got drowned, and died.

Jesus Christ tells us that for every idle word men may speak, they will give account of it in the Day of Judgment. For by your words you will be justified, and by your words you will be condemned (Matt. 12:36-37).

Your words can justify you, and it can also condemn or mar you. You can receive healing, financial breakthrough, marital well-being, and spiritual success by your words; and those areas of life can be cursed by your words.

Many people speak too much; they speak when it is not necessary. The Word says that sin is not absent in the multitude of words (Prov. 10:19).

Do you want to be perfect in words? Then learn when to speak and when not to speak. We should be quick to hear and slow to speak. Be slow to anger as well (Jas 1:19-20). Man's anger or wrath does not work out the Righteousness of God.

When you want to defend yourself, you will speak too much. I am not saying that you should not defend yourself, but know what to say to defend yourself when necessary, and learn to leave the rest to God.

Even Jesus Christ was criticized; who are you not to be criticized? Even when men may not believe you, God will justify you. Anyway, God is the Final Judge and not any man. Learn to be quiet and leave things to God (1 Thes. 4:11).

The Bible says that those who love the tongue, those who don't mind what they say, will reap the fruit of their work or word (Prov. 18:21). There are spiritual laws, just as they are natural laws.

When you speak against someone who is greater than you or who has authority over you, the person may punish you, and that will be your reward. If you curse someone who is on a higher spiritual level than you, the curse may return to you. When you say good or bad things about yourself, good or bad things will come to you.

The Bible says that the Servant of God must not quarrel (2 Tim. 2:24). I know, from experience, that if you make up your mind not to quarrel, the enemy will bring so much pressure and many temptations to lure you to quarrel, so that you will say bad things and offend God.

But, thanks to God that the devil will not have any place in your life, unless you let him, and he is not going to seize your mouth and speak with it. Hold fast to that which is good without wavering.

Some people say things that they neither understand nor are convinced of. People even affirm things they are not sure of, and this is not good. Reject profane and old wives fables. Do not rebuke an older man and an elder, but exhort him as a father.

Don't be a busybody in other people's affairs, or a gossip, saying things you should not say. Avoid the profane and idle babblings, and contradictions of what is falsely called knowledge. Speak evil of no man.

Do not strive about words to no profit, to the ruin of the hearers; shun profane and idle babblings, for they will increase to more ungodliness. Avoid foolish and ignorant disputes, knowing that they generate strife.

Beware of pride and boasting, shun blasphemy and slander. Speak the truth in love; let each one of you speak truth with his neighbours. Let no corrupt word proceed out of your mouth, but what is good for necessary edification, that it may impart grace to the hearers.

Let all bitterness, wrath, anger, clamour, and evil speaking be put away from you, with all malice. Refuse filthiness, foolish talk, and coarse jesting, which are not fitting, but rather giving of thanks. Remove filthy language out of your mouth.

Avoid foolish disputes, genealogies, contentions, and striving about the Law, for they are unprofitable and useless (Tit. 3:9). Do not allow negative confession out of your mouth, no matter how the situation may look like.

Speak the things which are proper for Sound Doctrine (Tit. 2:1). Speak sound speech which cannot be condemned. If any man does not stumble in word, he is a perfect man, able also to bridle the whole body. Bits in horses' mouths make them obey men, and men can turn their whole body.

Even though ships are very big, and are driven by fierce winds, they are turned by a very small rudder wherever the pilot desires. A forest is set on fire by a little fire. And the tongue is a fire, a world of iniquity.

No man can tame the tongue. It is an unruly evil, full of deadly poison. Don't bless God with your tongue and curse men with it also. Let the Spirit direct your tongue.

Use your tongue for effective prayer. Many will rather go about visiting and gossiping than pray. Preach and teach the Word of God, as God enables you. Don't be ashamed to speak of Jesus Christ.

Declare the Gospel in the public: blow the horn, let all men hear it! The Great Commission or world evangelism is still a priority with God and with us His children. Men, and not angels, are sent to preach the Gospel.

The tongue is so powerful that God created the heavens and the earth by His Words. God calls those things that do not exist by name as though they existed, and when He calls them, they come to existence. You are a god (Psa. 82:6).

Therefore, speak the Way God speaks, and you will see great results that will blow your mind. Maintain the profession or confession of your faith without wavering. If you believe, speak out what you believe, because it is the speaking that brings the physical manifestation!

Never Say That God Said What He Did Not Say!
THE SPIRITUAL CHRISTIAN

There is therefore now no condemnation to those who are in Christ Jesus, who do not walk according to the flesh, but according to the Spirit. For the Law of the Spirit of Life in Christ Jesus has made me free from the law of sin and death.

For what the Law could not do in that it was weak through the flesh, God did by sending His Own Son in the likeness of sinful flesh, on account of sin.

He condemned sin in the flesh, that the righteous requirement of the Law might be fulfilled in us who do not walk according to the flesh but according to the Spirit.

For those who live according to the flesh set their minds on the things of the flesh, but those who live according to the Spirit, the Things of the Spirit. For to be carnally minded is death, but to be spiritually minded is life and peace.

Because the carnal mind is enmity against God; for it is not subject to the Law of God, nor indeed can be. So then those who are in the flesh cannot please God. But you are not in the flesh but in the Spirit, if indeed the Spirit of God dwells in you.

Now if anyone does not have the Spirit of Christ, he is not His. And if Christ is in you, the body is dead because of sin, but the Spirit is Life because of righteousness.

But if the Spirit of Him Who raised Jesus Christ from the dead dwells in you, He Who raised Christ from the dead will also give life to your mortal bodies through His Spirit Who dwells in you.

Therefore, brethren, we are debtors – not to the flesh, to live according to the flesh. For if you live according to the flesh, you will die; but if by the Spirit you put to death the deeds of the body, you will live.

For as many as are led by the Spirit of God, these are the sons of God. The Spirit Himself bears witness with our spirit that we are children of God, and if children then heirs   heirs of God and joint-heirs with Christ, if indeed we suffer with Him, that we may also be glorified together.

For I consider that the sufferings of this present time are not worthy to be compared with the glory which shall be revealed in us. For the earnest expectation of the creation eagerly waits for the revealing of the sons of God.

The creation itself also will be delivered from the bondage of corruption into the glorious liberty of the children of God. For we know that the whole creation groans and labours with birth pangs together until now.

Not only that, but we also, even we ourselves groan within ourselves, eagerly waiting for the adoption, the redemption of our body.

The Spirit also helps in our weakness. For we do not know what we should pray for as we ought, but the Spirit Himself makes intercession for us with groanings which cannot be uttered.

Now He Who searches the hearts knows what the Mind of the Spirit is, because He makes intercession for the Saints according to the Will of God.

And we know that all things work together for good to those who love God, to those who are the called according to His Purpose.

For whom He foreknew, He also predestined to be conformed to the Image of His Son, that He might be the Firstborn among many brethren.

Moreover whom He predestined, these He also called; whom He called, these He also justified; and whom He justified, these He also glorified (Rom. 8:1-30).

If God has called you, make every effort to be chosen by Him also. As a chosen vessel of His, be faithful so that you will be commended, rewarded, and glorified at last, because the end of a matter is better than the beginning.

Walk in the Spirit, and you shall not fulfill the lust of the flesh. For the flesh lusts against the Spirit, and the Spirit against the flesh, and these are contrary to one another, so that you do not do the things that you wish. But if you are led by the Spirit, you are not under the Law.

The Fruit of the Spirit is love, joy, peace, longsuffering, kindness, goodness, faithfulness, gentleness, self-control. Against such there is no Law. And those who are Christ's have crucified the flesh with its passions and desires.

If we live in the Spirit, let us also walk in the Spirit. Let us not become conceited, provoking one another, envying one another. Bear one another's burdens and so fulfill the Law of Christ.

Do not be deceived, God is not mocked; whatever a man sows, that he will also reap. For he who sows to his flesh will also of the flesh reap corruption, but he who sows to the Spirit will of the Spirit reap Everlasting Life.

And let us not grow weary while doing good, for in due season, we shall reap if we do not lose heart. Therefore, as we have opportunity, let us do good to all, especially to those who are of the Household of Faith (Gal. 5 and 6).

God tells us that we should seek those things which are Above, where Christ is, sitting at the Right Hand of God. Set your mind on things Above, not on things on the earth. For you died, when you received Christ; and your life has been hidden with Christ in God.

When Christ Who is our Life appears, then we also will appear with Him in glory. Therefore put to death your members which are on the earth: fornication, uncleanness, passion, evil desire, and covetousness, which is idolatry. Put off all these: anger, wrath, malice, blasphemy, filthy language out of your mouth.

As the Elect of God, holy and beloved, put on tender mercies, kindness, humility, meekness, longsuffering; bearing with one another, and forgiving one another; if anyone has a complaint against another, even as Christ forgave you, so you also must do.

But above all these things put on love, which is the bond of perfection. And let the Peace of God rule in your hearts, and be thankful.

Let the Word of Christ dwell in you richly in all wisdom, teaching and admonishing one another in psalms and hymns and spiritual songs, singing with grace in your hearts to the Lord.

And whatever you do, in word or in deed, do all in the Name of the Lord Jesus, giving thanks to God the Father through Him. Continue earnestly in prayer, being vigilant in it with thanksgiving.

Walk in wisdom toward those who are outside, redeeming the time. Let your speech always be with grace, seasoned with salt, that you may know how you ought to answer each one (Col. 3 & 4).

Walk worthy of the calling with which you were called, with all lowliness and gentleness, with longsuffering, bearing with one another in love, endeavouring to keep the Unity of the Spirit in the bond of peace.

Put off, concerning your former conduct, the old man which grows corrupt according to the deceitful lusts, and be renewed in the spirit of your mind. Put on the new man who was created according to God, in true righteousness and holiness.

And do not grieve the Holy Spirit of God, by Whom you were sealed for the Day of Redemption. Be imitators of God as dear people of God. And walk in love, as Christ also has loved us and given Himself for us, an Offering and a Sacrifice to God for a sweet-smelling aroma.

Never Say That God Said What He Did Not Say!

See then that you walk circumspectly, not as fools but as wise, redeeming the time, because the days are evil. Therefore, do not be unwise, but understand what the Will of the Lord is. And do not be drunk with wine, in which is dissipation, but be filled with the Spirit.

Submit to one another in the fear of God. Be strong in the Lord and in the power of His Might. Put on the whole Armour of God that you may be able to stand against the wiles of the devil.

For we do not wrestle against flesh and blood; but we wrestle against principalities, against powers, and against the rulers of the darkness of this age, against spiritual hosts of wickedness in the heavenly places.

Therefore, take up the whole Armour of God that you may be able to withstand in the evil day, and having done all to stand.

Stand therefore, having girded your waist with truth, having put on the breastplate of righteousness, and having shod your feet with the preparation of the Gospel of Peace; above all, taking the shield of faith with which you will be able to quench all the fiery darts of the wicked one.

And take the helmet of salvation, and the Sword of the Spirit, which is the Word of God: praying always with all prayer and supplication in the Spirit, being watchful to this end with all perseverance and supplication for all the Saints (Eph. 4, 5, & 6).

Work out your salvation with fear and trembling: for it is God Who works in you both to will and to do for His Good Pleasure.

Do all things without complaining and disputing, that you may become blameless and harmless, children of God without fault in the midst of a crooked and perverse generation among whom you shine as lights in the world, holding fast the Word of Life, so that your salvation will not be in vain (Phil. 2:12-16).

Learn to build up yourself spiritually; be diligent to energize your spirit. Remember that weight hinders your Christian walk, while sin entangles you to the devil and the world. The Will of God for you in Jesus Christ is that you go and sin no more.

Also, you can't serve two masters at the same time. You can't serve God and money; you can't serve God and men. Live in all good conscience toward God and men.

Remember that your body is the Temple of God; therefore don't defile it. The Saints are to be perfected; they are to get matured and established in the Lord.

Love is the Great Commandment: to love the Lord your God with all your heart, with all your soul, and with all your strength; and to love your neighbour as yourself. This is the summary of the Law (Matt. 22:36-40).

The Word of the Lord commands us to love one another fervently, for love covers multitude of sins (1 Pet. 4:8). Let brotherly love continue (Heb.13:1). Be kindly affectionate to one another with brotherly love, in honour giving preference to one another (Rom. 12:10).

Let love be without hypocrisy. Abhor what is evil. Cling to what is good (Rom. 12:9). And let us not grow weary while doing good, for in due season, we shall reap, if we do not lose heart.

Therefore, as we have opportunity, let us do good to all, especially to those who are of the Household of Faith (Gal. 6:9-10).

People may not appreciate you, or even thank you, but God will reward you; you do it to God when you do it in the Name of God.

Love your enemies, bless those who curse you, do good to those who hate you, and pray for those who spitefully use you and persecute you, that you may be the sons of your Father in

Heaven; for He makes His sun to rise on the evil and on the good, and sends rain on the just and on the unjust.

For if you love those who love you, what reward have you? Do not even the sinners do the same? (Matt. 5:44-46). If you kill your enemy by prayer, and he dies and goes to Hell, is it God or the devil that gained?

Of course, Peter spoke by the anointing, and Ananias and Sapphira dropped dead, but it was as the Spirit led him. You don't just go about declaring that all your enemies die; if they die, the devil using them against you will leave and enter new people who will start to oppress you again.

Be a strong and prayerful Christian who is full of faith and the enemy will never harm you. But the problem is that many Christians are lukewarm.

Apostle Paul put temporary inability to see on Elymas by God's Power, and that led to getting the attention of the governor more (Acts 13:8-12). I like this style!

The Word of God speaks of the love of many waxing cold because of the abundance of iniquity (Matt. 24:12). The Ephesian Church was rebuked by the Lord because they had left their first love (Rev. 2:4).

They left it by failing to do the first works. The Laodicean Church was neither cold nor hot; they were lukewarm. If you are lukewarm, the Lord will spew you out of His Mouth (Rev. 3:15-16).

Get hot in your Christian life and maintain a red-hot Christian life. Be fervent in spirit, maintain the spiritual glow (Rom. 12:11).

The test or proof that you love the Lord is that you keep His Commandments (Jn 14:15; 1 Jn 2:4), and His Commandments are not burdensome (1 Jn 5:3).

They may look difficult, but they are not impossible, for God is a Just God. If you say that you love the Lord, and don't keep His Commandments, you lie and the truth is not in you.

If you say that you love the Lord and yet hate your brother, you are a big liar (1 Jn 4:20). Jesus Christ laid down His Life for us, and we too ought to lay down our lives for the brethren.

Love is a Fruit of the Spirit. The Love of God, having been shed abroad in our hearts by the Holy Spirit, we should bear the fruit of love and mature in it. We ought to be rooted and grounded in love (Eph. 3:17).

And we should forbear one another in love. Walk in love, as Christ also loved us. Faith and love represent our breastplate in the spiritual warfare (1 Thes. 5:8).

As many as the Lord loves, He rebukes so that they will not be disapproved and condemned (Rev. 3:19). Therefore, open rebuke is better than secret love. Rebuke evil and wrong-doing in love.

Do not love the world or anything in the world. If any man loves the world, the Love of the Father is not in him; for all that is in the world: the lust of the eyes, the lust of the flesh, and the pride of life come not from the Father, but from the world. And the world passes away with its lusts, but he who does the Will of the Father abides forever (1 Jn 2:15-17).

The love of money is the root of all evil, for which some have strayed from the faith in their greediness and pierced themselves through with many sorrows (1 Tim. 6:10).

Love suffers long and is kind; love does not envy; love does not parade itself, is not puffed up, does not behave rudely, does not seek its own, is not provoked, thinks no evil, does not rejoice in iniquity, but rejoices in the truth; bears all things, believes all things, hopes all things, endures all things.

Love never fails, even though spiritual gifts will fail and pass away. And now abide faith, hope, love, these three, but the greatest of these is love (1 Cor. 13).

Forgiveness is a term used in connection with sin and offence. We receive forgiveness from God when we repent of our sins and confess them to Him. If we confess our sins, He is faithful and just to forgive our sins, and to cleanse us from all unrighteousness (1 Jn 1:9).

He who covers his sins shall not prosper, but he who confesses and renounces them shall find mercy (Prov. 28:13). Take note of the renouncing factor; don't confess your sins with the intention to go back to it when you are tempted again.

As high as the heavens are above the earth, so great is the Father's Love. As far as the east is from the west, so far has He taken our sins from us (Psa. 103:11-12).

Our sins, He will forgive and remember them no more. The Blood of Jesus Christ is able to cleanse the vilest sinner who repents of his sins. And he that comes to God will not be cast away.

Consider the parable of the prodigal son; when the prodigal son was still afar off, as he was coming back, the father ran and embraced him, forgiving him his sins and making a big feast for him (Lk. 15:11-32).

There is no forgiveness in death. It is now that you have an opportunity to repent and be cleansed. Once death comes, a sinner goes straight to Hell, and all sinners belong to the devil.

Whether they are bishops, apostles, prophets, evangelists, pastors, teachers, musicians, prayer-warriors, clergy, laity, rich, poor, great, small, male, female, old, young, president, professor, director, or whatever position or title they may hold or have, all sinners are cursed forever.

Also, you must forgive others of the wrong they do to you. We are forgiven if we forgive others. If we don't forgive others, our Heavenly Father will not forgive us also (Matt. 6:14-15).

No matter the number of times he or she may sin against you, forgive him or her as he or she comes to you and says that he or she is sorry (Matt. 18:21-22).

Let no bitterness, hatred, and unforgiveness remain in your life, for they will block your blessings and make you spiritually wanting. Don't even hold grudges against the one that refuses to apologize.

Even, bitterness can cause sickness and heart-attack, just as worry and anxiety can cause heart-attack. Mental confusion will cause spiritual and physical problems to you.

Don't be like that unmerciful servant who was forgiven of a big debt, but when he saw his fellow servant who owed him a little, he sent him to the prison. His master punished him, calling him a wicked servant (Matt. 18:23-35). Mercy transcends over judgment.

Also, learn to forgive yourself of your past mistakes. Many are being overcome by their past mistakes because they do not forgive themselves, but allow their past sins and mistakes to hunt them, even when they would have confessed them to God.

Is God unfaithful to forgive your sins as He promised? You are not being more righteous by rejecting God's Word and doubting His Forgiveness. God cannot lie, and He has promised to forgive you when you confess your sins to Him.

God is Light and in Him is no darkness. If we say that we have fellowship with Him, and walk in darkness, we lie and do not practice the truth.

But if we walk in the light as He is in the light, we have fellowship with one another, and the Blood of Jesus Christ His Son cleanses us from all sin (1 Jn 1:5-7).

He who says he abides is Him ought himself also to walk just as He walked. He, who says he is in the light, and hates his brother, is in darkness until now.

Learn and train yourself to forgive others and forbear with men. Men are hard to deal with. Somebody can come to you saying one thing, while his mind is on another thing entirely.

Men hurt, but God heals and encourages. Learn to trust in the Lord always, and don't depend on men because they can fail you. But you, why not be trustworthy?

Never Say That God Said What He Did Not Say!

SECRETS TO SUCCESSFUL MINISTRY

We are surrounded by a great cloud of witnesses, those who had run this race before us. They succeeded and made God happy. We cannot fail God, because that will not be good at all.

If the people that went before us succeeded, we also can succeed; the God that enabled them is our God, and He cannot fail. He is all-powerful, and the host of Heaven is on our side.

The secret of successful ministry is obedience. You can't obey God fully and not be successful in ministry. But obedience presupposes foreknowledge of what to do. We know what to do in our Christian walk, in ministry, and in our present life by the Word of God and the Leading or Prompting of the Spirit of God.

Therefore, the secret of successful ministry is the Word of God and the Spirit of God. Actually, the Spirit of God inspired the writing of the Word of God, the Bible, and He also explains the Word to us, and brings it to our remembrance when we need it.

If you want to be successful (in God's Sight) in ministry, then you must make up your mind to obey God absolutely, no matter the cost or sacrifice. Whatever you may sacrifice for God and His Work, He is able to give it back to you many folds.

God did not call us to serve Him in vain. He will reward us very abundantly, both in this life, and in the life which is to come. Don't allow the devil deceive you with the temporal things of this world.

The Word of God tells us the Mind of God. The Word of God is forever settled in Heaven (Psa. 119:89). As a minister, the Word admonishes that you study the Bible to show yourself approved to God a workman that needs not to be ashamed, rightly dividing the Word of Truth.

To divide the Word of Truth the right way is to put every Word where it is supposed to be, and to compare Scripture with Scripture. It is to understand the Word of God clearly.

The devil misapplied the Scripture when he quoted ninety-first chapter of Psalm to Jesus Christ. Doing what the devil quoted would have amounted to testing God; but he quoted the Bible you carry.

In these days when occult men and agents of darkness carry Bible and call Jesus, you require a clear understanding of the Scripture so that you will not be led astray by fellow preachers. If you are led astray, you will also lead the people following you astray. If you lead them astray, God will hold you responsible.

Take heed to yourself and the Doctrine (the correct Doctrine); continue in them, for in doing this you will save both yourself and them that hear you (1 Tim. 4:16).

A demon may even speak to you audibly in the Name of (as if it is) the Holy Spirit, but with the Word, you can distinguish the Voice of the Holy Spirit from the voices of devils and manipulators. Let the Word of God dwell in you richly in all wisdom (Col. 3:16).

When you are full of the Word of God, no trial, scandal, or persecution will weigh you down; for the Word will give you strength and direction.

As said earlier, you need the Holy Spirit to function effectively in the ministry. Without the Holy Spirit you are a failure. It is not by power, nor by might, but by the Holy Spirit of the Living God (Zech. 4:6).

Jesus Christ never intended to leave us comfortless and helpless in life and ministry. That is why He sent the Holy Spirit to us after He left for Heaven. The Holy Spirit is our Comforter, Helper, Counselor, Intercessor, Advocate, Strengthener, and Standby. He is the Manifester of God's Power.

The Holy Spirit reveals Jesus Christ to us. He teaches us the Word and Will of God. He reminds us of what we had known before. The Holy Spirit reveals what is to come to us.

He helps our weaknesses; in prayer, the Spirit makes intercession for us with groanings that cannot be uttered (or uttered in an articulate speech), of which speaking in tongues is among.

Jesus Christ, after He was filled with the Holy Spirit, was led by the Spirit into the wilderness, and after being tempted by the devil (He ate nothing in those days), He returned in the Power of the Holy Ghost.

The Holy Spirit had anointed Him with the power He required to be fruitful and productive in His Ministry. You can't function any other way, except you want people to either neglect you or clap hands for you when God is not clapping for you.

Without the anointing, people will neglect your ministry, except you are keeping them with something else like traditions of men or demonic powers. I know some go to church to hear the Word of God for them, but you need the anointing to preach or teach effectively or more effectively.

If you are not prayerful, you can't be as effective in ministry as God wants you to be. Some ministers were very prayerful in the early years of their ministries, but when their ministries expanded and grew, they became too busy that they don't spend enough time with God in prayer again.

To maintain a strong anointing, you must be prayerful. No wonder the Word tells us to continue earnestly in prayer (Col. 4:2). Pray without ceasing. Men ought always to pray and not faint (Lk. 18:1).

Another booster to the ministry is fasting. As a matter of fact, there are levels of the anointing and empowerment by the Spirit of God that you will never reach in your life without fasting.

Of course, I am not saying that you can't be in the ministry without fasting, but why will it take someone a week or two to cast out a demon, while another can cast out same demon in few seconds?

The difference is the anointing. The difference is faith. I am not necessarily saying that someone who doesn't fast to a great extent can't have a larger church or ministry than another who fasts to a great extent.

First, there are other issues a minister should address, both in his life and in the lives of those who follow him, apart from fasting. If you fast long, but live in sin and disobedience, they will hinder your ministry.

Also, if you don't study the Word to increase your knowledge of God and His Word, it will also hinder your ministry, because there are levels of anointing God will not give you if you are a novice. Second, what you may judge as being large or big by human standard may be judged differently by God.

There are different ministries: an intercessor can sustain the ministry of a traveling evangelist, though the intercessor himself may not be well-known.

Holiness will also boost your ministry. All other things being equal, the holier you are, the more God will manifest His Power and Glory through you. There is perfecting or perfection in holiness. To perfect in holiness is to mature in holiness; it is to make your life of holiness steady.

Also, sin can stop the anointing from flowing through you. This is why many started as good ministers, but when they started living in sexual immorality, pride, and covetousness, they lost the anointing, and later went after demonic powers.

Obedience and righteousness will boost your ministry as well. By obedience, I mean doing what God tells you to do. By righteousness, I mean doing the right things at the right time.

If, for instance, you make up your mind to fast for seven days in order to minister to someone, and on the third day God tells you to go and minister to the person, obey God instead of obeying yourself.

He has the power, and the anointing is not your own. As a matter of fact, when you are filled with the Holy Ghost, you have all the potential power you need for life, Godliness, and the ministry.

But even though the potential is there, the Holy Spirit anoints people with different levels of the anointing. Why? There is a level of anointing God can give you at a certain state and that anointing will lead to your destruction: first of all, it can lead to pride, and you know that God hates pride, and will not share His Glory with another.

Secondly, there are levels of the anointing that will make satan mad, and if God gives it to you and you don't live the life of commitment and discipline required for it, satan will kill you. At any time and place, do what God tells you to do, and it will be well with you.

A minister ought to be able to tame his tongue and his emotions. Don't say anything that comes to your mind. Also, don't get depressed so that you will not get discouraged; and don't get too excited that you can't control your conduct.

You should be an example to your followers because they are watching you. Strike the shepherd and the sheep will scatter. There is something you will do and their trust for you will die. You are not a church-member but a leader or an overseer, as a pastor. There are things you can do and the church will scatter in a week.

Also, relate with other good ministers. Don't relate with someone your spirit feels uncomfortable with, except for casual relationships. Don't allow the devil pull you down through your wife or your children.

Show love, compassion, and kindness to those you minister to. Don't only receive: give also, as you are led. If you sow a little to your followers, they will be happy, and when God leads them to give you, they will be more sensitive to the Voice of God.

Avoid pride, for it destroys the minister. Be humble, patient, and diligent. Persevere, no matter what. The Christian life and the ministry require steadfastness and persistence. Operating in unity will boost your productivity and fruitfulness in the ministry.

Walk worthy of your Christian life and the calling that the Lord has called you! Run the race that the Lord has set before you with determination and commitment. Abstain from all appearances of evil.

Don't be lazy in the work that the Lord has committed to your trust. Avoid idleness, but commit your time to the Lord's Service and be dedicated to seeing that the Lord's Work does not suffer in your hand.

Don't sleep, don't slumber in the ministry that the Lord has committed to your trust. Be zealous for the work or task the Lord has committed into your hand. Expect persecutions and sufferings in the course of the ministerial work.

Beware of covetousness and love of money. Also, beware of women: avoid lust, fornication, and adultery. Always remember your reward in Heaven, for that will give you the zeal, passion, and endurance you require for this work. Don't be earthly minded but heavenly minded.

Never Say That God Said What He Did Not Say!

ABOUNDING IN THE FRUIT OF THE SPIRIT

The Fruit of the Spirit is in all goodness, righteousness, and truth. What the spirit of man produces by the Holy Spirit's Indwelling is in all that have to do with goodness, righteousness, and truth (Eph. 5:9).

When a sinner repents and gives his heart to the Lord Jesus Christ, confessing Him as his Saviour, the Holy Spirit of the Living God regenerates, recreates, and makes new that person's spirit. If any man is in Christ, he is a new creature (new creation); old things have passed away, and all things have become new (2 Cor. 5:17).

It is the spirit of man that is born again or recreated. Man is a tripartite being who is a spirit, has a soul, and lives in a body. Your soul which is the seat of your thinking, reasoning, and emotions, is not born again but is saved or restored by the renewing of your mind with the Word of God so that you begin to think God's Way.

Then you need to present your body and its members a living sacrifice to God, holy and acceptable to Him. Present your body and its members as instruments of obedience to holiness and righteousness (Rom. 12:1-2; Rom. 6:13,19).

The human spirit of a Christian wants to please God, but his body may still desire some things that displease God. Your mind is the point of decision where you decide whether to obey your spirit or your flesh.

If your mind has been renewed by the Word of God, it will agree with your spirit to please God. Apostle Paul said he beat his body and brought it to subjection.

It was his spirit, his inward man that controlled his body, because his mind took side with his spirit. To be spiritually minded is life, but to be carnally or fleshly minded is death. The carnal mind is enmity with God, for it is not subject to God's Commandments, and can never be subject to them.

This is why those that are in the flesh cannot please God. But you are not in the flesh (Rom. 8:6-9). Get rid of the works of the flesh out of your life. As Christians, we are good trees; and good trees are supposed to bear good fruits.

The Presence of the Holy Spirit in the human spirit enables the human spirit to produce, among other things: love, joy, peace, longsuffering, kindness, goodness, faithfulness, gentleness, self-control. Against such there is no Law (Gal. 5:22-23).

Love makes you obey God, no matter the cost, and gets you to do to others as you would have them do to you (as it will please you that they do to you, not as they will do to you). Joy makes you happy and to take pleasure in the Lord your God. No matter what may be surrounding you, you have joy in the Holy Spirit.

Peace will make you calm, removing worry and fear from you, no matter how harsh the external situations or circumstances may be. Longsuffering will make you patient in your Christian race, and to wait patiently for God's Time and Intervention. He that endures to the end will receive the promise; the same will be saved.

Kindness will make you say or do things that show you care about other people and want to help them or make them happy; you will have a compassionate feeling for people.

Goodness is the quality of being good. Being good will make you profitable and of advantage to others. Goodness has to do with actions or behaviours that are morally right or that follow the Christian Principles. Do not be weary in doing good, for in due time, you will reap your reward if you do not give up (Gal. 6:9).

Faithfulness will make you loyal and trustworthy. Integrity and honesty must be part of you. Gentleness will make you kind and careful in your character or behaviour and not at all violent or unpleasant. Self-control is the ability to behave calmly and sensibly, even when you feel very excited, angry, sad, etc.

Do not walk as the rest of the unbelievers walk, in the futility of their mind, having their understanding darkened, being alienated from the Life of God, because of the ignorance that is in them, because of blindness of their heart; who being past feeling, have given themselves over to lewdness, to work all uncleanness with greediness.

But you have not so learned Christ, if indeed you have heard Him and have been taught by Him, as the truth is in Jesus Christ.

Put off, concerning your former conduct, the old man which grows corrupt according to the deceitful lusts, and be renewed in the spirit of your mind; and put on the new man which was created according to God, in true righteousness and holiness.

Let no corrupt word proceed out of your mouth, but what is good for necessary edification, that it may impart grace to the hearers. Let all bitterness, wrath, anger, clamour, and evil-speaking be put away from you, with all malice. Be tenderhearted and forgive others as God forgave you.

Be imitators of God, as Christians: and walk in love, as Christ also has loved us and gave Himself for us. But fornication and all uncleanness or covetousness, let it not even be named among you, as is fitting for Saints; neither filthiness, nor foolish talking, nor coarse jesting, which are not fitting, but rather giving of thanks.

For this you know, that no fornicator, unclean person, nor covetous man, who is an idolater, has any inheritance in the Kingdom of Christ and of God.

Walk as children of light, finding out what is acceptable to the Lord. And have no fellowship with the unfruitful works of darkness, but rather expose them.

See then that you walk circumspectly, not as fools but as wise, redeeming the time because the days are evil. Submit to one another in the fear of God (Eph. 4 & 5). Walk in the Spirit, and you shall not fulfil the lust of the flesh.

If you are led by the Spirit, you are not under the Law. Those who are Christ's have crucified the flesh with its passions and desires. Let us not become conceited, provoking one another, envying one another.

Let your love abound more and more in knowledge and all discernment; approve the things that are excellent, and be sincere and without offence till the Day of Christ, and be filled with the fruits of righteousness which are by Jesus Christ (Phil. 1:9-11).

Be like-minded with the true brethren, having the same love, being of one accord, of one mind. Let nothing be done through selfish ambition or conceit, but in lowliness of mind, let each esteem others better than himself. Let each of you look out not only for his own interest, but also for the interest of others (Phil. 2:2-16).

Work out your own salvation with fear and trembling; for it is God Who works in you both to will and to do for His Good Pleasure.

Do all things without complaining and disputing, that you may become blameless and harmless, children of God without fault in the midst of a crooked and perverse generation, among whom you shine as lights in the world, holding fast the Word of Life.

Be anxious for nothing. Rejoice in the Lord always. Let your gentleness be known to all men. The Lord is at hand.

Whatever things are true, whatever things are noble, whatever things are just, whatever things are pure, whatever things are lovely, whatever things are of good report, if there is any virtue, and if there is anything praiseworthy, meditate on those things (Phil. 4:4-8).

The Foundation of God stands, having this seal: "The Lord knows those who are His," and "Let everyone who names the Name of Christ depart from iniquity." Flee youthful lusts; but pursue righteousness, faith, love, and peace with those who call on the Lord out of a pure heart.

In a great house there are not only vessels of gold and silver, but also of wood and clay, some for honour and some for dishonour. Therefore, if anyone cleanses himself from the later, he will be a vessel for honour, sanctified and useful for the Master, prepared for every good work.

Avoid foolish and ignorant disputes, knowing that they generate strife. And a Servant of the Lord must not quarrel, but be gentle to all, able to teach, patient (2 Tim. 2:19-24).

Whoever commits sin also commits lawlessness, and sin is lawlessness. Whoever abides in Him does not sin. Whoever sins has neither seen Him nor known Him. Let no one deceive you. He who practices righteousness is righteous, just as He is righteous.

He who sins is of the devil. Whoever has been Born of God does not sin, for His Seed remains in him, and he cannot sin, because he is Born of God. In this the children of God and the children of the devil are manifest: whoever does not practice righteousness is not of God, nor is he who does not love his brother (1 Jn 3:3-10).

Produce the Fruit of the Spirit in abundance! You have the ability, by the Holy Spirit to do so. Believers are to be like Christ (Christian); they are to be like God (Godly). Ask yourself, in every situation, what Jesus Christ would have done or what God would have you do in that same situation.

Never Say That God Said What He Did Not Say!

PLEASING GOD

The Heartbeat of God is that all men may come to the knowledge of His Son Jesus Christ, and that they obey and fear Him always. This is why we must evangelize to the ends of the world.

To please God should be your goal in life; it should be your highest priority. Why? Because this is the Whole Duty of man, and that is why man was made.

To fear God and keep His Commandments is the Whole Duty of man (Eccl. 12:13-14). To please God is to do those things that make Him happy and proud of you. If you do those things that please God always, He will never leave you, as He never left Jesus Christ (Jn 8:29).

But without faith, it is impossible to please Him, for he who comes to God must believe that He is, and that He is a Rewarder of those that diligently seek Him (Heb. 11:6).

This is to say that if you know that you will gain a lot from pleasing God, it will make you please Him so that, among other things, you will receive the reward. Of course, we have to please God because we love him, and not just because of what we can get from Him.

Jesus Christ had this attitude when the Bible says that Jesus Christ, for the Joy that was set before Him, endured the Cross, despising the shame, and has sat down at the Right Hand of the Throne of God (Heb. 12:2).

Because Jesus Christ humbled Himself and became obedient to the point of death, God also has highly exalted Him and given Him the Name which is above every other name, that at the Name of Jesus Christ every knee should bow, and every tongue confess that Jesus Christ is Lord, to the Glory of God the Father (Phil. 2:8-11).

Can you say, like Apostle Paul, "For me to live is Christ, and to die is gain?" To live for Christ is to surrender your will to His, so that, no matter how difficult His Will may seem to you, you will do it.

When you say that to die is gain, you are saying that you have lived for Christ, and if you die now, you will be ushered into Heaven by the angels of God. My brother, no one who died and went to Hell, or is cast out into the Outer Darkness, gained.

God has not called us to serve Him in vain; there are so many good things we gain by serving God and doing His Will, both in this life and in the life which is to come.

Being conscious of this will make you to do anything, and sacrifice anything (even your life) for the Name of the Lord. Christians do not love their lives to death as Christ also surrendered His (Rev. 12:11).

Another thing that you should be conscious of is that there are punishments associated with disobeying God and displeasing Him, both in this life and in the life which is to come.

Hence, Apostle Paul said that knowing the Terror of God, we persuade men everywhere to repent, for He has appointed one day when He will judge all men by Jesus Christ (2 Cor. 5:11).

It is a fearful thing to fall into the Hands of the Living God Who is a Consuming Fire (Heb. 10:31; Heb. 12:29).

Many don't care about God and His Christ because they don't know what lies ahead of them. If their eyes are opened to see 10% of what they will suffer for ignoring God and His Word, they will run for their lives to save themselves from Him Who can destroy both body and soul in Hell Fire.

Whether you know of it or not, great punishment is coming on you for despising God, for he that dishonours God, God will dishonour him also (1 Sam. 2:30).

If you love the Lord, then keep His Commandments: as a proof that you love Him (Jn 14:15). Love is the Great Commandment: loving God and your fellow human beings.

WARNINGS FROM THE LORD

To please God, you must bear fruits in your life. You must bear the Fruit of the Spirit which is in all goodness, righteousness, and truth (Eph. 5:9-10). The Fruit of the Spirit finds out what pleases the Lord.

The Fruit is love, joy, peace, longsuffering, kindness, goodness, faithfulness, gentleness, self-control. Against such there is no Law (Gal. 5:22-23). You must live the life of holiness and obedience to God.

Another area you must bear fruit is in the area of soulwinning. He who wins souls is wise and shall shine like stars forever. God had only One Son and He made Him a Soulwinner; but many parents will rather have it that their children are doctors, lawyers, engineers, accountants, business directors, and university-professors.

Well, in your own life, you must win souls for the Lord Jesus Christ, for that is why He died. Build your spirit up by the Word, by training, and by prayer, even praying in the Holy Spirit.

Walking by faith pleases God, for the righteous shall live by faith. We walk by faith and not by sight (2 Cor. 5:7). God called Abraham out of his father's place, and he obeyed God and went, not knowing where he was going to, because he believed God and walked by faith.

Thomas told the other apostles that he will never believe that Jesus Christ has risen until he sees Him by himself. That is not faith and it displeases God. Renew your mind with God's Word and live according to the Word.

To please God, you must not love your life to death. The Saints overcame the devil by the Blood of the Lamb and by the Word of their Testimony, and they did not love their lives to the death (Rev. 12:11).

You have not yet resisted to bloodshed striving against sin (Heb. 12:4). If you love any person or your own life more than Jesus Christ, you are not worthy of Him. You must take up your cross daily and follow Him (Lk. 9:23). Find out the Will of God for your life and follow it; don't compete with others.

To please God and make Him proud of you as He was proud of Job, you must not love the world or anything in the world. He who loves the world does not have the Love of the Father in him.

The things that are in the world are: the lust of flesh, the lust of the eyes, and the pride of life. The world will pass away with its entire works, but he who does the Will of God abides forever (1 Jn 2:15-17). What is there in the world that a Christian should envy?

Brethren, you have been called to liberty; only do not use your liberty as an opportunity for the flesh, but through love serve one another. Walk in the Spirit and you shall not fulfill the lust of the flesh.

For the flesh lusts against the Spirit, and the Spirit against the flesh; and these are contrary to one another, so that you do not do the things that you wish. But if you are led by the Spirit, you are not under the Law.

Now, the works of the flesh are evident, which are: adultery, fornication, uncleanness, lewdness, idolatry, sorcery, hatred, contentions, jealousies, outbursts of wrath, selfish ambitions, dissensions, and heresies.

The list continues with: envy, murders, drunkenness, revelries, and the like; of which the Bible declares that those who practice such things will not inherit the Kingdom of God (Gal. 5:13-21).

Let no corrupt word proceed out of your mouth, but what is good for necessary edification, that it may impart grace to the hearers. And do not grieve the Holy Spirit of God, by Whom you were sealed for the Day of Redemption.

Let all bitterness, wrath, anger, clamour, and evil speaking be put away from you, with all malice (Eph. 4:29-32). Crucify your flesh and its desires.

Be kind to one another, tenderhearted, forgiving one another, even as God in Christ forgave you. Therefore be imitators of God as dear children; walk in love.

But fornication and all uncleanness or covetousness, let it not even be named among you, as is fitting for Saints; neither filthiness, nor foolish talking nor coarse jesting, which are not fitting, but rather giving of thanks.

For this you know, that no fornicator, unclean person, nor covetous man, who is an idolater, has any inheritance in the Kingdom of Christ and of God.

Let no one deceive you with empty words, for because of these things the Wrath of God comes upon the sons of disobedience. Therefore do not be partakers with them (Eph. 5:1-7). Set your mind on things Above, not on things on the earth. When Christ Who is our Life appears, then you also will appear with Him in Glory.

Therefore, put to death your members which are on the earth: fornication, uncleanness, passion, evil desire, and covetousness. Put off all these things: anger, wrath, blasphemy, filthy language out of your mouth.

Do not lie to one another, since you have put off the old man with his deeds, and have put on the new man. Put on tender mercies, kindness, humility, meekness, longsuffering, bearing with one another, and forgiving one another.

To please God, you must remove pride, because pride goes before destruction. Be humble always, because God resists the proud, but gives grace to the humble. Learn to praise God always; worship and thank God, for He is worthy of our praise.

The Will of God in Christ Jesus for us is that we bring glory to Him. No matter how bad the surrounding circumstances may look like, praise and worship Him. God seeks those who will worship Him in spirit and in truth.

Renew your mind so that you can think and judge the Way God thinks and judges. If Enoch, Noah, Abraham, Elijah, Elisha, Samuel, Moses, Joshua, Caleb, Jeremiah, Daniel, Jesus Christ, Peter, John, Paul, and others could please God, you too can.

Can the Lord describe you as a burning and shining light as He described John the Baptist? John was described thus because he did what God called him to do effectively; he did not love the world, but lived a separated life.

The period you spent not pleasing God is a wasted period, and the years you spent not pleasing God are wasted years. Remember that there is a Crown of Righteousness to be given to those who please God at the Coming of the Lord.

The Word of God is our reference point to know what pleases Him. Prove all things. Don't walk and live according to your senses and reasoning!

As you please God, you are laying up treasures in Heaven, and nothing can happen to any treasure you store in Heaven. However, strive to endure to the end, so that no one takes your crown and reward.

It is the Lord Who works in you, both to will and to do according to His Will and Good Pleasure. It is not of him who runs, nor of him who wills; however, it is of the Lord who shows mercy. Therefore, be careful to give Him all the glory. You could become nothing without Jesus Christ. Life outside Jesus Christ is a mess.

One may plant, while another may water. But it is the Lord that makes His Work to grow. Therefore, both he who plants and he who waters are nothing; the One that should receive the glory is the Lord that makes His Work (the seed) to grow. And it is Him Who also gives seed to the planter, strength to the one who waters, and life to both of them.

Do not walk, sit, or stand among sinners. This is not to say that you will avoid them completely, for then, you will have to leave this world. Don't be unequally yoked together with unbelievers.

Remember that evil company corrupts good manners. Of course, you must have to preach to them so that they may be saved. Don't be an accomplice to their evil deeds.

Your number one enemy to pleasing God is your flesh, and not the devil, the world, or anything else. Therefore, if you can subdue your flesh and its passions, you will do well in every area. If you do that and discipline yourself, then you are already a champion, because you cannot fail!

The devil has used films to corrupt the world so much. Even some so-called Christian films are not directed by the Word of God and the Spirit of God. You see a lot of nudity in many of those films, and they corrupt your mind. You may call them home-movies, but it makes no difference.

Have you not observed that even when people want to do advertisement of their products, they use seductive pictures to attract people's attention? Some of them don't know what they are doing, but many of them are conscious of what they are doing, because agents of the kingdom of darkness are out to corrupt people's minds as they pass the roads.

Many spend their time in pornographic sites in the internet. Some websites will bring those seductive and destructive pictures to you by 'force' once you log in there. Many spend many hours watching films, but how long do they spend reading their Bibles and praying? Satan has destroyed many children and adults through films and movies.

The Bible says that it is not he that approves himself that is approved but whom the Lord approves (2 Cor. 10:18). It is not him that men approve that is approved, but whom the Lord approves. Do you know that a group of Christians may approve you, and yet God will not approve you?

This is why you should not seek the praise of men, but the Praise of God. To seek the approval of men is death, but to seek the Approval of God is life. Of course, if you do the right thing, good people will approve you and that is good.

When you please God, He will approve you. Enoch walked with God and pleased Him, and God approved him and took him away that he did not see death (Gen. 5:24; Heb. 11:5). Moses pleased God and received the testimony that he was faithful in all his house (Heb. 3:2).

Joshua and Caleb pleased God, and while the other adults that left Egypt with them died, two of them entered the land of Canaan. Daniel, Shadrach, Meshach and Abed-Nego pleased God when they refused to defile themselves, and God blessed them exceedingly in the land of Babylon.

The Word of God says that we should be diligent (King James Bible says, 'study') to show ourselves approved to God, workmen that need not be ashamed, rightly dividing (that is, correctly handling) the Word of God, the Word of Truth (2 Tim. 2:15).

This means that to be approved, you must be diligent, having made the decision. Approval by God requires sacrifice and self-discipline.

Ask yourself if you know what God wants you to be doing or to do. If you know, are you doing it? Have you done it? If you are doing it, are you doing it (did you do it) the Lord's Way?

Doing what God wants you to do the Lord's Way is what gets you His Total Approval. Don't settle for God's Permissive Will; go for His Perfect Will.

The minister that God will approve must be prayerful. It is said that prayer is the master-key. Jesus Christ prayed well during His Earthly Ministry and that was why He could fulfil God's Assignment for Him. Through prayer, He was able to know God's Will for His Life and was able to do it.

Jesus Christ prayed daily and His ministers must pray daily too. Don't pray well some days, and be prayerless the others. Maintain a consistent prayer-life. I think every minister should spend a minimum of two hours in prayer everyday.

The minister that God will approve should be full of the Word of God. No wonder the Word of God tells us to study to show ourselves approved to God, a workman that needs not be ashamed, rightly dividing the Word of Truth (2 Tim. 2:15).

Let the Word of Christ dwell in you richly in all wisdom (Col. 3:16). It has to dwell in you richly, and not just by manageable measure. Also, it must be in all wisdom: the Word of God says that we should rightly divide the Word of God and compare Scripture with Scripture (1 Cor. 2:13).

Apostle Paul told Timothy to preach the Word, to be instant in season and out of season. Timothy was to reprove, rebuke, exhort with all longsuffering and Doctrine (2 Tim. 4:2).

Timothy was to put the brethren in remembrance of good teaching to be a good minister of Jesus Christ, nourished up in the Words of Faith and of Good Doctrine, which he had attained (1 Tim. 4:6). He was to give attention to reading, to exhortation, to Doctrine (1 Tim. 4:13).

It is the Word that saves, sanctifies, and builds up. To be approved by God, you are to preach the message that works: you are to preach Jesus Christ, and not yourself. The message that works is the preaching and teaching of the Word of God, and not philosophy, psychology, and things of unbelief, doubt, and human wisdom.

If the Lord is going to approve you, you must do what you preach and teach. Don't be like the Pharisees who would say one thing and do the contradictory thing. God hates hypocrisy. Whatever may be hidden now will be brought to light at the Coming of the Lord Jesus Christ.

Ask God to give you the grace to practice what you preach. You have to be an example to the Believers and to your followers (1 Tim. 4:12). Let not God's Name be blasphemed for your sake (Rom. 2:24).

The Lord Jesus Christ tells us that we are to be doing the works that He did, even greater works (Jn 14:12). The Works of Jesus Christ include: preaching, teaching, healing, casting out devils, miracles, signs, and wonders.

Don't be afraid of the devil and his works because you are sitting with Christ at the Right Hand of God (Eph. 2:6). You have the power and authority to trample on serpents, scorpions, and all the power of the enemy, and nothing shall by any means hurt you (Lk. 10:19).

You must be holy, for the Lord is holy (1 Pet. 1:15). Be perfect as your Father in Heaven is perfect (Matt. 5:48). Be dedicated to God in absolute obedience and consecration. Jesus Christ came to save us from the power of sin and the effects of sin.

God may tell you to do a difficult thing, but never an impossible thing. His Commands are not grievous and burdensome (1 Jn 5:3). God's Yoke is easy and His Burden is light (Matt. 11:30). God will bless you abundantly if you are obedient to Him.

The minister that God is going to approve must be led by the Spirit of God. As many as are led by the Spirit of God, these are the sons of God (Rom. 8:14). Don't be like the horse that will run faster than is necessary; and don't be like the mule that will need to be pulled to move as needed (Psa. 32:9).

Be sensitive to the Holy Spirit's Promptings and Witness. He will teach you all things and show you things to come (Jn 14:26; Jn 16:13). He will remind you of what you had learned and known (Jn 14:26). It is not by power nor by might, but by the Spirit of God (Zech. 4:6).

The Word of God says that we are to prove all things, and hold on to the good (1 Thes. 5:21). Believe not all spirits, but test the spirits whether they are God's, for many false prophets have gone into the world (1 Jn 4:1).

Beware of the ministers you relate with, because evil company corrupts good manners (1 Cor. 15:33). Don't try to help God, and never try to get a substitute to God's Power and Blessings.

Patiently, wait on God for His Appointed Time. Don't be associated with demons, for whatever they offer is worthless.

If you want God to approve you, then you must be blameless, a husband of one wife, temperate, sober-minded, of good behaviour, hospitable, apt to preach and teach, not given to wine, not violent, not greedy for money, but gentle, not quarrelsome, not covetous.

You should rule your own house well, having your children in submission with all reverence. You must not be a novice, and you should have a good testimony among those who are outside (1 Tim. 3:2-7).

For God to approve you, you must be reverent, not double-tongued. You must hold the mystery of the faith with a pure conscience. Even, your wife ought to be reverent, not slanderer, temperate, faithful in all things (1 Tim. 3:8).

I used 'ought to' instead of 'must' for the minister's wife because the devil is fighting many ministers through their wives and trying to suppress their Christian lives and ministries through them. The wives of many of them are the ways they are, because many of them don't know how to handle them.

Of course, many ministers married before they were born again and their wives have refused to be born again also. But even believing wives are not exempted.

Of course, the King James Version italicized the word 'must,' showing that it is not in the original text, but was added for a better understanding. Take authority over your wife and break the power of the enemy over her life in the Name of Jesus Christ and you will see a change.

This is why a minister should not depend on physical appearance to marry someone. Pray well and depend on the Holy Spirit. That is not to say that your God-given wife may not give you headache.

As a matter of fact, God can allow your wife to trouble you (though the trouble was induced by the devil) to train you the way He wants to. But He will be there always to help you overcome.

The Christians and the ministers are responsible for many of the things we accuse satan and the unbelievers of. The work of the devil is to kill, steal, and destroy, while our work is to stop and destroy the works of the devil; if we don't do our part, the devil will succeed, and God will hold us responsible.

An unbeliever who dies in sin will be punished, but the Christian who refused to preach to him will be held responsible.

There is nothing like being approved by God. When God approves you, you can be sure of Heaven; and you will inherit the Kingdom of Heaven with great rewards.

Don't seek the praise of men, but do every thing you can to please God. If you are sure that God is moving you this way, then go the very way and it will be well with your soul.

From the Life of Jesus Christ, we learn that we should make prayer our priority; we also learn that we should submit ourselves to the Will of God, no matter the cost. From the life of Apostle Paul, we learn that if you sell yourself out to God to do His Will, you will go through severe trials and persecutions.

From the life of Moses, we learn that how you end is more important than how you started. The Old Testament heroes and heroines of faith, and the early New Testament Disciples and ministers left us a rich inheritance of examples to emulate.

Being approved by God is not in titles or names. You can be famous among Believers and yet not be approved by God. You can go by such titles as, 'pope,' 'archbishop,' 'bishop,' 'reverend,' 'apostle,' 'prophet,' 'evangelist,' 'pastor,' 'senior apostle,' 'prophetic evangelist,' 'reverend (doctor),' and the rest, and still not be approved by God.

Actually, some people assume someone took a particular title because of pride, but it is not always like that. By the way, ministry is not in names, but titles can help define your ministry and keep you focused.

Someone may use a big title and not be proud, while someone with a seemingly lesser title may be proud. Do you know that someone can even be proud to be humble without people's knowledge?

God is interested in our continuance with what He has called us to do. Many times, we obey God, but we don't continue with it. Sometimes, we may stop doing the right thing because we do not see the results we expect immediately. But be courageous because God's Word can never fail, though it may tarry.

Never leave your first love, and never stop doing your first works. Continue in them because, it is by forbearance that you inherit the promise.

It is him that endures to the end that will be saved. God is not a man and does not judge as men judge. You may be rich and holy in people's eyes, while before God, you are poor and corrupt.

If a sinner forsakes his sins and does righteousness, none of his sins will be remembered; rather, he will be remembered for his present righteousness.

Likewise, if a righteous man forsakes his righteousness and does evil and wickedness, none of his righteousness will be remembered; rather, he will die and suffer for his present sins and wickedness.

Whenever God calls you, follow Him. Whatever He tells you to do, do it. However the Lord tells you to do what He wants you to do, do it that way.

God knows better than any man, and He is more dependable than any other. Do not be wise in your own eyes, but trust in the Lord and do the right things.

As a leader, there are steps you must take. Remember that many are looking up to you, and if you fall and fail, they may fall and fail too. Follow the pathway to leadership to lead effectively. When you lead effectively, God will approve you and reward you abundantly.

Speak whatever the Lord has commanded you to speak, and don't be afraid. You have been called for rooting out and planting, pulling down and building up. None shall prevail against you. Neither devil nor man can stop you from doing what the Lord has commissioned you to do for Him, if you keep in pace with God.

Remember Lot's wife. She turned to a pillar of salt because she disobeyed the Commandment given to them. Who knows whether she looked back because she called to remembrance the much wealth they left behind! But life is more important than riches.

No one who puts his hand to the plough and looks back is fit for service in the Kingdom of God. Sit down and count the cost of being a Christian; consider the reward for obedience and the punishment for disobedience.

Never Say That God Said What He Did Not Say!

BEING FRUITFUL AND PRODUCTIVE

God wants us to be fruitful, and to produce the expected results. One area we should be fruitful in is in winning of souls. Jesus Christ is the True Vine and we are the branches. The Father, Who is the Vine-dresser, takes away every branch that does not bear fruit.

However, He prunes the branches that bear fruit, that they may bear more fruit. We are in Jesus Christ, and just as Jesus Christ bore Fruit by getting Followers and pleasing the Father, we too ought to win souls and please God.

Abide in Jesus Christ, and let Him abide in you. As the branch cannot bear fruit of itself, unless it abides in the vine, neither can you, unless you abide in the Lord. He who abides in Him, and He in him, bears much fruit; for without Him, you can do nothing.

Anyone who does not abide in Him is cast out as a branch and is withered and burnt. The Father is glorified when we bear much fruit, so as to confirm that we are Jesus Christ's Disciples.

If we abide in Him and His Words abide in us, we will ask what we desire, and it shall be done for us. If we keep His Commandment, we will abide and remain in His Love, just as He kept His Father's Commandments and abides in His Love.

We are His Friends if we do whatever He commands us. We did not choose Him, but He chose us and appointed us that we should go and bear fruit, and that our fruit should remain, that whatever we ask the Father in His Name He may give us (Jn 15).

For us to be fruitful and productive requires that we have patience, endurance, and longsuffering. Just as different crops and trees take different periods to mature and produce fruits, so is the Christian life and the ministry.

Therefore be patient, brethren, until the Coming of the Lord. See how the farmer waits for the precious fruit of the earth, waiting patiently for it until it receives the early and the latter rain (Jas 5:7).

Jesus Christ says that if we are ashamed of Him and His Word, especially before this sinful and adulterous generation, He Himself will be ashamed of us before His Father (Mk 8:38). If we confess Him before men, He will also confess us before His Heavenly Father and before the holy angels (Matt. 10:32-33).

Those who are wise shall shine like the brightness of the firmament, and those who turn many to righteousness like the stars forever and ever (Dan. 12:3). We must strive to win souls for the Lord no matter the cost.

Giving all diligence, add to your faith virtue, to virtue knowledge, to knowledge self-control, to self-control perseverance, to perseverance Godliness, to Godliness brotherly kindness, and to brotherly kindness love.

For if these things are in you and abound, you will be neither barren nor unfruitful in the knowledge of our Lord Jesus Christ. For he who lacks these things is short-sighted, even to blindness, and has forgotten that he was cleansed from his old sins.

Therefore, brethren, be even more diligent to make your call and election sure; for if you do these things, you will never stumble; for so you will be abundantly allowed to enter the Kingdom of Christ (2 Pet. 1:5-11).

Apostle Paul, writing to the Galatians, spoke of what Apostle Peter said in another way. The Book of Galatians speaks of what the Bible translators translated as the Fruit of the Spirit (Gal. 5:22), even though it is actually 'the fruit of the spirit (the human spirit).'

It is talking about what the recreated human spirit (by the Help of the Holy Spirit) produces. The fruit of the human spirit by the Holy Spirit is love, joy, peace, longsuffering, kindness, goodness, faithfulness, gentleness, self-control. Against such there is no Law (Gal. 5:22-23).

As you were once darkness, but now you are light in the Lord, walk as children of light (for the Fruit of the Spirit is in all goodness, righteousness, and truth), finding out what is acceptable to the Lord.

And have no fellowship with the unfruitful works of darkness, but rather expose them (Eph. 5:8-11). And those who are Christ's have crucified the flesh with its passions and desires. If we live in the Spirit, let us also walk in the Spirit (Gal. 5:24-25).

Father Abraham started as one person; God called him and as he believed God and obeyed Him, God multiplied him into a multitude as innumerable as the stars and as uncountable as the sand by the sea-shore (Heb. 11:12).

And today we are part of the offspring of Abraham through Jesus Christ. God will make great things out of anyone who trusts Him and does His Will.

Jesus Christ came alone, He followed God's Plan for His Life, and before He left for Heaven, He had got the twelve apostles and many other strong Disciples. Today, we are part of the Believers in Him; we are part of His Body (the Church) and the number of the sons brought to glory increases day by day.

This was made possible because He laid down His Life for the salvation of many. When you sacrifice for the Lord, and deny your body of its pleasures (as the Spirit leads), you can't be an ordinary person.

The early apostles and Disciples multiplied greatly, and that was God's Will for them. Apostle Peter's first preaching brought about three thousand souls to the Lord Jesus Christ. Another preaching brought more souls (in thousands) to repentance (Acts 2:41; Acts 4:4).

The story became the same as the days went by and the number of the Disciples multiplied greatly in Jerusalem and many of the priests were obedient to the faith (Acts 6:7). Even when serious persecutions came, the Disciples preached wherever they went.

You must preach the Word (the Gospel), in season and out of season; reprove, rebuke, exhort with all longsuffering and Doctrine (2 Tim. 4:2). If you are ashamed of Jesus Christ and His Gospel, He will also be ashamed of you.

If you confess Him before men, He also will confess you before His Father and before the holy angels (Lk. 9:26). God will reward you abundantly if you win souls, because Jesus Christ gave up His Life for that purpose.

In every area of your life, be fruitful and productive. Be fruitful and productive: spirit, soul, and body. God told Adam to be fruitful and multiply and replenish the earth.

That is still His Will for today: in finance, in health, in academics, in job, in ministry. Once you have found out God's Perfect Will for your life, work towards it and show God that He has not invested in you in vain, and He will be glad.

Fight the good fight of faith, lay hold on Eternal Life. Flee evil things and pursue righteousness, Godliness, faith, love, patience, gentleness (1 Tim. 6:11-12).

Let no one despise you, but be an example to the Believers in word, in conduct, in love, in spirit, in faith, in purity. Do not neglect the gift that is in you. Meditate on these things; give yourself entirely to them, that your progress may be evident to all.

Take heed to yourself and to the Doctrine. Continue in them, for in doing this, you will save both yourself and those who hear you (1 Tim. 4:12-16).

You must discipline your body and bring it to subjection in order to obey God and fulfil His Purpose for your life. Run so as to obtain: if people who take part in games train hard to excel, how much more you whose engagement and investment is eternal?

Love not the world or anything in the world. Without holiness, no eye shall see the Lord (Heb. 12:14). God is of a Purer Eyes than to behold iniquity (Habk. 1:13); and only the pure in heart shall see Him.

If God turned His Face away from Jesus Christ, as He hung on the Cross carrying the sins of the whole world, who are you that God will compromise His Standards? Be holy for the Lord is holy.

And if you call on the Father, Who without partiality judges according to each one's work, conduct yourselves throughout the time of your stay here in fear (1 Pet. 1:16-17). Work out your salvation with fear and trembling, for God is no respecter of persons.

Daniel and his friends feared God and God promoted them and delivered them. The Eyes of the Lord run to and fro the face of the earth to show Himself strong on behalf of anyone, who will believe Him, obey Him and cooperate with Him. With God, nothing shall be impossible.

The Church is marching on and the gates of Hades shall not prevail against it. The Letters that the Lord wrote to the seven Churches tell us what He expects from us, how some of us are, and the reward He has for us.

Break up your fallow ground, and do not sow among thorns. Stop procrastination and do what you are supposed to do now. Don't wait for tomorrow, for you don't know what tomorrow will bring forth.

WARNINGS FROM THE LORD

A HEAVEN TO GAIN AND A HELL TO AVOID

Heaven and Hell are real. I know many people don't believe in them. Some believe in literal Heaven but not in literal Hell. Some believe that Heaven and Hell are in this world; what a pity! Many think that a Loving God Who is full of mercy cannot throw someone into Hell Fire.

However, they might have not considered the fact that He is not only a Consuming Fire (Heb. 12:29), but it is also a fearful thing to fall into the Hands of the Living God (Heb. 10:31). God is no respecter of persons. Even though He is full of mercy, He is also the God of Justice. God is a Loving God, Who also is a Consuming Fire.

If God's Word says that there are Heaven and Hell, then they exist. God cannot lie and does not have the ability to deceive. It is the devil that lies and deceives people.

Jesus Christ told His apostles that if there were not many mansions in His Father's House, He would have told them (Jn 14:2). He went to prepare a Place for us and when He is through, He will come back to take us with Him, so that where He is, there we may be also.

Hell was not made for mankind. Hell was made for satan and his fallen angels and demons. Hell was made for them because they rebelled against God. When man disobeyed God and rebelled against Him, he put himself into the same position as them and so was destined for Hell.

It is only Jesus Christ that can save man from Hell. If you want to avoid Hell, then you must accept Jesus Christ and live to please God.

Heaven is a very good place. It is the Abode of God. Everything in Heaven is perfect. There is neither evil, sin, nor pain in Heaven. Our tears will be wiped out in Heaven. No human word can describe the beauty of Heaven.

You must do all you can to be there. It will profit you nothing if you gain the whole world and lose your own soul (Matt. 16:26). There is no devil or demon in Heaven.

Hell, on the other hand, is a very bad place. No human word can express the horror and suffering of Hell. The suffering of Hell cannot be equated to that of this world, except you are going to use an infinite relationship.

The fire of Hell does not quench and the worms of Hell do not die (Mk 9:43-48). In Hell, there is gnashing of teeth; if you enter there, you will thirst and thirst and thirst, and there will be no water to quench your thirst.

The Kingdom Of Heaven is eternal and forever, just as Hell Fire is eternal and forever. Once you enter any of them, there is no turning back. If you enter Heaven, you will spend eternity with God, and if you enter Hell Fire, you will spend eternity with satan.

Actually, God will neither put you into Heaven nor Hell; you are the one who chooses where you will go. Your life on earth and your relationship with Jesus Christ, the Word of God, and the Spirit of God, will determine where you will spend eternity.

The Word of God declares that He will make a New Heaven and a New Earth (Isa. 65:17). The Heaven it is talking about here is not the Third Heaven where God lives and where we will be. There is a first heaven (the sky), and there is the second heaven (the planetary bodies).

The Word says that when the Lord shall come again, the heavens shall pass away with a great noise and the element shall melt with fervent heat; the earth also and the works that are there shall be burned up (2 Pet. 3:10).

Seeing that these things shall be dissolved, what manner of persons ought you to be in all holy conversation and Godliness, looking for and hastening the coming of the Day of the Lord?

WARNINGS FROM THE LORD

We, according to His Promise, look for New Heavens and a New Earth wherein righteousness dwells. Seeing that you look for such things, be diligent that you may be found by Him in peace without spot, and blameless (2 Pet. 3:11-14).

One day is with the Lord as a thousand years, and a thousand years as one day. The Lord is not slack concerning His Promise, as some men count slackness, but is longsuffering towards us, not willing that any should perish but that all should come to repentance.

But the Day of the Lord will come as a thief in the night (2 Pet. 3:8-10). Don't reason within you that the Lord will not come again since He has not come all these while.

Follow peace with all men, and holiness without which no man shall see the Lord (Heb. 12:14). It is only the pure in heart that shall see the Lord (Matt. 5:8). Make up your mind and make every effort to be holy, righteous, obedient, spotless, and blameless.

No impure thing will enter either the Kingdom of Heaven or the New Earth. Sin leads you to Hell Fire. Don't live in sin; you have no reason to serve satan.

Many have been taken to Heaven and to Hell, and they have told us what they saw. We know that their testimonies are true because the Bible says so. Apostle Paul was taken to Heaven, the Third Heaven (2 Cor. 12:2).

Apostle John was taken to both Heaven and Hell (Rev. 19 to 22). It is because of God's Love for us that He shows us things ahead of time, and warns us to labour for Heaven and to avoid Hell. Don't be foolish but understand God's Plans. Apostle John also spoke of a New Heaven and a New Earth (Rev. 21:1).

Do not lay up for yourselves treasures upon the earth, where moth and rust do destroy, and where thieves break through and steal.

But lay up for yourselves treasures in Heaven, where neither moth nor rust do destroy, and where thieves do not break through and steal: for where your treasure is, there will your heart be also (Matt. 6:19-21).

And if either your right eye or your right hand will cause you to sin, pluck it out and cut it off, and cast them off: for it is profitable for thee that one of your members should perish than that your whole body be cast into Hell (Matt. 5:29-30).

Not everyone that calls on the Lord Jesus Christ shall enter the Kingdom of Heaven, but he that does the Will of our Heavenly Father. Many will say to the Lord in that Day, "Lord, Lord, have we not prophesied in Your Name? And in Your Name have cast out devils? And in Your Name done many wonderful works?"

And then will He say to them, "I never knew you: depart from Me, you that work iniquity" (Matt. 7:21-23). Why do you call Him, Lord, Lord, and do not do what He tells you to do? (Lk. 6:46).

The wicked shall be turned into Hell (Psa. 9:17). The way of the adulteress leads to Hell (Prov. 7:27). Because the sinners have increased themselves, Hell has enlarged itself to accommodate them (Isa. 5:14).

Do not fear them who can kill the body but are not able to kill the soul: but rather fear Him Who is able to destroy both soul and body in Hell (Matt. 10:28).

The story (not a parable, because Jesus Christ said, "There was a certain rich man...") of the rich man and Lazarus gives us an insight into the suffering of Hell (Lk. 16:19-31).

God took Enoch and Elijah to Heaven so that they did not see death because they pleased God. God's Presence fills the Heaven and the earth. If your name is written in the Book of Life, in Heaven, rejoice.

Heaven cannot be compared to anything on this earth. If all the gold, the silver, the oil, and whatever there is, are combined together and given to one person, they will not compare to the bliss of Heaven. The gold of Heaven is pure gold.

It is not the Will of God that any soul should perish but that all should come to repentance (2 Pet. 3:9). He would have all men to be saved. However, God will not force anyone: He has set before men good and bad, life and death, Heaven and Hell.

Men choose what they want and God implement them. You cannot run away from God; you cannot hide yourself from Him. Today is the acceptable time, the day of salvation (2 Cor. 6:2).

Don't say that you will change your ways tomorrow, because tomorrow may be too late. Your life is like a vapour that vanishes and a flower that withers easily (Jas 1:11; Jas 4:14). The Mill of God grinds so slowly, but it grinds so small.

Keep on doing good, and don't faint; God will surely reward you at last. He who is unjust, let him be unjust still; he who is filthy, let him be filthy still; he who is righteous, let him be righteous still; he who is holy, let him be holy still.

Behold, the Lord is coming quickly, and His Reward is with Him, to give to everyone according to his work. Are you ready for the Lord's Coming?

Be faithful till death and you can never lose anything. Whatever you may lose in this life, the Lord will replace for you many folds. He who finds his life will lose it, but he who loses his life for the Lord will save it. God knows everything about you, including your works of faith: the things you do for His Name.

The Bible says that if our hope in Christ is only in this world, we are of all men the most miserable (1 Cor. 15:19). Do you understand that?

It means that if the reason you are a Christian, if the reason you serve God is because of what He would do for you in this life only, you are miserable. No wonder the Bible says that if you gain the whole world and lose your soul, you profited nothing (Lk. 9:25; Mk 8:36).

What shall a man give in exchange for his soul? (Mk 8:37). The Lord that we serve has given us so many precious promises and inheritances both in this life and in the life to come (life after death) (1 Tim. 4:8).

If you were raised together with Christ Jesus, set your mind on things Above, and not on earthly things (Col. 3:1-2). When Christ Who is your Hope shall appear, you will reign with Him in Glory (Col. 3:4). The Word of God says that where your treasure is, is where your heart will be also (Matt. 6:21).

This is one reason you should labour for Christ. You should evangelize and win souls to the Kingdom of God. If you are ashamed of Jesus Christ and refuse to confess Him before men, He will be ashamed of you also when He will appear in Glory with His holy angels (Lk. 9:26).

If you are afraid that you will be persecuted or killed for preaching Jesus Christ, that means that you love your life more than Him. In that case, the Lord says that you are not worthy of Him (Lk. 14:26).

When many people come to church for healing, they are not interested in other things but the healing they need. They would want you to stop all other things so as to attend to them.

Whether you, as a pastor is talking about commitment, dedication, holiness, righteousness, prayer, the study of the Word, or whatever, you are on your own to them. All they want is for you to finish your preaching or teaching and give them their healing so that they can go.

God has given us and will give us so many good things. Every good and perfect gift comes from Above (Heaven); it comes from the Father (Jas 1:17). His Divine Power has given us all things we need for life and Godliness through our knowledge of Him Who has called us by His Power and Glory (2 Pet. 1:3-4).

The earth is the Lord's and all its fulness (Psa. 24:1). Silver and gold are His; even a thousand cattle by the hills belong to our God (Hag. 2:8).

There is nothing the Lord cannot give you. There is nothing that is impossible, either to God or with God. 'To God' because He has the Ability to do all things, having created the whole universe by His Word and Power (Gen.1).

'With God' because nothing is impossible to him that co-operates with God, to him who believes and does what God tells him to do (Mk 10:27). However, never you put the blessing before the Blesser.

Many go to the wrong churches, ministries, and ministers, because they are seeking for miracles instead of the God that works miracles.

Even when the Spirit of God may be prompting them and witnessing in their spirits that they are either in the wrong places or going to the wrong places, they do not pay attention to Him because they are following their minds that are bent on having what they want.

How can a pastor allow people to dress anyhow they want to his church if he doesn't have a hidden agenda? People wear mini-skirts and seductive dresses to some churches and the pastor tells them that it doesn't matter.

The men in the churches are seduced and lured into lust and fornication, and the atmosphere becomes non-conducive for the Spirit of God to operate, and the pastor is not touched. Beware of such pastors, prophets, and ministers.

What many people don't know is that many preachers and ministers are serving the interest of satan instead of that of God. Some do it without their conscious knowledge, while others do it consciously.

There are many satanic and occult churches, ministries, and ministers in the world today. Does this marvel you? You shouldn't be marveled because the Bible tells us that satan masquerades or poses as an angel of light when, in fact, he is the angel of darkness (2 Cor. 11:13-15).

It is, therefore, no big thing if his ministers come as ministers of Christ. In the Book of Revelation, the Lord Jesus Christ commended the Ephesian Church because the false apostles that claimed that they were apostles of Christ were tested by them and found out to be liars, fake, and impostors (Rev. 2:2).

The Word of God tells us to prove all things and to hold on to that which is good and true (1 Thes. 5:21). We are to test every spirit (1 Jn 4:1).

The issue is that no matter what you may receive from God, if you don't spend eternity with God, you lost everything. The Bible speaks of the children of the Kingdom of God being cast out to the Outer Darkness (Matt. 8:12).

These were people who were meant for Heaven, but because of sin and disobedience, they didn't make it. Because they wanted to please their fleshly passions, they were disapproved.

No wonder the man of God, Apostle Paul, after having been in the ministry for many years and having done mighty exploits through the Name of Jesus Christ and by the Power of the Holy Spirit of the Living God, still said that he beat his body and brought his body under subjection, so that after preaching to others, he will not be disqualified (1 Cor. 9:27).

Our hope in Christ Jesus is mainly in the life to come. No matter what He gives you or is able to give you, don't set your mind on them. God is able to give you healing and health; He is able to give you job and money.

The Lord will give you admission into institutions of learning so that you will obtain the certificates and qualifications that you want. Do you need children, wife, or husband? It is a small thing with God. He is able to do exceeding abundantly above all you can ask or imagine (Eph. 3:20).

"Ride on, pastor!" That statement or something like that is heard in churches often. However, the apostle, the prophet, the evangelist, the pastor, or the teacher is not the Judge. The Judge is the Lord Jesus Christ. He has said that you must be changed by His Word and His Spirit (Jn 3:5).

He has given you the Bible; and He told you that His Word (the Bible) will judge you on that Day (Jn 12:48). The Lord Jesus Christ says that the proof of the love you have for Him is that you obey Him (Jn 14:15).

His Commandments are not burdensome (1 Jn 5:3). They are meant to make you, and not to mar you. Why do you call Him, Lord, Lord, and do not do what He says? (Lk. 6:46). Only those who do the Will of the Father will enter the Kingdom of Heaven (Matt. 7:21).

God is no respecter of persons (Acts 10:34). Our God is a Consuming Fire, and it is a fearful thing to fall into His Hands (Heb. 10:31).

Make up your mind that whatever it takes, you are going to please God. You have not resisted to bloodshed, striving against sin (Heb. 12:4).

If your right eye will lead you to Hell, pluck it out; for it is better to enter the Kingdom of Heaven with one eye than to land into Hell with full body (Matt. 5:29).

BEING STRONG IN THE LORD

The Church is marching on, and the gates of Hades shall not prevail! Be strong in the Lord and in the power of His Might (Eph. 6:10). This is a Command which the Lord has given to us. If the Lord has commanded us to be strong in Him, then we must obey Him and do just that.

How do we get strong in the Lord? There are many ways to get strong in the Lord, but we will start with the way that is given to us in the same chapter, and that is by putting on the whole Armour of God.

Armour is a defensive weapon; this is why we talk of armoured cars or vehicles in warfare. But looking at the armour we are given, we notice that one of them is an offensive weapon, and that is the Word of God, which the Bible calls 'the Sword of the Spirit' (Eph. 6:17).

There are many more offensive weapons we use and can use in our spiritual warfare. You know that we do not war against flesh and blood but against spiritual entities. The weapons we fight with are not carnal but mighty through God to the pulling down of strongholds (2 Cor. 10:4).

Other weapons (defensive and offensive) that we will consider include: the Name of Jesus Christ, the Blood of Jesus Christ, the Fire of the Holy Spirit, the anointing, speaking in tongues, praises, fasting, etc.

God showed me, by revelation, that certain situations require certain weapons; therefore, don't expect to use only particular ones and say that others are not necessary. I might have thought the same way, but God showed me otherwise.

One mighty weapon to use in our Christian life and spiritual warfare is the weapon of obedience. We will be able to punish every act of disobedience when our own obedience is complete (2 Cor. 10:6).

Absolute obedience to God is holiness. Obedience is better than sacrifice and self-denial (1 Sam. 15:22).

According to the sixth chapter of the Book of Ephesians, we should be strong in the Lord and in the power of His Might. We should put on the whole Armour of God that we may be able to stand against the wiles of the devil.

For we wrestle not against flesh and blood, but against principalities, against powers, against the rulers of the darkness of this age, against spiritual hosts of wickedness in the heavenly places.

Therefore, take up the whole Armour of God, that you may be able to withstand in the evil day, and having done all, to stand.

We are to gird our waist with the belt of truth. It is the belt that holds your armour or wears together. The Word of God is the Word of Truth. The Word speaks of sanctification by the Word which is truth (Jn 17:17).

The Word of God cleanses us as we hear it (Jn 15:3). We are to rightly divide the Word of God (2 Tim. 2:15). To rightly divide the Word of Truth is to interpret the Word aright. It is to put Scripture where it belongs; and the Bible speaks of comparing Scripture with Scripture (1 Cor. 2:13).

Let the Word dwell in you richly in all wisdom (Col. 3:16). The belt of truth is a clear understanding of the Word of God.

Then, we should put on the breastplate of righteousness. The breastplate of righteousness protects your heart, your spirit, for your heart is located around your breast or chest. When we believed on the Lord Jesus Christ, we received the gift of righteousness from Him, which gave us a right-standing with God.

But the Bible says that he who does righteousness is righteous as Jesus Christ is righteous. If you commit sin, if you live in sin, you are of the devil (1 Jn 3:8). Righteousness is doing right; it is doing the good that you ought to do (Jas 4:17).

Then comes the shoeing of our feet with the preparation of the Gospel of Peace. It is the Gospel, the Good News of the Kingdom that brings peace to men; therefore, preach the Gospel, the Word of God, in season and out of season (2 Tim. 4:2).

Follow peace with all men (Heb. 12:14). Inasmuch as it lies with you, live peaceably with all (Rom. 12:18). Don't allow strife, envy, quarrels, and contentions into your life.

You must take the shield of faith with which you will be able to quench all the fiery darts of the wicked one. The devil throws many wicked arrows at us, and it is only faith that can protect us.

Faith is the assurance of things hoped for, the evidence of things not seen (Heb. 11:1). Faith comes by hearing and hearing by the Word of God (Rom. 10:17). Therefore, faith is being convinced of, being sure of the Word of God.

When you have faith, you are confident that your Almighty God will do for you what He says He will do for you.

Also, take the helmet of salvation. The Word speaks of the hope of salvation which shall be revealed in the Last Day (1 Thes. 5:8). It is the helmet that will protect your head; if your head is not protected, you may as soon become a dead man.

Many are walking around as Christians while they are already dead. In this age where evil abounds, it is your salvation, which is the hope of the Glory that shall be revealed when Christ comes, that will protect you.

Without such hope, your love will grow cold and you will backslide. But it is only those who endure to the end that shall be saved (Matt. 24:13).

Take the Sword of the Spirit which is the Word of God. The Sword of the Spirit is the offensive declaration and confession of the Word of God with your mouth.

As you speak the right Scriptures, in the spiritual realm, the Word you speak come out of your mouth as sword, piercing the devil. The Word of God comes out of your mouth as fire and as hammer (Jer. 23:29).

Then you are to pray always with all prayer and supplication in the Spirit, being watchful in prayer with all perseverance and supplication for all the Saints (Eph. 6:18).

Watch and pray that you may not fall into temptation. The spirit indeed is willing, but the flesh is weak (Matt. 26:41). Have you known that prayer is one of the things that Christians find very hard to do, even though it is indispensable and should be part of our lives?

Maintain a consistent prayer-life. Add fasting to your prayer, for fasting multiplies the power of prayer many times. If you say you can't fast, even till 12:00 p.m. or 4:00 p.m. because you are pregnant or sick, the day you may have miscarriage or die, you will judge for yourself whether you are wiser than God.

Other weapons include the Name of Jesus Christ. At the Name of Jesus Christ, every knee should bow, of things (beings) in heaven, and of things (beings) on earth, and of things (beings) under the earth, and every tongue should confess that Jesus Christ is Lord, to the Glory of God the Father (Phil. 2:9-11).

The Blood of Jesus Christ protects us from the attacks of the enemy. The Blood speaks better things than the blood of Abel (Heb. 12:24). Learn to plead the Blood of Jesus Christ; it is a good attitude. However, don't plead the Blood in fear, for the hosts of Heaven are for you and with you.

The Holy Ghost's Fire is a mighty weapon that is at our disposal. Many don't believe in it. However, inasmuch as there are ways people pray which I don't like, the Lord showed me the effectiveness of the Fire of the Holy Ghost in spiritual warfare (Matt. 3:11).

The anointing is another mighty weapon of spiritual warfare, and there are different kinds and levels of the anointing. The Anointing and Power of the Holy Spirit breaks every yoke (Isa. 10:27).

Speaking in tongues is another mighty weapon. When you speak in tongues, you speak mysteries (hidden things) to God, you confuse the devil, and you pray for what you don't know of, the right way (1 Cor. 14:2; Rom. 8:26).

Praise is a weapon that scatters devils and sets confusion into the kingdom of darkness. Use it always. The last weapon we will discuss is spiritual gifts. The Manifestation of the Spirit (spiritual gift) is given to everyone for the good of all (1 Cor. 12:7). Use your own spiritual gift(s) effectively.

But to put on any armour, you must be spiritually alive and strong. First, you must be born again. Then you should be filled with the Holy Spirit, for you are endued with God's Power when you are filled. Be sensitive to the Holy Spirit and let Him lead you.

Let the fruit of the recreated human spirit (or the Fruit of the Spirit, according to the King James Version and some other versions) be abundant in you (Gal. 5:22-23). Make every effort to stand so that you will not fall.

As Christians, we are supposed to be mighty in words and deeds. When people see us, they are supposed to see Jesus Christ. God does not expect us to remain as spiritual babies, but we are to grow and mature to the fulness of the Stature of Christ Jesus. Seek to know the Lord more than before; seek God more than anything else.

Learn to praise and worship God always. The angels in Heaven worship God always. They sing, "Holy, holy, holy, Lord God Almighty..." and they fear and bow down before the Lord. Worship the Lord in the beauty of holiness. The more you praise and worship God, the more satan will run away from you.

They that know their God shall be strong, and they shall do exploits. To know your God, you have to know His Word and also know Him personally and intimately in prayer.

Knowing God will lead to your doing exploits, in signs, wonders, and miracles. You shall do the works that Jesus Christ did, even greater works than them.

Don't live the normal life that everybody lives. Dare to live extra-ordinarily. That is God's Will for you: living the extra-ordinary life. That extra-ordinary life is the supernatural life, and it transcends natural laws. It is the life by the Spirit of God; it is living by faith, and not by sight.

Faith is the substance of things hoped for, the evidence of things not seen. (Heb. 11:1). Faith is believing that God exists and that His Word is true and sure. It is being confident that what the Lord promised, He will perform without failure.

Faith is obedience to the Word of God in any area, because you believe that you are committed to obey Him as your Lord and Master. Faith is acting on the Word, taking action as directed by His Word.

But faith comes by hearing the Word of God (or as Apostle Paul put it, "Faith comes by hearing and hearing by the Word of God" (Rom. 10:17). When you hear the Gospel, the Gospel tells you that Jesus Christ suffered and died for you, and that if you receive Him, He will wash away your sins and save you.

When you submit to the Gospel, you receive faith by the Gospel (the Good News or the Word of God concerning salvation); and through the faith, you are saved when you confess Jesus Christ.

Then you don't stop at that level of the knowledge of the Word of God; you progress by hearing, reading, studying, meditating on, and confessing the Word of God; and you increase your faith through those means. The Bible says that we should be filled with the Word of Christ in all wisdom (Col. 3:16).

The Word should dwell in us richly so that our faith will be stronger. We resist the devil steadfastly in faith, and faith is our shield that protects us from all the fiery arrows of the enemy. The righteous shall live by faith.

Faith works by love (Gal. 5:6). The Word of God says that if you have all faith that you can remove mountains, but have not love, you are nothing (1 Cor. 13:2). Among faith, hope, and love, the greatest is love.

Therefore, no matter the level of faith you may be operating in, you must love: first, love God with your all, so that you can keep His Commandments; second, you must love others as yourself, so that you can do to them as you would have them do to you, as you desire they do to you.

The Word of God commands us to have faith in God (or literally, to have the Faith of God). We ought to have absolute confidence in our God, so that even if the seas roar, though the mountains may crumble, though the earth may quake, we should never be afraid, because we are confident that the Lord is with us and will shield us.

This is why we have to obey God absolutely, because it is sin and disobedience that brings guilt.

The Faith of God is the faith that calls those things that do not exist by name as though they do exist. God Who gives life to the dead and calls those things which do not exist as though they did, told Abraham that He has made him a father of many nations, when, as yet, he didn't even have a son.

But thanks to God that Abraham, contrary to hope, in hope believed, so that he became the father of many nations. And not being weak in faith, he did not consider his own body, already dead (since he was about a hundred years old), and the deadness of Sarah's womb.

He did not waver at the Promise of God through unbelief, but was strengthened in faith, giving glory to God, and being fully convinced that what He had promised He was also able to perform.

And, therefore, it was counted to him for righteousness (Rom. 4:17-22). It was through the God-kind of faith that He created the heavens and the earth. Even though they were not in existence, God declared that they should be, and they came to be.

By faith we understand that the worlds were framed by the Word of God so that the things which are seen were not made of things which are visible (Heb. 11:3).

Whoever says to this mountain, "Be removed and be cast into the sea," and does not doubt in his heart, but believes that those things he says will be done, he will have whatever he says.

Whatever things you will ask when you pray, believe that you receive them, and you will have them (Mk 11:23-24). If you have faith, and do not doubt, if you say to a mountain, "Be removed and be cast into the sea," it will be done. And whatever thing you ask in prayer, believing, you will receive (Matt. 21:21-22).

Some people have thought that Jesus Christ went about healing anyone He wanted to heal, but this is not true. Even though Jesus Christ was anointed without measure, people received their miracles both by the demonstration of the anointing upon Him, and by the exercise of their own faith.

The woman with the issue of blood, for example, received her healing by exercising her faith, and Jesus Christ told her, "Your faith has made you whole." He told another that he will receive if he had faith, for all things are possible to him that believes (Matt. 9:22; Mk 9:23).

When He came to His Own place, His people despised Him, saying, "Is this not Jesus whose parents and brethren we know?" Their unbelief prevented Jesus Christ from doing mighty works among them (Matt. 13:54-58; Mk 6:1-6).

Unbelief, doubt, sin, disobedience, and fear are obstacles to faith. You must get rid of those things if you are going to excel in the faith-life, because the righteous one will live by faith. Faith will keep you free from the arrows and plans of the devil; and without faith, you give the devil a place in your life.

Faith and works go together. Faith without works is dead, and works without faith is self-righteousness and cannot save you or fulfil God's Purpose for your life.

If you believe that God will protect you and provide for you, then you must be prayerful and learn to give; and if you fail in prayer and in giving, you will be disappointed.

You believe that there is one God. You do well. Even the demons believe and tremble! Abraham was justified by works when he offered Isaac his son on the altar, and by works faith was made perfect (Jas 2:19-22).

Your faith is activated by prayer and confession. With the heart one believes to righteousness, and with the mouth confession is made to salvation (Rom. 10:10).

Whatever you believe God can do for you, pray for that: and when you ask, you receive; when you seek, you will find; and when you knock, the door will be opened to you (Matt. 7:7). Don't joke with prayer; it is one of the most important things in your life.

There is the gift of faith which the Holy Spirit imparts to a Spirit-filled Believer to help him receive a miracle from God. It is distinguished from the gift of the working of miracles in that the working of miracles works miracles actively, while the gift of faith receives miracles passively.

When Daniel was not hurt by the lions in the den, it was the gift of faith that was in operation, but when Jesus Christ commanded the waves of the sea and the wind to cease, it was the working of miracles that was in operation. But the gift of faith is given to Believers as the Spirit of God wills.

Faith is perfected through practice. It is like taking part in athletics or sports; you have to train and practice so that you can perfect in your area and be able to win the game. It is like lifting weights; you start with lighter ones, and you progress to heavier ones.

Even though you would be able to lift heavy objects in future, you wouldn't be able to lift them at the beginning. The Lord says that if you have faith as small as the mustard seed, you can remove mountains.

The practice is not necessarily to get more faith (and you need more faith; the Bible speaks of great faith), but to strengthen and activate the faith.

The elders of old, the Saints and Servants of old, received good reports or testimonies by faith. Without faith, it is impossible to please to God, for he who comes to God must believe that He is, and that He is a Rewarder of those who diligently seek Him (Heb. 11:2,6).

Abel gave to God by faith. Noah obeyed God by faith. Moses chose to suffer affliction with the people of God than to enjoy the passing pleasures of sin, esteeming the reproach of Christ greater riches than the treasures in Egypt.

Faith purifies the heart; the Word of God which is the truth sanctifies us; by the Word, we are made clean (Acts 14:9; Jn 17:17; Jn 15:3). There is strong faith (Rom. 4:17-20). There is weak faith (Rom. 14:1). There is shipwrecked faith (1 Tim. 1:19). There is unfeigned faith (1 Tim. 1:5).

Anything not done in faith is sin (Rom. 14:23). We walk by faith, and not by sight (2 Cor. 5:7). Don't deny the faith, and don't cast off your first faith. Do not err from the faith, but earnestly contend for the faith once delivered to the Saints (Jude 1:3).

Jesus Christ is the Way, the Truth, the Life, and the Door. He is the Way to God and anything you may desire. He is the Truth, and any other thing opposed to him is fake. Jesus Christ is the Source of life for anybody who desires life. Also, He is the Door to the Treasures of God.

Never Say That God Said What He Did Not Say!

BECOMING A PRAYER-WARRIOR

Jesus Christ told us a parable to the intent that we know that men ought always to pray and not faint (Lk. 18:1). The Word of God says that we should pray without ceasing, we should pray always (1 Thes. 5:17).

We are commanded to watch to prayer (1 Pet. 4:7), and to watch and pray (Matt. 26:41). Why should we pray? Because the Word of God says that we receive when we ask, we find when we seek, and we have an open door when we knock (Matt. 7:7).

If your son asks you of bread, you do not give him a stone; if he asks of a fish, you don't give him a snake. In the same vein, if he asks for an egg, you do not think of giving him a scorpion.

If we know to give good things to our children, how much more will our Father in Heaven give good things to us? (Matt. 7:9-11; Lk. 11:11-13). Do you trust man more than God? Cursed is he that puts his trust in man instead of in God (Jer. 17:5).

God, the Maker of all things, is able to do all things. He can neither lie nor fail to perform His Word (Heb. 6:18). Instead of one thing that has gone out of the Mouth of God not to come to pass, heaven and earth shall pass away (Matt. 24:35).

Has He said it? He will do it also. This is one reason we should obey the Instruction of the Lord that we should study the Word of God (2 Tim. 2:15) and be full of it (Col. 3:16).

If you know the Word of God, you will know His Provisions for you. If you are full of God's Word, you will know your rights, privileges, and inheritances in the Kingdom.

This will make you receive from God the things that you need, and to stop the works of the devil from coming to pass in your life. You will also be able to overcome tests, trials, and temptations.

The problem is that many Believers don't pray. Many don't maintain a consistent prayer-life. Many have made many decisions and resolutions which they failed to keep.

They decided that they will pray this long or that long every day, but they went back to prayerlessness after a short while. A prayerful Christian is a powerful Christian whereas a prayerless Christian is a powerless Christian.

Of course, everybody prays; even powerless Christians pray. But God has declared that the prayer of the sinner is an abomination to Him (Prov. 15:8). If you are a sinner, if you are not born again, the prayer that God wants from you right now is the prayer of repentance and acceptance of the Lord Jesus Christ into your life as your Lord and Saviour.

He came down from Heaven, suffered, died, and resurrected again for your sins, so that you may be justified and made righteous before God (Jn 1:12; Rom. 3:24).

Why don't people pray? Many don't pray because of laziness. They sleep too much and find it easier to do many other things than to pray.

Many don't pray because they feel, on the inside of them, that it really makes no difference whether or not they pray. They say that whatever will be, will be, and whatever will not be, will not be. But that is not true; the devil has subtly told people that.

Some don't pray because of business. My own definition of business is whatever makes you busy. Your job can keep you busy; your relationship can keep you busy; even preaching can keep you so busy that you won't pray as you are supposed to.

Ignorance of God and His Ways makes people not to pray as they are supposed to. Some don't know what the Bible teaches about prayer. Some teach about prayer very well and yet don't pray.

Satanic or demonic strongholds and obsession are other factors that make people not to pray. Have you ever wondered why you start feeling sleepy and weak when you want to pray or when you are praying?

You may see someone that will start sleeping when he starts praying, but when the same person wants to watch a football match in the television, the sleep leaves him. That is demonic remote-control.

This is one reason you don't need to eat too much (or even at all) in the night. When your body feels fasted in the night, it will be easier for you to overcome sleep in the night.

Also, eat at least three hours before going to bed. This will minimize or remove the ability of demons and their human agents to make you sleep and sleep and sleep. It will also make it hard for demons to force you have the experiences that you don't like in dreams.

Some people wake up early in the morning, and instead of rising up to pray, they decide to sleep a little more and they find out that they never wake up until it is late.

Some people decide to lie down on their beds and pray, and before long, they start sleeping and end up not praying effectively. To pray effectively, you must discipline yourself. You will need to plan and implement your prayer-time.

It is one thing to pray, and it is another thing to maintain a steady prayer-life. Some people, after listening to good messages or reading books on prayer, decide that they are going to pray two, three, or more hours everyday.

Some may do it for one, two, three, or more days, and before you know it, they get back to inconsistent prayer-life. Praying long is good, but if it is one or two hours you are able to pray everyday, maintain it and make it consistent: but increase the time, as you are able.

I recommend that every Believer should pray for at least two hours everyday, but it is not specifically written in the Bible. Take a day or more to do some personal fasting. Regular fasting with prayer will make you a spiritual giant.

Prayer should be very important to you as a Christian. Jesus Christ prayed effectively and always. Apostle Paul told us to pray always and without ceasing.

There are many conditions to receiving answers to your prayers. One condition is to pray in faith (Jas 1:6-8); another is to pray without doubting and wavering; another is to pray in the Name of Jesus Christ (Jn 16:24); another is to bear fruit that will remain (Jn 15:16); still, another is to do those things that please God (1 Jn 3:22).

Of course, prayer will not work in an unforgiving heart, because if you don't forgive, God will not forgive you also, and you will be sinful when screened spiritually (Mk 11:25-26). Pray according to the Will of God (1 Jn 5:14-15).

There are other conditions, but one thing you must realize is that the bottom-line lies in the fact that what we receive from God is as a result of the Sacrifice that Jesus Christ performed for us.

It is not of him that wills nor of him that runs, but of God that shows mercy (Rom. 9:15-16). Time and chance happen to everything on earth (Eccl. 9:11). Therefore, you should wait patiently for your answer if it delays. Delay is not denial, and God knows the best for you.

This is why it is necessary you pray according to the Will of God. Prayer is not "Give me this or that" only. Prayer is talking to God and waiting for Him to speak to you also.

Don't rush out of the Presence of God. Also, learn to pray in the Holy Ghost. Pray in tongues always and everyday. The Holy Spirit helps us to pray for the right things in the right way (Rom. 8:26-27).

We are a triumphant people, a triumphant Church, and we enforce the victory that the Lord has won for us by prayer and speaking forth of words of faith.

Learn to stay alone with God, praying to Him. Wait on God patiently. Speak to God and allow Him speak to you by listening and being quiet before the Lord.

Satan is afraid of the Gifts of the Holy Spirit; satan is afraid of good preaching and right teaching; yet, satan fears prayer more than all of them. It is prayer that holds all these things together and makes them effective.

Without prayer, even your spiritual activities will fail, be unproductive, or be less productive. Yet, remember that fasting increases the power and effectiveness of prayer many folds.

Prayer is very powerful, and we have to pray always with all kinds of prayer. The effectual fervent prayer of the righteous avails much and is powerful. Prayer is a force that many have refused to use, even though it is within their reach. Men of all ages and nations have been praying.

In fact, man has that instinct within him; man has the desire to communicate with His Creator; hence, even unbelievers pray. But the prayer of the wicked is an abomination to God (Prov. 15:8).

However, God (being a Good God) gives His rain, sun, children, air, etc to all men; and if they were to buy them, with what will they buy them? He will also hear the cry of the needy!

God gave man authority over the earth, though man lost that authority to the devil when he sinned against God by disobeying Him; hence, the Bible calls the devil the god of this world (2 Cor. 4:4).

This is why the devil can cause pains, sufferings, sicknesses, earthquakes, and such things. But when the Lord Jesus Christ rose up from the dead, He said that all authority in Heaven and on earth has been given to Him and He gave that authority to the Church, His Body, who represent Him on earth (Matt. 28:18-20).

We, the Church, individually and as a group, have authority over the earth and we exercise that authority by prayer. There are different kinds of prayer, and we will take them up later.

We are commanded to watch and pray that we do not fall into temptation (Matt. 26:41). To watch is to be alert, sober, and vigilant. We have to open our eyes and ears (physically and spiritually) to know what is happening around us so that we can pray intelligently and effectively.

It is not enough to just pray; you've got to pray to receive results. Hence, Apostle Paul said that he doesn't fight aimlessly like the one beating the air (1 Cor. 9:26).

When you know the strongholds and plans of the enemy, you will fight against him more effectively. And the devil, many times, does not want to be recognized so that his plans and purposes will neither be thwarted nor destroyed.

Ask, and you shall receive; seek, and you shall find; knock, and the door shall be opened to you. For he who asks, receives; he who seeks, finds; and to him that knocks, the door will be opened (Matt: 7:7-8).

You do not have, because you do not ask. When you ask, you do not receive because you ask amiss that you may spend them on your own pleasures (Jas 4:2-3). Asking or praying in doubt and with double-mind will also hinder your answers.

Another thing that can hinder your prayer is sin and disobedience. God's people suffer because of ignorance (Hos. 4:6); and ignorance leads to unbelief which is a great obstacle to receiving your answers.

This is why you have to study the Word of God for yourself, so that you may know what the Lord Jesus Christ purchased for you, and you will pray more effectively.

The Bible says that we are to pray always or without ceasing (1 Thes. 5:17). We are to be instant in prayer (Rom. 12:12). No one should be forcing you to pray, but you have to make prayer a habit and a duty; and you will have to discipline yourself to pray as supposed.

If you show a careless attitude to prayer, that is how your prayer-life will be: inconsistent. Therefore, just as athletes train to perform well, you have to discipline yourself and pray till you make it your lifestyle.

One condition to receiving answers to your prayer is faith, believing that God has answered your prayer. Whatever you ask of when you pray, believe that you receive it and you shall have it (Mk 11:24).

Another condition is to pray according to the Will of God (1 Jn 5:14). Another is to do those things that please Him. And you have to bear fruit, that whatever you ask the Father, He will give it to you (Jn 15:16). And don't live in sin, for the prayer of the sinner is abominable to God.

Throughout the Bible, we see the records of people who prayed. Abraham interceded for Sodom and Gomorrah, though at last, ten righteous people couldn't be found there (Gen. 18:32); Moses interceded for the children of Israel so that God did not wipe them out as He had intended (Exo. 32:7-14).

Elijah prayed, and it did not rain for three and half years, and when he prayed afterwards, it rained (1 Kgs 17 & 18). Jesus Christ prayed a lot. Apostle Paul prayed and showed us an example.

Now, we will consider the different kinds of prayer. There is praying in the Holy Ghost. Praying in the Holy Ghost includes praying in tongues, praying prophetically, and groaning in the Spirit (1 Cor. 14:14-15; Rom. 8:26). You build up your most holy faith by praying in the Holy Ghost (Jude 1:20).

And there is the prayer of intercession. In the prayer of intercession, you stand to intercede on behalf of others, especially in trying to keep them from being punished.

There is the prayer of supplication, which is to ask for God's Help, Supply, Provision, and Intervention on your behalf and on the behalf of others, especially Christians.

When you petition God, you are telling God to do this or that for yourself and others, according to His Word; hence, the Word says that you should plead your case (Mic. 6:1; Mic. 7:9; Isa. 41:21). Of course, many kinds of prayer are related, but they need to be separated for better understanding.

There is the prayer of faith. The prayer of faith is the prayer that you pray because God has specifically promised you or others something, and you stand on that provision and pray, believing that you receive; and you shall have it.

No matter how the situation may appear not to have changed, hold on to your belief and confession, and instead of praying again for it, keep on thanking God for the answer and you will see the manifestation in no distant time.

We now consider the prayer of consecration. This kind of prayer needs to be prayed always by every Christian, submitting himself/herself to the Will of God for his or her life as Jesus Christ did (Matt. 26:38-42).

Be willing and ready to do the Will of God, no matter how hard it may look like. I will consider the prayer of confession. First, confess your sins to God, for he that covers his sins shall not prosper, but he that confesses and renounces them shall find mercy (Prov. 28:13). This is very important for every Christian.

Of course, a Christian should not live in sin, but many don't repent of their sins and continue to pray. You are deceiving yourself. And you know that you have to forgive others for God to forgive you (Matt. 6:14-15).

Next is to confess or declare what you want to be, what you want to happen, without doubting. Whoever says to this mountain, "Be removed, and be cast into the sea," and does not doubt in his heart, but believes that those things he says will be done, he will have whatever he says (Mk 11:23).

There is the prayer of agreement, which involves two or more people praying together in agreement over this or that thing. The people involved will need to believe and not doubt, for maximum result; and the prayer can be made even if they are not together physically.

The prayer of binding and loosing involves destroying the works of devils by speaking directly to the devils responsible for them, and to their works, to pull down and to root out, to destroy and to throw down, to build and to plant (Jer. 1:10).

And the Lord says that whatever you bind on earth, will be bound in Heaven, and whatever you loose on earth, will be loosed in Heaven (Matt. 18:18). There is the prayer of commitment in which you cast your cares to the Lord (1 Pet. 5:7).

The prayer of worship involves showing respect and love for God. It is the prayer of adoration. Pray always with all kinds of prayer!

Never Say That God Said What He Did Not Say!

OBEDIENCE, HOLINESS, AND RIGHTEOUSNESS

God created the universe and everything in it. God created all men for His Good Pleasure. When the Lord God made man, He gave him all good things that he needed.

God gave Commandments to Adam on how he should live. However, when the devil tempted Eve, she ate of the forbidden fruit and gave to her husband, Adam, and Adam did eat. Due to that disobedience to God, man was separated from God and became God's enemy, even though God still loved him.

God demands our obedience to His Commandments. To disobey God's Commandments is to displease God. Disobedience is sin. Sin is the transgression of the Law; sin is lawlessness (1 Jn 3:4).

Sin is: knowing what to do and refusing to do it (Jas 4:7). Sin is anything done out of faith (Rom. 14:23). Faith comes by hearing and hearing by the Word of God (Rom. 10:17). Therefore, to do something out of faith is to do something contrary to the Word of God.

If God tells you to do something, do it. If He tells you to avoid something, avoid it: that is what obedience is. If you go to many Christian families, you will come to know that many don't understand what obedience is.

Will it surprise you to see a born-again wife whose husband tells to do something (something that is not contrary to God's Word) and she will not do it? Some will not only disobey their husbands that God has told them to submit to, but they will even abuse their husbands.

Now, those same women, if they are working in offices, will neither disobey nor abuse their bosses in the offices. Apart from the fact that the devil is using them to fight their husbands, that is demonic obsession.

Demonic obsession is a situation where, though someone is not demon-possessed, yet the person's mind is influenced by demons to dance to their tone. Even ministers' wives are not left out.

Do you know that many ministries and ministers are suffering and pressed down spiritually, because the devil is using the ministers' wives to torment, irritate, and discourage the ministers?

The same thing is seen in churches. Many people don't obey their pastors whom the Lord has set over them. Many talk to their pastors as if they are talking to church-members. However rich you may be in the church, the Lord has set the pastor over you and commanded you to obey your pastor.

Of course, I am not telling you to obey your pastor if your pastor tells you to do evil. If you make your pastor's work burdensome for him, you will give account of it to God on the Judgment Day (Rom. 14:12; Heb. 13:17).

Think of how a student will go out immediately to run an errand for his teacher or lecturer, even when the time is contrary to his schedule. Learn to respect and honour your pastor more than your boss at office or your lecturer at school.

You may have money more than them, but they represent God; and I tell you, they are higher than you spiritually. Even if you pray more than your pastor, there is a place of authority he has over you that you don't have.

In the military, people understand obedience and ranks. However, the devil fights in homes, churches and ministries to frustrate the leaders so that the leaders will not fulfill the God-given Assignments for them, and possibly offend God and perish in Hell.

But woe to him that will put a stumbling block to a Christian or to a minister of the Gospel (Matt. 18:6-7). If you can't obey your husband or your pastor, how will you obey God? Stop deceiving yourself before it will be too late for you. Of course, the husband must love his wife, and the pastor must take care of his members in love.

The Bible says that the Whole Duty of man is to fear God and keep His Commandments (Eccl. 12:13-14). You can't keep God's Commandments if you don't fear Him. If you don't have fear for your husband or your pastor, you can't obey him, and you wouldn't even know when you start insulting and abusing him.

The Lord Jesus Christ tells us that the proof that we love Him is our obeying Him and keeping His Commandments (Jn 14:21). Abide in the Lord Jesus Christ, by obeying His Word and His Spirit.

The Word of God says that without holiness, no man can see the Lord (Heb. 12:14). Only the pure in heart will see God (Matt. 5:8). The Church that the Lord is coming for is the Church that is without spot, wrinkle, or blemish (Eph. 5:27).

If you, as an individual, have spot, wrinkle, or blemish, you will not be raptured. May your whole spirit, soul, and body be kept blameless until the Coming of the Lord, because it is only those that endure to the end that will be saved (1 Thes. 5:23; Matt. 24:13).

What is holiness? Holiness is being without sin. It is sinlessness. Holiness is to be separated to God, to be consecrated or set apart for Him. Holiness is to be without spot, wrinkle, blemish, or any other thing that offends.

Holiness is complete and absolute obedience to God. The Bible talks of perfecting holiness (2 Cor. 7:1). To perfect holiness is to be complete in holiness; it is to mature in holiness. Some people live their lives confessing the same sins always. They confess, God forgives them, and they go back to it again and again.

Holiness and obedience involve making up your mind to be holy always and to obey God, no matter the cost. Some have chosen the ones they will obey and the ones they won't.

That type of attitude displeases God. Jesus Christ did not come to wash away your sins only: He also came to deliver you from the power of sins. As many as receive Him, to them He gives the power to become children of God (Jn 1:12). The power to become a child of God is the power to overcome sin and live above it.

Do you know that you are not bound to sin again? Don't let yourself to be overcome and enslaved again by the power of sin. If you do, the last state will be worse than the first (2 Pet. 2:20-21). There is nothing to envy in this world. If you gain the whole world and lose your soul, you gained nothing (Mk 8:36).

If you live to please your flesh, if you live according to the lust of the eyes and flesh, you will end in Hell Fire. Beware of the pride of life (1 Jn 2:15-17). God gave you life, but the life you are living is not your own.

We have heard it said that righteousness is right-standing with God. It is standing before God without a sense of guilt. When we are born again, we receive the Righteousness of Jesus Christ that makes us know that we are God's children.

Many have depended on this definition of righteousness alone and they live their lives anyhow, claiming that they have right-standing with God because of Jesus Christ. There are many unrighteous people who claim they are righteous.

When the Lord saves you and washes away your sins, He expects you to live a righteous life. The righteous life is the life that lives right. It is the life that does what it is supposed to do, and avoids what it should avoid. The Bible says that you should neither be deceived nor deceive others (Matt. 24:4; 1 Cor. 3:18; Eph. 5:6; 1 Jn 3:7).

He who does what is right is righteous just as Jesus Christ is righteous (1 Jn 3:7). He that lives in sin, he who sins is of the devil, for the devil has been sinning from the beginning (1 Jn 3:8).

Some believe that once you are saved, you are forever saved. But the Word says that some who are first will be last (Matt. 19:30), and that only those that endure to the end will be saved (Mk 13:13).

All the Israelites were delivered from the Egyptian bondage, all were baptized into Moses; they ate spiritual food and drank from the Rock (Christ) that followed them. Yet God was displeased with many of them and their bodies were scattered in the desert because God killed them.

It pays to serve God. It pays to be holy, righteous, and obedient. Remember that disobedience is like the sin of witchcraft (1 Sam. 15:23). It is better to obey than to sacrifice. God is bigger and greater than all, and He requires our absolute obedience.

Cry out to God concerning any area you find yourself weak in, and He will deliver you. Call to Him and He will answer you (Jer. 29:12-13; Jer. 33:3). If you have any habit you find difficult to break, take some time to fast as the Spirit leads you, and that bad habit will break and crumble.

In your relationship with others, don't repay evil with evil, but rather, reward evil with good. You should also be able to know the Good, the Acceptable, and the Perfect Will of God.

There is a difference between the Permissive and the Perfect Will of God; the Perfect Will of God is the best for anyone. If you diligently obey the Voice of God, you will be the head and not the tail; all people (and even devils) shall be afraid of you.

We operate by the law of liberty; we have been called to liberty, but we must not use our liberty as an occasion for the flesh. We are no more in bondage, but we must not live our lives anyhow, but offer the members of our body as instruments of righteousness to holiness.

God hates complaining, murmuring, and bearing of grudges. God has promised to meet all your needs, and not all your wants. Of course, He gives you your wants as well, but He knows the best for you. If you give a ten-year old boy your car to drive in the highway because he is your child and you love him, do you really love him? Also, God's Time is the best.

The Israelites asked for a king, because they wanted to be like the other nations and God gave them kings, but were they better under those kings? They complained of meat in the wilderness and God gave them quail, but while they ate it, the Anger of the Lord burned against them; this happened because, instead of asking in faith, they murmured and complained.

God corrects, rebukes, and reproves His children using different means, and for different reasons. He does these to make them better in different areas of their lives. There is nothing that is hidden from God; all the secrets of men are open to Him and they will be exposed at the appointed times.

God hates sensuality. By sensuality, I mean living according to your senses, and not according to the Spirit of God and His Word. Humans have five sense organs of eye, ear, nose, tongue, and skin, which are for sight, hearing, taste, smelling, and feeling respectively. In sensuality, we are concerned with walking by sight, hearing, and feeling.

Learn or study to be quiet. In the multitude of words, sin is not absent. He who can bridle his tongue can bridle his whole body; he who is faithful in money will be faithful in many other areas; and he who can avoid sexual immorality can avoid many other sins. Control your passions and motives, and bring them under subjection to the Word of God.

Sincerity is not enough. That you are sincere (which is very good) does not mean that you cannot make mistakes, that you cannot lose God's Blessings, and that the devil will not have a place in your life. God's people perish and suffer loss due to ignorance. You must, therefore, add knowledge and other Christian virtues to your sincerity.

BEING LED BY GOD

In these end times and last days, the need to be led by God cannot be overemphasized, if we must fulfil God's Task and Purpose for us, and avoid the devil's deception. Many times, Divine Plans are different from human plans. The sons of God are led by the Spirit of God (Rom. 8:14).

If you are not led by the Spirit of God, then you have some questions to ask yourself. Of course, the Spirit of God is always there to lead you if you allow Him. You have to follow the Leader to be led.

When the Spirit of God speaks to your heart, when He gives you a witness about something in your heart, it is your responsibility to sense that witness and to follow the witness.

Don't blame God when you refuse to be led. If the Spirit of God, for instance, sees danger ahead of you and gives you a warning, if you refuse to heed the warning and you are caught up in the danger, you are responsible for it.

God loves His children and He will not want them to fall into danger. God will do all He can to help you, but He cannot force His Will on you if you refuse.

Children of God should be sensitive to God's Leading always. Of course, the devil will want to speak to you, as if it is God. Satan parades himself as an angel of light just as his ministers pretend to be ministers of Christ (2 Cor. 11:13-15).

But the Bible tells us to prove all things and hold on to that which is good (1 Thes. 5:21). Believe not every spirit, but test the spirits whether they are of God; many false prophets have gone out into the world (1 Jn 4:1).

There are many voices in the world and none of them is without significance or meaning (1 Cor. 14:10). You need, therefore, to distinguish between the Voice of God and the voice of the devil. There are many ways God leads His people; the devil can fake some of them.

For instance, the devil may fake an audible voice. This is one reason you should be able to recognize the Inward Witness of the Holy Spirit in your spirit, for the devil does not live in your spirit, but the Spirit of God does.

The primary way or the number one way God leads all His children is by the inward witness or inward intuition. It is like a checking on the inside of you, whether your heart (not your mind) is at peace about something or whether you are uncomfortable with it.

If the more you think about or pray about the thing, you feel good about it, the Spirit of God is giving you a go-ahead signal. On the other hand, if you feel bad about it, it is a stop-signal. You know you are saved by an inward witness (Rom. 8:16).

Another way God leads His children is by the still-small voice or inward voice. Your spirit has a voice, just like your physical body. The voice of your human spirit is your conscience, your inward voice.

There is the Authoritative Voice of the Holy Spirit also, and God leads His children that way. For instance, after Peter had the vision of the sheet from Heaven, as he thought about the vision, the Spirit of God told him that three men sought for him. He was directed by the Holy Spirit's Voice to follow them. The Voice may seem audible, but it comes to your spirit (Acts 10:19-20).

God talks by Audible Voice, as well: after Jesus Christ was baptized (and baptism is by immersion: if you were baptized by sprinkling, re-baptize by immersion.

Any baptized Believer can re-baptize you in the Name of the Father, and of the Son, and of the Holy Spirit; in the Name of the Lord), as He came up, God spoke audibly from Heaven

(Matt. 3:17). Also, before the Lord went to the Cross, as He spoke to the people in Jerusalem, God spoke to Him from Heaven (Jn 12:23-33).

God can send an angel to direct and guide you; God sent an angel to speak to Mary (Lk 1:26-38). An angel spoke to the high-priest, Zechariah, before the birth of John the Baptist (Lk 1:11-22).

God spoke to Philip through an angel to go to where he would see the Ethiopian eunuch; when Philip obeyed and went there, God changed His Method by speaking to him again by His Holy Spirit (Acts 8:26-39). God has many methods; don't be too rigid.

Joseph, the husband of Mary, was spoken to by means of dreams many times. Through dream, he was told to take Mary as his wife, he was told to take Jesus Christ and Mary to Egypt, and he was told to come back to the land of Israel after the death of Herod (Matt. 1:20; Matt. 2:13; Matt. 2:19-20).

God spoke to King Solomon through dream (2 Chron. 7:12). Even, many of the prophets of the Old Testament received some of the things they said by means of dreams. However, dreams can come from your mind or from the devil.

Another way God speaks to His children is by vision. Of course, the Bible calls dreams 'visions of the night'; that is, the visions you see as you are asleep. There are three types of visions.

There is the inward vision in which your spirit sees things spiritually, while you are still conscious of your physical environment; this will happen even if your eyes are closed.

The vision that Peter had concerning the sheet from Heaven is by trance. Trance is a form of vision in which you see things when your physical senses are suspended (Acts 10:9-17). In a trance, you are not conscious of your physical environment while God speaks to you or shows you things supernaturally.

The last form of vision is the open vision. In the open vision, you are fully aware of your physical environment and yet you see supernaturally. In the open vision, you may see Jesus Christ, an angel, devils, and other beings or things. Many of the God's children are led by visions more often than angelic visitations and audible voices.

God leads by circumstances also. Check the circumstances surrounding you, because God can lead you by them. For instance, when you plan to travel, the circumstances may work out in such a way that the travel may not work out. The same may happen when you are pursuing a business endeavour.

There are angels who minister for the heirs of salvation (Heb. 1:14), and they can make circumstances favourable or unfavourable for you, to protect or guide you.

However, you must be careful to understand your circumstances aright, because the devil can also cause unfavourable circumstances for you. In that case, destroy the works of the devil in the Name of Jesus Christ, and at the Name of Jesus Christ every knee should bow (Phil. 2:10).

As I said, the devil may fake God's Method of leading His children. But don't be afraid, because you have the Word of God and the Spirit of God. You will not be led astray if you follow the Word and the Spirit.

God can also lead by prophecy, by tongues and interpretations, and by other means. He who prophesies speaks to men to exhortation, to edification, and to comfort (1 Cor. 14:3).

God even used a donkey to speak to Prophet Balaam (Num. 22:30). You can't limit God because He is not limited. Many times, the way God will speak to you will depend on you.

For instance, if you are not spiritually sensitive, He may use natural means to speak to you. But depending on natural means is risky, because the devil can easily imitate and fake it.

This is why you don't need to put out a fleece like Gideon did (Jdgs 6:11-40). If you tell God to open that door if He wants you to do something, the devil can open that door. Do you know that the devil can allow you to have good and legal things in order to deprive you of God's Best for you?

Always be sensitive. Don't seek voices, visions, or dreams, so that the devil will not mislead you. Ask God for direction and He will lead you the way He deems good and best.

The Word and the Spirit agree. The Bible, the Word of God, represents the Mind of God. Inasmuch as there are some things you may not find out from the Bible (for instance, which school to attend), nothing from God and His Spirit will contradict the Word of God, when properly interpreted in the right context.

The Word of God was written by the Inspiration of God (2 Tim. 3:16), and the holy men that spoke the Mind of God spoke as they were moved by the Holy Spirit of the Living God (2 Pet. 1:21).

The hardened heart cannot work out the Righteousness of God; the hardened heart will stand against God's Leading and Prompting. Learn to wait on God with open heart and mind. God wants to lead and guide you more than you want Him to lead and guide you.

God reveals secrets to us. The Holy Spirit tells us things to come; He tells us of past things also. The secret things belong to God, but the things that are revealed belong to us. God does nothing without revealing it to His Servants, the prophets.

However, God reveals what He wants us to know. He will reveal what He wants you to know to you; therefore, don't go around for prophecies so that you will not be deceived.

God is still in the business of revealing secrets and mysteries to His people. He still speaks to His children. My God is not a dumb God; He speaks even today.

You only have to tune in to the frequency that He speaks, and you will hear Him clearly. Even as God gives revelations and visions, the devil also has been working hard to give counterfeit revelations and visions to people.

The devil, sometimes, comes as an angel of light to deceive people. He can even speak to you to deceive you. All visions and voices are not God's.

This is why the Scripture instructs us to prove all things and hold on to that which is good, true, and Godly. We are told to test every spirit to see whether they are from God. Why? Because many false prophets have gone out into the world (1 Jn 4:1). God is Spirit; the devil is a spirit too.

1 Corinthians 14:22-33 reads thus, "Therefore, tongues are for a sign, not to those who believe, but to unbelievers; but prophesying is not for unbelievers, but for those who believe. Therefore, if the whole church comes together in one place, and all speak with tongues, and there come in those who are uniformed or unbelievers, will they not say that you are out of your mind?

"But if all prophesy, and an unbeliever or an uninformed person comes in, he is convinced by all, is convicted by all. And thus the secrets of his heart are revealed; and so, falling down on his face, he will worship God and report that God is truly among you.

"How is it then, brethren? Whenever you come together, each of you has a psalm, has a teaching, has a tongue, has a revelation, has an interpretation. Let all things be done for edification.

"If anyone speaks in a tongue, let there be two or at the most three, each in turn, and let one interpret. But if there is no interpreter, let him keep silent in the church, and let him speak to himself and to God.

"Let two or three prophets speak, and let the others judge. But if anything is revealed to another who sits by, let the first keep silent. For you can all prophesy one by one, that all may learn and all may be encouraged.

"And the spirits of the prophets are subject to the prophets. For God is not the author of confusion but of peace, as in all the churches of the Saints."

Earlier, Apostle Paul said, "There are, it may be, so many kinds of languages (or voices) in the world, and none of them is without significance. Let him who speaks in a tongue pray that he may interpret (1 Cor. 14:10,13).

"For if I pray in a tongue, my spirit prays, but my understanding is unfruitful. What is the conclusion then? I will pray with the spirit, and I will also pray with the understanding. I will sing with the spirit, and I will also sing with the understanding" (1 Cor. 14:14-15).

We see, from verse 10, that there are many voices in the world. There are also many languages in the world. There are the Voice of God, the voice of an angel, the voice of the devil, the voices of demons, the voices of people, the voice of the mind, etc.

If you speak in tongues, pray that you may also interpret. However, if everybody in the church is praying individually (to be summarized by one person), you are free to speak in tongues or to pray with your understanding.

But the leader can tell you people to stop praying privately at any time; then, obey and be orderly, by stopping. If you must speak in tongues apart from when everyone is praying individually, then there should be an interpreter (which can be you yourself) or else speak silently or quietly.

But the Spirit has a lot to teach us that we might have not known. There are so many things in the Bible that we have not understood. We will understand many later, and we will understand others when the Lord comes.

Speaking in tongues plus interpretation equals prophecy. Interpretation will help others know what you spoke, so that the whole Church may be edified. He who prophesies speaks edification, exhortation, and comfort to men.

He who speaks in a tongue does not speak to men but to God, for no one understands him; however, in the Spirit he speaks mysteries. He who speaks in a tongue edifies himself, but he who prophesies edifies the Church (1 Cor. 14:2-4).

Therefore, brethren, desire earnestly to prophesy, and do not forbid to speak with tongues (verse 39). Let all things be done decently and in order.

Many are so much interested in prophecies, revelations, visions, and voices that they do not pay attention to the Inner Witness of the Holy Spirit Who indwells them and witnesses with their spirit to make them know what to do and what not to do, what to believe and what not to believe, and who to pay attention to and who not to pay attention to.

Many value prophecy, revelation, vision, and audible voice more than they value the Word of God. Ministries and churches established on prophecies, healings, and miracles without a strong base on the Word of God will sooner or later diminish, wane, or stop entirely.

Such ministries can easily be scattered by rumours. Even the deaths of the founders can bring them to stopping ends. To be on a safer side, put the Word of God (the Bible) first, and put the Spirit of God second.

Yes, the Spirit of God inspired the Word (2 Tim. 3:16); He moved the holy men who prophesied in the Old Testament, and the Early New Testament (and even now) (2 Pet. 1:20-21); and the Spirit, the water (the Word), and the Blood agree as one.

The Father, the Word, and the Holy Spirit are One (1 Jn 5:7-8). Man is born again of water (the Word) and of the Spirit (the Holy Spirit).

Apostle Peter said that the Prophetic Word of the Old Testament is surer, in confirming the Personality of Jesus Christ, than their Testimony of being with Jesus Christ on the mountain of transfiguration where Jesus Christ's Countenance changed and shone with light, and the Voice of God spoke to them (2 Pet. 1:16-21).

Brother, the Scripture was given to us so that we may know the Mind and Will of God. If you put the Bible you see behind you, if you don't stick to that Bible, how can you follow the Holy Spirit of the Living God?

Over the years, people have been deceived by visions, dreams, prophecies, revelations, and voices. Even though God still speaks, demons will try to deceive us, as if it is God that is speaking, and it is when we know the Word well and understand the Witness and Promptings of Holy Spirit well, that we can detect His Voice from their voices.

They sincerely believed that they came from God, even when a moderate knowledge of the Bible would have given them a better understanding. People go to camps and retreat grounds, and pray, pray, and pray to hear God's Voice, and they wouldn't even spend one hour a day to study the Bible during that retreat, when they can spend six hours praying daily during the retreat.

Believe me; many of them are deceived by visions and voices. Many can't distinguish God's Leading from devilish voices.

I am not encouraging you to be fearful, because God can always top the devil in everything. But please, pray and ask God to lead, direct, and guide you, and let Him do it the way He wants to do it.

You may be looking for a writing on the sky while the inner witness or the inward voice by the Holy Spirit has always been with you; but because you are not paying attention, you wouldn't get it; and if one devil speaks to you with a shout, you will value it more than that Voice or Leading of God that is in you.

I believe in prophecy, revelation, vision, and audible voice; I like them. But we are not ignorant of the devices of the devil (2 Cor. 2:11). Therefore, you have to know the truth, because it is better to be late than to be late: it is better to delay than to be found dead.

It is also better to follow God some distance behind, than to rush ahead of God and move towards the west, while He is moving towards the north. God loves us and does not want us to be deceived; but the responsibility lies with us.

People run around looking for those who will give them a Word from the Lord. Why not trust in God and get sensitive to the Holy Spirit Who lives inside you? But woe to the man who will say that the Lord said this or that when the Lord has not spoken.

This is how people get preyed by deceivers, hypocrites, and demonic prophets who come as ministers of Christ. Do you not know that even satan comes as an angel of light? (2 Cor. 11: 14-15).

God leads His people by: the inner witness or prompting in their spirit by the Holy Spirit; the inner or inward voice of their spirit by the Spirit of God; the Authoritative Voice of the Holy Spirit; and by visions, dreams, prophecies, audible voices, angelic visitations, and tongues and interpretation.

However He chooses to lead you, be sensitive and submit. It is important to obey God promptly. Obedience is better than sacrifice; and to hearken than the fat of rams (1 Sam. 15:22).

JESUS CHRIST COMES VERY SOON

The Lord Jesus Christ comes quickly, and His Reward is with Him, to give to everyone according to his work (Rev. 22:12). The Lord Jesus Christ is very great and greater than all. He was before all, and He is the End.

It pleased the Father that His Fulness should dwell in Him, and the Father has committed all things into His Hands. The Lord Jesus Christ is the King of kings and the Lord of lords.

But of the times and the season, brethren, you have no need that I write to you. For you yourselves know perfectly that the Day of the Lord so comes as a thief in the night.

For when they say, "Peace and safety!" then sudden destruction comes upon them, as labour pains upon a pregnant woman. And they shall not escape. But you, brethren, are not in darkness, so that this Day should overtake you as a thief (1 Thes. 5:1-4).

The Coming of the Lord Jesus Christ shall be like in the days of Noah. Before the Flood, people were doing normal things; they were doing business, building houses, and enjoying themselves.

People were overtaken with the cares of this life, and they never listened to Noah, who the Bible calls a 'preacher of righteousness,' until the Flood came and took them away. May it not be so with us!

The Day of Judgment is coming. That Day shall overtake the children of men like the thief in the night. When they say, 'Peace and safety,' sudden destruction will overtake them; and they will not escape it.

The Great White Throne Judgment is coming on all the people of the world. Even Christians will be judged by the Lord at His Coming according to their works, so that each will receive his reward according to what he has done.

Beloved, now we are children of God, and it has not yet been revealed what we shall be, but we know that when He is revealed (when He shall appear), we shall be like Him, for we shall see Him as He is.

And everyone who has this hope in Him purifies himself, just as He is pure. Whoever commits sin also commits lawlessness, and sin is lawlessness. And you know that He was manifested to take away our sins, and in Him is no sin.

Whoever abides in Him does not sin. Whoever sins has neither seen Him nor known Him (1 Jn 3:2-6).

When the Lord Jesus Christ ascended to Heaven, while His Disciples stood and watched, two angels appeared to them and told them that He will come back the same way they saw Him go up (Acts 1:9-11).

We are expecting the Coming of the Lord Jesus Christ. However, the most important part to it, is to be ready for His Coming. He will come like a thief in the night.

The Bible says that blessed are the pure in heart for they shall see God. Is your heart pure? Will you see Him? Without holiness, no man shall see the Lord (Heb. 12:14). Holiness is absolute obedience and dedication to God.

The Word says that we must not love the world or anything in the world, because if anyone loves the world, the Love of the Father is not in him.

The Saints will be raptured to meet the Lord in the air. If we believe that our Lord Jesus Christ died and rose again, even so God will bring with Him those who sleep in Jesus Christ. By the Word of the Lord, we who are alive and remain until the Coming of the Lord will by no means precede those who are asleep.

For the Lord Himself will descend from Heaven with a Shout, with the voice of the archangel, and with the Trumpet of God. And the dead in Christ will rise first.

Then we who are alive and remain shall be caught up together with them in the clouds to meet the Lord in the air. And thus we shall always be with the Lord. Therefore, comfort one another with these Words (1 Thes. 4:14-18).

When the Rapture takes place, there will be commotion and crying in this world, for people will run helter-skelter, but then, it would have been too late. Unbelievers will beat themselves and blame one another for their situation. Then, people will seek to die, but death will be far from them.

Even, carnal and worldly Christians will be left behind, and they will say, "Had I known, I would have...." And the Holy Spirit would have gone. Then the devil will torment and persecute those who have been left behind.

The antichrist will deal with people mercilessly; and people will cry and look for death, but death will not be around. Brethren, this is the time anyone can amend his or her ways.

How will you feel if when the Saints leave, you are left behind? How will your unbelieving neighbours see that you were left behind? The Servant who knew His Master's Commandment and did not do it will be beaten with more stripes.

No wonder Apostle Peter said that if after one is born again, and has known the truth, if he gets entangled in sin and overcome by it, his later state will be worse than the former state. It would have been better if he never came to Christ at all (2 Pet. 2:20).

If your hand or foot causes you to sin, cut it off and cast it from you. It is better for you to enter into life lame or maimed, rather than having two hands or two feet, to be cast into the Everlasting Fire.

And if your eye causes you to sin, pluck it out and cast it from you. It is better for you to enter into life with one eye, rather than having two eyes, to be cast into Hell Fire (Matt. 18:8-9). Many are called but few are chosen. Whatever it will cost you, strive to be chosen.

The Coming of Jesus Christ will be as the days of Noah were. For, as in the days before the Flood, they were eating and drinking, marrying, and giving in marriage, until the day came and took them all away; so also will the Coming of the Son of Man be.

Then two will be in the field: one will be taken and the other left. Two women will be grinding at the mill: one will be taken and the other left.

Watch therefore, for you do not know what Hour your Lord is coming. But know this that if the master of the house had known what hour the thief would come, he would have watched and not allowed his house to be broken into. Therefore, you also be ready, for the Son of Man is coming at an Hour you do not expect.

Blessed is that Servant whom His Master, when He comes, will find ready. But if the Servant is not ready, the Master will punish him and appoint him his portion with the hypocrites. There shall be weeping and gnashing of teeth (Matt. 24:37-51).

When Jesus Christ comes in His Glory, and all the holy angels with Him, then He will seat on the Throne of His Glory. All the nations will be gathered before Him, and He will separate them one from another, as a shepherd divides his sheep from the goats.

And He will set the sheep on His Right Hand, but the goats on the Left. Then the King will say to those on His Right Hand, "Come, you blessed of My Father, inherit the Kingdom prepared for you from the foundation of the world.

"For I was hungry and you gave Me food, I was thirsty and you gave Me drink, I was a Stranger and you took Me in, I was naked and you clothed Me, I was sick and you visited Me, I was in prison and you came to Me."

Then the righteous will answer Him saying, "Lord, when did we do those things to You?" And the King will answer and say to them, "Assuredly, I say to you, inasmuch as you did it to one of the least of these My brethren, you did it to Me."

Then He will also say to those on the Left Hand, "Depart from Me, you cursed, into the Everlasting Fire prepared for the devil and his angels. For I was hungry and you gave Me no food,

"I was thirsty and you gave Me no drink, I was a Stranger and you did not take Me in, naked and you did not cloth Me, sick and in prison and you did not visit Me."

Then they also will answer Him, saying, "Lord, when did we see You in those conditions and did not minister to You?" Then He will answer them, saying, "Assuredly, I say to you, inasmuch as you did not do it to one of the least of these, you did not do it to Me."

And these will go away into Everlasting Punishment, but the righteous into Eternal Life (Matt. 25:31-46). Heaven and earth shall pass away, but the Word of the Lord will not pass away.

But of that Day and Hour, no one knows, not even the angels in Heaven, nor the Son, but only the Father. Take heed, watch and pray; for you do not know when the Time is.

It is like a man going to a far country, who left his house and gave authority to his servants, and to each of his work, and commanded the doorkeeper to watch.

Watch, therefore, for you do not know when the Master of the house is coming in the evening, at midnight, at the crowing of the rooster, or in the morning lest, coming suddenly, He finds you sleeping (Mk 13:31-36).

When Jesus Christ comes, everyone, great or small, will be judged. Anyone not found written in the Book of Life will be cast into the Lake of Fire. He who overcomes shall inherit all things, and the Lord will be his God and he will be His son.

But the cowardly, unbelieving, abominable, murderers, sexually immoral, sorcerers, idolaters, and all liars shall have their part in the Lake which burns with fire and brimstone, which is the Second Death (Rev. 21:8).

He who is unjust, let him be unjust still; he who is filthy, let him be filthy still; he who is righteous, let him be righteous still; he who is holy, let him be holy still. Jesus Christ is coming very soon!

The Lord has given us many warnings in things pertaining to this life, Godliness, and the life to come. God is wiser than all; therefore, let us heed to these warnings and it will be well with us.

Jesus Christ is coming for His Saints and Elects. The Saints of God are His holy and separated people. The Elects of God are those who follow God's Word and Spirit.

Whatever you do in this life, be conscious of life after death; be conscious of eternity. The Saints will be raptured at the Coming of the Lord Jesus Christ, and they will spend eternity in the Presence of God.

The Gospel is the only hope of man: the Good News that Jesus Christ died for the sins of the world so that whoever believes in Him and confesses Him as his Lord and personal Saviour will be saved.

We must send more missionaries into the ends of the world, and we must support the work of missions with all our heart. Whenever Jesus Christ comes, unsaved men will be lost forever.

If we disobey God in the spreading of the Gospel, we are rebelling against God. Disobedience, rebellion, and witchcraft are alike; therefore, we must obey God. Souls mean more to God than any other thing in this world.

There is joy in Heaven over one soul that repents. Jesus Christ came not to condemn the world, but that the world through Him might be saved.

Covetousness and idolatry are alike. Let us not live our lives in greed and covetousness, pursuing the things of this world, that we forget or neglect what the Lord has called us to do.

The more dedicated we are to the Work of the Lord, especially in the spreading of the Gospel, the more reward we will get from God. We will live eternally with Jesus Christ in God's Kingdom.

In stewardship, it is expected that a man be found faithful. Stewardship refers to the way in which someone controls and looks after an event or an organization. A steward is a man whose job is to look after a place with the things in it, like a farm, an estate, etc.

In Christianity or ministry, stewardship refers to looking after or taking control of what God has committed to your hands: His Assignment for you, the ministry He has committed to your trust.

How do you take care of your churches, as an apostle? How do you manage or administer the words or revelations God has given you for others, as a prophet? How do you dedicate yourself to the salvation of souls, as an evangelist?

How do you take care of or shepherd your flock, your members, as a pastor? How do you dedicate yourself to studying and teaching, as a teacher? How much time do you give to intercession as an intercessor? As a musician, how do you prepare yourself before you sing?

No matter what God has committed to your hands, be diligent in doing it, and make sure He finds you faithful in it.

Now is the time for action and service. Stop delaying; whatever your hands finds to do, do it now with all your strength. Preach in season and out of season. The Lord Jesus Christ is coming very soon, and He will reward each one according to his work.

It is not men that will judge you. It is not even Christians or your pastor that will judge you.

Some people have succeeded in buying or winning the favour of people so that whatever they do, the people applaud and support them. Some pastors buy the conscience of their deacons. But God is the One that will judge.

All men shall stand before God and give account to Him of all He has committed to their trust. Even sinners and unbelievers will tell God how they handled or lived the life that He gave to them.

How have you handled the health that God has given to you? How do you appreciate and praise Him for it and use it for His Glory? Many are in the hospitals and cannot walk or work as you do.

The Bible says that Moses was faithful in all His House (Heb. 3:5). Moses was faithful to what God called him to do. In going to Pharaoh, in demonstrating the Power of God, he was faithful.

Moses was faithful in teaching the people the Commandments of the Lord; he was faithful in keeping the things God told him to do. Moses built the tabernacle exactly as he was shown. He interceded for the children of Israel so that God did not wipe them away as He had intended.

Moses walked with God. Even though the people provoked him, that he used the rod on the rock, instead of speaking to the rock, as God directed him. God forgave him and took him to Heaven.

Faithfulness is among the Fruit of the Spirit as recorded in the fifth chapter of the Book of Galatians. Faithfulness means trustworthiness.

Can God trust you with the assignment He has for you? Will you be faithful to what the Lord has called you to do? Have you been faithful to what He had committed to your trust?

He that is faithful in small things will be faithful in big things. If you are not faithful in the little God gave you, how can you be faithful in the big things you want to do for Him?

In the parable of the talents, the one that received five talents traded with it, and got five more talents. The one that received two talents got two talents extra as well. But the one that received one talent buried it, for whatever reason he considered, and was punished at last.

Don't despise anything that the Lord has given to you, and don't be proud of whatever big thing He may commit to your trust. Be faithful in it and let Him be proud of you as he was with Jesus Christ and with Job (Matt. 17:5; Job 1:8).

It is he that endures to the end that shall be saved. You may start well, but if you don't finish well, you will regret at last. Don't say, "Had I known…." It will be too late.

Don't think that the devil will not fight you or bring temptations to your way. You are not greater than Jesus Christ or Paul. But don't drift back because of trials and temptations.

As a minister the devil will fight you through your wife, children, neighbours, and even colleagues. But never mind, all will be well. God is with you in trouble and out of trouble.

The Call of God is a high call. God gave His Only Son to die for the sins of the world. He made Him a Soulwinner. The Lord Jesus Christ accomplished the Task that the Father had for Him. He did the Assignment faithfully.

As Christians, we are supposed to be Christ-like; therefore, we should be faithful in God's Assignments for us. Apostle Paul was happy towards the end of his ministry and until his death. He said that he had fought the good fight and finished the race. (2 Tim. 4:6-8).

No matter what it takes, answer the Call of God for you. It may not be easy for you; in fact, you will have to suffer persecutions for the Cause of Christ. You must have to take up your cross daily and follow Him.

There will be rewards for obedience and punishments for disobedience. God will neither leave you nor forsake you. God helped the holy Saints of Old, His past holy Servants, to fulfill the ministry He had for them, and yours will not be an exception.

Be strong in the grace that is in Christ Jesus. You, therefore, must endure hardship as a good soldier of Jesus Christ.

No one engaged in warfare entangles himself with the affairs of this life, that he may please him who enlisted him as a soldier. And also, if anyone competes in athletics, he is not crowned unless he competes according to the rules.

The hard-working farmer must be first to partake of the crops. Consider these things and may the Lord give you understanding in all things.

If we die with Him, we shall live with Him; if we endure, we shall also reign with Him. If we deny Him, He will also deny us. If we are faithless, He will remain faithful; He cannot deny Himself.

Be diligent to present yourself approved to God, a worker who does not need to be ashamed, rightly dividing the Word of Truth (2 Tim. 2:3-15).

Giving all diligence, add to your faith virtue, to virtue knowledge, to knowledge self-control, to self-control perseverance, to perseverance Godliness, to Godliness brotherly kindness, and to brotherly kindness love.

For if these things are yours and abound, you will be neither barren nor unfruitful in the knowledge of our Lord Jesus Christ. For he who lacks these things is short-sighted, to blindness and has forgotten that he was cleansed from his old sins.

Therefore, brethren, be even more diligent to make your call and election sure, for if you do these things, you will never stumble; for so an entrance will be supplied to you abundantly into the Everlasting Kingdom of our Lord and Saviour Jesus Christ (2 Pet. 1:5-11).

Keep your heart with all diligence, for out of it spring the issues of life (Prov. 4:23). If you lead, do it with diligence (Rom. 12:8).

God is not unjust to forget your work and labour of love which you have shown towards His Name, in that you have ministered to the Saints and do minister. Show the same diligence to the full assurance of hope until the end (Heb. 6:10-11).

If you diligently heed the Voice of the Lord your God and do what is right in His Sight, give ears to His Commandments, and keep all His Statutes, He will remove sickness and disease from you (Exo. 15:26).

You shall diligently keep the Commandments of the Lord your God, His Testimonies and His Statutes which He has commanded you (Deut. 6:17). Follow good works diligently (1 Tim. 5:10).

God rewards those that diligently seek Him (Heb. 11:6). He who has a slack hand becomes poor, but the hand of the diligent makes rich (Prov. 10:4). The hand of the diligent will rule, but the lazy man will be put to forced labour (Prov. 12:24).

The soul of the diligent shall be made rich. The plans of the diligent lead surely to plenty. Have you seen a man diligent in his works, he shall stand before kings, and not before ordinary men (Prov. 22:29).

Be diligent to know the state of your flocks, and attend to your herds; for riches are not forever, nor does a crown endure to all generations (Prov. 29:23-24).

Be diligent in whatever the Lord has given you to do and be found faithful in it. God has not called you to serve Him for nothing. He will reward you abundantly.

But know that there is punishment for laziness and unfaithfulness. Diligence and faithfulness shall be our watch-word.

Do not rob God. Robbing God is not in tithes and offerings alone. To rob someone is to deprive or relieve him of what belongs to him in his presence. It is distinct from stealing, in that stealing is done in the absence of that person.

God is ever present, and when you deny Him of what belongs to him, you are robbing Him. When you don't give God the time that belongs to Him, it is robbery.

Never Say That God Said What He Did Not Say!

FALSE MINISTERS AND AGENTS OF DARKNESS

Take heed that no one deceives you. Many will come in the Name of Jesus Christ, saying, "I am Christ," and will deceive many. Many false prophets will rise up and deceive many (Matt. 24: 4-14).

False christs and false prophets will arise and show signs and wonders to deceive, if possible, even the Elect (Mk 13:22). These were the Words of Jesus Christ when He foretold what will happen at the end of times. And if you have not known it, these things are happening today.

People are using the Name of Jesus Christ and the Bible to deceive many. But thanks to God that it is not possible to deceive the Elect.

Who are the Elects? Has God selected some people and abandoned others? The Elects are those who are led by the Spirit of God, and whose lives are guided by the Word of God.

Some of these false ministers were called by God, but due to sexual immorality, pride, love of the world, and other things, they lost the anointing, and either went after strange gods to get negative powers or began to do wrong things to deceive the simple and exploit men.

False religions, beliefs, and teachings abound in the world today. But if we follow the Word of God and the Spirit of God, we will not be deceived. Even as we know that the antichrist is coming, there are many antichrists in the world today; they are even inside churches.

When you preach and teach things contrary to the Word of God and His Christ, you make yourself an antichrist. When you encourage people, by teaching or practice, to live lives contrary to the Word and Will of God, you are against Christ.

The Word of God says that we should prove all things and hold on to that which is true. We should not believe every spirit, but test the spirits whether they are of God. Let the prophets speak two or three, and let the others judge (1 Cor. 14:29).

We should no longer be children who are deceived easily. Don't run after miracles and prophecies; follow the Spirit of God and His Word so that you will not be deceived. Evil abounds these days. Don't relate with the one you are sure is a false minister.

This is love, that we walk according to His Commandments. This is the Commandment, that as you have heard from the beginning, you should walk in it; for many deceivers have gone out into the world.

Look to yourselves, that we do not lose those things we worked for, but that we may receive a full reward. Whoever transgresses and does not abide in the Doctrine of Christ, does not have God.

He who abides in the Doctrine of Christ has both the Father and the Son. If anyone comes to you and does not bring the Right Doctrine, do not receive him into your house nor greet him; for he who greets him shares in his evil deeds (2 Jn 1:10-11).

According to Apostle Paul, some preach Christ even from envy and strife, and some also from goodwill. People preach Christ out of selfish ambition, not sincerely, but some preach him out of love.

According to him, whether Christ is preached in pretence or in truth, Christ is preached, and he rejoices (Phil. 1:15-18). However, it is not good for you, as a minister, to finish preaching Christ and be cast away into Hell.

Jesus Christ says that in the Day of Judgment, He is going to tell many who prophesied and did mighty works in His Name that He never knew them, for they were workers of iniquity, though they were in the ministry (Matt. 7:21-23).

Don't be marveled because satan himself transforms himself into an angel of light. Therefore, it is no great thing if his ministers also transform themselves into ministers of righteousness, whose end will be according to their works. Such are false ministers, deceitful workers, transforming themselves into ministers of Christ (2 Cor. 10:13-15).

Beware of false prophets, who come to you in sheep's clothing, but inwardly they are ravenous wolves. You will know them by their fruits. Every good tree bears good fruit, but a bad tree bears bad fruit (Matt. 7:15-17).

Another parable Jesus Christ put forth to the people, saying, "The Kingdom of Heaven is like a man who sowed good seed in his field; but while men slept, his enemy came and sowed tares among the wheat and went his way. But when the grain had sprouted and produced a crop, then the tares also appeared.

"So the servants of the owner came to him, and said, 'Sir, did you not sow good seed in your field? How then does it have tares?' He said to them, 'An enemy has done this.'

"The servants said to him, 'Do you want us then to go and gather them up?' But he said, 'No, lest while you gather up the tares you also uproot the wheat with them. Let both grow together until the harvest'" (Matt. 13:24-30). Then there will be separation and burning of the tares.

The coming of the antichrist will be preceded by false prophets and false ministers. The Day of the Lord will not come until the Falling Away comes first, and the man of sin is revealed, the son of perdition.

He opposes and exalts himself above all that is called God or that is worshiped, so that he sits as God in the Temple of God, showing himself that he is God. The mystery of lawlessness is already at work; only He Who now restrains will do so until He is taken out of the way.

The coming of the lawless one is according to the working of satan, with all power, signs, and lying wonders, and with all unrighteous deception among those who perish, because they did not receive the love of the truth, that they may be saved (2 Thes. 2:3-10).

Miracles and prophecies are not proofs that the Spirit of God is with somebody. You need to go beyond them to checking their fruits and comparing their sayings and works with the Word of God. He, who has an ear, let him hear what the Spirit of God says to the Church.

False ministers are bent to deceive and they compromise God's Word. They are sent by satan, directly or indirectly, whether or not they are aware of it; and people like what satisfies their flesh. People like to come to church and still live the way they like.

They may not have problem with you when you tell them to come to church (they even want to be regarded as good persons because they go church), but when you speak against sin in their lives, many of them will get offended.

Some will go church for as long as ten years and yet not be born again. Some desire to be teachers when they understand neither what they say nor the things which they affirm.

Now the Spirit expressly says that some have departed (and others will still depart) from the faith, giving heed to deceiving spirits and doctrines of demons, speaking lies in hypocrisy, having their own conscience seared with a hot iron (1 Tim. 4:1-2).

These days are perilous times, when men love themselves, love money, boast, are proud, blaspheme, and do all sorts of ungodly things. They have the form of Godliness, but deny its power. Turn away from such people (2 Tim. 3:1-5).

Preach the Word! Be ready in season and out of season. Convince, rebuke, exhort, with all longsuffering and teaching.

For the time has come when they do not endure Sound Doctrine, but according to their own desires, because they have itching ears, they heap up for themselves teachers; and they turn their ears away from the truth, and are turned aside to fables.

But you be watchful in all things, endure afflictions, do the work of an evangelist (evangelists preach the Gospel and get sinners saved by the demonstration of God's Power), fulfill your ministry (2 Tim. 4:2-5).

Many are sent to churches from the kingdom of darkness as agents of darkness to do one thing or the other there. Many of them operate as prophets, pastors, elders, deacons, musicians, departmental leaders, interpreters, choristers, organizers, and other functions.

They may appear to be zealous for God, but they are after one assignment or the other. They can pretend so much, to deceive, because they are after specific Christians or ministers to bring them down. But thanks to God that we have God's Word and His Spirit, and we know that they are there.

We should never be afraid of false ministers, but avoid them when we recognize them because we will be wasting our time following them. Remember also that evil company corrupts good manners.

Attack them by prayer and fasting, if perhaps they happen to maneuver their ways to positions of authority in your church. You have the host of Heaven behind you. God is with you, in you, and for you. Greater are they that are with us than they that are with them.

The Church is marching on and the gates of Hades will not prevail against it. We have power and authority to trample on serpents and scorpions and over all the powers of the enemy; and nothing shall by any means harm us. There is neither divination nor enchantment against us.

Be sensitive to the Holy Spirit's Promptings, Urges, and Witness. Always obey the Voice of the Spirit of God instantly; never argue because He knows better than you do know.

False ministers are servants of corruption and bondage. They live to please the devil and themselves. Their minds have been corrupted and held in bondage by the devil, the wicked one.

Be careful who you allow to lay hands on you because, by the laying on of hands on you by a minister operating with a wrong spirit, you can be enslaved or affected by wrong spirits. This is why you must be prayerful and maintain a red-hot Christian life and spirituality.

Just as a good minister can impart something from the Spirit of God in him on you, a false minister can also do the same if you are not red-hot spiritually.

There are people who serve the interest of the devil in this world. Just as God needs people to work with Him, the devil needs people to work with him also.

The devil (satan) comes to steal, to kill, and to destroy. However, Jesus Christ came to give us life and more abundant life (Jn 10:10).

The Word of God says that we wrestle not against flesh and blood but against principalities, against powers, against rulers of the darkness of this world and against spiritual wickedness in high places (Eph. 6:12).

The devil and his associates (his fallen angels and demons) have ranks in their operation, the highest being the spiritual wickedness in high places. Those kinds operate in the heavenlies, and they direct the rulers of the darkness of this world who, in turn, give orders to the powers.

The principalities receive instructions from the powers. Apart from these spiritual entities, there are human beings that work with them to achieve their purposes.

The human agents are the witches and the wizards. Though the witches refer to the female agents while the wizards refer to the male agents, for the purpose of our study, the witches will serve for both of them.

Even the human agents also operate in ranks, and there are different cults and secret societies: some operate in the air, some operate in the water, and others operate on the land. They do travel to the outer space through astral projections and soul-travels.

Even though there is the likeliness that there are more female agents of satan than there are the male agents, especially in the marine kingdom, the male agents occupy higher positions often. Of course, there are many female agents who occupy greater positions than many male agents, depending on the society or cult one operates in.

This can also happen due to their levels of advancement. However, there are levels they don't allow females to pass, except in few instances; because they recognize that females are weaker and may expose their higher secrets easily, more than males.

As noted earlier, the devil comes to steal, kill, and destroy. The devil, his fallen angels and demons, and his human agents have those three things in mind, directly or indirectly. They fight the ministers of the Gospel.

They tempt them with different things and in different ways to make them sin. They also try to harm them physically. They are sworn enemies of Christians; they do whatever they can to pull the Christians down, hurt them, and, if possible, to kill them.

They take Christians as criminals and ministers as their most wanted criminals. This is because the ministers are leaders who are followed by many, and when one minister falls or dies, many are affected. They are in different arms of churches.

The devil and his agents use ministers' spouses and children against them. This is why some minister's wives will pick up quarrels often with their husbands to get their husbands angry, and maybe overreact.

For women-ministers, their husbands can also be used to frustrate their ministries, though the devil's usage of wives in this connection is more. Also, they try to make ministers' children ungodly and stubborn to frustrate them and give them bad image in the public.

This is why you must pray and study the Bible with your family always. Pray for each member of your family in your private prayer-life.

In churches, they pretend to be children of God and carry out their assignments under cover. Of course, some may be more evident to be agents of darkness, depending on their assignments and works.

Some of the assignments may be to cause sicknesses, sleep, lukewarmness, sexual immorality and lust, strife and quarrels, and such things.

Some agents appear violent while others appear quiet. Therefore, don't be deceived by appearance, let the Holy Spirit lead you concerning this.

This is why you, individually or as a group, need the gifts of the word of knowledge and the discerning of spirits so that the devil won't deceive you easily.

However, even without the gifts, your knowledge of God and His Word, and your being able to be sensitive to the Inward Witness of the Holy Spirit in your spirit will safe-guard you.

Never be afraid of witches, for, before the Holy Spirit in you, they are powerless. The Fire of the Holy Spirit, the Blood of Jesus Christ, and the angels of God are there for you, so that no evil will harm you.

Witches cause accidents to take human lives. They do this to send more people to Hell and to get enough blood in their blood-banks, because they feed on blood. They cause poverty and calamities in the lives of people.

During their initiations, their original God-given heart is removed and a stony heart is given them spiritually, so that they begin to desire and feel like the devil with great passion. This is why someone can turn very wicked overnight.

Therefore, parents, be careful with the type of associations your children keep, because children and youths are easily initiated through different things like gifts, borrowing, and lending.

They do this in nursery, primary, secondary, and tertiary schools. They do this in churches, markets, streets, clubs, and everywhere. You must always pray for your children and cover them with the Blood of Jesus Christ.

This is why you should train them in the Way of the Lord, so that when they are old, they will not depart from it. Make sure they are committed Christians, even at early age.

Some people use the gifts or alms given them to make some incantations in their covens and enslave the activities of their donors. They may come to you as beggars or those in need.

This doesn't mean that you should not give or lend, but always cover the gifts with the Blood of Jesus Christ before you give them out. Remember that when you give or lend in the Name of the Lord, you are doing it for the Lord Jesus Christ Himself.

If they lend money to you or sell goods to you in credit, they can use the credit-contact to remote-control your money and business, except you are prayerful. He who goes on borrowing will go on sorrowing. Also, the borrower is a servant to the lender (Prov. 22:7).

Pray over the food and meat you take; bless them in the Name of Jesus Christ, and they will be blessed by prayer and by the Word of God (1 Tim. 4:5). Be careful how you allow people touch you; but, don't be afraid.

Even, many rulers of different categories in the government of the nations are in different cults, and they use them to frustrate the economies of the nations of the world.

This is why many of them are very wicked and are uncaring; because when people are frustrated, many look for negative powers to solve their problems and go into robbery, prostitution, pursuit of money, wrong company, and others.

To this end, the Word of God says that we should pray for all men, especially those in authority, that we may live a Godly and peaceable life (1 Tim. 2:1-4). It is only the prayers of Christians that can save their countries.

Satan appears as an angel of light, and it is no wonder if his agents and ministers do the same (2 Cor. 11:14-15). Many of the false brethren in churches, ministries, and fellowships are nothing but agents of satan, and they cause confusion there.

Actually, if you serve the will of satan, you make yourself his agent, whether you are a witch or not. Therefore, husbands, wives, children, friends, pastors, members, do not allow the devil to use you fulfill his work.

When you speak lies in hypocrisy, you are serving the interest of the devil. When you preach and teach things that are contrary to the Word of God, you are serving the interest of the devil.

Many have been deceived, and many are deceiving others. Demons deceive people, even Believers, so that those who have been deceived will be used to deceive others.

Jezebel was used by the devil to cause God's children commit immorality (Rev. 2:20). False apostles of the Ephesian Church were tested and found liars (Rev. 2:2).

He who believes shall not be in haste (Isa. 28:16). Try the spirits and prove all things. Before you marry, make sure you are spiritually sensitive to God's Direction and Leading. Favour is deceitful and beauty is vain.

WARNINGS FROM THE LORD

Even many products in markets are produced in the demonic world and sold to our world, physically. They include: cosmetics, dresses, food items, and many others; therefore, pray over the things you use before using them.

Some say we should not talk about the devil; however, if their eyes are opened, they will not say so. How would a demonic lady lure a highly anointed man of God into sexual immorality, without the man recognizing it?

Be prayerful always; add fasting to your prayers. Also, increase in your knowledge of God and His Word. Fellowship with other sincere Believers and let the Peace of God be with you. Amen.

When you cause strife and division in the House of God, you are serving the interest of the devil. Therefore, as a Believer, don't allow the devil to use you fulfil his purpose.

Never Say That God Said What He Did Not Say!

INDECENT DRESSING AND OUTWARD APPEARANCE

People dress indecently and seductively these days, especially girls, ladies, and women. Of course, some men dress indecently also.

But whereas even unbelieving men dress decently, many ladies who claim they are Christians, who go to different churches and call on the Name of the Lord, dress indecently to work, school, shopping, and even church.

Most of them will tell you that it doesn't matter, if they want to speak with respect to that. But doesn't it matter? It may not matter with you; but does it not matter with God?

No wonder the Lord Jesus Christ asks, "Why do you call Me, Lord, Lord and do not do what I say?"(Lk. 6:46).

He says that many will say to Him on the Day of Judgment, "Lord, Lord, have we not prophesied, cast out demons, and did mighty miracles in Your Name?" But He will tell them, "I never knew you, depart from Me, you workers of iniquity" (Matt. 7:21-23).

What will happen to you on the Day of Judgment if you realize that many of the things you thought didn't matter actually matter? Then, there will be no second chance.

How will you feel if you are cast into Hell Fire, where the fire does not quench, and the worms do not die? What will be your experience when a demon or your unbelieving neighbour asks you, "So you later came here?"

The Lord Jesus Christ tells us that if we love our lives more than Him, then we are not worthy of Him (Lk. 14:26). If you can't sacrifice your dressing for the Lord, can you sacrifice your life for Him? Don't be foolish but understand what the Will of the Lord is.

The dressing and outward appearance of Christians must be different from those of unbelievers. If a Muslim will value covering herself well, how much more should you value it?

The problem is that many people will find it easier to manage bondage than liberty. But do not use your liberty as an opportunity for sin and disobedience (Gal. 5:13).

The Bible tells us that man looks at outward appearance (1 Sam. 16:7). Even in the secular world, appearance can decide your acceptability in many areas of life.

Escape for your dear life; run before it is too late. The five foolish virgins lost their target. Remember that they were virgins, but they lacked something they didn't remember or deem necessary.

Please, open your eyes well, well; the devil has intruded into the Church: his ministers now parade themselves as ministers of Jesus Christ, to deceive and destroy the souls of the children of men.

Be careful of any church where people are allowed to dress anyhow to, no matter how anointed you may think the preacher is or how knowledgeable he is concerning the Bible. It is a different case when unbelievers dress anyhow to crusades, maybe, for the first time.

The Bible says that out of the abundance of the heart, the mouth speaks. Your actions and your words show what is on the inside of you. Your physical appearance reveals your inner man.

If you don't care about what people think about your indecent dressing, then your spirit has a serious problem, and your mind has been corrupted. I don't care what you may think about it.

Even unbelievers will find it difficult to believe you are a Christian when you dress indecently as they do. There must be a difference between the dressing of a Christian and a non-Christian.

Many ladies think that they attract marriage partners by dressing seductively. Well, you can only attract a carnal man when you dress that way. How can a reasonable spiritual man decide to marry someone that is worldly in appearance?

WARNINGS FROM THE LORD

Even Queen Esther who was in a heathen nation of Babylon asked nothing but what Hegai the king's eunuch, the custodian of the women, advised. Yet she obtained favour in the sight of all who saw her, and the king loved her more than all the other women.

It is true that she took part in the compulsory preparations and purifications that all of them underwent; however, besides what their custodian advised, she requested for nothing (Esth. 2:15-17).

Esther took part in those things because they were in a foreign heathen land. In fact, they were captives, and Mordecai had charged her not to reveal that she was a Jew. Even if she had not used them, she would have been chosen, except that it might have revealed her identity.

It was the beauty that God gave her, it was God's Favour and Glory that attracted the king to her. The Glory of God will attract your husband to you.

Apostle Paul asked that women should adorn themselves in modest apparel with propriety and moderation, not with braided hair or gold or pearls or costly clothing, but which is proper for women professing Godliness with good works (1 Tim. 2:9-10).

Did you notice that there is an appearance that is proper for women professing Godliness? But many people will want us to believe that all that God looks at is your heart. The lie is from the devil, the father of lies.

The heathen of their days spent their time, money, and energy in decorating themselves to look charming and expensive. However, Paul discouraged that among Christians; and they were to do everything in moderation.

The word 'propriety' means the correctness of social or moral behaviour. Whatever Godly women do should be what is morally accepted among Godly Christians.

I am not speaking about what is accepted among people who have departed from the faith, giving heed to deceiving spirits and doctrines of demons; they speak lies in hypocrisy, having their own conscience seared with a hot iron (1 Tim. 4:1-2).

I am not speaking of what is accepted among those who do not endure Sound Doctrine, but according to their own desires, because they have itching ears, heap up for themselves teachers who teach them what they want to hear (2 Tim. 4:3).

Apostle Peter said, "Do not let your adornment be merely outward arranging the hair, wearing gold, or putting on fine apparel rather let it be the hidden person of the heart, with the incorruptible beauty of a gentle and quiet spirit which is very precious in the Sight of God (1 Pet. 3:3-4).

In the first place, the word 'merely', is not in the original text, and that is why it is italicized in the New King James Version. The King James Version says, "…whose adorning let it not be that of outward adorning of…."

Well, Apostles Paul and Peter are not necessarily saying that you should neither arrange your hairs, wear costly dresses, nor put on fine apparels. If you can't go to work, school or church without a costly dress or fine apparel, something is wrong with you; you now love the world.

There is a level you may be and what is costly to others may not be costly to you: however, even at that level, position, or wealth, never put your mind on costly things. Whatever God gives you, use it for His Glory and don't allow it enter your head.

Understand what I am saying here. You can use a costly car without putting your mind on costly things. If you are in a position to use costly things, use it to the Glory of God, and not for pride or to show off.

Concerning the dressing or arranging of the hair, using of weavons and attachments is devilish and worldly. Many of those weavons are actual human hairs that were cut and sold. Many of the weavons and attachments are manufactured with demonic materials to enslave the children of men.

Also, when you use weavons and attachments, when you perm and jerry curl your hair, you are saying that God is stupid to have made your hair the way He made it. When people refuse to cover their hairs, they resort to worldly means of weavons for a covering.

Much of those things women use for their hair, in perming and jerry-curling, is manufactured from alantoin extracted from aborted babies. The worst is that some men even fry their hair.

Satan has entered the Church and has deceived many. Many are sincerely deceived. Those cortexes, lipsticks, make-ups, and many other painting materials, apart from being worldly, are manufactured from demonic materials, aborted babies' placentas, and human blood.

This is a mystery that many have not realized. When people use those things, they get demonic problems they don't know where they came from.

Blouses that show too much of your back; tight-fitting and revealing dresses; mini-skirts; spaghetti or line-sleeve and transparent dresses; blouses showing your breast; cobweb and body-hug dresses; blouses revealing your belly; and any such dresses are devilish, satanic, demonic, and worldly.

Sagging your trousers and dread-locking your hair are satanic also. Women shouldn't put on trousers because they look more decent in skirts and gowns. In biology, when women mature, their buttocks get enlarged, this is why when they wear trousers, they reveal their body contours and look seductive.

Any attire or dress that glorifies the devil and does not glorify God is worldly and devilish. There are no two ways about this matter.

We now come to the issue of earrings, necklaces, and bangles. These things are worldly also. God made you look fine, what advantage is it in decorating your body, which is the Temple of the Holy Spirit, with those things?

We wear cloths and dresses to cover our nakedness. Before Adam sinned, we didn't even need dresses, for God's Glory covered us. Earrings were classified among foreign and ungodly things when Jacob purified his household (Gen. 35:1-15). The knowledge of God advanced from Abraham, Isaac, to Jacob.

Even though you may argue, can you prove to me why you need them when God made you beautiful? The problem is that many of these things have continued for so long that many don't even know why they do what they do. Personally, I don't see those things as beauty, and God does not like them.

Take it to the whole world and quote me: these sleeveless or very short-sleeved blouses which women and ladies wear, which show their arm-pits when they raise their hands are satanic, worldly, seductive, and deceptive. It is deceptive because many assume that since it is for fresh air and not for direct attraction, nothing is wrong with it.

That is why you say you want to worship and praise God while you show the men your arm-pits. That is why you wear skirts and gowns that will show the men that came to worship God your laps as you sit down, because you want to look sharp and modern. Many are deceived with the thought that since God touched me, nothing is wrong with me.

Don't you know that God touches unbelievers also? Is it not written in your Bible that God gives sun and rain to the evil and the good, to the just and the unjust? (Matt. 5:45). Don't you know that even unbelievers fall down under the anointing? Maybe you have never seen where God spoke to Prophet Balaam through an ordinary donkey (Num. 22:15-35). The Spirit of the Lord came upon Prophet Balaam in Num. 24:2.

Many read the Bible, and it appears that they don't understand simple and clear language. No wonder the Holy Spirit, through Apostle Paul, said that some will depart from the faith, giving heed to deceiving spirits and doctrines of devils, speaking lies in hypocrisy... (1 Tim. 4:1-2).

No wonder God spoke through Apostle Paul to tell us that the time will come when they will not endure sound doctrine, but according to their own desires, because they have itching ears, they will heap up for themselves teachers; and they will turn their ears away from the truth... (2 Tim. 4:3-4).

Look at what I mean: many are so much interested in miracles, prophecies, signs, and wonders that they seem never to have seen it in their Bible that the Lord Jesus Christ will tell many that prophesied, cast out demons, and did mighty works in His Name that He never knew them, because they were workers of iniquity (Matt. 7:21-23). This situation pains the Lord so much that He asks, "Why do you call Me 'Lord, Lord,' and not do the things which I say? (Lk 6:46).

Even you young men that want to appear however you want to appear. You don't want restrictions. God put the tree of the knowledge of good and evil in the Garden of Eden to teach man the need for restrictions and obedience. When you want unlimited access and unrestricted freedom, you are not ready for Heaven.

That is why some of you men wear earrings and noserings. I have seen a church in America where men wear those things. They even wear caps right inside church programmes. God has become your mate: is it not so? These have nothing to do with civilization and modernization as far as God is concerned. Have you not seen ladies that follow men so that people will not take them as uncivilized? You want to look like a Rastafarian?

Young men dress and unbutton their shirts to show people their chests. I went to one church, and it was their youth day. During their mass choir, their leader flied his shirt and unbuttoned it to show his chest. Neither the bishop nor any of their pastors said anything, at least to my hearing.

I think many people don't really believe in Heaven and Hell. Forget about what they claim; if they really believed that the Word of God is unchangeable and forever settled in Heaven, if they really believe in Heaven and Hell in their innermost beings, we wouldn't have been seeing many of the things we see. God is waiting for many people at His Judgment Seat!

Many ladies appear to be stubborn when it comes to how they will dress. Many are bent on having what they want, and don't care about what God or people think about them. And the devil has succeeded in making many indecent ways people dress look harmless. Have you ever seen how indecently many dress during wedding, in the name of wedding gowns?

Never Say That God Said What He Did Not Say!

THE BELIEVER SHOULD NOT PERISH

For God so loved the world that He gave His Only Begotten Son that whoever believes in Him should not perish but have Eternal Life (Jn 3:16).

I want you to notice, particularly, that the verse declares that the Believer should not perish and not that the Believer shall not perish. The one that believes on the Lord Jesus Christ should not perish.

If you believe on the Lord Jesus Christ, if you are born again, you are not supposed to perish. When someone or something should not perish, it means that the person or thing ought not to (is not supposed) to perish. It also means that the person or thing may perish.

If you are hanging on a strong and stable crane, high above the ground level, you should not fall down and crash by the influence of the force of gravity. However, if you separate yourself from the crane, you will crash on the ground.

People of God perish because of lack of knowledge (Hos. 4:6). Ignorance of God and His Ways will make you perish; though, in this case, the perishing is not applicable to perishing in Hell Fire alone; in fact, this place is talking about losing God's Provisions for you, among other applications.

The devil is no good entity; if you don't know your rights and privileges in Christ Jesus, he will steal from you, kill you, and even destroy you (Jn 10:10).

Don't allow the enemy to succeed in prevailing over you. Let none of his works come to pass in your life. Give no place to the devil (Eph. 4:27).

This is why you have to study the Bible, because, in reading and studying it, in meditating on and speaking forth its contents (the things applicable to you), you overcome the devil and his devils. You are sitting with Christ at the Right Hand of God (Eph. 2:6).

Well, my topic is that the Believer should not perish in Hell Fire. However, many Believers will perish in Hell Fire. Casual reading of the New Testament will reveal this truth to you. God does not intend that it should be so, but it will be so to many.

The Bible says that it is not the Will of God that any soul should perish, but those that refuse Jesus Christ will perish in Hell Fire. Those that live in sin and disobedience will perish in Hell Fire.

As a matter of fact, God is not the one that sends people to Heaven or Hell; actually, people choose where they will go, even without their knowledge. Where you go is dependent on what you do with Jesus Christ, His Holy Spirit, and God's Word.

God sets before you life and death, blessing and curse (good and bad), and you choose the one you want (Deut. 30:19). God does not force anyone. Of course, He can change circumstances and conditions around you to help you take the decision to obey; however, He still, will not force you.

Hell Fire was not made for man. Hell was made for satan and his fallen angels, his demons. Why? Because they rebelled against God.

However, the man that rebels against God is putting himself in the same position as the devil, and the Bible says that he will suffer the same condemnation and punishment in Hell Fire. The punishment of Hell Fire is everlasting and eternal.

The fire of Hell does not quench and its worms do not die. If all the sufferings in this world are put together, and one person is made to carry them and bear them, yet it will not equal what someone will suffer in Hell for 24 hours.

My brother, run from the damnation of Hell Fire while there is time. After death, there is no room for repentance; neither is there room for forgiveness.

WARNINGS FROM THE LORD

The Lord Jesus Christ asks, "Why do you call Me, Lord, Lord, and do not do what I say?" (Lk. 6:46). Many will say to Him on that Day, "Lord, Lord, have we not done this or that in Your Name?" But He will tell them that He never knew them (Matt. 7:21-23).

Notice that many of them even prophesied. It is only those that do the Will of the Father that will enter the Kingdom of Heaven (verse 21). You may be baptized and confirmed in your church, but that is not the answer.

If you want to enter the Kingdom of Heaven, you must be born of water and of the Spirit (Jn 3:5). That is a higher level of "I am born again" (Jn 3:3). The water is the Word of God (Eph. 5:26), and the Spirit is the Holy Ghost.

You must obey the Word of God, and you must listen to the Spirit of God. Many who are first will be the last, and the last first (Matt. 19:30). Let this not be your portion.

Some people argue and say that God knows those who will go to Heaven and those who will go to Hell. In other words, they say that some are meant for Heaven and some are meant for Hell. This is no truth.

Of course, the Bible says that God will have mercy on whom He would have mercy (Rom. 9:14-20). The Bible says that God loved Jacob and hated Esau (Rom. 9:9-14). But you've got to interpret that Scripture well, in order not to misdirect yourself.

The Bible says that it is those that endure to the end that will be saved (Matt. 24:13). In other words, if you fall by the wayside, you will not be saved. He who despises God, He will despise (1 Sam. 2:30).

The end of a matter is better than the beginning (Eccl. 7:8). It is one thing to start well, but it is another to end well. Don't fall by the roadside. Many are called but few are chosen (Matt. 20:16).

Why were they chosen? It is because they were faithful. Count yourself to be death with Christ and alive for Him. The life that you live now should be for Him.

The Word of God talks of the children of the Kingdom being cast away into the Outer Darkness wherein is gnashing of teeth (Matt. 8:12). Those children were meant for the Kingdom of Heaven, but due to sin, disobedience, and unrighteousness, they lost their place in it.

God, after saving the children of Israel from the Egyptian bondage and allowing them to have many spiritual and mighty experiences, destroyed those that sinned and did not believe (1 Cor. 10:1-13).

The Word of God says that because iniquity shall abound in the last days, the love of many shall wax cold; however, some people's love will not wax cold and they will endure to the end (Matt. 24:12-13).

It is those that endure to the end that will be saved. Without holiness, no man can see the Lord (Heb. 12:14). Blessed are the pure in heart, for they shall see God (Matt. 5:8). If you are not holy and pure, forget Heaven.

However, whatever you might have done, repent now; confess your sins to God and make the necessary restitutions; and God will wipe away your sins and unrighteousness.

If you confess your sins, He is faithful and just to forgive your sins and cleanse you from all unrighteousness (1 Jn 1:9). There is no hard-man with God.

All your pride and boasting is because your time is not up. When your time expires, God will judge you and He is no respecter of persons (Rev. 2:20-23). God says, "Return to me, you backslider!" Obey Him now so that you will not say, "Had I known...."

This is not a question of whether you are an apostle, a prophet, an evangelist, a pastor, a teacher, a bishop, or an archbishop, a president and founder, a general overseer, an elder, a deacon or a deaconess, a men's or women's leader, a Sunday School teacher, a singer, an intercessor or whatever you may be; if you don't obey God and His Word, forget Heaven and prepare to live with the devil eternally.

Abstain from the lust of the flesh which war against your soul. Flee youthful lusts. God will not allow any temptation that is greater than you to come to you, but don't go where angels fear to tread on. Man can never be wiser than God; when God says, 'Flee,' do just that.

When you are enticed, do not give in to the enticement or temptation. Don't get entangled with sin and disobedience. There are many errors among Believers today; avoid those errors so that it will be well with your soul.

Examine yourself to see whether you are still standing in the faith. If you judge yourself, you will not be judged. Beware of hypocrisy and compromise. All hypocrites will end in eternal separation from God.

Unfaithful servants will be cast into the Outer Darkness. Those who compromise the Word and Standard of God will find themselves in the Lake of Fire which burns with fire and brimstone.

Wives, submit to your husbands, in the Lord; husbands, love your wives as your own bodies. If you put a stumbling block to your spouse, so that your words and actions cause him or her to live contrary to the Word and Will of God, God will require it from you: you will give account of your relationship with your spouse to God.

Abhor what is evil; cling to that which is good and true. You must forgive others so that God will forgive you your own sin. Awake to righteousness and shun sin and immorality.

Many have already been corrupted by the lust of the flesh, the lust of the eyes, and the pride of life. The minds of many have already been polluted by demonic suggestions.

He who overcomes will inherit all things. The overcomer will be blessed forever. Let your inward man direct and control your outward man, and not vice versa.

If you live according to your flesh, you shall die; but if through the Spirit, you put to death the deeds of the flesh, you shall live.

God did not call us to serve Him for nothing. He will reward our obedience and punish the disobedient. Cease to do evil, learn to do well.

If you live your life anyhow, you will be devoured by the sword of God's Judgment. If you judge yourself, you will not be judged. Walk in the highway of righteousness, the way that pleases God and does His Good Will.

The world is changing very fast, especially now. Many modern inventions and technologies have amazed all of us. Of course, the Lord God told us that knowledge will increase in the last days (Dan. 12:4).

The inventions in aircrafts, computers, electronics, digital communications, medicine, and many other fields are noteworthy. While many of the advancements in science and technology are great, some serve good purposes, while some serve bad purposes.

Think of the advancement in the production of weapons of war: a whole city can be wiped out within a small space of time by using weapons of mass destruction.

While computers and the television are good for the storage, processing, and retrieval of data and information, and for communication, think of the pornography that is associated with them. Many have run after the things of this world so much so that they have little or no time for God.

Many pursue after flashy cars, attractive buildings, education, and certificates, and they give their time, energy, and mind to these things, but have no time for God.

However, when I talk of a changing world, I am not talking about these inventions, even though many of them have something to do with what I am talking about.

The advancement in cosmetics which make people to paint their faces and other parts of the body that they look horrible and worldly is part of what I am talking about.

God says that we should fear Him and not to mingle with those who are given to change. Their calamity, according to God, shall come quickly (Prov. 24:21-22).

If you look at many churches today, you see a lot of worldliness among people who go to church. Even Believers are not left out; many Believers live like the people of the world. Many of them dress and appear like unbelievers.

There must be a difference between the Believer and the unbeliever. Their lives must be different; their desires and priorities must be different; and their appearances should be different.

You can't dress like a harlot and expect me to believe that you are a Christian. Man looks at outward appearance; and I am a man, even though I am not an ordinary man, I still look at outward appearance.

But you must know that God sees the outward appearance too. The Word of God says that out of the abundance of the heart, the mouth speaks (Matt. 12:34). As a man thinks in his heart, so is he (Prov. 23:7).

If you dress and appear anyhow before the public and you don't care about what people think of you, something is seriously wrong with you. You need to repent and change, and God will forgive you (Acts 3:19).

I tell you that God is not an American. He is not a European either. God is not from any nation, rather all men in all nations are from God, because He created and formed them. However, God is not a Father to all men.

He is a Father to those who have accepted the Lord Jesus Christ as their Saviour. If you are not born again, ask the Lord Jesus Christ to come into your life as your Lord and personal Saviour.

Having recognized that you are a sinner who cannot save himself, believe that Jesus Christ came to this world, died for your sins, and was raised again for your justification (Rom. 4:25). He who comes to God, God will not cast him away (Jn 6:37).

No matter how dirty or sinful you may be, He is able to wash you and remember your sins no more (Isa. 1:18; Isa. 43:25). Don't wait till tomorrow, because you may not see tomorrow (Heb. 3:7-8).

If God is not pleased with you, He is not pleased with you. Simply because Believers in America or in London do those things do not make them right. Just as perversion in dressing is a problem in Nigeria today, the same had applied to them some years ago, even today.

After many years, some have thought that this or that is their culture, but the devil introduced those things over there some years back, even as he is doing today.

God is no respecter of persons. Whether you are an apostle, a prophet, an evangelist, a pastor, a bishop, an archbishop, a reverend or what, if you disobey God's Word and His Holy Spirit, you are disobedient.

Of course, because of Jesus Christ's Intercession for us at the Right Hand of the Father, God's Judgment and Punishment may not come on you now, but once the time God gave you is gone (as He gives time to everybody), God's Punishment will catch up with you.

Remember that no sinner will ever enter the Kingdom of Heaven (Eph. 5:5; 1 Cor. 6:9-10). A minister of the Gospel who lives in sin is a sinner, and all sinners will inherit Hell Fire. Many have said that many things don't matter.

What of if on the Day of Judgment, you find out that they finally mattered, and by that time, I tell you, it will be too late. Then, no matter how you repent, confess, and plead for mercy, God's Ears will not be open to your cries.

Some say that God never said that you should not drink alcohol at all, but that you should not drink it too much. But think of it, how could Apostle Paul tell Timothy to use little wine for his stomach's sake instead of using only water if he was already drinking little.

Certainly, Apostle Paul needed to advise him to take a little for medicinal purpose since he was taking none of it, because the other Believers were not taking it. Of course, their level of medical development those two thousand years ago was crude and unrefined.

Give strong drink to those who are perishing (Prov. 20:1; Prov. 31:3-7). Medical science and technology have advanced today that you don't need alcohol, even for stomach ache.

If alcohol will make your brother to stumble, why drink it? Even, the unbelievers will doubt your repentance or faith when they see you drink or buy it.

Let the Spirit of God lead you always and don't be overcome by the lust of the flesh. Don't do something, simply because someone else is doing it. Anything not done in faith is sin (Rom. 14:23).

Some sects or groups of Christians or Believers despise some other sects of Christians, saying that the others are legalistic and conscious of the Law. Well, Jesus Christ came not to destroy the Law and the Prophets, but to fulfil them (Matt. 5:17).

They say that the others are religious. Well, inasmuch as I don't believe in religion, but in Christianity (in a life changed by the Word and the Spirit of God, because someone has accepted Jesus Christ and the authenticity of the Word of God), yet "pure and undefiled religion before God and the Father is this..." (Jas 1:26-27, KJV & NKJV).

You've got to know the difference between the ritual Laws which have been done away with and the moral Laws which still stand today. Rightly divide the Word of Truth!

God can neither lie nor change His Mind (Num. 23:19) God's Standard has never changed and can never change for any people. Therefore, don't deceive yourself and don't deceive others, for we must all stand before the Judgment Seat of Christ to give account of ourselves (Rom. 14:10-12).

Don't be deceived by anyone (Eph. 5:6). He who does what is right is righteous just as God is righteous; he who lives in sin, he who does unrighteousness belongs to the devil (1 Jn 3:7).

But no matter what you might have done, contrary to the Word of God, repent now and ask for His Forgiveness and He will abundantly cleanse and pardon you. Remember that there is a Heaven to gain, and there is a Hell to shun. The Peace of the Lord Jesus Christ be with your spirit. Amen.

RECEIVING, THINKING, BELIEVING, CONFESSION, AND POSSESSION

Man is made up of the human spirit, the soul, and the body (1 Thes. 5:23). Many people are more conscious of their body than they are of their spirit, but the truth is that man was made in the Image and Likeness of God (Gen. 1:26-27).

If man was made in the Likeness of God and God is Spirit (Jn 4:24), man must of necessity be a spirit also. You are, actually, a spirit, and you have a soul (the soul is the seat of reasoning, emotions, thoughts, etc).

Your body accommodates both your spirit and your soul. Your spirit exists within your heart, your belly position (Prov. 20:27). On the other hand, your soul (that is your mind) is within your brain area.

However, what is most important is that you know that you consist of these three parts or areas, and for you to be conscious of the fact that your spirit-man is the main man. Your spirit-man is your inner man (1 Pet. 3:4) or your inward man (2 Cor. 4:16).

When Adam disobeyed God, his spirit died and he got separated from God and became His enemy, even though God still loved him. God made provision for Adam's restoration which was consummated at the Coming, Death, and Resurrection of the Lord Jesus Christ.

When someone believes and confesses Jesus Christ, his spirit is regenerated or made alive by the Holy Spirit of the Living God.

This is what is meant by being born again; and the Lord says that except a man is born again, he can neither see nor enter the Kingdom of Heaven (Jn 3:3,5).

If any man be in Christ, he is a new creature, old things are passed away and all things have become new (2 Cor. 5:17). It is your spirit that was born again and became a new creature.

It is not your mind, your soul, that is born again. You may still think imperfect thoughts even after you are born again. That is why the Word of God tells born again, Spirit-filled Believers to renew their minds (Rom. 12:2).

Your mind is renewed, is saved, by the Word of God (Jas 1:21). The more you read or hear the Word, the more you meditate on it and believe it, the more your mind is renewed; you see yourself thinking and speaking like God God's Word is God.

It is not your body that is born again. Your body remains the same: the same height and complexion. Some have tried to change their complexion by bleaching their skin. That is satanic.

What will you tell God when you stand before His Judgment Seat on the Judgment Day and He asks you, "Why did you call Me an imperfect Creator?" Some have changed their hair, face, and other parts of the body.

The Word of God tells us to present our bodies a living sacrifice, holy, acceptable to God which is our reasonable service (Rom. 12:1). Presenting your body is a good sacrifice; it involves self-denial and self-control.

We are to present our members, parts of our body as instruments of righteousness and obedience to holiness and pleasing God (Rom. 6:13,19). Your body is the Temple of the Holy Spirit and you must keep it holy for the Lord.

Our topic is about receiving, thinking, believing, confession, and possession. Our body has five sense-organs. The organs include: the eye (for sight), the nose (for smelling), the tongue (for taste), the skin (for touch), and the ear (for hearing).

It is actually from these senses that we receive information into our brains (our brain is a giant and complex computer: it receives, stores, processes, and gives out information). God is a Wonderful God!

You must be careful of what you receive, especially through your eyes and your ears. What you receive and keep receiving will influence your beliefs. Your beliefs will influence your actions, confession, and possession.

Actually, your actions are a form of your confession. Your confession is your available action, and your action is your visible confession.

The impure images and information you receive and keep receiving will tempt you with impure thoughts and actions. Godly words and information will make you think Godly thoughts.

Be careful of what you allow into your mind, for it will greatly influence your thoughts, beliefs, confessions, and actions; and they, in turn, will influence your possessions and your ability to fulfill your destiny.

God has a great destiny for you. Receive the grace to fulfill your destiny in Jesus Christ's Name. Amen.

When you spend your time in pornographic images, messages full of unbelief and doubt, and gossiping, your Christian life will be messed up. Evil communication and company corrupts good manners (1 Cor. 15:33).

Don't be wiser than God. The Bible says that you must flee from youthful lusts (2 Tim. 2:22). You must pursue God and Godliness also.

Don't stay in a locked room, in a dark room, alone with somebody of the opposite sex because you think you are very much anointed. The man may force you, and the lady may seduce you.

The Word of God tells us to think on good, pleasant, loving, truthful, praiseworthy, and Godly things (Phil. 4:8). Don't spend your time meditating on evil and ungodly things because they will mar you. What you ponder on will make or mar you.

Think on the Word of God. Meditate on God's Word day and night (Josh. 1:8). Keep looking at the Word (Prov. 4:20-21). Keep your eyes on Jesus Christ and you will never sink (Matt. 14:28-31; Heb. 12:2).

Also, have absolute confidence and belief in the Word of God. God can neither lie nor fail to perform His Word (Heb. 6:18). He is the Almighty Jehovah, the Maker of all things and there is nothing impossible with Him (Lk. 1:37).

They that trust in the Lord shall be like Mount Zion, which cannot be removed but abides forever (Psa. 125:1). Believe and don't doubt in your heart. When you pray, believe that you receive and you shall have your request (Mk 11:24).

Your confession will expose your belief, for out of the abundance of the heart, the mouth speaks (Lk. 6:45). Even in salvation, believing is to righteousness, while confession is to salvation (Rom. 10:10).

Keep confessing the Word of God, no matter how dark and difficult your path and situation may be like. Always be positive and never be negative, no matter what you may be seeing or hearing. Always be moved by what you believe, by what God says.

Coming to your possession, the Lord God Almighty has given us all things that pertain to life and Godliness through our knowledge of Jesus Christ Who has called us by His Own Power and Glory (2 Pet. 1:3,4).

We are given exceeding great and precious promises, and all the Promises of God in Christ Jesus are 'Yes,' and 'Amen' (2 Cor. 1:20).

If you maintain the confession of your faith, no matter how bad the circumstance may look like, you will overcome and have your expectations.

The Word tells us to fight the good fight of faith, to lay hold on Eternal Life (1 Tim. 6:12). Eternal Life is the Life and Nature of God.

Even when it seems you are seeing the opposite of what you expect, if you don't waver, if you don't doubt but believe, I tell you, you will have all that you need, all that you require, and all that Christ Jesus has provided for you.

Check whether your plans, desires, purposes, and pursuits correspond with those of the Lord over your life. God's Plans and Will for our lives are always the best. But you get to know about them by waiting on God and listening to Him, by prayer and meditation.

Don't harden your heart, but be open to God, so that you will receive His Direction. Don't say that you have made up your mind on this issue, and can't change it. Also, don't wait to have God stamp your decision; let Him, rather, direct you on what to do, so that demons will not deceive you by stamping it for you.

A time came in David's life that the Amalekites invaded Ziklag, and burned it with fire, taking captives their women (wives), their sons, and their daughters.

David and the people that were with him lifted up their voice and wept, until they had no more power to weep. What a calamity! Have your sufferings reached that extent?

David's two wives were taken captive. And David was greatly distressed; for the people spoke of stoning him, but David encouraged himself in the Lord his God.

David enquired of the Lord, saying, "Shall I pursue after this troop? Shall I overtake them?" And He answered him, "Pursue, for you shall surely overtake them, and without fail recover all."

So David went, he and his men. But David pursued, even though some of them who were very weak stayed behind when they could not cross the Brook Besor.

Along the way, they found someone who had not eaten for three days and fed him. When he had got his strength back, he directed David and his men to where the invading troops were.

Then David attacked them and recovered all that they had taken away. What would have happened if David had not pursued and attacked them? He would have lost all.

What would have happened if he had not enquired of the Lord? He might have not had the courage to pursue and attack them. God knows of your losses and predicaments, and He will make a way for you.

Even the Amalekite's servant that fell sick so that his master abandoned him (he directed David) was in God's Plan for the whole thing (1 Sam. 30:1-20).

This was also demonstrated by Abraham when he recovered Lot. When Sodom and other cities were attacked, the invading army took all the goods of Sodom, and all their provisions, and went their way.

They also took Lot, Abraham's brother's son who dwelt in Sodom, and his goods and departed. Then one who had escaped came and told Abraham, the Hebrew. When Abraham heard that his brother was taken captive, he armed his men and pursued the captors.

Abraham armed his three hundred and eighteen trained servants, who were born in his own house, and went in pursuit as far as Dan. He divided his forces against them by night, and he and his servants attacked them and pursued them.

So he brought back all the goods, and also brought back his brother Lot and his goods, as well as the women and the people (Gen. 14).

After his return, he gave tithe to Melchizedek who blessed him and said, "Blessed be Abram of God Most High, possessor of Heaven and earth; and blessed be God Most High, Who delivered your enemies into your hand."

Abraham would have lost Lot if he had remained in his place comfortably and not pursued. But he refused to remain at ease, and chose rather to act; and when he acted, he brought glory to the Name of the Lord.

The Word of God says that we should occupy till the Lord comes (Lk. 19:13). To occupy is to take charge and control of what you have been given to oversee. It is to enter a place and keep control of it. For example, by a military force.

In this case, the Lord wants us to oversee and do what He has entrusted into our hands, and keep it from interference by an enemy.

Then, even if due to one reason or the other, an enemy invaded our ground and took away anything, we should pursue, overtake, and recover all. To occupy is to do the Father's Business (the Lord's Business).

Some reason that since their income is enough, they will be buying medicine to control the disease they are passing through, which might have been termed 'incurable.'

Some may say, "Since I have this church or ministry, even if it is not flourishing well, at least let me maintain it." Inasmuch as we should give thanks to God in any situation we find ourselves in, yet it is the Lord's Will that you enjoy the fullness of His Provisions for you.

However, we must recognize that some deprivations and harsh states are brought about or allowed by the Lord Himself for different purposes.

What I am saying is that you should know when to pursue and when not to pursue. Even David enquired of the Lord and pursued when the Lord told him to pursue.

Some harsh conditions may be a test or a trial for you, and in that case, pursuing will not help matters, because it will not change it.

God told me that it is not every time that you have to bind and loose in prayers to correct a negative situation. He cited the case of Abraham whose wife was barren. Abraham prayed to God about the situation and God gave him a son, without binding and loosing (or dealing with demons).

If you study your Bible well, you will come to know that the prayer of binding and losing (or casting out demons) will not solve some undesirable conditions. For example, do you think that Prophet Jonah would have cast out that big fish that swallowed him?

His was a case of sin and disobedience, and what he needed to do to be free was repentance, confession, and mercy. Some will not come out of their conditions until their knowledge and wisdom have been developed to a level that God is satisfied.

Some will not come out until they learn humility and despise pride. You may not like the situation, but God allowed it for your own good, for your development and promotion.

There is a case in the Bible where the Israelites said, "The time has not come, the time that the Lord's House should be built." The Lord asked them, saying, "Is it time for you yourselves to dwell in your paneled houses, and this Temple to lie in ruins?"

The Lord went on, "Consider your ways! You have sown much, and bring in little; you eat but do not have enough; you drink, but you are not filled with drink; you clothe yourselves, but no one is warm; and he who earns wages, earns wages to put them into a bag with holes."

The Lord told them, "Consider your ways! Go up to the mountains and bring wood and build the Temple, that I may take pleasure in it and be glorified. You looked for much, but indeed it came to little; when you brought it home, I blew it away.

"Why? Because of My House that is in ruins, while every one of you runs to his own house. Therefore the heavens above you withhold the dew, and the earth withholds its fruit.

"For I called for a drought on the land and the mountains…on whatever the ground brings forth, on men and livestock, and on all the labour of your hands" (Hag. 1).

However, whatever the enemy, who comes not but to steal, kill, and destroy, might have taken away from you will be restored to you. But you have to pursue him and overtake him so that you can recover all.

When you believe, you speak and confess so that you can possess your possession. Confront your confrontations! Pray through; pray until you have a witness that you have prayed through.

Some prayers require fastings. You may have to do some days or weeks of night-vigils, maybe some three hours every night.

The violent takes his inheritance and possession by force. The Spirit of God lifts up a standard against the devil. Greater is He that is in you than he that is in the world. Confront the devil. God has not given you a spirit of fear, but of power and of love and of sound mind (2 Tim. 1:7).

The Lord is with you, and He will never leave you. They that are with you are more than they that are against you. One angel destroyed one hundred and eighty-five thousand Assyrian soldiers in one night (2 Kgs 19:35).

Be glad then, you children of Zion, and rejoice in the Lord your God; for He has given you the former rain faithfully, and He will cause the rain to come down for you the former rain and the later rain in the first month.

The threshing floors shall be full of wheat, and the vats shall overflow with new wine and oil. So the Lord will restore to you the years that the swarming locust has eaten, the crawling locust, the consuming locust, and the chewing locust, His great army which He sent among you.

You shall eat in plenty and be satisfied, and praise the Name of the Lord your God, Who has dealt wondrously with you, and God's people shall never be put to shame.

Then you shall know that He is in the midst of Israel. He is the Lord your God and there is no other. God's people shall never be put to shame (Joel 2: 23-27).

Learn to distinguish when to wait on God and when to pursue and overtake the invaders and spoilers.

We must understand the strategies of the enemy, so that he will not gain an advantage over us. God's people perish because of ignorance.

We should not even give him the opportunity to strike in the first place, to take away anything from us; however, if he succeeds in depriving us of anything, we must pursue him and recover all by force.

Are you possessing your inheritance in Christ Jesus the way you should? How will you feel, if when you get to Heaven, you realize that you deprived yourself of many things the Lord purchased and provided for you?

Whatever you have lost shall be found. Whatever the enemy has stolen or robbed from you shall be found and recovered. But you have your part to play; and you know that God cannot fail to fulfil His Own Part.

The Kingdom of God suffers violence, and the violent take it by force. Don't sit back and watch the devil deprive you of God's Blessings for you without doing anything. Pursue, overtake, and recover all!

WATCHFULNESS, VIGILANCE, AND SOBRIETY

To be watchful is to be careful to notice what is happening, in case anything bad happens. To watch is to look carefully, in order to avoid any danger.

To be vigilant is to give careful attention to what is happening, so that you will notice any danger. Sobriety refers to behaviour that shows a serious attitude to life.

These three words require seriousness; that is, to be watchful, vigilant, and sober, you've got to be sensible and quiet. We live in evil days; therefore, you must be watchful, vigilant, and sober.

The Word of God tells us to watch and pray so that we will not enter into temptation. The reason is that the spirit is willing, but the flesh is weak (Matt. 26:41).

You can watch without praying, and you can pray without watching. You must watch and pray. If you watch without praying, you can know of danger, but you may not avoid it.

If you pray without watching, you can pray amiss, and you can be caught up in the temptation or danger. Be sober, be vigilant, because your adversary, the devil, walks about like a roaring lion, seeking whom he may devour.

Resist him, steadfast in the faith, knowing that the same sufferings are experienced by your Brotherhood in the world (1 Pet. 5:8-9).

To be sober is to have a serious attitude to life; it is not to take things or life for granted, but to be careful and sensitive. The devil is looking for any loophole in your life so that he may strike.

Therefore, don't create any loophole for him. Your faith (steadfast faith) is the shield with which you can stop all the arrows of the devil.

The parable of the wheat and the tares tells us the need for watchfulness (Matt. 13:24-30). A man sowed good seeds in his field; but in the night, because he had no watchman who was watching, an enemy went to that field of his and sowed tares and left.

Neither the man nor his servants knew about the tares until when they sprouted and grew alongside the wheat. Without watchfulness, vigilance, and sobriety, the devil can spoil the good things you are doing for God.

Their unwatchfulness led to a loss; because, for fear of damaging the wheat, the owner advised his servants to allow both of them to grow together till the harvest. The wheat and the tares, therefore, had to share the soil nutrient in the field.

The wheat would have grown better if the competition for the available nutrients and conditions was not there. This same thing is happening in churches today.

Due to carelessness, agents of the kingdom of darkness have entered many churches to do their destructive and bad works among the Believers while posing as fellow Believers.

There are many bad and sinful doctrines and ways of life that have been introduced into churches because satanic agents entered among Christians.

For instance, let's consider the issue of Christian ladies using weavons. There are many reasons why Christians should not use weavons. Using weavon is like telling God that He is stupid and imperfect for giving you the kind of hair you have.

It is like bleaching which many do; they feel that God should have made them fair in complexion instead of dark. But on the Day of Judgment, you will find out that you tried to degrade God.

Also, many of those weavons are real human hair which were cut and sold. How can you be wearing another person's hair as a Christian lady or woman? This is worldliness; this is satanic and demonic; sister, the ground you are treading on is dangerous.

Then, even though some of those weavons may be synthetic or artificial (which the first point still condemns), many of those weavons ladies use are manufactured in the water-kingdom of darkness and brought to this earth for sales to contaminate the people of the world.

The thing that some people don't know is that some companies which exist physically on this earth came from the dark kingdom of satan, especially the water-world of the devil.

It may surprise you to know that an occult man who wants to construct a building can do it using workers from the dark kingdom who will manifest physically. Occult companies use satanic agents as workers and people wouldn't know.

In fact, many things we see physically came from the dark kingdom. Even many legal and morally good things we see are manufactured in the dark kingdom, some of which I wouldn't mention here.

This is why you need to pray over and sanctify the things that you use, especially edible things. But how will you want to sanctify things that the Lord has rejected and condemned?

Everything is not demonic, don't misunderstand me; don't live in fear either, because greater is He that is in us than he that is in the world.

The anointing breaks every yoke of the enemy. But many Christians create loopholes for the devil through sin, disobedience, and worldliness.

You need to be watchful and sober, because if you are not, the devil can lead you into sin and worldliness, and if the Lord Jesus Christ meets you in that state at His Coming, or you die in that state, you will miss Heaven and go to Hell.

But that is not God's Plan for you, and He did not bring you out of the world to condemn you later. Therefore, don't condemn yourself. You condemn yourself by despising His Word and the Promptings His Spirit.

The Bible recommends that a bishop must be vigilant (1 Tim. 3:2). Every minister of the Gospel must be vigilant. As a pastor, you need to walk with God.

You need to be vigilant and watchful; and you need to know the Voice or Leading of the Spirit of God. Do you know that somebody can be sent to your church or ministry by the powers of darkness to pull you down?

That person may come in and become very zealous in your activities, and you may start promoting the person to responsible positions. After some months or years, he or she may do or say things that can destroy your ministry.

The fellow can lie against you, and may say things that you may not be able to explain. People, even your members, may believe him or her, saying that if he or she was fake and lying, he or she wouldn't have been with you for so long.

This is why you don't need to believe everything you hear about someone. Don't believe every good or bad thing people say about a minister, except you have the witness inside you.

Watch, for you do not know what Hour your Lord is coming. But know this, that if the master of the house had known what hour the thief would come, he would have watched and not allowed his house to be broken into (Matt. 24:42-43).

Take heed, watch and pray; for you do not know when the Time is. It is like a man going to a far country, who left his house and gave authority to his servants, and to each his work and commanded the doorkeeper to watch.

Watch, therefore, for you do not know when the Master of the House is coming in the evening, at midnight, at the crowing of the rooster, or in the morning, lest coming suddenly, He finds you sleeping (Mk 13:33-36).

The Bible tells us to be watchful in all things (2 Tim. 4:5). Watch your tongue, watch your words, watch your actions, watch your relationships, watch your life, watch your ministry.

Watch your environment, watch your commitments, and watch in everything. Don't be taken by surprise unnecessarily.

Remember that the Spirit of God will tell you things to come. The Word says that we should not sleep, as others do, but should watch and be sober.

For those who sleep, sleep at night, and those who get drunk are drunk at night. But let us who are of the day be sober, putting on the breastplate of faith and love, and as a helmet the hope of salvation (1 Thes. 5:6-8).

Therefore, gird up the loins of your mind, be sober, and rest your hope fully upon the grace that is to be brought to you at the Revelation of Jesus Christ;

As obedient children, not conforming yourselves to the former lusts, as in your ignorance; but as He Who called you is holy, you also be holy in all your conduct (1 Pet. 1:13-15).

But the end of all things is at hand; therefore, be serious and watchful in your prayers. And above all things have fervent love for one another, for love will cover a multitude of sins (1 Pet. 4:7-8).

God doesn't want us to be at a disadvantage at any time and in any thing. No wonder Apostle Paul declared that we are not ignorant of the devices of the devil (2 Cor. 2:11).

If you are ignorant, he will take advantage of you; and he does not come, but to steal, kill, and destroy. God's people perish because of ignorance; therefore, go for more and right knowledge.

Remember that you are a watchman; therefore, watch in all things. The souls of men are tied to you; if you don't watch over their souls, they will perish. Therefore, give diligence to being committed to winning souls for the Lord.

Know your friends, and be careful of your enemies. It is good to keep friends, but know that your friends will either make or mar you. Therefore, be careful with the type of friends you keep. Also, know that your enemies may be looking for the slightest opportunity to strike. Therefore, watch always.

We are in the End Time; you must be watchful the more as you see the Day of the Lord approaching. There are many End-time realities, things that the Lord told us will happen before He comes.

As He has warned us ahead of time, so that the Day of the Lord will not overtake us unexpectedly, we must be more alert. We must prepare for the Lord's Coming; we must be ready to welcome Him.

As a born-again child of God, you need to fellowship with other Believers. The Bible tells us not to forsake the assembling together of ourselves, the fellowship of other Believers (Heb. 10:25).

When you fellowship with other Believers, you gain a lot of things. First, the Lord tells us that wherever two or three are gathered together in the Name of Jesus Christ (in His Name), He is there with them in their midst (Matt. 18:20).

He is there in their midst, and not just in them, upon them, for them, or with them. God is for us (Rom. 8:31); God is with us (Matt. 28:20); God is in us (1 Jn 4:4); and God is upon us (Acts 1:8).

The Lord works with us, both as individuals and as a group of Believers (Mk 16:20). God inhabits the praises of His people, both as an individual Christian and as a group of Christians (Psa. 22:3). However, in this case, God is in their midst, in the midst of a Body of Believers.

There is something about the corporate anointing of a Body of Believers gathered together with one mind, in one accord, and in unity. When they pray and praise together, a strong corporate anointing is released; and this corporate anointing is stronger than any individual anointing of anyone present there.

When that corporate anointing is in operation, healings, miracles, signs, and wonders take place, even without specific pronouncements.

When the 120 Disciples in the upper room were gathered together with one accord in one place, the Holy Ghost fell on them strongly as a group; and tongues of fire appeared and sat upon each of them so that they were filled with the Holy Spirit and spoke in other tongues as the Spirit gave them utterance (Acts 2:1-4).

As the apostles prayed together after they had been persecuted, the place where they were gathered was shaken by God's Power (Acts 4:31).

When Paul and Silas were beaten and imprisoned, they prayed and sang, and the Power of God came down and shook the prison, so that their chains fell off and the prison's doors opened (Acts 16:22-34).

Of course, an individual Christian can still experience Mighty Moves and Demonstrations of God as he prays and sings alone.

However, there is something about the corporate Refreshment of the Holy Spirit that makes it wonderful. This is one reason you get so much excited as you listen to good music, either from cassette players or from a group of Christians.

Behold, how good and how pleasant it is for brethren to gather together in unity (Psa. 133:1). The problem of many churches and fellowships is that people gather together and their minds are not together in one accord.

Many gather together without being united in heart and spirit. Many set their minds on different things, even though they are together physically. This attitude hinders the Move of the Spirit of God.

Try to bring your fellowship, service, or meeting to that place of unity that God desires, because the more we are united, the greater the Manifestation of God's Spirit among us.

Even when a strong and highly anointed minister of the Gospel is invited to minister in a church, the Operation of God's Spirit will be by higher dimension if the people present are united in heart and in mind.

The atmosphere of a service can increase or decrease the anointing in a man of God. Even music played in the fellowship can increase or hinder the anointing on the man of God and on the Body of the Believers as a whole.

Good music brought the Hand of God upon Prophet Elisha so that he prophesied (2 Kgs 3:15). Even today, it is still the same with us: good, anointed, and Holy Spirit's inspired music brings the Anointing and Power of God on us.

The Bible says that iron sharpens iron, as one man the countenance of the other (Prov. 27:17). The Word of God tells us to bear with the weak and the feeble-minded (1 Thes. 5:14). As we gather together, the strong is encouraged and the weak is strengthened.

Just as the body is one but has many parts, so also is the Body of Christ. Each member has different functions and when those functions are carried out, we are strengthened.

This is why the Bible says that when we are gathered together, we should come with different things. Some can come with teaching, others with songs, others with revelations, other with psalms, others with prophecies, and many other things, that the Church may be edified and built up (1 Cor. 14:26).

The ear will not do the work of the eye; neither will the hand do the work of the mouth. Do you know that someone can live a hundred years without an eye? Yet if your anus is blocked permanently, it will not be long before you die.

As a Believer, don't stay alone; fellowship with others. Of course, your own private Christian life should be strong. Your prayer-life, your Bible-study life, your fasting life, etc should be strong.

If you spend a lot of time in Church services and fellowships, while your private Christian life is nothing to be appreciated, you will still be a weak Christian. Inasmuch as the fellowship of other Believers is very necessary, your own Christian life is more important.

Our topic talks of a good fellowship, a good church. This is to say that there are bad and not-so-good ones. You have to seek God's Face in prayer and waiting on Him concerning the church or the fellowship you should be associated with.

The Holy Spirit may direct you to change church or fellowship, or He may lead you to remain in the one you are already in. What is most important is that you are open to His Direction. Don't insist on your own. Don't say that you were born there; and therefore, should die there.

Your church should be a Full Gospel church. I am not just talking about whether it is called a Pentecostal, charismatic, evangelical, holiness, orthodox, or whatever name it may go by.

I know that there are some churches that are called Pentecostal that are no Pentecostal at all. There are churches that are (or were) regarded as orthodox that have even gone more Pentecostal than some traditional Pentecostals. It is not all that glitters that is gold; have this in mind.

The Bible says that sinners shall not stand in the congregation of the righteous (Psa. 1:5). Many churches are lukewarm and cold, and that is why agents of the dark kingdom stay there for long comfortably without being exposed, or forced to go out by God's Power and Fire.

Someone may ask of Judas Iscariot who dwelt with Jesus Christ. Read your Bible very well; you will know that Jesus Christ knew of him: but those people stay and operate without those in authority knowing about them, such that they regard them as Christians and even promote them.

Yes, satan came with the sons of God (Job 1:6); but God and the others recognized him. He is the accuser of the brethren, and God allowed him for that purpose. However, it is not everything a man of God may know, but the things God reveals to him.

Also, even when God wants to reveal a thing, people may not be available for the revelation because they do not seek God's Face. The trial of Job was not revealed to him because it was his own examination. So, God may choose not to reveal something for a particular purpose, or to work out something.

Your church should teach the Whole Counsel of God. Your church should teach the Word of God as it is, without adding to it and without subtracting from it. Teaching it is not enough; they should practice it.

It is knowledge applied that is beneficial: if you know all things and apply none of them, what have you gained? The church you attend is very important because your Christian maturity will be affected by it. Even, your making Heaven at last depends on it also.

Just as evil communication or company corrupts good manners (1 Cor. 15:33), your associating with a church that is not good is harmful to your Christian life.

Many are in the ministry today, serving their flesh and belly, instead of serving God. Many are so much interested in money that they will not tell people the truth. When a pastor tells you or allows you to dress anyhow you want to church, beware of that church.

The thing that many don't know is that there are ministers who serve the interest of satan, instead of the Interest of God. Some do it knowingly and others unknowingly. If you don't know, know it that many ministers operate with occult and satanic powers.

Many do miracles with satanic powers. They even prophesy with satanic powers. This is one reason you should seek God, instead of seeking miracles or prophecies (2 Cor. 11:15; 2 Pet. 2:19; Phil. 3:18-20; Rom. 16:17-18).

Do you know that someone can preach and teach the Bible, and still be a false minister? Someone can even say, "In Jesus Christ's name," and would either not be talking about your Jesus Christ or is just using it to imitate and camouflage (Mk 13:21-23).

Some answer Jesus as a name. Jesus Christ Himself told us that false christs shall appear (Matt. 24:24). Some worship satan as God, and many have come in the Name of the Son of God. Therefore, I tell you, someone can even say "In the name of Jesus, the son of God," and not be talking about your Jesus Christ of Nazareth, the Son of the Living God.

If you are open to God, His Spirit will lead you to a good church and out of a bad one. But don't harden your heart.

If it was only the preaching and the naming that are involved, I may not disturb myself (Phil. 1:18), but many are enslaved into demonism and ungodliness, even without their knowledge.

Never Say That God Said What He Did Not Say!

THE WRONG MENTALITY

I am interested in the wrong mentality among Christians or people who profess Christianity. The Word of God is a lamp to our feet and a light to our path (Psa. 119:105). Forever, the Word of God has been settled in Heaven.

By living according to the Word of God, each and every Christian will be blameless, spotless, and wrinkleless. However, when a Believer operates according to his thoughts and senses, he is bound to displease God, whether or not he is aware of it.

The Anointing (Holy Spirit) we have received teaches us all things, and we don't need that any person teach us anything (1 Jn 2:20,27). The Holy Spirit passes God's Thoughts to our minds through our spirit.

The devil tries to pass his thoughts to our minds through our senses and flesh. If we know all that the Holy Spirit tells us, we wouldn't need others to teach us.

However, because somebody can mistake God's Thoughts for the devils thoughts, and vice versa, God has given us His Word (the Bible) and teachers to expound and teach us the Bible.

It is by the Bible that we can differentiate God's Voice from the devil's voice. This is why we should be full of the Word of God, in all wisdom, and divide God's Word rightly. Prove all things and hold on to that which is good.

The Bible is a more solid foundation than any teaching, voice, revelation, vision, prophecy, or leading. The Word was inspired by the Holy Spirit, and the Spirit can never contradict the Word.

No matter how anointed a man of God may be, no matter the length of time in God's service, and no matter the title you may have, if what you preach or teach contradicts the Bible (when interpreted well by comparing Scripture with Scripture), you have either listened to the voice of your mind, the voice of the devil, the voice of people, or any other different voice.

One area that Believers have wrong mentality in, is in the area of prosperity, as compared with the Christian character.

Many ministers and preachers spend most of their time talking about prosperity, breakthrough, miracles, healings, etc than they speak of Godliness, holiness, obedience, and the likes. Many of them don't even speak about God's Judgment and Punishment of sinners in Hell Fire.

While it is true that there are many false ministers that satan has sent to deceive people and corrupt their minds so that they will be more interested in the things of the world than in Heavenly things, many real ministers have fallen into this error because of ignorance, immaturity , deception, and lack of purpose.

Even though Jesus Christ and the early apostles demonstrated God's Power through the gifts of healings, working of miracles, casting out of devils, and prophetic ministrations, they spent more time teaching about things related to the Christian character and eternity.

Take the Bible and study for yourself. Check the teachings in the Gospels, the Acts of the Apostles, the Epistles, and the Book of Revelation.

If you have indeed risen with Christ, set your minds on things Above, not on earthly things; and when Jesus Christ Who is your Hope shall appear, you will also appear with Him in Glory.

The things of this earth are temporal and deceitful, and they war against our souls. The cares of this world and deceitfulness of riches choked the seed (the Word) that fell among thorns so that it did not bear fruit (Matt. 13:22).

When you don't understand the Word that you hear, the devil will snatch it away from you, and it will not even grow, not to talk of bearing fruit.

If you have no root in you, if you are not rooted in God, you will endure for a while; for when persecutions and trials come, you will fall by the wayside. When you hear the Word and the Word is choked with the cares, riches, and pleasures of this life, you will bring no fruit to perfection.

However, when you have an honest and a good heart, the Word will bear much fruit (Lk. 8:11-15). This isGod's Will and Purpose for His children, and for all men.

Another area that Believers have the wrong mentality in is in the area of suffering. Many assume that Christianity is a bed of roses.

No matter how you see it, it is not; however, when Jesus Christ shall come again, all pains and tears will be taken away from us, and we will dwell forever in the Bliss of Glory which cannot be compared with the bed of roses.

Yes, if you must follow Christ, you must take up your cross daily and follow Him. Jesus Christ Himself says that difficult is the way which leads to life and there are few who find it (Matt. 7:14, NKJV).

Think about it: to pray for two, three, or more hours daily is certainly not a bed of roses. To wake up by 3:00 a.m. to study God's Word when others are enjoying their sleep is certainly not a bed of roses. To go into that remote village to win souls for Christ is not a merry adventure.

What of persecutions and trials you will receive because you gave your heart to the Lord Jesus Christ, and live to obey Him? In fact, even Believers who misunderstand you will criticize you. To teach that there is no suffering in Christianity is to be an enemy of the Cross of Jesus Christ.

Now, we come to the area of punishment, discipline, or chastening. Many have so much spoken about God's Love, Mercy, and Forgiveness, that they don't know that God chastens His children.

His Purpose for chastening us is to make us mature in Him and live to please Him. The Lord will scourge and beat you to make you a good child of His. If all God does is to forgive you and have mercy on you, you will remain a spiritual child throughout your life and never get to maturity.

But the Lord is wiser than any of us and His Thoughts are higher than our thoughts. Whatever the Lord does is for our good, and He has no bad thought for us!

Do not despise the Chastening of the Lord, nor His Rebuke (don't be discouraged). The Lord chastens those He loves, and scourges every son whom He receives. If you endure chastening, God deals with you as with sons; for what son is there whom a father does not chasten?

But if you are without chastening, of which all have become partakers, then you are illegitimate and not sons. Furthermore, we have had human fathers who corrected us, and we paid them respect.

Shall we not much more readily be in subjection to the Father of spirits and live? For they indeed for a few days chastened us as seemed best to them, but He for our profit, that we may be partakers of His Holiness.

Now no chastening seems to be joyful for the present, but painful; nevertheless, afterward it yields the peaceable fruit of righteousness to those who have been trained by it.

It is out of God's Love for us that He chastens and scourges us; He wants us to be Godly (like Him) (Heb. 12). Don't be annoyed with God because He chastens you; He loves you more than you love yourself!

Another area I want to address is the area of it-doesn't-matter. There are many things that Believers do and say that they make no difference to Christianity.

When a Believer dresses anyhow to school, work, or church, and says that there is no problem, the devil has got him or her. Indecent dressing is more rampant among ladies, even though some young men engage in this also.

What the men call 'sagging' is devilish and satanic; wearing of body-hug dresses is not good for both males and females. Indecent dressing does not glorify my God and Father.

Another wrong mentality is the idea that whatever will be, will be. This idea insinuates that whether or not we pray, God will do what He wants to do and achieve what He wants to achieve.

Listen, if you don't pray, the devil will be successful (or more successful) in his work, and you will suffer unnecessarily. If you don't preach the Gospel, many more souls will get into Hell Fire. If you don't obey God's Word, you are disobedient.

We should obey God without reservations. We should not be wise in our own eyes. Avoid procrastination; because, by doing so, the devil will gain more grounds, and Heaven will be disappointed.

God loves us so much, and He has given us His Word to show us His Mind and Will. Take time to study His Word (the Bible) so that you will know God more. God's Word is God Himself. Be sensitive to the Voice of the Spirit of God, and obey God promptly, and it will be well with your soul. Amen.

There are many things we can learn from Job. There are things we go through which are not actually caused by us, even when we may blame ourselves for them.

Though people may criticize us unjustly for some things they see in our lives, yet that doesn't mean that they are justified. Also, whatever we may lose for God, God will restore to us many folds.

Expect accusations, slander, criticisms, and gossips. Even the members of your family will accuse and criticize you. When brethren slander you and gossip in your name, don't be discouraged, for that is the handiwork of the enemy.

Inasmuch as you do the Will of God concerning your life, the devil will incite people against you. They did the same to Jesus Christ our Lord, and who are you to escape these things when our Lord and Saviour experienced them?

Many assume that the name you bear does not make any difference to your life, but this is wrong; the name you bear affects you negatively or positively. A good name is better than choice silver.

There is something about names that makes them distinguishable as good and bad ones, both in terms of character and in the name one is called by. Even in the Bible many people's names were changed for better ones.

What of vows, oaths, pledges, and swearing? Pay your vows; it is better not to vow than to vow and not pay. Don't give grudgingly or out of persuasion; but give cheerfully and willingly. Above all, don't swear, but let your "Yes" be "Yes," and your "No," "No."

Another wrong mentality among Believers is in the area of ministerial training and ordination. Some believe that ministerial training is not necessary, while others believe that except you go to Bible College or Theological school, you are not qualified to be a minister.

Those two thoughts are wrong. Bible College is good and necessary, but it is not compulsory. It is not all ministers that must attend Bible school, before being recognized as ministers. When God calls you, He anoints you for the work He calls you to do. Ministerial training is good for improvement.

Also, Believers reason that they will do this or that, but they will do it later. Procrastination has destroyed a lot of things in the Christendom and made the devil gain. Whatever your hands find to do, do it now with all your being; you don't know what tomorrow will bring about.

Of course, in many things, you have to wait on God for His Timing; but why will you leave praying or Bible reading/study today so that you will do them tomorrow?

Many assume that restitution is not necessary to repentance, but this assumption is wrong. There are things that require restitution after repentance, and there are things that don't require restitution. Make the necessary restitutions if you have repented.

Also, many assume that God will not sponsor His Work effectively, but our God is more than able to supply what we need for the ministry. The Strength of the Lord is made perfect in man's weakness. Let the weak say that he is strong. Learn to tap into the Strength of the Lord God Almighty.

You can't subdue by your own strength, but by the Lord's Strength. It is not by might nor by power, but by the Spirit of God.

Many don't know that their identity means a lot. If you live in sin, it will cause the works of the devil come to pass in your life, no matter how you pray and fast. If a curse is following you, you will struggle and achieve little or nothing.

If you keep close relationship with God and obey Him, devils and witches will fear you, even without having prayed 'Holy Ghost's Fire.' God and the Fire of His Spirit will become your identity when you follow and obey Him.

Another wrong assumption is that God will always give you everything you ask Him the time you want them. God can, in His Wisdom withhold some things from you, even though you may want them. He may give you that thing later, and not at the time you want it. There is time for everything.

God is not like the devil who is selfish. God will withhold the blessing that will destroy you from you, because He loves you. Learn to walk with God in patience.

Patience is a very great Christian virtue that many don't like to hear of; they want it now. But why did Jesus Christ have to wait for thirty years before taking up a Task that took Him less than four years?

Some Believers have followed the way of the world, which says that the end justifies the means. Many don't care how they obtain this or that; they are interested in their having it. This is why someone will steal and come to church to give testimony of what he has stolen, without fear or shame.

A good name is better than choice silver. It is better to eat a dry morsel with quietness, than to feast with many troubles. Strive to obey God fully in all things.

Some people get angry with God when things don't work out the way they want it. There are many things about your life you can't explain now until we get to Heaven.

The Bible says that time and chance happen to all things. The battle is not to the strong, nor the race to the swift. Allow God to lead and guide you. Remove your human wisdom.

God is the Maker of the whole universe and everything in it. God is omnipotent, omnipresent, and omniscient. He is my God and Father. God is in the Heaven of heavens, from where He oversees the whole universe.

That is not to say that God is responsible for everything that happens in the universe; He may permit what happens, even when it is not His Perfect Will. For instance, it is the Will of God that all men be saved (1 Tim. 2:4), but for you to be saved, you must have to submit your will to the Message of the Gospel.

God declares that He has set before men life and death, good and bad, and He has encouraged you to choose good and life (Deut. 30:19). However, what you choose will affect what you become.

God may allow the devil to cause an earthquake which may claim many lives, even though He doesn't want their death, because of sin, prayerlessness, faithlessness, and non-dependence on God.

There is the Good and Acceptable and Perfect Will of God in everything, just as the good, the better and the best in things. If men co-operate with God, His Will will come to pass on earth.

The more we co-operate with Him, the more His Will will be done on this earth. We co-operate with God through obedience, prayer, and faith. No matter how God may want to help us, our beliefs, actions, and confessions can stop Him.

God is not from any nation and He owns all nations. Though we know, from the Bible, that God has a special link with the nation of Israel, yet, He is not from Israel; Israel cannot dictate for Him, and He will not change His Standard because of Israel.

God cannot change His Standard for anyone and for any church. No matter how anointed you are, no matter what you may have, all came from God.

Many people do the things they do because they think that since this or that nation does the same things, they must be right; but this is not true in the ultimate sense. The thing that many fail to understand is that the devil is working in every nation of the earth.

No matter the nation you may come from, the devil had been working in your nation before you were born, and he will continue to work there. The devil has succeeded to work in many nations without being recognized.

There are many things that are being done in some nations of the world which people don't see as having come from the devil. For instance, when a country legalizes abortion, whether or not they know it, the work of the devil is being fulfilled in their midst.

God hates abortion; for no one has right to take any other person's life. No matter the theory or proposition medical science may make to make abortion look good, they are just dancing to the tone of the devil's deception. Once the zygote has been formed, a human being has come.

Let us consider the issue of women liberation movements. Have you noticed the rate of divorce and juvenile delinquencies these days? These are the long-term effects of women liberation movements.

When women decide to abandon their basic responsibilities in pursuit of secondary issues, the devil is at work, whether they recognize it or not. Women have the responsibility to be helpers suitable to their husbands.

I am not saying that women must not work, but most women have worked at the expense of their families. They get jobs that do not give them time to train their children well. Many cannot make their husbands happy because of their commitment to work and business.

Even if your husband is happy because of the money you are making, when your children are living however they want, both of you are wrong. I know many men don't take up their responsibilities, but allow the wife to fend for the family; this is wrong.

It is the responsibility of the husband to fend for the family, even though both of them should put their trust in God for their provisions.

This is why the devil has worked so hard, and he is still working, to frustrate the economy of the nations of the world so that what the man will get will not be able to support his family well, and the wife will start working (on her own) as well.

I know some women work to avoid idleness, and this is good, if the work doesn't stop you from doing your elementary job well. Every woman should spend at least two hours everyday in prayer and Bible study, apart from the normal family prayer-time.

You won't even be idle if you do your house work well. But many have left the maids to do what they should do. Why does a woman want to be the president of her country? Some will ask about Deborah. She was a prophetess who judged and God was their King.

Many women hide under the shadow of avoiding idleness to work, when, in fact, their real motive is to make money. Inasmuch as making money is good, what will it profit you if you make big money and your house (husband, children) is not in order?

Women should find enough time to pray for their husbands and children, even though the husband should pray as well. I tell you, even if your husband is a multimillionaire, the devil's attack through a witch or a wizard can reduce him to a poor man in a short while. But your diligence in prayer can avert it.

We will now consider the issue of whether it is good for women to put on trousers. One thing about dresses is that they are meant to cover the person putting them on, whether they are men or women.

Gowns, wrappers, skirts, blouses, trousers, shirts, etc are to cover the person wearing them. I want you to know that over the years, in every continent (America, Europe, Africa, Asia, etc), there have been changes in the modes of their dressing.

However, any dressing or change in dressing that does not glorify God is satanic and demonic, no matter what any person may think or say, even though you may not have it in mind as you put them on. That is the truth. The devil prefers to work under cover and without being noticed.

When women put on sleeveless blouses, mini-skirts, tight-fitting and partly transparent (revealing) dresses, they are glorifying satan, and helping him to fulfil his purpose, whether or not they know it.

Considering the biological features of women, I believe that women should not use pairs of trousers. Why? When a woman is matured sexually, one of the features that biologists tell us will be noticed in her is enlarged buttocks. Have you never noticed that trousers show their body contours for everybody to see? Trousers reveal their buttocks and laps seductively.

Now, don't say that you are going to allow your children wear pairs of trousers and when they mature, they will stop using them. If you train them up that way, when they are old, they will not depart from it (Prov. 22:6).

I know some may not be happy with me for saying this; but think of this, the Bible says that if doing something will cause your brother sin, you should avoid it (Rom. 14:15-23).

Of course, anyone can decide to sin because of what you did or do, even when the situation shouldn't have warranted it. You know that the Jews spoke against Jesus Christ and the Holy Spirit, even though Jesus Christ was just doing the Assignment God had given Him.

But seductive dresses or dressing seductively helps the devil spread his lust wave, and people get into the sins of lust, fornication, adultery, etc. Some will say that whoever wants to fall will fall, but you and I know that some things can make someone fall, when he wouldn't have fallen without them.

Let the Spirit of God lead you, and do not be led by your mind and thought. Trousers are neither an American culture nor a British culture.

It started at a time and got so much opposition there then; but over so many years later, the opposition has waned so much that some think it is their culture. After all, was there anything like America until Amerigo sailed past the Atlantic Ocean and found the land which was later developed to be America?

My conclusion is this: any dressing that helps the devil fulfil his will, plan, and purpose is from him. If you can't stop dressing this or that way because of Jesus Christ, can you lay down your life for Him? (Matt. 10:39).

THE IMMUTABILITY OF GOD'S WORD AND STANDARD

The Word of God is forever settled in Heaven. God is not a man to lie, and He is not a son of man to change His Mind. Has He spoken and shall He not bring it to pass? Instead of one Word from God to fail, heaven and earth shall pass away.

People try to change the Word of God to suit their desires. They use the Bible to defend themselves, when it is actually the devil that is quoting the Scripture to them wrongly, as he did to Jesus Christ. But God cannot be mocked; whatever you sow, that you will reap.

Brethren, contend earnestly for the faith which was once for all delivered to the Saints. For certain men have crept in unnoticed who long ago were marked out for this condemnation, ungodly men who turn the Grace of our God into lewdness, and deny the only Lord God and our Lord Jesus Christ.

But remember that the Lord, having saved the people out of the land of Egypt, afterward destroyed those who did not believe.

All the fathers of the Israelites were under the cloud, all passed through the sea, all were baptized into Moses in the cloud and in the sea, all ate the same spiritual food, and all drank the same spiritual drink.

But with most of them, God was not well-pleased, for their bodies were scattered in the wilderness. Now, these things became our examples, to the intent that we should not lust after evil things as they also lusted.

And do not become idolaters, as were some of them. Nor let us commit sexual immorality, as some of them did, and in one day twenty-three thousand fell; nor let us tempt Christ, as some of them also tempted, and were destroyed by serpents; nor complain, as some of them also complained, and were destroyed by the destroyer.

Now all these things happened to them as examples, and they were written for our admonition, upon whom the ends of the ages have come. Therefore, let him who thinks he stands take heed lest he fall.

No temptation has overtaken you, except such as is common to man; but God is faithful, Who will not allow you to be tempted beyond what you are able, but with the temptation will also make the way of escape, that you may be able to bear it (1 Cor. 10:1-13).

Therefore, we must give the more earnest heed to the things we have heard, lest we drift away. For if the Word spoken through angels proved steadfast, and every transgression and disobedience received a just recompense or reward, how shall we escape if we neglect so great a salvation;

Which at the first began to be spoken by the Lord, and was confirmed to us by those who heard Him. God also bearing witness both with signs and wonders, with various miracles, and Gifts of the Holy Spirit, according to His Own Will? (Heb. 2:1-4).

Beware, brethren, lest there be in any of you an evil heart of unbelief in departing from the Living God, but exhort one another daily, while it is called "Today," lest any of you be hardened through the deceitfulness of sin.

For we have become partakers of Christ, if we hold the beginning of our confidence steadfast to the end, while it is said "Today, if you will hear His Voice, do not harden your hearts, as in the rebellion." For who, having heard, rebelled? Indeed, was it not all who came out of Egypt, led by Moses?

Now, with whom was He angry forty years? Was it not with those who sinned, whose corpses fell in the wilderness? And to whom did He swear that they would not enter His Rest, but to those who did not obey?

So we see that they could not enter in because of unbelief. Therefore, since a promise remains of entering His Rest, let us fear, lest any of you seem to have come short of it. For indeed, the Gospel was preached to us, as well as to them;

But the Word which they heard did not profit them, not being mixed with faith in those who heard it. For we who have believed do enter that rest (Heb. 3:12-4:3).

The angels who did not keep their proper domain, but left their own abode, He has reserved in everlasting chains under darkness for judgment of the Great Day. For God did not spare the angels who sinned, but cast them down to Hell; and delivered them into chains of darkness to be reserved for judgment.

God did not spare the ancient world, but saved Noah, one of eight people, a preacher of righteousness, bringing in the Flood on the worlds of the ungodly.

As Sodom and Gomorrah, and the cities around them, in a similar manner to these, having given themselves over to sexual immorality and gone after strange flesh, are set forth as an example, suffering the vengeance of Eternal Fire.

God turned the cities of Sodom and Gomorrah into ashes, condemned them to destruction, making them an example to those who afterward would live ungodly; and delivered righteous Lot, who was oppressed by the filthy conduct of the wicked (for that righteous man, dwelling among them tormented his righteous soul from day to day, by seeing and hearing their lawless deeds).

These dreamers defile the flesh, reject authority, and speak evil of dignitaries. They speak evil of whatever they do not know; and whatever they know naturally, like brute beast, in these things they corrupt themselves. Woe to them!

This is because they have gone into the way of Cain, have turned greedily in the error of Balaam for profit, and perished in the rebellion of Korah.

These are spots in your love-feasts, while they feast with you without fear, serving only themselves. They are clouds without water, carried about by the winds; late autumn trees without fruit, twice dead, pulled up by the roots.

These are raging waves of the sea, foaming up their own shame; wandering stars for whom is reserved the Blackness of Darkness forever.

Behold, the Lord comes with ten thousand of His Saints, to execute judgment on all, to convict all who are ungodly among them of all their ungodly deeds, which they have committed in an ungodly way, and of all the harsh things which ungodly sinners have spoken against Him.

These are grumblers, complainers, walking according to their own lusts; and they mouth great swelling word, flattering people to gain advantage. Many walk according to their own ungodly lusts. These are sensual persons, who cause divisions, not having the Spirit.

But you beloved, building yourselves up on your most holy faith, praying in the Holy Spirit; keep yourselves in the Love of God. On some have compassion, making a distinction, but others save with fear, pulling them out of fire.

There were false prophets among the Israelites of Old, just as they are false teachers among the Church today, who secretly bring in destructive heresies, even denying the Lord Who bought them, and bring on themselves swift destruction.

And many follow their destructive ways, because of whom the way of truth is blasphemed. By covetousness, they exploit you with deceptive words. The Lord knows how to deliver the Godly out of temptations and to reserve the unjust under punishment for the Day of Judgment.

The Lord will judge those who walk according to the flesh in the lust of uncleanness and despise authority. They are presumptuous, self-willed. They are not afraid to speak evil of dignitaries.

They speak evil of the things they do not understand, and will utterly perish in their own corruption, and will receive the wages of unrighteousness.

They are spots and blemishes, carousing in their own deceptions while they feast with you, having eyes full of adultery and that cannot cease from sin, enticing unstable souls.

They have a heart trained in covetous practices, and are accursed children. They have forsaken the right way and gone astray. While they promise them liberty, they themselves are slaves of corruption; for by whom a person is overcome, by him also he is brought into bondage.

For if after they have escaped the pollutions of this world through the knowledge of the Lord and Saviour Jesus Christ, they are again entangled and overcome, the latter end is worse for them than the beginning.

For it would have been better for them not to have known the way of righteousness, than having known it, to turn from the Holy Commandments delivered to them (Jude 1 and 2 Pet. 2).

God cannot change His Word and Standard for anyone. God is of Purer Eyes than to behold sin, disobedience, unrighteousness, and iniquity.

If God could turn His Face away from Jesus Christ Himself when He was carrying the sins of the world on the Cross of Calvary, who are you that God will allow you into His Kingdom with sin? All the ungodly, the unrighteous, and sinners will be cast into the Lake of Fire, Hell Fire.

God can never lie nor fail to fulfil His Word. God has promised that He will provide all that you need. He has also promised to protect you. Therefore, do not worry; do not be anxious for anything. Anyway, worrying will not solve the problem. Commit your cares to the Lord for He cares for you.

By the Stripes of Jesus Christ you have been healed. The Bible says that you were healed by the Stripes of Jesus Christ (1 Pet. 2:24). That means that even when you may be feeling the symptom of the sickness, you were healed.

Learn to walk by faith, and don't accept the package of the devil. Speak according to the Word of God, and believe the same, and the plans of the devil will fail to come to fruition in your life. The Promises of the Almighty can never fail; hold on to anything He has promised you.

Preach and teach the Gospel of the Kingdom of God. Don't preach or teach human wisdom and reasoning. Don't preach psychology, philosophy, or faithlessness. God's Word can never fail, and if you preach and teach it, you will see outstanding results of it, both in your life and in the lives of those who hear you.

Where is your heart? This is one of the most important questions anyone can ask you. Where your heart is, has a lot to do with you.

No wonder the Bible says that if you were raised with Christ, seek those things which are Above, where Christ Jesus is sitting at the Right Hand of God. Set your mind on things Above, not on things on the earth.

If you do that, when Jesus Christ Who is our Life appears, then you also will appear with Him in Glory (Col. 3:1-4).

Where do you put your treasure? Is it in banks, in property-development, or in investments? The Lord Jesus Christ tells us that where your treasure is, is where your heart will be also (Lk. 12:34).

If you don't labour for the Lord, how will your heart be in Heaven? If you seek the praise of men, instead of that of God, how will your heart be in Heaven? If you don't win souls for the Lord, if you don't support the Work of the Lord, if you don't obey the Lord, your heart will not be in Heaven.

Where your heart is has a lot to do with you. This is because the Word of God says that out of the abundance of the heart the mouth speaks (Matt. 12:34). Your words and actions are a reflection of what is in your heart.

If your heart is filled with good things, your heart will produce words and actions that will prepare you for Heaven. If your heart is full of the Word of God (Col. 3:16), and you are obedient to the Word you know, your reward will be abundant in Heaven and your heart will be there.

Those who are rich in this present age should not be haughty and proud, nor trust in uncertain riches but in the Living God, Who gives us richly all things to enjoy.

They should do good, be rich in good works, ready to give, willing to share, storing up for themselves a good foundation for the time to come, that they may lay hold on Eternal Life (1 Tim. 6:17-19). Then will their hearts be in Heaven.

The Bible teaches that it is easier for a camel to pass through a needle's hole than for a rich man to enter the Kingdom of Heaven (Mk 10:24-27). With men, that is impossible, but not with God; for with God, all things are possible (verse 27).

If a rich man will submit to the Word of God, the Word of God will remove his heart from the things of this world, and he will begin to set his heart on things Above, which only can make him please God. Do you remember the rich young ruler who could not obey Jesus Christ? (Matt. 19:16-26).

The rich man went away sorrowful because his heart was on his riches. If you are rich, God gave you the riches; therefore, instead of trusting on the riches, trust the Giver. Remember that riches have wings, and they do fly away (Prov. 23:5).

Some may trust in horses and some may trust in chariots, but we will trust in the Name of our God (Psa. 20:7). Cursed is the man that puts his trust on men and on money (Jer. 17:5-6).

The Bible says that if you lay up treasures for yourself in this world, you may lose them to the hands of thieves and robbers. Even, rust and moth do destroy material things. However, if you lay them up in Heaven, be sure that neither thieves, robbers, rust, nor moths are there (Matt. 6:19-21).

Furthermore, in nakedness you came and in nakedness you will go at death (Job 1:21). Remember the rich man that died the night after he had made plans to enjoy his riches and wealth. The Lord called him a fool (Lk. 12:20).

He was called a fool because he had no heart for God. To have a heart for God is not to come to church and make a donation of one million dollar when you have no plan to serve and obey God.

No matter how rich you may be, you will have one room, one car, one pair of shoes at a time; and finally, you will have one grave. Don't allow the riches that the Lord has given you or allowed you to possess lead to your Eternal Destruction.

Some people's hearts are on their past mistakes, the disappointments of the past, their past sins and hurts they received from people. Some people have vowed not to forgive this or that person.

If you don't forgive, God will not forgive you also; and you will remain a sinner, no matter how you confess (Matt. 6:15). Bitterness in your heart will hinder your spiritual life and can result to mental or physical sickness.

The Bible says that if you confess your sins, God is faithful and just to forgive your sins and to cleanse you from all unrighteousness (1 Jn 1:9).

If you repented and confessed your sins, God has forgiven you: go ahead and live the good life that Christ Jesus has provided for you. Putting your heart and mind on your past sins will greatly affect your Christian walk; forgive yourself.

Your past mistakes and disappointments can be turned into a great future. Even though the devil steals from you (and you can stop or could have stopped it through prayer), know that all things work together for good to them that love God, to them who are called according to His Good Purpose (Rom. 8:28).

The Lord God is able to restore the years that the cankerworm and the palmerworm have eaten (Joel 2:25-26). Nothing is impossible with God (Mk 10:27).

Some people's hearts are on education and certificates. Education is good, and certificates are good; but they should not stop you from doing what you are supposed to be doing for God.

I tell you, there are many people in institutions of higher learning, like universities, polytechnics, and colleges of education, today who the Lord would have they had entered Theological schools (and note that there are many wrong and bad Theological schools) and prepare for ministry immediately after high or secondary schools.

God pleads with you to give Him your heart (Prov. 23:26). If He has your heart, He has your all. Walk with God in perfect heart, the perfect heart that says, "Since God has said that this should be this way, it should be this way."

Walking with God in perfect heart made God to add fifteen more years to King Hezekiah, when he prayed (2 Kgs 20:1-7). Your heart is your spirit-man. Apostle Paul said that he has always walked with (or followed) God with all pure conscience since his youth (Acts 23:1).

Did you notice that he was saying that even when he was killing and imprisoning Christians, he did what he did with a perfect heart? No wonder he told us later that he did what he did ignorantly in unbelief (1 Tim. 1:13).

And we know that God forgave him when he repented and submitted to God. Even though you may still be making some mistakes now, don't be discouraged: follow God with a perfect heart and make every effort to know God and His Word the more so that you can avoid those mistakes.

The heart of a sinner is deceitful and desperately wicked (Jer. 17:9). All the ways of a man seem right to him, but the Lord tries and weighs his heart (Prov. 21:2).

If men disappoint or hurt you, know that they are men. If they criticize, slander, or backbite you, learn to swallow up the negative effects the devil will want to bring your way through them. Don't allow any stumbling block of the enemy knock you down.

God loves you very much. Give Him your all; give Him your heart. If He has your heart, it will be easy to correct and instruct you. Don't say that you know everything. When you get to know more, you will realize that you had known little.

Don't let the devil have your heart. Don't sell your soul to the devil for anything. Don't be like Esau, who for a single meal sold his birthright and lost it forever.

SIN AND DISOBEDIENCE

Sin is going contrary to the Word of God. Sin is disobedience, and disobedience is sin. When God tells you to do something, if you don't do it, it is sin. If He tells you to avoid something, if you don't avoid it, if you do it, it is sin.

Sin entered the world by one man (Adam), and one Man (Jesus Christ) came to take away sin. Sin came from the devil but righteousness, peace, and joy came from the Lord.

There are three basic definitions of sin, as found in the Bible. Sin is lawlessness, the transgression of the Law (1 Jn 3:4). Sin is anything not done in faith (Rom. 14:23). Sin is knowing what you should do and not doing it (Jas 4:17).

These three definitions of sin are comprehensive and they touch many different things. God hates sin, though He loves the sinner. God is of Purer Eyes than to behold sin (Habk. 1:13).

Sin will keep you far from God. God will do everything to save the sinner, but if he refuses, he bears the consequences.

Sin is the transgression of the Law. To transgress the Law is to go against the Law. When the Law is mentioned, some think that the Law has been done away with. This needs proper interpretation. Jesus Christ came to fulfil the Law and the Prophets, and not to destroy them (Matt. 5:17).

The ritual Laws of the Old Testament have been done away with, but not the moral Laws. Today, instead of resting and worshipping God on the Sabbath (Saturday), we rest and worship on the first day of the week (Sunday) (1 Cor. 16:2; Acts 20:7).

The important thing there, is that God loves us and wants us to rest. He gives His beloved rest. It is not because we work every time that we succeed. God is able to supply all our needs.

Actually, we are supposed to worship God everyday. So, everyday is our day of worship. But unlike in the Old Testament where they couldn't even cook on the Sabbath, we know now that the Law was made for man and not man for the Law (Mk 2:27).

But we know that "You shall have no other god before Me" still exists. "You shall honour your father and your mother," "You shall not commit adultery," etc still exist today. But even when we do these things, we do them out of love for God and for man.

All the Law is summed up in love: you shall love the Lord God with all your heart, with all your mind, and with all your strength, and you shall love your neighbour as yourself (Deut. 6:5; Matt. 22:37).

We live by the Law of Liberty (Jas 1:25; Jas 2:12), and we do not use our liberty as an opportunity for the flesh (Gal. 5:13).

Sin is anything not done in faith. The Bible says that if you do something in doubt, it is sin, and sin leads to condemnation (Rom. 14:23). Think of the many it-doesn't-matters among Christians today.

I have snapped pictures in a university and you see a lot of things with respect to dressing in the environment. In fact, a time came that I stopped snapping normal pictures except passports, apart from special cases, there. In the university environment, you see a lot of indecent dressings, both among ladies and among young men.

Even among people who call themselves Believers, you see a lot of indecent dressings. People dress indecently to many campus fellowships and churches.

People paint themselves and look like unbelievers, and yet these are people who had been born again and washed with Christ's Precious Blood. Later, they despised the Blood, and live however they want in the name of it-doesn't-matter.

They wear body-hugs and transparent dresses. The worst is that when many of them came in newly in their first year, they used to dress decently, but as time went on, they disappointed both God Who gave them the admission and their parents who sponsor them.

There are many other areas where people live in doubt and say that it makes no difference. Right in their heart, they are not confident of what they are doing, even though many people tell them that it is sinful.

Students live the life of examination malpractice, and yet they are Believers. Do you know why, after Jesus Christ had talked about regeneration in John 3:3, He talked of living by the Word and the Spirit in John 3:5?

The last definition of sin is not doing the good that you know that you should do. In the Epistle of James, James speaks of a case in which a brother comes to you for help and you know that you can and should help him, but instead of helping him, you tell him to go in peace (Jas 2:14-17).

This definition of sin holds many Christians. For instance, if the Spirit of God speaks to your heart to go out for evangelism or to preach to a particular person, if you don't do it, it is sin and disobedience.

No wonder the Word of God says that if the Christian refuses to preach to and warn the sinner, and that sinner dies in his sin, the sinner will go to Hell Fire for his sins, but his blood will be required from the Christian (Ezek. 33:6-9).

If the Spirit witnesses to your heart to pray, then pray; if He tells you to study the Bible, do just that. Preach the Word of God. Be prepared in season and out of season (2 Tim. 4:2). If you know you should love your wife and refuse to love her, it is sin to you.

Of course, I had said that sin is disobedience and disobedience is sin. When God gives us His Commandments, He expects us to obey them. Our obedience to God's Word is for our own good. If we obey Him, He will bless us.

Also, our obedience to the Word of God will keep us from harms. For instance, when God tells you not to commit fornication, He expects you to obey Him, and He will bless you for obeying Him. However, apart from that, it will save you from many venereal diseases.

Disobedience to the Word of God will receive punishment, both in this life and after death. It is true that because of Jesus Christ's Intercession for us at the Right Hand of the Father, God's Judgment does not fall on us immediately like in the Old Testament.

However, when the time of grace God gives you expires, you will be judged (Rev. 2:21). Furthermore, Hell Fire is reserved for sinners and the disobedient.

Has the Lord as great delight in burnt offerings and sacrifices, as in obeying the Voice of the Lord? Behold, to obey is better than sacrifice, and to hearken than fat of rams. Rebellion is as the sin of witchcraft; and stubbornness is as iniquity and idolatry (1 Sam. 15:22-23).

Those were the Words Prophet Samuel spoke to King Saul, after the king disobeyed God's Commandment to him. What is worthy of note in this place is that the king obeyed God but his obedience was partial.

We can then deduce, from God's Reaction, that partial obedience is disobedience. His disobedience cost him the kingdom of Israel, for he was dethroned as a king without an offspring to succeed him. Apart from that, he died in the battle field.

The devil wants to destroy you, he wants to kill you and steal from you. Don't give him a place through disobedience (Eph. 4:27). He that breaks the hedge shall be bitten by the serpent (Eccl. 10:8).

The problem is that many don't value our inheritance in Christ Jesus. Many Christians have despised Esau and spoken badly of him. But do you know that many have behaved and acted worse than Esau?

Some have sacrificed their souls and inheritance for an employment. Some have lost their destinies for a ten-minute sex. Can you lose your life for the Cause of Christ? (Heb. 12:16-17; Matt. 10:39).

Shadrach, Meshach and Abed-Nego told King Nebuchadnezzar that their God was able to deliver them, and He will deliver them. However, they went on to tell the king that they will not bow to his golden image, they will not disobey their God, even though their God refuses to deliver them (Dan. 3:16-30).

You have not yet resisted to bloodshed, striving against sin (Heb. 12:4). Jesus Christ was tempted at all points, and yet He did not sin. You are a Christian; therefore, be like Christ!

True freedom is freedom from sin and disobedience. True gain is making Heaven at last and receiving abundant reward from God in His Eternal Kingdom. If you say you are free, when you are still bound by sin and disobedience, you are in bondage.

If you gain the whole world and lose your soul at last, you gained nothing. Make up your mind to obey God at all time, no matter the cost and sacrifice.

The Bible says that all other sins that a man commits are outside the body, but he that commits fornication sins against his own body. The Word of God tells us to flee fornication. It did not say that we should avoid fornication, but that we should flee fornication.

To flee is to run away from something as though you are afraid (in fear) of it. Do you not know that your body is the Temple of the Holy Spirit, Who is in you, Who you received from God, and you are not your own? (1 Cor. 6:18-20).

You were bought with a Price; therefore, glorify God in your body, and in your spirit, which are God's. The body is earthly and physical. With my spirit, I contact the spiritual realm; with my soul, I contact the mental realm; and with my body, I contact the physical realm.

You should always allow your spirit, who is born again, to rule your life. Your body is not born again, and if you allow the dictates and desires of the body to govern you, you will be a carnal Believer.

The body wants three basic things which are: food, sex, and comfort. Comfort is connected to rest, relaxation, and sleep. All those appetites were given us by God, and we have to use them the right way.

Food is good, but if you are not careful, you will become gluttonous. Love of food will keep you from fasting, and you will become less sensitive spiritually.

Sleep and relaxation can make you become lazy if you love them. Too much sleep will affect your prayer-life and your obedience to God. Of course, he who loves sleep will not be rich.

You must work to excel in life and in ministry. Don't be idle, for the idle mind is the devil's workshop: when he is through with the mental planning and luring, he will execute it.

Sex has its moral and legal use. Let's forget about the legal use, for now, because many laws existing in many countries of the world were inspired by the devil and his demons. When a country approves same-sex marriage, the devil is at work in that country.

When a country says that nothing is wrong with sex outside marriage, if both partners give their consent, that is satan at work. Christians should pray against the approval of sinful bills or laws in their nations.

WARNINGS FROM THE LORD

However, there is the moral and Biblical use of sex, and that is that sex must be within marriage. Do you know that some people are living together as husbands and wives without marriage?

The Samaritan woman that Jesus Christ had conversation with was living with someone who was not her husband (Jn 4:16-19). My dear, if you are like that, you better get married before you end in Hell Fire.

Sexual immorality is a sin against God, and it has many forms and associates. They include: fornication, adultery, masturbation, lust, lesbianism, homosexuality, incest, voyeurism, pornography, bestiality, necrophilia, orgies, paedophile, bisexuality, heterosexuality, etc.

If you indulge in any of these, you are heading towards Hell. No sexually immoral person will inherit the Kingdom of God and of Christ (Eph. 5:3-6).

Fornication is to have sex with someone you are not married to. Adultery is for a married person to have sex with someone he or she is not married to. Masturbation is to make yourself sexually excited by touching or rubbing your sexual organs.

Lust is to have very strong sexual desire for someone even when you have not actually had the physical intercourse. Lesbianism is for a woman to be sexually attracted to another woman.

Homosexuality is a man being attracted sexually to another man. Incest is illegal sex between people who are closely related, like a brother and his sister, or a father and his daughter. Voyeurism is getting sexual pleasure from secretly watching other people's sexual activities.

Pornography is the treatment of sexual acts in pictures, film, or writing in a way that is intended to make people feel sexually excited. Bestiality is sexual relations between a person and an animal.

Necrophilia is sexual interest in dead bodies. Orgy is sexual activity in a group; that is, having sex with more than one person at a time. Paedophile is someone who is sexually attracted to small children. Bisexuality is to be sexually attracted to both men and women. Heterosexuality is to be sexually attracted to people of the opposite sex.

The Word of God tells us to flee fornication. Don't say that you cannot fall and remain in a closed dark room with the opposite sex.

In the Bible, sexual immorality made people to lose their God-given purposes. Reuben who was the first son of Jacob lost his first place because of sexual immorality (Gen. 49:3-4). King David brought immorality and sword to his family by adultery and murder (2 Sam. 11 & 12).

Because of lust and pride, King Solomon despised the Law of God and married foreign women who turned his heart from following the Lord in his old age. Sampson, that Old Testament strong man, lost his power and mission due to sex (1 Kgs 11; Jgs. 16).

There are many diseases associated with sexual immorality or sex. The sexually transmitted diseases (STD's) include: syphilis, gonorrhea, HIV/AIDS, and others. Do you see that God loves you when He tells you to flee fornication?

Joseph fled from fornication when Portiphar's wife tried all she could to get Joseph into that sin. Joseph said that to do that would amount to sinning against God and Portiphar (Gen. 39:4-23). If you deny God because of sexual urge, can you lay down your life for Him?

Many ladies dress indecently and seductively. Many say that they are Christians and your appearance does not matter but your heart. But man looks at outward appearance (1 Sam. 16:7). Woe to him or her that will cause a brother or a sister to fall (Matt. 18:6).

Dress decently and you will receive the Acceptance of God and of men. Body-hugs (tight-fitting dresses), sleeveless blouses, revealing dresses, mini-skirts, hanging blouses that show your belly, the ones that reveal your breasts, and many others are satanic, devilish, and demonic.

The Bible says that because iniquity shall abound, the love of many shall wax cold (Matt. 24:12). Some even get involved in sexual immorality so that people will not say that they are not civilized and matured.

Do not give your strength to women (Prov. 31:3). He that keeps company with harlots spends his substance (Prov. 29:3). There is the attire of a harlot (Prov. 7:10). Do not let your heart decline to the harlot's paths.

The immoral woman has cast down many wounded: yea, many strong men have been slain by her. Her house is the way to Hell, going down to the chambers of death.

Don't sell your birthright and inheritance for sex, no matter the pressure and urge. God is able to help you overcome. Depend on the Holy Spirit, and not on the strength of the flesh. By the arms of the flesh shall no one prevail (1 Sam. 2:9).

Some sexually immoral tendencies are as a result of demonic strongholds. If you find that you won't overcome the urge to have sex, please, take some time and fast, pray, study the Bible, and wait on God.

Let's mean business here; if you fast for three days and nights straight, you will not die. If you fast till 3:00 p.m. or 6:00 p.m. for seven days, you will not die either. Many want a quick-fix method.

Inasmuch as there is deliverance that can be received by prayer, many have gone into the hands of false ministers in the name of deliverance ministries. What about telling your pastor?

PSALMS ABOUT HOLINESS, OBEDIENCE, GOODNESS, AND RIGHTEOUSNESS AND THE REWARDS

"Lord, who may abide in Your Tabernacle? Who may dwell in Your Holy Hill? He who walks uprightly, and works righteousness, and speaks the truth in his heart; he who does not backbite with his tongue, nor does evil to his neighbour, nor does he take up a reproach against his friend;

"In whose eyes a vile person is despised, but he honours those who fear the Lord; he who swears to his own hurt and does not change; he who does not put out his money at usury, nor does he take a bribe against the innocent. He who does these things shall never be moved (Psa. 15).

"My heart is overflowing with a good theme; I recite my composition concerning the King; my tongue is the pen of a ready writer. You are fairer than the sons of men; grace is poured upon Your Lips; therefore God has blessed You forever.

"Gird Your Sword upon Your Thigh, O Mighty One, with Your Glory and Your Majesty. And in Your Majesty ride prosperously because of truth, humility, and righteousness; and Your Right Hand shall teach You awesome things.

"Your Arrows are sharp in the heart of the King's enemies; the peoples fall under You. Your Throne, O God, is forever and ever; a scepter of righteousness is the scepter of Your Kingdom.

"You love righteousness and hate wickedness; therefore God, Your God, has anointed You with the oil of gladness more than Your companions. All Your Garments are scented with myrrh and aloes and cassia, out of the ivory palaces, by which they have made You glad.

"Kings' daughters are among Your honourable women; at Your Right Hand stands the queen in gold from Ophir. Listen, O daughter, consider and incline your ear; forget your own people also, and your father's house; so the King will greatly desire your beauty; because He is your Lord, worship Him.

"And the daughter of Tyre will come with a gift; the rich among the people will seek your favour. The royal daughter is all glorious within the palace; her clothing is woven with gold. She shall be brought to the King in robes of many colours; the virgins, her companions who follow her, shall be brought to You.

"With gladness and rejoicing they shall be brought; they shall enter the King's Palace. Instead of Your fathers shall be Your sons, whom You shall make princes in all the earth. I will make Your Name to be remembered in all generations; therefore the people shall praise You forever and ever (Psa. 45).

"Behold, how good and how pleasant it is for brethren to dwell together in unity! It is like the precious oil upon the head, running down on the beard, the beard of Aaron, running down on the edge of his garments. It is like the dew of Hermon, descending upon the mountains of Zion; for there the Lord commanded the blessing – life forevermore (Psa. 133).

"Lord, I cry out to You; make haste to me! Give ear to my voice when I cry out to You. Let my prayer be set before You as incense, the lifting up of my hands as the evening sacrifice. Set a guard, O Lord, over my mouth; keep watch over the door of my lips.

"Do not incline my heart to any evil thing, to practice wicked works with men who work iniquity; and do not let me eat of their delicacies. Let the righteous strike me; it shall be a kindness. And let him rebuke me; it shall be as excellent oil; let my head not refuse it. For still my prayer is against the deeds of the wicked.

"Their judges are overthrown by the sides of the cliff, and they hear my words, for they are sweet. Our bones are scattered at the mouth of the grave, as when one ploughs and breaks up the earth.

"But my eyes are upon You, O God the Lord; in You I take refuge; do not leave my soul destitute. Keep me from the snares they have laid for me, and from the traps of the workers of iniquity. Let the wicked fall into their own nets, while I escape safely (Psa. 141).

"Blessed is he who considers the poor; the Lord will deliver him in time of trouble. The Lord will preserve him and keep him alive, and he will be blessed on the earth; You will not deliver him to the will of his enemies.

"The Lord will strengthen him on his bed of illness; You will sustain him on his sickbed. I said, 'Lord, be merciful to me; heal my soul, for I have sinned against You.' My enemies speak evil of me: 'When will he die, and his name perish?'

"And if he comes to see me, he speaks lies; his heart gathers iniquity to itself; when he goes out, he tells it. All who hate me whisper together against me; against me they devise my hurt. 'An evil disease,' they say, 'clings to him. And now that he lies down, he will rise up no more.'

"Even my own familiar friend in whom I trusted, who ate my bread, has lifted up his heel against me. But You, O Lord, be merciful to me, and raise me up, that I may repay them. By this I know that You are well pleased with me, because my enemy does not triumph over me.

"As for me, You uphold me in my integrity, and set me before Your Face forever. Blessed be the Lord God of Israel from everlasting to everlasting! Amen and Amen (Psa. 41).

"Do not fret because of evildoers, nor be envious of the workers of iniquity. For they shall soon be cut down like the grass, and wither as the green herb. Trust in the Lord, and do good; dwell in the land, and feed on His Faithfulness.

"Delight yourself also in the Lord, and He shall give you the desires of your heart. Commit your way to the Lord, trust also in Him, and He shall bring it to pass. He shall bring forth your righteousness as the light, and your justice as the noonday.

"Rest in the Lord, and wait patiently for Him; do not fret because of him who prospers in his way, because of the man who brings wicked schemes to pass. Cease from anger, and forsake wrath; do not fret – it only causes harm.

"For evildoers shall be cut off; but those who wait on the Lord, they shall inherit the earth. For yet a little while and the wicked shall be no more; INDEED, you will look carefully for his place, but it shall be no more.

"But the meek shall inherit the earth, and shall delight themselves in the abundance of peace. The wicked plots against the just, and gnashes at him with his teeth. The Lord laughs at him, for He sees that his day is coming.

"The wicked have drawn the sword and have bent their bow, to cast down the poor and needy, to slay those who are of upright conduct. Their sword shall enter their own heart, and their bows shall be broken. A little that a righteous man has is better than the riches of many wicked.

"For the arms of the wicked shall be broken, but the Lord upholds the righteous. The Lord knows the days of the upright, and their inheritance shall be forever. They shall not be ashamed in the evil time, and in the days of famine they shall be satisfied.

"But the wicked shall perish; and the enemies of the Lord, like the splendour of the meadows, shall vanish. Into smoke they shall vanish away. The wicked borrows and does not repay, but the righteous shows mercy and gives.

"For those blessed by Him shall inherit the earth, but those cursed by Him shall be cut off. The steps of a good man are ordered by the Lord, and He delights in his way. Though he fall, he shall not be utterly cast down; for the Lord upholds him with His Hand.

"I have been young, and now am old; yet I have not seen the righteous forsaken, nor his descendants begging bread. He is ever merciful, and lends; and his descendants are blessed. Depart from evil, and do good; and dwell forevermore.

"For the Lord loves justice, and does not forsake His Saints; they are preserved forever, but the descendants of the wicked shall be cut off. The righteous shall inherit the land, and dwell in it forever. The mouth of the righteous speaks wisdom, and his tongue talks of justice.

"The Law of his God is in his heart; none of his steps shall slide. The wicked watches the righteous, and seeks to slay him. The Lord will not leave him in his hand, nor condemn him when he is judged.

"Wait on the Lord, and keep His Way, and He shall exalt you to inherit the land; when the wicked are cut off, you shall see it. I have seen the wicked in great power, and spreading himself like a native green tree.

"Yet he passed away, and behold, he was no more; indeed I sought him, but he could not be found. Mark the blameless man, and observe the upright; for the future of that man is peace. But the transgressors shall be destroyed together; the future of the wicked shall be cut off.

"But the salvation of the righteous is from the Lord; He is their Strength in the time of trouble. And the Lord shall help them and deliver them; He shall deliver them from the wicked, and save them, because they trust in Him (Psa. 37).

As a general rule, you should be able to know the difference between the Old Testament and the New Testament. There are some things that were allowed in the Old Testament dispensation, which are not allowed in the New Testament dispensation.

For instance, whereas people were rewarded according to their works in the Old Testament, we are not to reward evil with evil in the New Testament. The Bible says, "You have heard that it was said, 'An eye for an eye and a tooth for a tooth.' But I tell you not to resist an evil person. But whoever slaps you on your right cheek, turn the other to him also.

"If anyone wants to sue you and take away your tunic, let him have your cloak also. And whoever compels you to go one mile, go with him two. Give to him who asks you, and from him who wants to borrow from you do not turn away.

"You have heard that it was said, 'You shall love your neighbour and hate your enemy.' But I say to you, love your enemies, bless those who curse you, do good to those who hate you, and pray for those who spitefully use you and persecute you,

"That you may be sons of your Father in Heaven; for He makes His sun rise on the evil and on the good, and sends rain on the just and on the unjust. For if you love those who love you, what reward have you? Do not even the tax collectors do the same?

"And if you greet your brethren only, what do you do more than others? Do not even the tax collectors do so? Therefore you shall be perfect, just as your Father in Heaven is perfect" (Matt. 5:38-48).

Also, in the Old Testament, they lived by their righteousness; but in the New Testament, even though we are to live in holiness and obey God, as a prove that we truly love Him, yet we live by the Righteousness and Sacrifice of Jesus Christ. To this end, the Bible says, "For Christ is the End of the Law for righteousness to everyone who believes.

"For Moses writes about the righteousness which is of the Law, 'The man who does those things shall live by them.' But the righteousness of faith speaks in this way, 'Do not say in your heart, "Who will ascend into Heaven?"' (that is, to bring Christ down from Above) or, '"Who will descend into the abyss?"' (that is, to bring Christ up from the dead).

"But what does it say? 'The Word is near you, in your mouth and in your heart' (that is, the Word of Faith which we preach): that if you confess with your mouth the Lord Jesus and believe in your heart that God has raised Him from the dead, you will be saved.

"For with the heart one believes unto righteousness, and with the mouth confession is made unto salvation. For the Scripture says, 'Whoever believes on Him will not be put to shame.' For there is no distinction between Jew and Greek, for the Same Lord over all is rich to all who call upon Him. For 'whoever calls on the Name of the Lord shall be saved'" (Rom. 10:4-13).

In this New Testament, we operate with the spirit of love, mercy, forgiveness, and love, unlike in the Old Testament, where they operated with the spirit of judgment. This why the Bible says, "Now it came to pass, when the time had come for Him to be received Up, that He steadfastly set His Face to go to Jerusalem, and sent messengers before His Face.

"And as they went, they entered a village of the Samaritans, to prepare for Him. But they did not receive Him, because His Face was set for the journey to Jerusalem. And when His Disciples James and John saw this, they said, 'Lord, do You want us to command fire to come down from Heaven and consume them, just as Elijah did?'

"But He turned and rebuked them, and said, 'You do not know what manner of spirit you are of. For the Son of Man did not come to destroy men's lives but to save them.' And they went to another village (Lk. 9:51-56).

"If it is possible, as much as depends on you, live peaceably with all men. Beloved, do not avenge yourselves, but rather give place to wrath; for it is written, 'Vengeance is Mine, I will repay,' says the Lord.

"Therefore 'if your enemy is hungry, feed him; if he is thirsty, give him a drink; for in so doing you will heap coals of fire on his head.' Do not be overcome by evil, but overcome evil with good" (Rom. 12:18-21).

Never Say That God Said What He Did Not Say!

DEMONIC AND SATANIC ACTIVITIES TODAY

The Bible says that the works of satan and his hosts are stealing, killing, and destroying (Jn 10:10). And the reason Jesus Christ came was that He might destroy the works of the devil (1 Jn 3:8). Therefore, our work, as Christians, is to destroy the works of the devil.

In these days of concentrated satanic and demonic activities, we have to be wise and operate according to the Word of God in order to be free from the plans, purposes, and works of the devil and his hosts. Yes, Jesus Christ has freed us from the power of the devil; but the Bible tells us what to do in order to maintain and enjoy that freedom and victory that our Lord got for us.

This is why the Bible says, "Nor give place to the devil" (Eph. 4:27), and "Resist the devil and he will flee from you" (Jas 4:7). This is talking of the responsibility that God gave you as a Christian: it is not God that will resist the devil for you, but you yourself. And He has given you the resources you need to resist the devil. If you give the devil a place in your life, then the devil will gladly have that place.

Yet, "Behold, I give you the authority to trample on serpents and scorpions, and over all the power of the enemy, and nothing shall by any means hurt you" (Lk. 10:19). And, "No weapon formed against you shall prosper, and every tongue which rises against you in judgment, you shall condemn. This is the heritage of the Servants of the LORD, and their righteousness is from Me," says the LORD (Isa. 54:17).

Also, "And these signs will follow those who believe: in My Name they will cast out demons; they will speak with new tongues; they will take up serpents; and if they drink anything deadly, it will by no means hurt them; they will lay hands on the sick, and they will recover" (Mk 16:17-18). These and many others are God's Provisions for us as His children; but we must also take up our responsibilities, so that we will enjoy the things that Jesus Christ has provided for us to the fullest.

In these end-times, learn and get used to studying the Word of God (in order to know your rights, privileges, power, and authority as a Believer in Christ Jesus); and apply what you know, because it is applied knowledge that brings the desired results. Learn to fast and pray in these days of concentrated demonic activities. But don't be afraid, for God is with you and for you! Flies do not perch on boiling oil, even as serpents do not coil around red-hot iron. Therefore, maintain a red-hot spiritual life always.

Learn to pray over and bless your food and water. The Bible says, "For it is sanctified by the Word of God and prayer" (1 Tim. 4:1-2). Many products in the market are polluted by witches and demons. Pray and bless the things you buy in the market, especially edible things and pre-packed and canned foods. Pray over yourself when you go for such services as barbing and hair-keeping. Be sensitive to know who you should not patronize, even for things like dry-cleaning.

Please, no matter how I may sound, before you take any drug or medicine (for those who like taking drugs/medicine), pray over them. There are satanic and demonic products in the form of drugs and medicine; and there are also satanic, demonic, and occult doctors, pharmacists, and nurses in many hospitals, whether public or private, local or foreign. If you want to go to hospital, pray over yourself and cover yourself with the Blood of Jesus Christ before you go. You may also tell a trusted person to pray for you; but never forget to pray by yourself.

No matter how urgent the case may be, if you can't pray, then don't go! Many people have lost their lives in hospitals, not because of the sickness or disease that attacked them, but because of satanic medicine and medical practitioners. It will even be difficult for police to detect these practices, because they are spiritually remoted and performed. And you know that many policemen are not spiritually sensitive; therefore, even if a policeman is there, the doctor can do what he wants to do, and the security agent can't even notice it.

Please, pray over the clothes and wears you buy, especially the second-hand ones, because many of them actually come from the underworld. Someone may doubt the possibility; but do you know that the Bible says that God created the physical world from the spiritual world (things that exist from things that do not exist)? (Heb. 11:3). The spiritual controls the physical, whether the good realm or the bad realm. Even unbelievers believe that after performing some demonic rituals, they can disappear and reappear at will.

In geography, we are told that the 70% of the earth's surface is covered with water. Do you know the vastness of the expanse of water in the Atlantic Ocean, for example? If a ship appears from the mermaid kingdom in that great expanse of sea and sails to the seaport, how do you know where it came from? Yes, it can carry any national flag they want it to carry.

And you know that there are submarines which go under water and come up when they want; so if the one from the underworld appears as a submarine, how do you know where it came from? They will come with whatever paper for the goods that you may want at the seaport, and they can interfere with whatever signal you may send or receive. Yes, they can operate physical shipping industries that will carry their goods at whatever point in the sea. Even if you may argue that the signal or information says that the ship came from another physical seaport, it makes no difference, because they can always outsmart you.

Don't be deceived: they will still have physical clearing agents for the goods, and distributing or marketing companies and agents for their materials. You may even work in a physical satanic company without your knowledge; and you will say, "I know how these things are produced." Do you also know how they got many of the 'imported' chemicals and materials they use in the factory?

Pray over your meat and fish. Please, pastor, when people bring life-animals for thanksgiving and gifts, pray over them and sanctify them. As odd as I may sound, some of those animals are more than animals. And even many of those ones which are normal animals might have been dedicated to devils (with different proclamations and curses) before they bring them to you. This is also applicable to the ones you buy in the market by yourself, even the ones you use for general cooking in camps, ceremonies, and retreats.

Before you travel, pray. Many of the accidents you hear of are not mechanical, but spiritually remote-controlled. Many plane-crashes, motor-accidents, and shipwrecks, which are blamed on mechanics, vehicle producers, and transport companies are actually caused by witches and devils. This is not for you to be afraid, because angels are guarding you; in fact, fear can open a way for the devil. Entertain no fear, because satan is nobody before your Almighty God!

Pray for your children and family, because witches want to enslave and initiate them if they have the opportunity. There are many conscious agents of satan in nursery schools, primary schools, secondary schools, universities, work-places, streets, and markets. Train your children to refuse edible things from strangers, and to pray over what they eat and drink. Pray over gifts you receive and the things you buy in the market. During/after your ceremonies and weddings, pray over the gifts you receive.

The devil and his devils are desperate these days more than before, because he knows that his time is short. If he can't destroy you, he will want to kill you; and if he can't kill you, he will want to steal from you. Therefore, watch and pray, lest you enter into temptation (Matt. 26:41).

The Bible says, "Owe no man anything…" (Rom. 13:8) and, "…the borrower is servant to the lender" (Prov. 22:7). It is not that it is sinful to borrow, because the Word also says, "…and from him who wants to borrow from you do not turn away" Matt. 5:42). But to borrow and refuse to pay is evil. It is also not good to postpone paying your debts when you are in the position to pay the debt.

Also, debt has spiritual significance; therefore, if you are not prayerful, somebody can use the credit-contact to drain your money or influence your life financially. He who goes on borrowing, goes on sorrowing. Learn to trust in God, instead of trusting in men and creditors. Also, the time, energy, and effort you put in to borrow and think on how to pay can bring stress and shame on you.

Pray for your newborn child and children; cover them with Blood of Jesus Christ. Pray over what you give out to strangers like beggars: cover it with the Blood of Jesus Christ.

Pray and cover yourself, your family, business, occupation, and property with the Blood of Jesus Christ. Believers need to pray a lot these days (and also fast), especially in group prayers.

Pray before you embark on journeys by land, air, or water. And if you have an uneasy feeling as you want to travel, then pray through before traveling. But this is not to tell you to live in fear, because angels are already guarding you. However, be prayerful generally.

Never Say That God Said What He Did Not Say!

DIVINE REVELATIONS AND NEAR-DEATH EXPERIENCES (NDE'S)

If it is contrary to the Word of God, then it is from satan – the devil and God's archenemy – who deceived Eve (from the beginning) with: "Did God really say…." That which is against God and His Word cannot be from God, the Maker of all things, Who holds the whole world in His Hand, because God's Word and His Spirit agree. The Lord Jesus Christ, Who defeated satan on the Cross of Calvary about two thousand years ago, is the Same – yesterday, today, and forever. He is coming very soon; get ready to meet Him: Heaven and Hell are real; let no one deceive you.

And the Word says, "Beware of false prophets, who come to you in sheep's clothing, but inwardly they are ravenous wolves. You will know them by their fruits. Do men gather grapes from thornbushes or figs from thistles? Even so, every good tree bears good fruit, but a bad tree bears bad fruit. A good tree cannot bear bad fruit, nor can a bad tree bear good fruit. Every tree that does not bear good fruit is cut down and thrown into the Fire. Therefore by their fruits you will know them.

"Not everyone who says to Me, 'Lord, Lord,' shall enter the Kingdom of Heaven, but he who does the Will of My Father in Heaven. Many will say to Me in that Day, 'Lord, Lord, have we not prophesied in Your Name, cast out demons in Your Name, and done many wonders in Your Name?' And then I will declare to them, 'I never knew you; depart from Me, you who practice lawlessness!'" (Matt. 7:15-23).

To tell you the truth, a lot of the noise made by many Believers means little or nothing to God. Many Believers and ministers cause God more pain and heartbreak than unbelievers. Many ministers preach and teach what God never thought of, not to talk of saying it: Many of them preach, teach, and practice the mind of the devil. Many Believers live however they want, while shouting, "Praise the Lord!" and "The Lord is good!" Well, let all of us amend our ways while there is still time, because God cannot change His Word for any person.

One time, I went to an open-air crusade which was titled: Mega Fire Crusade with one celebrated evangelist. It was a two-day crusade. I went the last day; and I stayed from the beginning of the preaching till the closing of the crusade. Brethren, the man didn't even mention or pray about either receiving Jesus Christ or avoiding sin. But he mentioned and prayed about car, building, marriage, factory, business, healing, and giving.

And he took two sets of offerings/donations, and invited people to the church that organized the crusade, telling them that he would anoint them during the church service. I was so unhappy that I met him after he came down, while they were about carrying him to his hotel room. He asked what my problem was, thinking that I came for prayer. I told him what I observed in his ministration, telling him that I am an evangelist and the primary aim of crusades should be to draw souls to Jesus Christ.

Guess what? He never even regretted or apologized, but defended himself, saying that sometimes it is like that. But, brethren, the crusade was only for two days. This is not a story that somebody told me, but what I experienced myself.

When I walk along the street and see how many ladies and women dress, I weep. And when you pass through beer parlours and joints, and see our young men, you will wail. What about the things happening among Believers, ministries, and churches?

Jesus Christ is coming very soon: Heaven and Hell are real. Let us get ready for His Return, knowing that the Christian race and God's Judgment are individual, and not collective. There is Only One Jesus Christ; and there is only one Bible. If you love the Kingdom of Heaven, then start reading and studying your own Bible for yourself, so that when those who teach you lies are condemned by God, you will not be condemned alongside with them.

It is not every place that is called by the name of church, ministry, fellowship, or mission that is preparing people for Heaven. Many of them are preparing people for Hell Fire. You will come to terms with the reality in the end. And the great regret is that by then, there will not be a second chance.

It is not just a matter of, "Thank You Jesus!" It is a matter of obeying His Word and Commandments, not being hypocrites who claim to be Believers, but live and act however we want, not regarding the things contained in the Bible, which He gave us. God is no respecter of any person; He will judge all men using His Word as His Standard. Remember that the righteous Lucifer became His archenemy by sin, and the holy Adam became separated from Him by disobedience.

Someone can accuse others of spreading the 'gospel of sin', and of making people sin-conscious. Read 1 Cor. 10:1-14, and see who the 'gospel' of sin is meant for (even though there is no such thing as 'the gospel of sin'). But beware, that you do not run and labour in vain! Also, know that idolatry does not only mean the worship of carved and molten images (Jas 4:4-5). Refer to Rom. 6:1 and 2 Cor. 6:1. May God open the eyes of your understanding, so that those who follow you may enter the Kingdom of Heaven!

NOW, I AM NOT JUDGING ANYONE, NOR AM I ENCOURAGING JUDGING ANYONE; but we must speak to warn those who are derailing, not to judge them; because they can still repent, as long as they are still alive, if they open themselves to the Holy Spirit's Promptings. And this applies to both the leaders and the led!

Read: Matthew 7:15-27; 2 Corinthians 11:13-15; 2 Peter 2:1-22; 1 John 4:1; Jude 1:3-13; and see that Jesus Christ, Paul, Peter, John, and Jude spoke against false preachers, teachers, prophets, and ministers. Did they do it to condemn them? No; rather, they did it to warn their followers and those who may be deceived by them.

Many people speak against Divine Revelations from God (including the testimonies of those who had Near-death Experiences) about Heaven and Hell. God has chosen to do it His Own Way, as He had been doing before. Why not believe God? Revelations like these are meant to encourage the faithful and warn the faithless (unfaithful). "The Bible is our standard and guide"; but, many people use this statement to trample on and work against the Will and Purpose of God.

The true testimony-bearers did not say that dressing a particular way alone will take you to Heaven; they emphasized on salvation, holiness, and total obedience to the Word of God. And be mindful that holiness and righteousness is both inward (of the heart and the mind) and outward (of the body). Refer to 2 Corinthians 7:1 and Romans 12:1-2.

And as for whether they should sell the testimonies, they are to allow God lead them in that area. By the way, if a true man of God is invited to preach to people (or teach them), inasmuch as he has his transport fare (or can get there) or is transported to the place of the ministration, he goes there and preaches free of charge to all who are there to listen; and he does so joyfully to win and establish souls for the Lord. If you give him some money after the ministration, and he collects it, is it evil?

Even if you don't give him, God will take good care of him; but if he comes with compact discs (CDs), DVDs, books, or tapes, must he give them to you free of charge? Your buying (willingly) any material, is it not for your own good and future use/revision? Can you mention one man of God that gives all his materials free of charge to people, except where (in some instances) the minister himself, someone else, a group of people, or the ministry/church pays for them (or for some of them)? Or, are they selling them at exorbitant prices?

And if the compact discs, tapes, and books are not produced, how will those within the vicinity of the programme who didn't attend the programme hear from the man of God directly? Or, is it better for them to hear misinterpreted and misinformed reports from those who attended the programme? And what about the areas the man of God may not speak on for that time; is it not from the materials he came with (or his materials that are sold by traders) that people will learn? By the way, the Bible you have and read, did you get it free of charge?

Unbelievers and businessmen spend money to buy or get what they want; should Christians complain, because they paid small money to get books, CDs, and tapes? Many Believers/Christians will spend a lot of money on food, clothes, schools and certificates, and other physical and mental things; but when it comes to spending money for spiritual things, they will hypocritically complain. Don't they know that "man shall not live by bread alone, but by every Word that comes out of the Mouth of God"?

And on the case of knowing who is in Heaven or in Hell (after having died), even the person you think you know may have a hidden (inward) sin or a grave 'mistake' which you will not know. By the way, the finally dead person has died, and cannot change his or her situation of everlasting friendship or separation from God.

When Apostle John heard something(s) in the Book of Revelation and wanted to write it (them) down, he was commanded not to write it (them) (Rev. 10:4). When Apostle Paul went to Heaven (Paradise), there were things he heard and saw, which he was not allowed to say or write (2 Cor. 12:4). Prophet Daniel was told to seal up part of the revelations he got (Dan. 12:4). Even Jesus Christ Himself knew many things which He didn't tell His apostles, as at the time He was with them (Jn 16:12).

However, they all revealed and said many of the things that they heard, saw, and knew! And read what was told Prophet Daniel in that place: he was told to seal it up until the time of the end. This means that at the appointed time, maybe in the time of the end (the last days), they will no longer be sealed up, but be revealed. Also, remember that it also says that knowledge will increase in the last days.

Apostle John, in the Book of Revelation, chapters 2 & 3, mentioned the names of specific churches. Except you want to deceive yourself, Apostle John, mentioning: the church of Ephesus, the church in Smyrna, the church in Pergamos, the church in Thyatira, the church in Sadis, the church in Philadelphia, and the church of the Laodiceans, is the same as mentioning names of specific churches. Therefore, God can mention names of specific churches – it is Scriptural! And that your church's name was not mentioned does not guarantee that it is better than those that might have been mentioned: so, check yourself, and correct anything that is to be corrected.

Now that one person is controlling all the branches of the churches, ministries, or fellowships in a particular country (or even in the whole world), why wouldn't his name be mentioned by God? Apostle Paul rebuked Apostle Peter publicly (Gal. 2:11-14); did he judge or condemn him by that? Was he not trying to put him in the right order out of brotherly love?

If you hadn't known it, Apostle Peter had greater authority than Apostle Paul in the Church. "Do not rebuke an older man (an elder, the KJV), but exhort him as a father (1 Tim. 5:1)," must be interpreted well. Advising Timothy on the administration of the church, Paul said, "Those who are sinning rebuke in the presence of all, that the rest may also fear (1 Tim. 5:20)".

What of where an elder is sinning and committing sin that is open to everybody and leading them astray?

Remember that the purpose of rebuking before all, according to the Bible, is for others to fear and avoid doing the same (or similar) things. And Jesus Christ, after saying, "Do not judge (Matt. 7:1)," also said, "Judge with righteous judgment (Jn 7:24)." So, learn to interpret the Word of God well in every situation.

That Apostle Paul wrote more books, and did extended Gospel work among the Gentiles, didn't make him rise above Peter. Think of it, even though Elisha got the double portion of Elijah's anointing (or the Holy Spirit upon him), he didn't rise above Elijah. And you know that Elijah was carried alive to Heaven, while Elisha died from sickness, and had his body decayed. Though John the Baptist didn't perform any recorded healing miracle, yet the miracle-working Moses didn't rise above him. And John the Baptist came in the spirit of Elijah, and not of Elisha!

For those who may say, "Never listen to any of those revelations," if revelations and visions (or listening to them) will be discouraged, because false revelations and visions exist, then reading Christian books and literatures, or listening to preachings and teachings must also be discouraged, since false preachings, teachings, and 'Christian' books and literatures also abound.

And you know that God Himself put preachers and teachers in His Church (even after having given us the Bible and Scriptures), just as He also put prophets too. No one man has all the inspirations, preachings, teachings, and ministries that God wants to pass across to His people. Yes, the devil and his demons can also give dreams, visions, revelations, audible voices, prophecies, and miracles; therefore, always study your Bible to know the Mind of God.

But do not let any person – preacher or what – stop you from hearing what God wants to tell you! And you can be sure that the devil doesn't promote the Cause of God and His Word, when analyzed, summarized, and weighed very well. And those from God don't and can't contradict the Word of God, when well interpreted and understood. In the last days, visions and revelations will abound – both good and bad, God-Sent and devil-sent.

And one of the signs of the last days is that people (even Believers) will harden their hearts from God's Voice and Messages, and try to disprove them with such misleading questions and comments as: (1) "In the Bible when the rich man asked Abraham to send Lazarus to his living brothers, Abraham said, 'If they don't hear Moses and the prophets, neither will they be persuaded though one rise from the dead' (Lk. 16:31)." Was it Abraham or Jesus Christ that made the statement? Certainly, it was Abraham, and not Jesus Christ.

Read the story very well, as told by Jesus Christ. Abraham didn't even have the ability to make Lazarus pass the gulf that was between the Paradise (where they were) and Hades (where the rich man was) to give the rich man a drop of water if Abraham had wanted to send Lazarus to the rich man. How then could that level of decision of sending Lazarus to the rich man's brothers be taken by an ordinary 'dead' (though living) Abraham? Abraham neither had the authority to send Lazarus to them, nor the power to raise Lazarus from the dead.

This was before Jesus Christ's Death and Resurrection, when both Paradise (for righteous men) and Hades (for sinners) were still beneath the earth and 'near' each other; now, only Hades is beneath the earth: Paradise is now Above. Jesus Christ took the righteous people who were in the underneath Paradise up to Above after His Resurrection.

The Bible says, "And Jesus said to him, 'Assuredly, I say to you, today, you will be with Me in Paradise'" (Lk. 23:43). The forgiven criminal was going to the underneath Paradise, from where he was taken to an Above Paradise – Heaven – after the Resurrection of Jesus Christ. And the Word says, "And Jesus cried out again with a loud Voice, and yielded up His Spirit.

"Then, behold, the veil of the temple was torn in two from top to bottom; and the earth quaked, and the rocks were split, and the graves were opened; and many bodies of the Saints who had fallen asleep were raised; and coming out of the graves after His Resurrection, they went into the holy city and appeared to many" (Matt. 27:50-53). Notice that they could only come out of their graves after Jesus Christ's Resurrection. And they were taken to an Above Paradise!

Of course, you can see the level of the rich man's torment in Hell. But I want you to notice that Abraham, based on the rich man's request, told him that his brothers have Moses and the Prophets, that they should hear them. Abraham was saying that the living should obey the Word of God, to avoid going to Hell. Therefore, those who do not obey the Word of God, but live to please the desires of their hearts and minds, will end in Hell.

Then again, when the rich man told Abraham that his brothers would hear if someone rises from the dead to preach to them, Abraham told him that if they did not hear Moses and the Prophets (the Word of God being preached and taught), neither would they be persuaded though someone rose from the dead. First, it was Abraham, and not God or Jesus Christ, who told the rich man that. God knows better than Abraham; and if He knows that people will listen to someone that rises from the dead, He can send the person.

Abraham couldn't even cross the gulf between Paradise and Hell; how then could he send Lazarus back to the earth? He did not have that level of authority or power to send a dead person to the living; but God has the power, ability, and authority to do that. Also, notice that Abraham did not say that nobody (none) could/would hear the dead that rises from the dead, but that the rich man's brothers would not hear. Why would they not hear? Because they had made up their minds on what they wanted; and they might have even scorned the fellow, saying that he did not actually die. (And, being hardened, they could have even said that it was a spirit posing as a human, who was dead, if Lazarus had appeared to them physically).

But many people will believe the story that would be told them by someone who rises from the dead; and many people will still not believe the story told them by someone who rises from the dead, no matter what, because the devil has hardened their hearts and they have made up their minds on what they want. The Bible says, "And behold, there was a great earthquake; for an angel of the Lord descended from Heaven, and came and rolled back the stone from the door, and sat on it.

"His countenance was like lightning, and his clothing as white as snow. And the guards shook for fear of him, and became like dead men. …Now while they were going, behold, some of the guards came into the city and reported to the chief priests all the things that had happened. When they had assembled with the elders and consulted together, they gave a large sum of money to the soldiers,

"Saying, 'Tell them, "His Disciples came at night and stole Him away while we slept." And if this comes to the governor's ears, we will appease him and make you secure.' So they took the money and did as they were instructed; and this saying is commonly reported among the Jews until this day" (Matt. 28:2-15). Can you imagine the hardness of men's (some men's) hearts and minds?

Instead of being grateful to God for saving them from death, and also giving them the opportunity to witness such a great sight, they decided to accept money and spread false story.

Who will blame God when He judges and punishes sinners with Eternal Death in His Great Wrath? But His Hands are still open now for whoever will submit to His Word and Grace!

Notice also that it was some of the guards (not all of them) that went to report; some of them might have repented from that incident. Yet the religious chief priests and elders hardened their hearts. Abraham was right when he told the rich man that his brothers would not hear though someone rises from the dead, because whereas some people will accept the testimony of the person who rises from the dead, many will still never believe his testimony, because their minds are made up.

(2) "That person said that she didn't know of this particular church, how then did she say that she heard the church is a holiness church?" Even with common sense, when the person was called by a woman on Monday to enquire about the very church, having given the woman answers, what stops her from asking about the church between Monday and Wednesday before the Lord spoke to her (as she said) on that Wednesday when the statement she made applied?

(3) "This is not the Bible (or even Koran) Jesus." The person was saying that Jesus Christ can't be too harsh with people to punish them the way described by the testifier(s) {or, maybe, the person was speaking of the way one of the testifiers was punished by God}, without knowing that our God, Who is also a Consuming Fire, destroyed everybody with the Flood (except Noah and his family), rained down fire to destroy all the dwellers of Sodom and Gomorrah (except Lot and his family), and even judges Believers with death, because they eat at the Lord's Table unworthily.

(4) "That person said, 'I Am That I Am,' on coming out of the experience; therefore, it can't be from God." When the prophets prophesied in the Name of the Lord, didn't they speak on Behalf of God? (5) "That testifier said that the only woman in Heaven is Mary, the mother of Jesus." When on earth did the person say such a thing? The person actually said that only a small percentage of people that left the earth made Heaven; and out of the people that made Heaven, only a small percentage of them are women, partly due to their attachment to jewellery, indecent dressing, make-up, and weavons/attachments.

(6) "If God really wanted to speak to the world through that person, He would have made her death and coming back public." Do you see the sense of man, when he decides to allow the devil to deceive him? (7) "Those people just used that boy to organize previous testimonies (reports) from others." Man, why do you want to be lost in Eternal Damnation in Hell Fire? (8) "The (those) testimonies are (were) made to make money." Make money from you by lying to get you ready for Heaven, and ending in Hell themselves?

(9) "Who has gone to Heaven and come back?" They wilfully forget that Apostle Paul and Apostle John went to Heaven and came back. (10) "No one can see God and live." Forgetting that Moses, Isaiah, Ezekiel, and John saw the Similitude of God (and hence saw God), and lived. (11) And one 'preacher' said, "If God wants to tell Believers or people something, He wouldn't use a dead or/and 'risen' person, but He will use pastors (or preachers)." Is that pride or deception?

These are few questions (or related statements) which people asked (or made) to disprove those Divine Revelations. And somebody (or some people) called them DEVELATIONS, trying to indicate that they came from the devil. People, why do you want satan, the devil, to take you to Hell Fire? And somebody may say that the Bible is our final authority (which is a very true statement).

But why do very many different persons, Believers, preachers, teachers, and ministers all say that the Bible is our final authority and standard, and also declare that they are preaching and teaching the raw and undiluted Word of God; and yet, in practice, they preach, teach, and practice different things? This is the more reason why you should maintain a tender heart, and allow the Holy Spirit speak to you.

Yes, the Bible is the final say and standard for all of us. Yet the things in the Bible were got by visions, revelations, dreams, audible voices, and inward inspirations/revelations. Can the Bible tell you which school to attend, which supermarket to shop in, or which vehicle to board? The Bible goes alongside with the Leading of the Holy Spirit.

However, we must disregard whatever contradicts the Bible. But true reports do not contradict the Bible; rather, their reports promote the Bible, except when you had allowed yourself to be loaded/filled with whatever false and misapplied teachings and doctrines you desire, because they suit your flesh; and you don't want to change.

The Bible tells us about Heaven and Hell: what we should do to gain Heaven, and what we must avoid to avoid Hell. But many Believers don't even regard and obey the Bible as they should. This is why God, seeing that many people have entered (and are heading towards) Hell, is giving more revelations and visions to spur us into taking the Bible serious (or more serious).

Someone may say, "How do you know that they have actually gone to Heaven?" Does asking that question not confirm and guarantee that God did not tell you that they didn't go to Heaven? And if you say that you were told that they didn't go to Heaven or/and Hell, who told you that – God or satan?

Many of those testimonies have been shared (or posted) in the Internet. Things shared in the Internet are read by many people. If one person who reads the post(s) gets and receives the Message being passed across, he may run with it, by spreading it to others; by that, the knowledge is more widely spread. There are millions of people who are following some preachers and ministers, even those outside their ministries and churches; and many of them think that because they prophesy and perform miracles, then all the things that they preach, teach, and practice are right.

But this is not true, in the ultimate sense. Therefore, instead of keeping quiet, and allowing them to follow anyone to Hell Fire, while Jesus Christ is crying for the abundance of lost souls, we are to stand up for God and warn the people. Much of the corruption in the church-world today is because people say that they want to mind their own business, even when the Lord wants them to mind His Own Business.

We are labourers together with God; and we have divisions and inter-mingleness of labour in the Kingdom of God. One may receive a Message from God; another may run with the Message to spread it; while another may be involved with fighting the devil, who may want to stop or hinder the spreading of the Message; another may be involved with taking care of those who were wounded by the devil in the course of doing their duty in the Kingdom; yet, we are working for the Same God.

Brother, if you had not known it, it is not an impossible thing that any of those testifiers can still backslide, if we don't give them any helping hand and support (but our God will hold them strong in Him!). Some of those testifiers are spiritual babies, who don't know the Bible well; and they need those who would prove, by the Bible, that their revelations are Biblical. I remember what Jesus Christ told one converted Muslim when he was taken to Heaven (or beyond the earth) and shown/told some things.

The Muslim (who turned to a preacher) had been a very rich Muslim, who was also involved in many secret societies (his conversion and testimony were not hidden and secret; he is from Northern Nigeria, Sokoto, and had Saudi Arabian citizenship: And Muslims fought hard to kill him after his conversion, because of the many things he exposed about Islam).

Now, after showing/telling him some things, and giving him a commission, Jesus Christ asked him, saying, "Will you be faithful to do what I have told you to do?" He answered Him with a Yes. The Lord Jesus Christ told him that He was asking him, because He had taken many people, both from his country (Nigeria) and from other countries of the world, and shown them extra-terrestrial things (like Heaven and Hell); yet, after they had gone back to the world, after some times, some (or many) of them started thinking that it was just a dream that they had.

And we will not sit back and watch those, who don't want to hear the Spirit of God, destroy these Heavenly Messages. So, we will not fold our hands and leave the testifiers stranded; but we will (by the Help of the Holy Spirit) use the Bible and inward inspirations to support and help them.

The Church is marching on; and gates of Hades shall not prevail against the Church of Jesus Christ, the Son of the Living God! The issue is: whether you yourself, as a preacher, was mentioned or not, or the church you attend was mentioned or not, let each and every one of us correct himself/herself of whatever is Biblically wrong – of whatever is wrong in the Sight of God. And for those who might have been mentioned, what have they done to correct themselves? God is calling, because He loves us!

Also, know that the churches and ministers that might have been mentioned are just samples, because there are thousands of needing-revival, requiring-purging, backslidden, half-bred, falsely indoctrinated, fake, satanic, demonic, and false ministers, apostles, prophets, evangelists, pastors, teachers, deacons, elders, musicians, church workers, church members, churches, ministries, and fellowships in our different countries and the whole world at large.

Let me include some things the Lord Jesus Christ told the seven churches in the second and third chapters of the Book of Revelation. The seven churches were in Asia Minor. They included the churches in Ephesus, in Smyrna, in Pergamos, in Thyatira, in Sardis, in Philadelphia, and in Laodicea. The churches were in different states of spirituality and carnality, just as the churches of today. The Lord had to encourage them, and warn them, by the hand of Apostle John.

The Lord was happy with those who did well (or, their good deeds); and He was unhappy with those who did not do well (or, their evil deeds/conditions). Even some who did well still had areas they had to correct. Because He desired that all of them do well, He had to send Messages to them according to their works and needs. The Messages sent to these churches are of benefit to us in this present age, if we open our hearts and minds to the Holy Spirit, and allow Him to purge, sanctify, consecrate, and edify us, so that we may become what the Lord wants us to be.

He was not happy with some of them; and He rebuked them. Some of them had left their first love. Some held to the doctrine of Balaam, who taught Balak to put a stumbling block before the children of Israel, to eat things sacrificed to idols, and to commit sexual immorality. They had also those who held the doctrine of the Nicolaitans, which thing He hates (hated). They allowed one Jezebel, who called herself a prophetess, to teach and seduce His Servants to commit sexual immorality and eat things sacrificed to idols.

Some had name that they were alive, but they were dead. He did not find the works of many of them perfect before God. Many of them were neither cold nor hot. The Lord wished that they were either cold or hot. And because they were lukewarm, and neither cold nor hot, He was going to vomit them out of His Mouth.

Some said that they were rich and had become wealthy, and had need of nothing. They did not know that they were wretched, miserable, poor, blind, and naked. No wonder the Bible says that we should neither be wise in our own eyes nor lean on our own understanding (Prov. 3:5-7). There is a way that seems good to a man, but the end of that road is death and destruction (Prov. 14:12). If we judge ourselves, we would not be judged (1 Cor. 11:31).

He warned them to remember where they had fallen from. He told them to repent and do the first works, else He would come to them quickly and remove their lampstand from its place – unless they repented. He told (and tells) anyone that had (and has) ear to hear to hear what the Spirit said (and is saying) to the churches. He advised them to not fear any of those things which they were about to suffer.

Indeed, the devil was about to throw some of them into prison, that they might be tested; and they were to have tribulation ten days. He commanded them to be faithful until death. The Lord told many of them to repent, or else He would come to them quickly and would fight against them with the sword of His Mouth. If Jesus Christ rebuked those churches, for them to repent and become faithful Believers, who are you to get annoyed when God decides to rebuke you? He rebukes and chastens those that He loves.

By the way, neither me nor anyone needs to approve or recognize the testimonies before they become true; for none of us is God! This race needs God's Grace and Mercy. Even as I write, I myself needs God's Grace and Mercy to make it to the end, because these last days are perilous. As an apostle who has evangelistic and teaching ministries, I need the grace to do what I teach.

When you teach or preach the Word of God sincerely, you teach and preach under the Anointing of the Holy Spirit. But when you finish, you have become that 'small' and 'ordinary' Christian, who must also discipline himself and bring his body under subjection to his spirit, to be able to obey God like every other Believer. To this end, Apostle Paul said, "But I discipline my body and bring it into subjection, lest, when I have preached to others, I myself should become disqualified" (1 Cor. 9:27).

Now, I say these things for the wellbeing of Christianity: If all these people who troop to crusades, ministries, and churches live to please God with perfect hearts, I tell you that Jesus Christ may be coming sooner! I would want to have a church of one hundred members, where about ninety of them are ready for the Coming of Jesus Christ, than to pastor ten thousand members, of which God may not even find five people who are ready for the Coming of His Son.

And it is better to have a mini crusade, where people sincerely repent and are faithful to God, than to organize a mega crusade, where thousands come out for altar call and go back to live however they want. Therefore, we evangelists, if we are troubled by the decadence in Christianity, knowing that many people trust us, should also use the opportunity we have to, at least, point out these things to, at least, the ministers and church-workers.

Some ministers say that they have special revelations on particular areas. Well, I myself have the revelation to help people understand the Truth of the Word of God and to follow the Leading of God's Holy Spirit. It is like I used to think a certain man of God was a 'holiness preacher/teacher' until listened to some of his messages I collected from one of his pastors. Then I understood that he is not a 'holiness preacher/teacher,' but a man of God who teaches the Word of God (of which holiness, which he emphasizes on, is included) and also demonstrates the Spirit and power.

The man demonstrates (has demonstrated) great miracles, signs, and wonders that many of the people we celebrate haven't done. But the thing is that he doesn't like proclaiming himself but God, Who does (did) those things; and he found out early enough that without holiness, no eye shall see the Lord. He found out that if one has all the miracles, healings, breakthroughs, deliverances, and anointing, and loses Heaven, the fellow lost everything and gained nothing.

Therefore, no matter the area you may say that you are called to 'specialize' on, preach, teach, and practice the Whole Counsel of God. And whatever we may have or achieve, we are nothing before God; and we must know that without holiness no one can see the Lord. Let us and those who follow us be aware of this real Truth.

Some people 'want' revelations, visions, and prophecies to be tested by the Word of God. Those people know whether they are sincere or whether they want to deceive others, having been deceived. I am a strong believer in this approach, because it is Biblical. The Bible says, "Prove all things; hold on to that which is good (1 Thes. 5:21). Beloved, do not believe every spirit, but test the spirits, whether they are of God... (1 Jn 4:1). Let two or three prophets speak, and let the others judge (1 Cor. 14:29)."

To explain some things, Jude speaks of sinners being reserved for the blackness of darkness forever (Jude 1:13). Jesus Christ Himself speaks of the sons of the Kingdom being cast into the Outer Darkness; and there will be weeping and gnashing of teeth (Matt. 8:12). Of course, you are already familiar with the heat of the fire of Hell. The Word says that their worm does not die, and the fire is not quenched (Mk 9:44).

Hell is a combination of fire, worms, darkness, etc. This does not mean, however, that you cannot see/notice/recognize someone in Hell, because you are more sensitive in Hell than you are on earth. This is why your spirit and soul can know things you didn't really perceive with your physical senses. Some people say that since they will be many in Hell Fire, they will put off the fire of Hell; but they don't know that the God, Who can mix fire and darkness, knows the frequency and magnitude of the fire which can comfortably absorb even trillions of entities! I hope you know that human beings have neither filled up the earth's surface nor used up all the oxygen, in spite of thousands of years of occupying the earth!

You have got to know that the time of the demons has not come; hence they spoke to Jesus Christ, saying, "Have You come to torment us before the time?" (Matt. 8:29). It is not the devil that formed Hell; it is God that formed it. It is not the devil that sends people to Hell; but God is the One Who sends people to Hell, as a way of punishing sinners and the disobedient. Even though a demon may carry or take you to Hell; but it is just because God has sent you there by releasing you to them. But on the case of men, it is appointed unto men to die once, and after that the judgment (Heb. 9:27).

Yes, the fire of Hell may not touch the demons now, because their time has not come; but when their time comes, God will either change their bodies to feel the effect of the fire, remove/neutralize the power that makes them not to feel the heat, or change the power and mode of the fire to burn them. Or, don't you know that even now someone can enter into physical fire and not feel the effect, because of demonic and satanic powers, after having performed some satanic rituals?

Even on the positive side, the fire of Nebuchadnezzar refused the bodies of Shadrach, Meshach, Abed-Nego, because God was there with them. And remember that the Bible says that Death and Hell will be cast into the Lake of Fire (Rev. 20:14). Therefore, if the demons don't feel the fire of Hell, they will certainly burn, cry, wail, and weep in the fire of the Lake of Fire. Understood?

Know that Hell or Hades is a temporary place of suffering for the dead sinner. The Lake of Fire, which the devils and sinners will be put into later, is actually the permanent place of extreme suffering for both the devils and human sinners. And the devil and his demons, for now, may be tormenting those who are presently suffering in Hell. But at the fulness of time, the devil and his fallen angels and demons will be cast into the Lake of Fire. And any person whose name is not found written in the Book of Life will also be cast into the Lake of Fire.

It is true that the time of fallen angels and demons has not come; but when their time comes, they will know that God has the kind of fire, that is available in the Lake of Fire and Brimstone, which will burn and torment them to wail and cry. The Bible says, "The devil, who deceived them, was cast into the Lake of Fire and Brimstone where the beast and the false prophet are. And they will be tormented day and night forever and ever.

"Then I saw a Great White Throne and Him Who sat on it, from Whose Face the earth and the heaven fled away. And there was found no place for them. And I saw the dead, small and great, standing before God, and books were opened. And another Book was opened, which is the Book of Life. And the dead were judged according to their works, by things which were written in the books.

"The sea gave up the dead who were in it, and Death and Hades delivered up the dead who were in them. And they were judged, each one according to his works. Then Death and Hades were cast into the Lake of Fire. This is the Second Death. And anyone not found written in the Book of Life was cast into the Lake of Fire" (Rev. 20:10-15).

As for whether Jesus Christ can accompany someone to Hell to show the person something in Hell, as someone said: "How can Jesus, as holy as He is, enter Hell with the guy, as if they are going on excursion; and don't you know that people in Hell can't see God's Face, how come the woman had the opportunity to be asking Jesus for forgiveness while she was already in Hell?" Bible and spiritual knowledge will tell you that it is possible.

If satan could come to where the sons of God came to present themselves to God (Job 1:6), and even spoke to God, how can't someone in Hell see Jesus Christ when He goes there on a mission to show someone mysteries about Hell? Yes, sinners cannot see God's Face; but you have to know that even though Jesus Christ is God, yet He is the Son of God and Mediator between God and men; and many sinners who couldn't see God saw Jesus Christ while He was on earth.

God created Hell, and He can enter there if He wants to; and the fire and heat of Hell cannot touch Him, even as the Fourth Person (Who had the Form of the Son of God) (Dan. 3:25) entered the fire of Nebuchadnezzar. And remember that God is everywhere (though His Manifest Presence is not everywhere). The Word says, "Where can I go from Your Spirit? Or where can I flee from Your Presence? If I ascend into Heaven, You are there; if I make my bed in Hell, behold, You are there" (Psa. 139:7-8).

The magnitude of the pain, either from the heat of the fire of Hell or the torments of the demons of Hell, is irrelevant for now; because Hell is a place of great suffering and torment; and no one will want to suffer, either from the heat or from the torments.

No one church is the only bearer of the Truth of the Word of God. And it is not only the churches that might have been mentioned for disobedience or rebellion that are taking their members to Hell by their teachings and practices.

Evil people do not have Eternal Life but eternal death. Men's souls are eternal; and demons and devils are eternal beings also: Therefore, they will suffer forever in the Lake of Fire. We see that Jesus Christ states in the Book of Mark that their worm does not die and the fire is not quenched (Mk 9:44). Did (Does) our Lord lie when He said (says) that the fire is not quenched? Hell Fire is forever!

WARNINGS FROM THE LORD

To clear doubts, the Bible itself says that Hell Fire is eternal (and not just forever). Let me say this, because of those who say that Hell Fire is forever but not eternal. Yes, everlasting or forever can stand for a period of time or for eternity. Everlasting or forever actually means till the stated time expires, and eternity means that there is no time limit.

But the Bible tells us specifically that the everlasting and forever of Hell Fire (the Lake of Fire) is eternity. The Word says, "...are set forth as an example, suffering the vengeance of eternal fire" (Jude 1:7). Therefore, Hell Fire is everlasting, forever, and eternal.

Yes, evil people go to Hell or Hades immediately after death, even though there is a corridor between death and either Heaven or Hell. And some people have actually come back from that corridor without either entering Heaven or Hell, but having seen them; though God actually takes some people (either in vision or in death) to Heaven or/and Hell to show them things they will report to the children of men when they come back.

He does these things, because He loves men and does not want any person to enter Hell. But many people are so hardened like the brothers of the rich man, of whom Abraham said, "If they do not hear Moses and the Prophets, neither will they be persuaded though one rise from the dead" (Lk. 16:31).

On the case of the possibility of increasing the heat or fire of Hell, God has different functions for His creatures, including angels. But have you ever seen it in the Bible where King Nebuchadnezzar told his men to increase his own fire seven times? (Dan. 3:19). Even in physics, though water boils at 100 degrees Celsius (which temperature human beings cannot withstand), yet it takes higher degrees of Celsius temperature to melt aluminum or iron into liquid form, not talk of vapourizing any of them.

For one particular testifier, at the point of her death, she was not born again, and so was left to the power of the demons; and demons torture people who are dead in Hell, which God formed for the torment of the disobedient. Yes, there are torture places in the kingdom of darkness for those who disobey their rules; but these are not (necessarily) the same place where those who are dead are tortured.

And after the devil and his fallen angels have tortured those that go contrary to their commands, when they actually die physically, they go to be punished and tortured in God's Own torture place, which is Hell (though devils increase people's torments there). The fact that there are prisons and death sentences and executions by men for criminals and murderers does not negate God's Own 'prison' and Hell.

Yes, the final Judgment has not come; but dying without Jesus Christ, or in sin, is as good as having been judged. God sees differently, and says, "...but he who does not believe is condemned already..." (Jn 3:16). Now and the final Judgment are the same, as long as the fellow is dead and appointed for judgment. Therefore, a sinner who dies now goes to Hell (and even if you hang for some time, you will still go to Hell after some time).

And even when you are still alive and have made up your mind that nothing can make you change your evil ways, then you are as good as having been judged, in a way, because the Bible says that it is the Word of God that will judge people on the Last Day; though with God, nothing shall be impossible.

Are there not many agents of the kingdom of darkness, who, though will experience what should show them that God's Power is superior to the power of devil, yet they do not change or embrace Jesus Christ, because their hearts (minds) have been hardened by satan? And satan can also harden the heart (mind) of someone, who may be carrying Bible in pretence (or, might have even known Christ).

When one particular testifier spoke of a force pulling her out of Hell, that was God's Power that pulled her out of that torment, because of His Mercy, so that she could come back to the earth, repent, accept Jesus Christ, and testify. Remember that God will have mercy on whom He chooses to have mercy on.

As for cleansing, you have got to know that our God is high and highly lifted up! He doesn't do everything by Himself: He has assigned different functions to different beings, including men and angels. When the devil rebelled against Him, He didn't fight the devil; that would have been giving much credit to satan. What God just did was to empower Michael the archangel and His warring angels; and they expelled the former Lucifer from Heaven.

God used one of the seraphim to touch Isaiah's tongue or mouth with the coal of fire (live coal) so that his iniquity was taken away and his sin purged (Isa. 6:6-7). When satan withstood Joshua, the high priest, because he was wearing filthy garments, the Angel of the Lord (God Himself) spoke and said to those who stood before Him, saying, "Take away the filthy garments from him" (Zech. 3).

I tell you that if she had not come back to life, she couldn't have been saved, because God cannot contradict His Word. However, God sees the end from the beginning. This is why, speaking to Abraham, He said, "I have made you father of many nations," when as yet he didn't have Isaac. He didn't say, "I will make you father of many nations." God had (has) a special mission for her, out His Love and Mercy, not because she is better than others.

This is why God can overshadow His chosen vessels with His Spirit, even before they actually submit to Jesus Christ; but if they refuse to submit, He will destroy them. Did God not call and speak to Adam even after he had sinned? God created and formed all things; therefore, He can relate with sinners (in some ways), just as He spoke to satan himself on the case of Job. Angels of God protect even the unbelievers to an extent; if not, the devil would have wiped them out.

Our 'headache' shouldn't be whether we will be in Heaven or in the New Earth. Our concern should be to please God and make His Kingdom at last. Angels come to earth from Heaven; and they also go to Heaven from the earth. And Jesus Christ says that we shall be like the angels, if we are counted worthy for the Resurrection from the dead (Lk. 20:35-36). Do you think that it is not possible for us to live both in Heaven and the New Earth?

In Hell Fire, worms, which do not die, eat (pass through) people's bodies. I have already stated that Hell Fire is eternal, as the Book of Jude tells us. God told Adam that he will die in the day that he eats of the forbidden fruit. Did Adam cease to exist on the day he ate the forbidden fruit? But he died spiritually, being separated from the Life of God. There are spiritual death (separation from God), physical death (ceasing to live physically), and the Second Death (Eternal Torment in Hell Fire or the Lake of Fire).

Sin separates you from God (spiritual death); and at death, spiritual death leads to eternal suffering of God's Punishment (Second Death) in Hell Fire. The Bible says, "…are set forth as an example, suffering the vengeance of Eternal Fire" (Jude 1:7). If you had been thinking that when people are cast into the Lake of Fire, then they are annihilated forever by way of being cut off from existence, then you had been making a great mistake.

And I tell you, if it all ends with the Judgment, then sinners somehow may assume they didn't 'lose.' If you 'enjoy' your life on earth, living in disobedience to God, and after the Judgment you cease to exist, do you think you 'really lost' anything, though losing Heaven is losing a very great thing? Then many more people can start living however they want; after all, when they are judged, they cease to exist! Then why didn't God wipe out the entire human race and create another set of good human beings?

The Bible says, "And they shall go forth and look upon the corpses of the men who have transgressed against Me. For their worm does not die, and their fire is not quenched. They shall be an abhorrence to all flesh" (Isaiah 66:24). So, God is going to leave a reminder for the good and faithful resurrected humans and the angels, in order to discourage any future disobedience or rebellion!

If you thought that when satan and his cohorts are cast into the Lake of Fire, then they will cease to exist, then what did they 'really lose'? And why did God allow them to continue to exist in the world, deceiving people and causing problems for human beings, and trying to destroy God's Plans? When then will they taste their torment? Don't misinterpret the Bible. The Bible didn't say that Hell and death have an end, but that they will be cast into the Lake of Fire; and the Lake of Fire is forever and eternal, according to the Book of Jude.

God does not tell us to follow man-made denomination; anyone whose preaching or teaching is not focused on the Kingdom of God, but on denomination, belongs to the group which will not make Heaven, but Hell. The fellow is not working for God, but for satan. However, be careful that you are not misinterpreting the preaching, teaching, action, or practice of some of those testifiers.

When you are lying down and sleeping, you don't know what is happening around you; yet you see yourself doing or saying things in your dream: God has used dreams to tell you that you are not all about that sleeping body, but you have got a soul and a spirit; why not be wise and learn from your dream experiences? Or you think your dreams are meaningless and non-existent?

When Adam lost the Life of God by disobedience, it was enough death; when somebody is tormented in the Lake of Fire, along with the devil and his fallen angels, that is great death in operation! When you die without Jesus Christ, or in sin, you are as good as having been judged (Jn 3:18). God, being the God of order, has given time to all humans (who die after some period of time), and when that time expires, He will call all of them (living and dead) for the Final Judgment.

You are actually judged at your death, and counted as holy, righteous, and justified, or sinful, evil, and condemned; the Final Judgment is actually for formality (Heb. 9:27; Jn 3:18).

The things that we need to know have been given and revealed to us. Even God taking people (through visions and death) to show them Heaven or/and Hell is just because we don't take His Word serious, because those things are found in the Bible, and can be known if we are open to the Spirit of God.

Concerning the resurrection from the dead at the Last Day, you need to ask yourself: "Is it resurrection from what/where to what/where?" Your soul does not die; so also is your spirit. Those people that they said they saw in Hell are not there with their physical bodies, but with their souls (which do not die). And just as you feel the effect of your enjoyment or suffering in your dreams, that is how you will feel the joy of Heaven (Paradise) or the suffering of Hell, when you die, as you wait for the resurrection.

Now, that resurrection is the resurrection of your soul putting on physical body again to be judged physically by God, because you existed as a physical being. But that is not now. Of course, before the Final Judgment and expiration of man's time, there would have been the Rapture of the Saints and the Millennium Reign of Jesus Christ with His faithful Saints.

But, whereas the Saints will resurrect with glorified bodies, the sinners will resurrect with the ordinary fallen bodies. Prophet Daniel said: "And many of those who sleep in the dust of the earth shall awake, some to Everlasting Life, some to shame and everlasting contempt" (Dan. 12:2). Here the Bible says that the state of both the righteous and the unrighteous (after resurrection) will be everlasting, but opposite to each other (just as light and darkness, or good and evil, are opposite to each other).

Jesus Christ Himself tells us that in Hell Fire, you do not cease to exist, but you will be going through on-going suffering, torment, and pain; and you will have your full sensitivity (even greater) there. Refer to the Book of Luke, chapter sixteen, and verses nineteen to thirty-one.

If you gain the whole world, and lose your soul in the end, you gained nothing. To tell you the truth, if you have all the miracles and prophecies you want from God, and in the end, hear, "Get behind Me, you worker of iniquity," you lost everything. If you live contrary to the Word of God, you better get ready for the Coming of Jesus Christ, because that your prophet or pastor, who tells you what the devil inspired him to say, will not save you from the Wrath of God.

God is no respecter of persons, whether you carry Bible or call Jesus. "But why do you call Me, 'Lord, Lord,' and do not do what I say?" (Lk. 6:46). And for those who put their trust of being saved on church attendance, baptism, communion, full membership, payment of big tithes and big donations to church projects, and friendship with the pastor, somebody should tell you that you are on your way to Hell Fire without a living relationship with Jesus Christ as your Lord and personal Saviour, and living to please Him.

Those of you who spread pornographic images in the internet, Hell Fire does not respect film actors, actresses, producers, and directors: get ready, because you will come to realize that worldly fame is satanic deception! God loves you and does not take delight in your perishing in Hell Fire; but if God turned His Face away from Jesus Christ Himself when He was carrying the sins of the world at the Cross of Calvary, who are you that God will allow you into His Kingdom with sin?

If you want to know the terror of Hell Fire, look at the Suffering of Jesus Christ (God Himself). And for those of you who don't believe in Hell Fire, no matter what you chose to believe, you will come to terms with the reality in the end. Let no one deceive you; and don't deceive anyone!

Many are called, but few are chosen; and it is not all those who are chosen that will be glorified, because the Bible says that it is the faithful that will be glorified. Therefore, among the few that are chosen, it is the fewer, who will be faithful and obedient, that will be glorified. The Word says, "Enter by the narrow gate, for wide is the gate and broad is the way that leads to destruction, and there are many who go in by it.

"Because narrow is the gate and difficult is the way which leads to life, and there are few who find it. Beware of false prophets, who come to you in sheep's clothing, but inwardly they are ravenous wolves. You will know them by their fruits…" (Matt. 7:13-16). It is not by their miracles or prophecies, because many false prophets will rise up and deceive many. False christs and false prophets will rise and show great signs and wonders to deceive, if possible, even the Elect (Matt. 24:11,24).

And because lawlessness (iniquity) will abound in the last days, the love of many will grow cold. But he who endures to the end shall be saved (verses 12 & 13). The Bible states: "For such are false apostles, deceitful workers, transforming themselves into apostles of Christ. And no wonder! For satan himself transforms himself into an angel of light. Therefore it is no great thing if his ministers transform themselves into ministers of righteousness, whose end will be according to their works (2 Cor. 11:13-15).

"Now the Spirit expressly says that in latter times some will depart from the Faith, giving heed to deceiving spirits and doctrines of demons, speaking lies in hypocrisy, having their own conscience seared with a hot iron (1 Tim. 4:1-2). For the time will come when they will not endure Sound Doctrine, but according to their own desires, because they have itching ears, they will heap up for themselves teachers; and they will turn their ears away from the Truth, and be turned aside to fables (2 Tim. 4:4).

"Take heed to yourself and to the Doctrine. Continue in them, for in doing this you will save both yourself and those who hear you (1 Tim. 4:16). But there were also false prophets among the people, even as there will be false teachers among you, who will secretly bring in destructive heresies, even denying the Lord Who bought them, and bring on themselves swift destruction. And many will follow their destructive ways, because of whom the way of Truth will be blasphemed" (2 Pet. 2:1-2).

I maintain that, by my understanding of the Scriptures and the inward conviction by the Holy Spirit of the Living God, that perming, jerry curling, or frying your hair (male or female) and the use of weavons and wigs are sinful, satanic, demonic, of mermaid, against God, anti-Christ, worldly, and Hell-attracting. Why? Because, when you perm your hair or use weavon, you are accusing God (consciously or unconsciously) that He is an imperfect Creator.

And it is inferiority complex, which says that the hair of the whites is superior to the hair of the blacks, that makes people insult our Awesome God. There is no difference between frying your hair and bleaching your skin (which some people do, to tell God that He is stupid for giving them the skin complexion that they have), whether or not you agree with the Truth.

Of course, you can still repent and correct your ways before death or the Coming of our Lord Jesus Christ; because, except you repent, you cannot enter Heaven but Hell, because no sin can enter Heaven. That is iniquity and living in sin. Many people say that they don't believe in Hell Fire: whatever you choose to believe, you will come to terms with the reality of Hell Fire in the end; then, you will have no second chance, but to suffer everlasting suffering in Hell Fire.

But if you will listen to the Voice of the Holy Spirit, you will escape the punishment of Hell Fire and eternal separation from the Almighty God. Many people like the thought that Hell Fire doesn't exist in order to comfort themselves in their sins. Who is satan, the devil? Was he not the Lucifer who was very close to God and well-honoured? Who was Adam? Was he not the one that was made in God's Image and represented God on earth? How come two of them became God's enemies?

Two of them, who were holy and perfect before God, made themselves sinners and God's enemies by pride and disobedience. Whoever makes himself a friend of the world makes himself an enemy of God (Jas 4:4). It doesn't matter how long you have been a Believer, how much of the Bible you know, how big your church or ministry is in people's eyes (because all those multitude of people may be going to Hell Fire with you), or how much anointing you have.

Perhaps you may need to be reminded that God made an ass to speak to Balaam in a human voice; and He used a heathen King Cyrus to build His Temple in Jerusalem. What is very different if God uses you to perform miracles? Maybe, you need to be told that Jesus Christ Himself said that, because of iniquity, He will reject many people who had prophesied, cast out demons, and done many wonders in His Name (Matt. 7:21-23).

And the Lord says, "STRIVE to enter through the NARROW GATE, for many, I say to you, will SEEK to ENTER and WILL NOT BE ABLE" (Lk. 13:24). Brothers and sisters, don't be deceived by all these miracles, falling down, breakthroughs, and deliverances. Healings, deliverances, signs, wonders, miracles, breakthroughs, and prosperity are small things to God. The One Who made the whole universe, what can He not do? His Concern is your soul, because He has determined, by an everlasting decision, that no sin, unrighteousness, or iniquity will cross the gate of Heaven.

The Business of God is drawing people to Jesus Christ, and getting them prepared for the Rapture and Heaven. Every other thing is extra and secondary. Think of it! God loved man so much that He sent His Son to die for men. Why didn't He wipe out all sins, since His Son has died? Why does He still require that you MUST believe in His Son?

If you have not understood the horror and penalty of Hell Fire, consider the terrible nature of Hell Fire by considering that Jesus Christ allowed Himself to be insulted and crucified by ordinary men, so that men will not enter Hell Fire. Just as God values a soul more than all the gold and silver of this world, He did not consider His Life dear to Him; but He gave His Life up for you, so that you will not end in Hell Fire.

But if you chose to spend everlasting torment and punishment in Hell Fire, God will execute it for you. Of all the multitude of people in the world in Noah's time, only Noah and his family were saved from the Flood that destroyed the whole world. It was only Lot and his family that escaped the fire from Heaven, of all the multitude of people in Sodom and Gomorrah.

Though God delivered all the Israelites with a Mighty Hand, and they experienced Divine and supernatural manifestations, yet, God destroyed all of them (who had come to age) that sinned against Him, except Joshua and Caleb. And even in this dispensation, He has told us that it is only few people that will be saved. Why? Is it because He does not love them? No!

Rather, it is because men (even when they call themselves Believers and preachers) are stubborn and obstinate; they choose what they want to obey, and despise God's Word and Spirit. But the Word of God has this for the Believers: "You believe that there is One God. You do well. Even the demons believe – and tremble!" (Jas 2:19). God will wait for everybody at His Judgment.

And those of you women that design your blouses to show us your breasts and armpits, get ready to face the Judgment Seat of God. Those of you that cut and divide your skirts to show us your laps, to help and encourage the devil to spread his lust-wave, prepare for your eternity.

Those who paint their faces and wear artificial nails, encouraging the activities of satan, who invented those lipsticks and cortexes, what will you do if when you appear before God's Judgment, He tells you, "You said these things didn't matter, but they matter to Me; depart to Hell Fire, which is prepared for satan and those that obey him"? And any design of dressing (male or female) that glorifies the devil and encourages his desires and works are from him.

The spirit of the antichrist tells people to combine Christianity with worldliness; they decide what they want, and use Bible quotations to deaden their consciences (as satan quoted the Scriptures to Jesus Christ). And, inasmuch as many people dress and appear like Godly ladies and women, while keeping hatred, bitterness, unforgiveness, etc in their hearts (which will still send you to Hell Fire if you don't repent), how much more will the inside of many of those who don't care about their outward appearance be worse!

When you hear some preachers say that they preach and teach the Word of God, you need to pity them; because they have been blinded by the devil to put materials things before the souls of men. In the last chapter of the Bible, the Word says, "He who is unjust, let him be unjust still;

WARNINGS FROM THE LORD

he who is filthy, let him be filthy still; he who is righteous, let him be righteous still; he who is holy, let him be holy still.

"'And behold, I am coming quickly, and My Reward is with Me, to give to every one according to his work'" (Rev. 22:11-12). THE WISE WILL LISTEN TO THE SPIRIT OF GOD, BUT THE STUBBORN WILL LAUGH OVER THESE THINGS AND RIDICULE THE LORD; BUT WAIT TILL THE COMING OF JESUS CHRIST!

To be sincere with you, if you have all the blessing, anointing and falling down, deliverance, healing, breakthrough, and miracles that God can give to any person, if you lose Heaven, you lost everything and gained nothing. Let no one deceive you: Many agents of the kingdom of darkness pretend to be ministers of Jesus Christ; and the devil uses them to keep people's focus out of Heaven, but on earthly and material things.

Even, many ministers who were called by God have been led astray by the devil, so that they are used to deceive other Believers by making them to set their minds on the things of the earth. Study the Bible by yourself to find out what God wants from you: what you should do and avoid. Be open to the Spirit of God, and don't harden your heart to what you want, so that He can lead and direct you to please God. Jesus Christ died for us; what have we done for Him?

The highest achievement you can have in life is that you are in Christ, and when Jesus Christ looks at you, He doesn't see any impediment which can withhold you from being raptured if He were to come now! Therefore, let us cleanse ourselves from all filthiness (sin) of the flesh and spirit, perfecting holiness in the Fear of God (2 Cor. 7:1).

The highest thing that separates God from satan is holiness; and this is why the angels sing, "Holy, Holy, Holy, Lord God Almighty…" and not, "Power, Power, Power, Holy Lord God…." God will allow you into His Heaven if you are poor, sick, and suffering without sin; but if you have all the miracles, deliverance, breakthrough, success, prosperity, healing, health, and prophecies with sin or disobedience, He will tell you: "Without holiness, no eye shall see the Lord."

If you love the Lord, then keep His Commandments (Jn 14:15). And why will you, after you have spoken in tongues, prophesied, cast out demons, and done mighty works in His Name, hear, "I never knew you; depart from Me, you who practice lawlessness"? A word is enough for the wise!

Satan, the devil, has blinded and gripped the Roman Catholics with idolatry, and taken captive many Pentecostals and charismatics with worldliness and it-doesn't-matter. Some people are concerned with, "Do not judge." But if you knew the millions of people who are going to Hell Fire, because of false, fake, half-bred, unbiblical, selfish, hardened, satanic, and demonic apostles, prophets, evangelists, pastors, teachers, and ministers, you would have long gone to seek God's Face in Bible study and prayer with fasting.

Others are of, "Let the wheat and the tares grow together till the Last Day," without knowing that the wheat and the tares will always grow together till the Last Day. But God Himself has sent many people to emphasize strongly that not all the plants are wheat; but there are tares among the wheat and in the church-world, so that people can decide beforehand whether to be a wheat (and plan for Heaven) or a tare (and wait for Hell)!

However, still know that it is not all supernatural revelations that come from God and His Spirit. In these days when God is revealing mysteries and hidden things to many people, to warn us of eternal realities (though the Bible contains eternal realities in it), know that the devil will also be giving his own revelations and visions to people.

The purpose of the devil in doing this is to lead men to sin and stubbornness, to put confusion among Christians, and to make Believers to not believe God-given revelations and visions. Originals are imitated; but we do not have to do away with the original because of the imitation!

Also, if you are listening to a testimony of someone telling you what Jesus Christ told him (or what he believes that Jesus Christ told him), you should be sensitive enough to separate (detect) what the Lord Jesus Christ told him and what he himself might add, in attempt to explain something to clarify issues.

However, many times, visions may be symbolic with the actual interpretation being given to the person in his heart/spirit. This is one danger of dreams' interpretations; some people have even made books of interpretations of different kinds of dreams.

Whereas they may be right (or nearly right) in many cases, yet some things are symbolic; and they can mean different things to different people. But even at that, the person who had the dream, vision, or even heard the audible voice, can add or subtract something(s) in attempt to tell us what he received, consciously or unconsciously.

A Biblical example may be seen in the about three places in the Book of Acts of the Apostles, where the encounter of Saul (Paul) with Jesus Christ is narrated by Paul himself (with Luke or and Luke). If you are very sensitive, you will perceive that the three accounts are not exactly the same, even though it was the same Paul or/and Luke who gave the report/testimony.

The spirit of man works with the mind and brain of man while he is giving a testimony; and there are things which you may not remember in some occasions. Similar examples are seen in the four Gospels Books.

Mathew and John were among the apostles of Jesus Christ; but Mark and Luke were not among the twelve apostles of the Lord. You may realize, if you are careful and sensitive, that there are times when more than one of them reported the same incidents, but the accounts were not exactly the same.

It is not that any of them lied, but whereas Mathew and John might have heard directly from the Mouth of Jesus Christ, Mark and Luke might have heard from a report of what Jesus Christ said.

And even the ones, who heard directly from His Mouth and saw the miracles, healings, and encounters, with their own eyes, had different levels of mental understanding and spiritual development, not to talk of the possibility (as humans) of forgetting some things at some times.

And John himself said, "And Thomas answered and said to Him, 'My Lord and my God!' Jesus said to him, 'Thomas, because you have seen Me, you have believed. Blessed are those who have not seen and yet have believed.'

"And truly Jesus did many other signs in the presence of His Disciples, which are not written in this Book; but these are written that you may believe that Jesus is the Christ, the Son of God, and that believing you may have life in His Name (Jn 20:28-31).

"Then Peter, turning around, saw the Disciple whom Jesus loved following, who also had leaned on His Breast at the supper, and said, 'Lord, who is the one who betrays You?' Peter, seeing him, said to Jesus, 'But Lord, what about this man?'

"Jesus said to him, 'If I will that he remain till I come, what is that to you? You follow Me.' Then this saying went out among the brethren that this Disciple would not die. Yet Jesus did not say to him that he would not die, but, 'If I will that he remain till I come, what is that to you?'

"This is the Disciple who testifies of these things, and wrote these things; and we know that his testimony is true. And there are also many other things that Jesus did, which if they were written one by one, I suppose that even the world itself could not contain the books that would be written. Amen" (Jn 21:20-25).

Notice that in the issue concerning Jesus Christ, Peter, and John (who was writing), the Lord's Statement was misunderstood. And this can also happen in giving of testimonies of revelations, visions, and mysteries.

But unconsciously, unknowing, and unwillingly misinterpreting, misunderstanding, mispresenting, adding to, or subtracting from the vision or revelation given to you is different from when you consciously, carefully, and knowingly misinterpret, mispresent, add to, or subtract from the revelation or vision given to you or to somebody else.

To this end, the Bible says, "For I testify to everyone who hears the Words of the prophecy of this Book: If anyone adds to these things, God will add to him the plagues that are written in this Book;

"And if anyone takes away from the Words of the Book of this prophecy, God shall take away his part from the Book of Life, from the Holy City, and from the things which are written in this Book" (Rev. 22:18-19).

However, this is not an excuse for you to say, interpret, or present what you do not understand, unconsciously or unknowingly, because the Bible also says, "My brethren, let not many of you become teachers, knowing that we shall receive a stricter judgment.

"For we all stumble in many things. If anyone does not stumble in word, he is a perfect man, able also to bridle the whole body" (Jas 3:1-2).

INDECENT DRESSING AND WORLDLY APPEARANCE

Writing to Timothy, Apostle Paul said, "Take heed to yourself and to the Doctrine. Continue in them, for in doing this you will save both yourself and those who hear you" (1 Tim. 4:16). This means that it is possible for both you and those who believe (look up to) you to not be saved, because of wrong doctrine and practice. And you know that he was writing to a preacher and minister of the Gospel who had some (many) Believers (people of God) under him.

A New Testament apostle, writing to New Testament Believers, wrote: "Therefore, having these promises, beloved, let us cleanse ourselves from all filthiness of the flesh and spirit, perfecting holiness in the Fear of God" (2 Cor. 7:1). Notice that Apostle Paul spoke of the filthiness of the flesh and spirit. Surprisingly, he put the filthiness of the flesh before the filthiness of spirit. But many will forget (or wilfully ignore) the filthiness of the flesh, while many will still not make their followers to be conscious of the filthiness of spirit.

And the Word of God, which cannot be broken, but endures forever, says, "...present your bodies a living sacrifice, holy, acceptable to God, which is your reasonable service. And do not be conformed to this world..." (Rom. 12:1-2). God looks at your heart, as well as your body, which is to be presented holy and acceptable to Him as a living sacrifice.

If the devil doesn't get you with lying, he will try to get you with pride; if he doesn't get you with fornication, he will try to get you with bitterness, hatred, unforgiveness, cheating, or stealing. If he doesn't get you with murder, he will try to get you with examination malpractice or falsification of result or age. If you say that you will not do this or that, because God told you not to do it, he will tell you to do it just once, confess, and God will mercifully, lovingly, and faithfully forgive you.

The devil tries as much as possible to take you to Hell Fire, because he knows that God can neither compromise His Standard nor condole sin. The devil, satan, was created as the holy Lucifer; but he became the wicked and evil satan, because of pride and rebellion.

Adam was formed as the pure and holy Adam; but due to disobedience to the Commandment of God, he became the sinful Adam. Do you know that the Father even removed His Face from Jesus Christ, as He carried the sins of the world on the Cross of Calvary, so that Jesus Christ cried out, saying, "My God, My God, why have You forsaken Me?"

The same blindness that holds many Roman Catholics, so that no matter how you tell them that worshipping images and praying to (or through) Mary (or, do they call it honouring her?) is unbiblical and anti-God, they do not seem to understand, is also holding many Pentecostals, orthodoxes, evangelicals, and charismatics, so that no matter how you tell them that indecent dressing and worldly appearance is unbiblical and anti-Christ, they hope and say that it doesn't matter.

But the devil will try as much as he can to hold you blind, captive, and disobedient until you find yourself in Hell Fire with no second chance. And many people don't even know that many people who carry Bible and call Jesus are actually agents of satan in disguise.

To this end, the Bible says, "For such are false apostles, deceitful workers, transforming themselves into apostles of Christ. And no wonder! For satan himself transforms himself into an angel of light. Therefore it is no great thing if his ministers also transform themselves into ministers of righteousness, whose end will be according to their works" (2 Cor. 11:13-15).

Apostle Peter, writing in the New Testament, to those who were born again, said, "Now if the righteous one is scarcely saved, where will the ungodly and the sinner appear?" (1 Pet. 4:18). When our Lord Jesus Christ says that He will tell many people on the Day of Judgment that He never knew them because they were workers of iniquity, He was speaking of those who had been born again, filled with the Holy Spirit, spoken in tongues, prophesied, cast out demons, and done mighty signs and wonders in His Name (Matt. 7:21-23).

I was passing a church when I saw somebody who was leading a prayer session speaking in tongues. She was seriously speaking in tongues, walking to and fro; but, behold, though I was inside a bus along the road (there was a kind of traffic slowdown, or rather, the bus was moving slowly), I saw part of her breasts all the way from the road due to the 'open-breast' blouse she was wearing; how much more the people with her there inside the church! Hell Fire has enlarged itself to accommodate very many people (Isa. 5:14).

The devil will tell you that there is no God; if you overcome him, he will say, "Okay, there is God, but there is no Jesus Christ." If you say that there is Jesus Christ Who died for you, he will say, "Okay, there is Jesus Christ, but wait till tomorrow before you give your life to Him." If you win him by giving your life to Jesus Christ, he will tell you: "You have the Righteousness of Jesus Christ; it is not by your righteousness that you were saved; therefore, don't worry how you live your life because you are the Righteousness of God; and as for outward appearance, what God looks at is the heart."

If you can't sacrifice small things like your dressing and appearance for Jesus Christ, can you lay down your life for His Sake? And He tells us that anyone who loves his life more than Him is not worthy of Him. Jesus Christ is coming very soon; get ready to receive Him.

If it is contrary to the Word of God, then it is from satan – the devil and God's archenemy – who deceived Eve (from the beginning) with: "Did God really say…." That which is against God and His Word cannot be from God, the Maker of all things Who holds the whole world in His Hands, because God's Word and His Spirit agree. Whatever glorifies the devil, and does not glorify God, is not of God.

The Lord Jesus Christ, Who defeated satan on the Cross of Calvary about two thousand years ago, is the Same – yesterday, today, and forever. He is coming very soon; get ready to meet Him: Heaven and Hell are real; let no one deceive you!

Many of those girls, ladies, and women, that expose their breasts (or breast cleavages), laps, and armpits in churches, in streets, at schools, in your compounds, in buses and cars, in markets, on Facebook, etc, are not just people who dressed seductively; make no mistakes about it! Many of them are agents of the kingdom of darkness, who have sold their souls to the queen of the coast and satan, the devil (who is their chief coordinator), to destroy the souls of men through lust, fornication, and adultery, because they want to entice, persuade, force, and drag people to Hell at any cost.

They may pretend to be Christians, harmless, good people, and ignorant of what they are doing; but they are out to serve the intent, plan, and purpose of the devil. This is one reason why many of them will not adhere to any preaching, teaching, instruction, or advice to get them dress like girls, ladies, and women who appreciate God's Work in them and value their bodies.

Many of them are blind agents of satan (because they do not know that satan is directly using them), while many of them are conscious agents of the kingdom of darkness and witches (who are doing and carrying out what they were told to do in the kingdom of satan, the fallen Lucifer). For many of them, only deliverance can change their mentality and mindset.

The Bible says, "For you were bought at a price; therefore glorify God in your body and in your spirit, which are God's" (1 Cor. 6:20). The Bible says that you should glorify God with both your body and your spirit, the two of which belong to God. When you are washing your plate, do you wash only the inside? No; but you wash both the inside and the outside, to be happy and satisfied. Why will you think otherwise with God?

The Bible says that if your eye causes you to sin, you should pluck it out (Matt. 5:29). If you can't leave lipstick, cortex, earrings, and weavon, can you pluck out your eye for the salvation of your soul if necessary? Your eye and lipstick, cortex, earring, or weavon, which one do you esteem above the other?

The Bible says, "Do not love the world or anything in the world. If any man loves the world, the Love of the Father is not in him; for all that is in the world: the lust of the eyes, the lust of the flesh, and the pride of life come not from the Father, but from the world. And the world passes away with its lusts, but he who does the Will of God abides forever" (1 Jn 2:15-17).

Adulteries, fornications, murders, and thefts are outward acts; yet the Lord says that they come from the heart and defile a man (Matt. 15:17-20). Eating with unwashed hand will not defile you, because you did not have evil thoughts to eat the food. But you can also eat with evil thoughts, like: gluttony and drunkenness.

Therefore using of lipsticks, weavons (wigs), artificial nails, etc defiles you, because it comes from evil thoughts of accusing God of imperfect creation and loving worldliness. And wearing seductive dresses and attire of the harlot come from the evil thoughts of wanting to expose your sensitive parts to command ungodly attention.

God calls hatred murder, calls lust fornication, calls changing your nature worldliness, calls dressing seductively causing your brother to fall, and calls painting yourself works of the flesh and of the devil. Lust is desire to fornicate; and God calls both the desire and the act the same thing – fornication. Using weavons and applying lipsticks and cortexes is to change God's Image which He made.

The Bible says, "A good tree cannot bear bad fruit, nor can a bad tree bear good fruit. Every tree that does not bear good fruit is cut down and thrown into the Fire. Therefore by their fruits you will know them. Not everyone who says to Me, 'Lord, Lord,' shall enter the Kingdom of Heaven, but he who does the Will of My Father in Heaven.

"Many will say to Me in that Day, 'Lord, Lord, have we not prophesied in Your Name, cast out demons in Your Name, and done many wonders in Your Name?' And then I will declare to them, 'I never knew you; depart from Me, you who practice lawlessness!'" (Matt. 7:18-23).

In some churches, people collect up to two, three, or more different kinds of offerings on Sundays; but they fail to tell their members to dress well. Is this hypocrisy or compromise? People put time, energy, and other kinds of efforts to convince (or will I say, pressurize?) people to give tithes/offerings and sow seed-faith; but when it comes to dressing, they will hypocritically say that the Holy Spirit will teach the Believers in Christ how to dress well.

Being born again is of the spirit (heart) of man by the acceptance of the Lord Jesus Christ (Jn 3:6). So someone can receive Jesus Christ while she is indecently dressed. Jn 3:3 says that unless one is born again, he cannot see the Kingdom of God. Jn 3:5 says that unless one is born of water and the Spirit, he cannot enter the Kingdom of God. The water there refers to the Word of God, according to Eph. 5:26. Being born again gives you the ability to become a child of God (Jn 1:12), so that you can live the way that God wants.

So whoever wants to enter (and not just to see) the Kingdom of God must be born again (led and directed) of the water (the Word of God) and the Spirit of God (Jn 3:5). To this end, Paul wrote to born again Believers to present their bodies a living sacrifice, holy and acceptable to God, and to renew their minds (Rom. 12:1-2). They themselves were to do the presenting and the renewing (God was not going to do it for them). This is why Paul himself said that he beat his body and brought it under subjection to his spirit, so that after he had preached to others, he himself will not be a castaway (1 Cor. 9:27).

So the one who knows the good he or she is to do, and does not do it, is sinning (Jas 4:17). And sinners spend eternity in Hell Fire. He who refuses to present his body a living sacrifice, holy and acceptable to God, is disobedient; and disobedient people go to Hell Fire. Remember that Adam was pure before God until he disobeyed God; and Lucifer was holy before God until iniquity was found in him.

Yes, if you receive Jesus Christ now with all your heart, while you are indecently dressed, God will wash away your sins and make you His child, and can even fill you with the Holy Spirit. But when you go to your house, the Spirit of God will speak to your heart to dress decently; if you refuse to obey, you will become a disobedient person (a fallen Adam). If you don't repent before you die or Jesus Christ comes, disobedient people go to.... Paul did not only preach faith towards Jesus Christ; rather, he preached faith towards Jesus Christ and repentance from dead works (Acts 20:21).

And the Word says, "Beware of false prophets, who come to you in sheep's clothing, but inwardly they are ravenous wolves. You will know them by their fruits. Do men gather grapes from thornbushes or figs from thistles? Even so, every good tree bears good fruit, but a bad tree bears bad fruit. A good tree cannot bear bad fruit, nor can a bad tree bear good fruit. Every tree that does not bear good fruit is cut down and thrown into the Fire. Therefore by their fruits you will know them.

"Not everyone who says to Me, 'Lord, Lord,' shall enter the Kingdom of Heaven, but he who does the Will of My Father in Heaven. Many will say to Me in that Day, 'Lord, Lord, have we not prophesied in Your Name, cast out demons in Your Name, and done many wonders in Your Name?' And then I will declare to them, 'I never knew you; depart from Me, you who practice lawlessness!'" (Matt. 7:15-23).

Apostle Paul, writing under the Unction, Anointing, and Inspiration of the Holy Spirit, said, "In like manner also, that the women adorn themselves in modest apparel (New International Version says, "Dress modestly, with decency and propriety"), with propriety and moderation, not with braided hair or gold or pearls or costly clothing, but which is proper for women professing Godliness, with good works" (1 Tim. 2:9-10, the New King James Version).

And Apostle Peter, being another witness, said, "Whose adorning, let it not be that outward adorning of plaiting the hair, and wearing of gold, or of putting on of apparel; but let it be the hidden man of the heart, in that which is not corruptible, even the ornament of a meek and quiet spirit, which is in the Sight of God of great price" (1 Pet. 3:3-4, the King James Version).

May you be changed by the Word of God! And may you learn to listen to the inner voice and witness in your spirit by the Holy Spirit, instead of following the multitude. May the Almighty Lord God give you wisdom and understanding in all things! Amen!

And instead of putting these things aside, criticizing them, or even getting annoyed over them, open your heart to the Holy Spirit and let Him speak to you further in your inner man: don't follow the multitude of disobedient and hardened people!

For the benefit of doubt, the things I have written down, as inspired by the Holy Spirit, are applicable to any tribe, people, nation, or country of the world, whether they are civilized or uncivilized, advanced or not advanced, developed or underdeveloped. To clarify you further, these things are applicable to Americans, Europeans, Asians, Africans, and others.

Let me state, categorically and without mincing words, that any preacher (no matter how anointed you may be, no matter your Knowledge of God, and no matter the years of service in the Kingdom of God), who encourages the use of cortex, lipstick, wigs or weavons, jewellery (jewelry), artificial nails, etc is encouraging the activities of the mermaid.

Never Say That God Said What He Did Not Say!

Much of the current wave of sexual immorality came from these things, even as they also use their demonic ladies and women to pull men into lust, fornication, and adultery. The only woman in the Bible who painted herself was Jezebel; and do you like the Jezebelic lifestyle and spirit? Beware of the attire of the harlot and prostitute! (Prov. 7).

If you do, you are encouraging, knowingly or unknowingly, the purposes and plans of the marine (water) kingdom of darkness, and the activities of the devil (satan), who is their chief-coordinator. You can fight against God without your knowledge; and you can encourage the devil without your knowledge.

And I will add that we preachers are responsible for most of the things happening in the world today, both on the positive side and on the negative side. All these people who misbehave and live their lives however they want, don't they go to churches?

When someone comes to church with his sin-partner (what many people call girl-friend), and leaves the church with the same sin-partner, without fear or shame, is it not enough to prove to you that the preachers are responsible for much of the evil in the society?

There is a way that seems right to a man, but its end is the way of death (Prov. 14:12; Prov. 16:25). God is warning us, because He loves us and does not want anyone to perish. But just as they never listened to Noah, many will not listen to the Truth; and just as Sodom and Gomorrah perished without Lot, those that will listen to God and do His Word and Will, will be saved!

Concerning the Bible passages we read before, I want you to see that there is the ornament or beauty of the spirit (heart). The word – fine – is not in the original text; and that is why it is italicized in the New King James Version. Apparel (according to the King James Version) or fine apparel (according to the New King James Version) refers to fashion and worldly ways of designing clothing. God wants you to look 'good'; but He detests worldly fashions.

Putting your mind on costly clothing makes clothing your idol. But how costly is the costly? Costly and expensive clothes encourage pride and idolization. For instance, if they make this clothing material as a material for the 'reigning' or 'current' people, then you have to remove yourself from it, because you are a different person – God's son or daughter.

People dress indecently and seductively these days, especially girls, ladies, and women. Of course, some men dress indecently also. But whereas even unbelieving men dress decently, many ladies who claim they are Christians, who go to different churches and call on the Name of the Lord, dress indecently to work, school, shopping, and even church.

The dressing and outward appearance of Christians must be different from those of unbelievers. If a Muslim will value covering herself well, how much more should you value it? The problem is that many people will find it easier to manage bondage than liberty. But do not use your liberty as an opportunity for sin and disobedience (Gal. 5:13).

Concerning jewellery (jewellery is British English, while jewelry is American English), Apostle Paul stated, "…that the women adorn themselves…not with…gold or pearls…" (1 Tim. 2:9, the New King James Version). The King James Version also says, "…women adorn themselves…not with…gold, or pearls…." Apostle Peter stated: "Do not let your adornment be merely outward…wearing gold…" (1 Pet. 3:3, the New King James Version). Now, take up your own New King James Version of the Bible, and read this portion of the Scripture. There you will see that the word 'merely' is italicized, which is to say that it is not in the original Greek text of the Bible.

Italicized words in the King James Version (which is the authorized version) or the New King James Version of the Bible are added for clearer understanding, and are not in the original Greek text; but I believe that this 'merely' added in the New King James Version, which, I thank

God, is not added in the only authorized version of the Bible – the King James Version – was added because of human acceptance over time based on demonic deception.

This is why you may see some versions of the Bible which will add 'merely' or 'only' without even italicizing it, which will make someone who doesn't have a certain level of understanding of versions and editions of the Bible to think that the words 'merely' or 'only' are in the original Greek text (and it is not there). Versions of the Bible (like KJV, NKJV, NIV, ASV, etc) are 'straight' translations of the Bible from the original Greek text, while editions of the Bible (like the Living Bible, Good News, etc) are 'interpreted' translations/descriptions of the Bible, either from the original Greek text or from a version of the Bible.

For your confirmation, the King James Version says, "Whose adorning let it not be that outward...wearing of gold...." There is no 'only' or 'merely' there. Apostle Peter said, "Let it not be outward wearing of gold (which is jewellery)." And Apostle Paul said, "Women are not to adorn themselves with gold or pearls (which, also, is jewellery). For the benefit of doubt, first, Apostle Peter didn't say anything about modesty. Secondly, hear Apostle Paul himself: "...women adorn themselves in modest apparel..." (1 Tim. 2:9).

Read it again from your own Bible, and you will see that he spoke of modest apparel, and not modest braiding of the hair or of wearing of gold or pearls (There is no such thing as modest braiding of the hair or modest wearing of jewels for Christians and Believers who want to make Heaven). We will see apparel and modest apparel, in dressing or clothing, later.

Some translations used 'modest appearance' instead of 'modest apparel', saying that the women should adorn themselves in modest appearance; but any translation, edition, or version of the Bible that uses 'appearance' either made mistake or purposely put it there to deceive people. Don't you know that some translations, editions, or versions of the Bible were done by some people to represent what they believe and accept? And you have got to know that the devil has agents (conscious or no conscious) in this regard. The Greek word used there is katastole, which means: apparel, dress, or clothing; it does not mean appearance.

Concerning plaiting or braiding of the hair (plaiting is British English, while braiding is American English), Apostle Paul clearly stated: "...that the women adorn themselves...not with braided hair..." (1 Tim. 2:9). Apostle Peter stated: "Whose adorning let it not be that outward adorning of plaiting the hair..." (1 Pet. 3:3, the King James Version). Apostle Peter said, "Don't adorn yourself by plaiting your hair." Apostle Paul said, "Don't adorn yourself with braided hair."

Neither Peter nor Paul spoke of modest plaiting or braiding of the hair, though Paul spoke of modest apparel. There is no modest braided or plaited hair. Your hair is to be natural as God made it. If it grows to the extent you find it difficult to comb it, then you can reduce it, but not as low as men's hair. Braiding or plaiting of the hair didn't come from God, but from the devil.

American, European, African, Asian, and Australian demons can give (or has given) American, European, African, Asian, and Australian methods and systems of braiding or plaiting of the hair. No matter how long the custom or culture has existed, the Bible says, "No braiding or plaiting of your hair, as a Christian woman." To dress the hair is to arrange someone's hair into a special style; and the devil has given braiding, plaiting, and weaving of the hair as ways in which many women and ladies dress or arrange their hair.

Concerning apparel or clothing, Apostle Paul clearly stated: "...that the women adorn themselves...not with...costly clothing" (1 Tim. 2:9, the New King James Version). The King James Version says, "...not with...costly array." Apostle Peter stated: "Whose adorning let it not be that outward adorning of...putting on apparel" (1 Pet. 3:3, the King James Version). The New

King James Version says, "Do not let your adornment be…putting on fine apparel." If you read the New King James Version, you will see that the word 'fine' is italicized, which means that it is not in the original Greek text. Therefore, Apostle Peter says, "Don't adorn yourself with apparel."

Apostle Paul said, "Don't adorn yourself with costly clothing or array." He said, "Adorn yourself in modest apparel." According to the Longman Dictionary of Contemporary English, 1995 edition, apparel is a formal word used for clothes, especially those worn for special occasions. So, apparel refers to special clothes. This not talking of normal clothes, but special clothes: this is talking of fashion and/or costly clothing. They are to use inexpensive or moderately priced clothes or clothing.

The Bible commands women to use modest apparel (1 Tim. 2:9). This particular, "In like manner also, that the women adorn themselves in modest apparel…" is not even talking of its price, but its style. According to the Longman Dictionary of Contemporary English, 1995 edition, modest clothing covers the body in a way that does not attract sexual interest. How many of our women, ladies, and girls dress modestly – in ways that do not attract sexual interest?

God hates dressing like the people of the world. He said: "And it shall be, in the day of the Lord's Sacrifice, that I will punish…all such as are clothed with foreign apparel" (Zeph. 1:8). Foreign apparel speaks of the kind of dressing that is not for God's people.

The Bible says, "Now when Jehu had come to Jezreel, Jezebel heard of it, and she put paint on her eyes…and looked through the window" (2 Kgs 9:30, the New King James Version). The King James Version says, "…she painted her face…." Painting your eyes, lips, and face is demonic and Jezebelic.

The Word says, "Now when Jehu had come to Jezreel, Jezebel heard of it, and she…adorned her head, and looked through the window" (2 Kgs 9:30, the New King James Version). The King James Version says, "…she…tired her head…." The New International Version says, "…she…arranged her hair…." Arranging, adorning, plaiting, braiding, or weaving the hair is demonic and Jezebelic.

Why didn't the Bible say, "Now when Jehu had come to Jezreel, Jezebel heard of it, and she looked through the window," but, "Now when Jehu had come to Jezreel, Jezebel heard of it, and she painted her face and adorned her head, and looked through the window." It was because she painted her face and adorned her head (or, arranged her hair) to look seductive and unnaturally attractive to seduce Jehu.

The Bible tells us that man looks at outward appearance (1 Sam. 16:7). Even in the secular world, appearance can decide your acceptability in many areas of life. Escape for your dear life; run before it is too late. The five foolish virgins lost their target. Remember that they were virgins, but they lacked something they didn't remember or deem necessary.

Please, open your eyes well, well; the devil has intruded into the Church: his ministers now parade themselves as ministers of Jesus Christ, to deceive and destroy the souls of the children of men.

Be careful of any church where people are allowed to dress anyhow to, no matter how anointed you may think the preacher is or how knowledgeable he is concerning the Bible. It is a different case when unbelievers dress anyhow to crusades, maybe, for the first time.

The Bible says that out of the abundance of the heart, the mouth speaks. Your actions and your words show what is on the inside of you. Your physical appearance reveals your inner man. If you don't care about what people think about your indecent dressing, then your spirit has a serious problem, and your mind has been corrupted. I don't care what you may think about it.

Even unbelievers will find it difficult to believe you are a Christian when you dress indecently as they do. There must be a difference between the dressing of a Christian and a non-Christian.

Many ladies think that they attract marriage partners by dressing seductively. Well, you can only attract a carnal man when you dress that way. How can a reasonable spiritual man decide to marry someone that is worldly in appearance? Will you paint your face with lipstick, eye-pencil, and decorative powder as the wicked and ungodly women, Jezebel, painted hers (2 Kgs 9:30)?

Concerning the dressing or arranging of the hair, using of weavons (or wigs) and attachments is devilish and worldly. Many of those weavons are actual human hairs that were cut and sold. Many of the weavons and attachments are manufactured with demonic materials to enslave the children of men.

I don't care whether you call it wool or what; it is still an attachment. You can't confuse God; He knows more than you do! Even, the using of thread to wind your hair (as many Believers do) is still attachment and unnatural hair. If you don't know, it is not a Christian style of hair-style but traditional style.

If you doubt this, check it out and see that traditional unbelievers use thread for their hair too. As a woman, wash your hair and comb it; there are suitable combs made for long hairs. Allow your hair to be natural; and you can pack it or allow it fly. And I am not telling you to cut your hair low like the general size of that of men of the same race as you, except you are going to cover it or wear cap on it, even outside the church.

Also, when you use weavons and attachments, when you perm and jerry curl your hair, you are saying that God is stupid (or, is an imperfect Creator) to have made your hair the way He made it. Relaxing your hair artificially (whether you call it science or technology) is of the devil. When people refuse to cover their hairs, they resort to worldly means of weavons for a covering. Of course, your must have a sign of authority on your head in church meetings or gatherings, as a woman. What do you lose by veiling your hair?

Much of those things women use for beauty and for their hair, in perming and jerry-curling, is manufactured from alantoin extracted from aborted babies. The worst is that some men even fry their hair.

I read a story of a woman who when she was still a young sister was warned by God to desist from using attachments on her hair. And anytime she disobeyed that Instruction, God will chastise her. She told God that there were other good Christians that were using attachments, and referred to one particular woman who was a spiritual mother to them, whom she saw as a model.

The story had it that then (as at the time of the reporting) the sister is married to a pastor for many years then, and she is a strong pillar in the ministry doing exploits for the Lord. On the other hand, she then makes her hair with attachment, weavons, and other materials without any further warning from the Lord. And she said that her relationship with the Lord is still intact.

This story, though 'funny', is painful. Can you see how someone who believes in Jesus Christ can so much love the things of this world to the extent that her conscience will get hardened to do what God told her not to do, and even make God to give her over to a reprobate mind, and also refuse to speak to her again, because she loves doing her own thing instead of God's Thing? And she still 'believes' that God is happy with her!

Start appreciating your hair the natural way God made it. If you find it difficult to comb it, then reduce it to manageable or easily-combable size, but not as low as the general size of that of men from the same race as you (the men who have the kind of hair that you have). This will solve all these problems of perming the hair, relaxing the hair, 'jerry-curling' the hair, wearing of weavons or wigs, braiding or plaiting your hair with natural hair, attachments, wool, and thread.

If your hair is very long, as a woman, it is good; but the Bible says, "If a woman has a long hair," and not, "When a woman has a long hair." If you have the kind of strong hair that will not be long (or very long) in its natural state without relaxing it artificially, then reduce it to manageable or easily-combable size, but not as low as the general size of that of men from the same race as you (the men who have the kind of hair that you have). Also, the use of veil, hair scarf, and caps can help you remove unnecessary worries.

Satan has entered the Church and has deceived many. Many are sincerely deceived. Those cortexes, lipsticks, make-ups, and many other painting materials and cosmetics, apart from being worldly, are manufactured from demonic materials, aborted babies' placentas, and human fat and blood. This is a mystery that many have not realized. When people use those things, they get demonic problems they don't know where they came from.

Blouses that show too much of your back; tight-fitting and revealing dresses; mini-skirts; spaghetti or line-sleeve and transparent dresses; blouses showing your breast; cobweb and body-hug dresses; blouses revealing your belly; and any such dresses are devilish, satanic, demonic, and worldly.

For men, sagging your trousers and dread-locking your hair are satanic also. Women shouldn't put on trousers, because they look more decent in skirts and gowns. In biology, when women mature, their buttocks get enlarged; this is why when they wear trousers, they reveal their body contours and look seductive.

Any attire or dress that glorifies the devil, and does not glorify God, is worldly and devilish. There are no two ways about this matter. If you doubt this, wait till the Day of Reckoning when you will cry and wail in Hell Fire! Then you will repent one thousand times in a short while without any second chance.

We now come to the issue of earrings, necklaces, and bangles. These things are worldly also. God made you look fine; what advantage is it in decorating your body, which is the Temple of the Holy Spirit, with those things?

We wear cloths and dresses to cover our nakedness. Before Adam sinned, we didn't even need dresses, for God's Glory covered us. Earrings were classified among foreign and ungodly things which Jacob purified his household from; and he buried them, after he had collected them from all the members of his household and those that were with him (Gen. 35:1-5). The Knowledge of God advanced from Abraham, to Isaac, and to Jacob.

God hates jewellery (jewelry) and ornamenting your body. Get rid of rings, chains, bangles, necklaces, and such things. Jewellery is designing your body with jewels. To God, it is idolatry; and the devil uses it to make women look worldly and seductive. By this, he seduces our men into lust, fornication, and adultery more easily.

Even though you may argue, can you prove to me why you need them when God made you beautiful? The problem is that many of these things have continued for so long that many don't even know why they do what they do. Personally, I don't see those things as beauty; and God does not like them.

Some argue that God told the Israelites to collect those things from the Egyptians as they departed from Egypt. Well, if you had not known it, God did not tell them to collect them from them because He wanted them to be given to jewellery. Those things were Egyptian and foreign, even though the Israelites might have been influenced by them after having stayed there for four hundred years.

He told them to collect them from them because they were made from gold, silver, and other materials; and they were to plunder Egypt. Those materials were needed for construction and other works by them and for the Work of God. Where do you think that they would have got the gold for the construction of the sanctuary and tabernacle?

See the Bible speak: "And when the people heard this bad news, they mourned, and no one put on his ornaments. For the Lord had said to Moses, 'Say to the children of Israel, "you are a stiff-necked people. I could come into your midst in one moment and consume you. Now therefore, take off your ornaments, that I may know what to do with you."' So the children of Israel stripped themselves of their ornaments by Mount Horeb" (Exo. 33:4-6).

God spoke to His people, after they had used their ornaments to make a calf and worshipped it as the god that brought them out of Egypt, and said, "...take off your ornaments...." Is it not clear enough? The Israelites removed their jewellery and stripped themselves of their ornaments, because God commanded them to do so; will you yourself obey God's Voice today and save your soul from Hell?

Also, notice that verse 5 didn't say, "The Lord said to Moses..." but, "For the Lord had said to Moses...." In order words, they didn't just remove the ornaments on their own in verse 4. Verse 4 happened because the Lord had instructed it. And verse 6 affirms that they stripped themselves of their ornaments.

Also, notice that because they still needed the materials from which the ornaments were made – gold, silver, etc – for construction purposes, God didn't tell them to throw away those ornaments; they kept them, not for future wearing of them, but for the preservation of the materials of gold, silver, etc, for which purpose He told them to collect them from the Egyptians in the first place – to be used for construction works.

To this end, the Bible says, "'Take from among you an offering to the Lord. Whoever is of a willing heart, let him bring it as an offering to the Lord: gold, silver, and bronze....' They came, both men and women, as many as had a willing heart, and brought earrings and nose rings, rings and necklaces, all jewellery of gold, that is, every man who made an offering of gold to the Lord.

"Everyone who offered an offering of silver or bronze brought the Lord's Offering. And everyone with whom was found acacia wood for any work of the service, brought it" (Exo. 35:5,22,24). I didn't say this for you to keep your jewels, because you must not.

Someone may ask, "But why did God tell the Israelites to put the jewellery on their wives, sons, and daughters?" The answer is not hard, if you are sincere and God opens your eyes. Many times, we don't see the Truth of the Word of God when we read the Bible, because we already have what we want it to say in our minds, and we force it to say the very thing!

Hear God: "And I will give the people favour in the sight of the Egyptians; and it shall be, when you go, that you shall not go empty-handed. But every woman shall ask of her neighbour, namely, of her who dwells near her house, articles of silver, articles gold, and clothing; and you shall put them on your sons and your daughters. So you shall plunder the Egyptians" (Exo. 3:21-22, the New King James Version).

The King James Version (which is the only authorized version of the Bible) says, "But every woman shall borrow of her neighbour, and of her that sojourneth in her house, jewels of silver, and jewels of gold, and raiment: and ye shall put them upon your sons, and upon your daughters; and ye shall spoil the Egyptians" (Exo. 3:22).

Notice that the purpose of the borrowing and the putting on was to plunder the Egyptians. The Hebrew word used there is 'shaal'. It means 'borrow', and in some instances, may be rendered/translated as 'ask' or 'request'. It is true that the NKJV used 'ask' instead of 'borrow'; but what God told them was to borrow them from them. Why?

Hear the Bible: "Afterwards Moses and Aaron went in and told Pharaoh, 'Thus says the Lord God of Israel: "Let My people go, that they may hold a feast to Me in the wilderness."' And Pharaoh said, 'Who is the Lord that I should obey His Voice to let Israel go? I do not know the Lord, nor will I let Israel go.'

"So they said, 'The God of the Hebrews has met with us. Please, let us go three days' journey into the desert and sacrifice to the Lord our God, lest He fall upon us with pestilence or with the sword'" (Exo. 5:1-3). Look at what Pharaoh said, "You are idle! Idle! Therefore you say, 'Let us go and sacrifice to the Lord'" (Exo. 5:17).

After some plagues, Pharaoh said, "Go, sacrifice to your God in the land." And Moses said, "It is not right to do so, for we would be sacrificing the abomination of the Egyptians to the Lord our God. If we sacrifice the abomination of the Egyptians before their eyes, then will they not stone us?

"We will go three days' journey into the wilderness and sacrifice to the Lord our God as He will command us." So Pharaoh said, "I will let you go, that you may sacrifice to the Lord your God in the wilderness; only you shall not go very far away. Intercede for me" (Exo. 8:25-28).

After other plagues, Pharaoh said, "Go, serve the Lord; only let your flocks and your herds be kept back. Let your little ones also go with you." But Moses said, "You must also give us sacrifices and burnt offerings, that we may sacrifice to the Lord our God. Our livestock also shall go with us; not a hoof shall be left behind. For we must take some of them to serve the Lord our God, and even we do not know with what we must serve the Lord until we arrive there" (Exo. 10:24-26).

I put those portions of the Scripture to help you understand why they were to borrow the jewels. In what they told Pharaoh, they were going on a three-day journey into the wilderness to sacrifice to the Lord their God. And it seems that what Pharaoh understood from their statement(s), was that they were going on a three-day journey into the wilderness to sacrifice to the Lord their God, and after the sacrifice, they would come back to Egypt.

Was God deceiving the Egyptians then? No, He is God; and that was His Method of plundering the Egyptians, as He had told Abraham that his descendants, after serving a foreign land, would come out with great possessions (Gen. 15:14). And notice that neither God nor Moses told any of them that they would come back after the sacrifice!

In God's Sight, the Egyptians were paying for having held His people for hundreds of years in their land. He was punishing them for punishing His people. The same kind of thing happened when Jesus Christ was crucified. The devil, in his desperation, killed Jesus Christ; but it was after He was killed that satan realized that Jesus Christ had to shed His Blood in order to redeem mankind.

Then satan, wanting Jesus Christ to come down from the Cross, entered some people, and they said, "If You are the Son of God, come down from the Cross, and we will believe You (Matt. 27:41-43)"; but it was too late! The Bible says, "Which none of the rulers of this age knew; for had they known, they would not have crucified the Lord of Glory" (1 Cor. 2:8).

What I want you to know is that it was after the Israelites had left Egypt that the Egyptians actually realized that Israel was gone! And this added to their punishments, because there were drown in the Red Sea when they pursued Israel. The Bible says, "Now it was told the king of Egypt that the people had fled, and the heart of Pharaoh and his servants were turned against the people; and they said, 'Why have we done this, that we have let Israel go from serving us?'" (Exo. 14:5).

So, you can see, if you want to, why God said, "Borrow those articles and put them on your wives, sons, and daughters." They were not going to ask for it and keep it in their purses; you borrow things for urgent need. And that was why they had to put the articles on them: It was borrowed articles, which their wives and children were in urgent need for use in the special sacrifice they were going to make for their God in the wilderness after a three-day journey.

For those who want to wear wrist watch, it must not be with chains, for it would be the same as wearing chains. If you want to wear wrist watch (not for beauty, but for keeping time), use the one that is made of plastic, rubber, or leather belt; and let it be of simple and inexpensive type, because it is for checking time and not for fashion. For this same reason, your waist belt must not be the chain type; and it is to be the simple type. And don't even wear the rubber or plastic wrist bangles which carry different kinds of advertisement/write-ups, whether of church, ministry, Bible, Christianity, or whatever.

The Bible says that God looks at the heart (I Sam 16:7). The Word of the Lord says that the Almighty does not look as man looks. How does man look? He looks at the outward appearance. This means that outward appearance is very important in our relationship with men, because they would look at our appearance. Could it be that God does not see in the physical? How can He, Who created the physical out of the spiritual, not see the physical, while we that were created see it?

The Bible says that out of the abundance of the heart, the mouth speaks. This means that what we say has something to do with what is in our heart (which we don't see). The appearance of men could be deceitful. An armed robber could dress like a banker or a pastor. Why will he do that? Because he knows that the appearance of the banker or the pastor is appreciated by responsible people.

However, the banker or the pastor will never want to dress like the armed robber (if there is how they dress). Why would he not want to dress like that? Because he knows that armed robbery is one of the ills of the society.

My brethren, how you dress and how you appear matter before people (responsible people) even when they don't confront you. From this day, make up your mind to glorify God in your dressing no matter the cost. Make up your mind not to offend God through your dressing.

I tell you, many of the girls, ladies, women, boys, young men, and grown up men you see in the towns are agents of the kingdom of darkness. Even many children are witches, and they have direct and conscious relationships with the dark kingdom. Of course, there are blind witches, who don't have conscious relationship with demons and fallen angels, but are demonically remote-controlled.

Will it surprise you to be told that there are many agents of the kingdom of darkness in many churches? Many operate as preachers; some operate as deacons, deaconesses, and elders; others operate as group leaders; still, many are in the choir and in other departments.

It is not that God wants it to be so, or that it is so in every church. It is because many churches, fellowships, and ministries are not at the place God wants them to be, that agents of the kingdom of darkness come into their midst and relax. This is not just saying that we are the Pentecostals or the charismatics, and we speak in tongues always.

Brother, have you ever asked yourself where all those people that flood into your church are going to? People will come to church with their girl-friends, and leave the church with their girl-friends, without fear and shame. If they had tried it in the Early Church, they would have seen what would have happened to them!

The increase of evil in these last days is not only because of the desperation of the devil. As a matter of fact, the devil has always been desperate since the time of Adam. Preachers are responsible for much of it. Apart from preachers who are direct agents of satan, many preachers who were called by God have compromised the Word of God and Christian standards, because of ignorance, fame, and love of money.

Many want to be known as the most popular preacher, the richest preacher, or the most influential preacher. Others want to have the largest congregation, the fastest growing church, or the biggest cathedral. Many ministers have lost the vision of the souls of men, and they are interested in money and other material things.

Why do Christians dress and appear like the people of the world? It is because there are many Jezebels and agents of the kingdom of darkness (especially the mermaid water kingdom) in many churches. This is why many preachers and churches have accepted what they used to call sin before, as being good and harmless now.

Many of them get committed in church activities, that the pastors wouldn't even know that they are agents of the kingdom of darkness; and the pastors begin to promote them, thereby helping them in their seductive and destructive works. When they dress that way and speak their demonic tongues, giving their demonic prophecies, the pastor and others will welcome them.

They will say, "Since this sister dresses like this, wears this, and paints this way, and yet is too spiritual, then nothing is really wrong with these things." And the devil will ask the other Believers and Christians, "Did God really say that it is sinful to dress this way, wear weavons, and paint this way?"

Then the other Believers and Christians will become 'sincerely' deceived (if sincerity is applicable at all, because many of them want it; and if you stop or forbid them, they will criticize and hate you). And when the pastor sees that many or majority of his members are like that, it will be as if water was poured on his spiritual energy to speak against those things.

I have observed that girls, ladies, and women like what appeals to the eyes. I am talking of believing girls, ladies, and women. In fact, the Christianity of many of them doesn't reach that side. If you speak against their worldly appearance, you will become their enemy. They will try as much as possible to find what they will use to justify themselves, because they want to look attractive and 'sharp.'

This is the same thing that put the world into the mess it is in today. In the beginning: "The woman saw (and they still see) that the tree was good for food, that it was pleasant to the eyes (Have you seen and confirmed what I am saying?), and a tree desirable to make one wise, she took of its fruit and ate" (Gen. 3:6).

My sister, whether or not you like it, the way to Heaven is a narrow way. And the Bible says, "Enter by the narrow gate; for wide is the gate and broad is the way that leads to destruction, and there are many who go in by it. Because narrow is the gate and difficult is the way which leads to life, and there are few who find it" (Matt. 7:13-14).

Luke added something when he said, "Strive to enter through the narrow gate, for many, I say to you, will seek to enter and will not be able" (Lk. 13:24). How many people are willing and ready to strive to enter through the narrow gate?

Yet, don't be deceived by appearance, because many agents of the kingdom of darkness dress like Christian ladies, to deceive people into thinking that they are Christians. To this end, know that some of them wear long skirts, tie headties, and wouldn't paint their lips. Be careful, so that the devil will not trap you down!

These days are last days, and the devil is fighting tooth and nail to draw as many people as he can to Hell Fire, to suffer eternal torment and punishment with him. The devil hates the human race with great passion; the human agents he uses are deceived into thinking that he loves them.

We are talking of indecent dressing and outward appearance. And what we have said so far concerns other areas of the life of a Christian. There are many things that people (Believers) do today, and say that they do not matter. It may strike your mind to know that even many unbelievers know that Christians should not live or be those ways.

You have to decide what you want. Do you want to please God or yourself? Do you want to obey the Truth or false teaching? Do you want to make it to Heaven or Hell? Do you want to receive abundant reward from the Lord or suffer loss? Make your decision now before it becomes too late!

Worldliness has crept into the lives of many Believers, especially in these last days. But one thing is that God's Word and Standard cannot change for any person or group of persons. God's Word is forever settled in Heaven: God hates worldliness. Worldliness is living like the people of the world. And concerning what we are discussing, it is appearing like the people of the world.

One of the major problems in many churches today is what somebody called 'churchiality without Christianity.' It is going to church, without being born again. It is being born again, without being committed to the Lord Jesus Christ. It is to be led and directed by the flesh, instead of being led and directed by the Word of God and His Holy Spirit.

Because many are in the churches, without being born again and committed to the Lordship of Jesus Christ, they live and appear like the people of the world; and before you know it, many Believers start joining or following them to live and appear like the people of the world, because they assume that those people, since they are members of our churches, are fellow Believers.

James put this matter in a strong form: "Adulterers and adulteresses! Do you not know that friendship with the world is enmity with God? Whoever therefore wants to be a friend of the world makes himself an enemy of God. Or do you think that the Scripture says in vain, 'The Spirit Who dwells in us yearns jealously (or, lusteth to envy, KJV)?'" (Jas 4:4-5).

What are you thinking, as you are reading this material? That you will change tomorrow? Tomorrow may be too late. Furthermore, if you don't make up your mind and take the right decision, accompanied by prayer, the devil can come and remove the Word from you. You may find out that the same Word that is burning in your heart now will not be felt much by you tomorrow.

How did people who rejected worldliness before accept it latter? By carelessness, lust of the flesh and the eyes, and by false teachings. A woman told me that she can never use weavon (or, is it attachment?) again, not just because I said it, but because she has known the truth about it. Brother, before you know what happened, she had started using it again. God told me the woman loved the world.

When preachings go forth, the women and ladies repent, cry, weep, and sob more than the men. Yet they are the ones that are easily deceived and led astray more than the men. Why is this the case? Apostle Paul said that it was not the man that was deceived, but the woman (1 Tim. 2:14).

If you see the kinds and appearances of dresses that parents put on their children, you will weep, if your understanding has been sharpened along this line. And those parents will expect those children to stop wearing those kinds of dresses when they grow up. They have been deceived, and they think they are wiser than God, Who said, "Train up the child in the way he should go, and when he/she is old he/she will not depart from it" (Prov. 22:6).

Any skirt or gown that is at the knee level as you are standing, which when you sit down, people can see your laps (even if it is a small part of your laps) is from the devil. Any skirt or gown that will require your covering yourself with handkerchief when you sit down is of demons (demon-inspired design). Any skirt or gown which when you sit down in a car, either as the driver or as a passenger, somebody can see your laps, originated from the wisdom of satan.

Read Exodus 20:26. Read also Exodus 28:42. If God was so much interested in the nakedness of His priests (which were even men) not being seen by people, how much more in this New Testament does He not want the nakedness of His daughters to be seen by men! And you say that you are a New Testament priest: why then are you not happy with making your gowns and skirts to be long enough to prevent people from seeing your laps (even when you are sitting down)?

Many women and ladies live in hypocrisy: when there is cold, the women cover themselves well to avoid it; but they will not care if their dressing is instigating lust and causing men to go Hell. Do they love Jesus Christ in reality?

In clearer words, the gown or skirt of a Christian and Godly woman, lady, or girl should not be shorter than halfway between her knee and her ankle, as she is standing up. This will guard against people seeing her laps when she sits down. These modern-day short (knee-level) gowns and skirts came from the wisdom and plans of the devil and his devils, whether or not you believe this Truth! The devil is very subtle and crafty.

If God is not interested in your body (or how you appear), why do you ask for (or claim) bodily healing or Divine health on your body? Many Believers allow the devil to deceive and mislead them with foolishness. How can you do try-and-luck (bet) with your eternal destiny in Heaven or Hell, when there wouldn't be any second chance?

What many people bind the devil of, are nothing but the works of the flesh. If you refuse to take up your responsibility, by obeying the Word of God, you will open a way for the devil; because he, who breaks the hedge, will be bitten by the serpent. Obey God, and those devils will leave by themselves! This will make it possible for you to have fewer things to pray and fast about.

The problem of many churches today is the presence of mixed multitude and great multitude. Yes, great multitude is good; but are you directing their hearts to the Lord and His Word? Today, you see unbelieving chorus leaders and musicians in the church. Many of them sing under the influence of drugs and alcohol. Some of them smoke. What a pity!

This is why you see worldly tones of music being played in many churches today. When you hear worldly tones of reggae, disco, awilo, makosa, etc, you should know that the end time is here with us. They will call God, Jesus, and speak Biblical things in the music; but the tone and beat is demonically programmed and attracts demons.

Choreographic dance is of the devil, for at least two reasons. First, it sends lustful impulses and thoughts to male watchers, which is one of the reasons why the devil introduced it into churches. Also, it makes people to put and focus their attention on the dancers and their body movements instead of focusing on worshipping God. Also, traditional dances are not to be used in the church, because they originated from demons who inspired those heathen traditions.

Concerning music and dancing, the Bible says, "Now the works of the flesh are evident, which are…revelries…of which I tell you beforehand, just as I also told you in time past, that those who practice such things will not inherit the Kingdom of God (Gal. 5:19-21).

"For we have spent enough of our past time in doing the will of the Gentiles – when we walked in…revelries…" (1 Pet. 4:3). According to the Longman Dictionary of Contemporary English, revelry means wild noisy dancing. God is against worldly, satanic, and demonic dancing, music, and tones, even in the church!

The Word of God tells us to prove or test all things, and to hold fast what is good (1 Thes. 5:21). Apostle John put it this way: "Beloved, do not believe every spirit, but test the spirits whether they are of God; because many false prophets have gone out into the world (1 Jn 4:1). Apostle Paul gave us another striking Word when he said, "Let two or three prophets speak, and let others judge" (1 Cor. 14:29).

Have you seen that even prophecies are to be judged and tested with the Word of God and the intuition or witness in your spirit by the Holy Spirit? When we talk of false prophets, many people seem to detect or suspect possible false prophets from their states or countries, and they count the foreign preachers as true ministers. My brother, they exist – locally, nationally, and internationally.

If they were preaching and teaching the Truth, without bringing people into satanic and demonic bondages, I wouldn't have been so much concerned. Why? Because Jesus Christ spoke to His Disciples, saying, "The scribes and the Pharisees sit in Moses' seat. Therefore whatever they tell you to observe, that observe and do, but do not do according to their works; for they say, and do not do" (Matt. 23:2-3).

They also use the Bible, quoting it to you, as the devil quoted it to Jesus Christ in the wilderness, to deceive people. They mix the Bible with the doctrines and teachings of demons and seducing spirits, and they deceive many. People hear them and say, "That is a great man of God!" People clap hands for them, and say, "Ride on, pastor!"

How do you know a false minister? By his words and practices. If his teachings and practices are against Sound Doctrine, run away from him. If he is interested in your money and not your soul, run away from him.

I am not just talking about somebody who may be making a minor mistake, because somebody may make a mistake (though God doesn't want it). But many of them know what they are doing. They know that they are working for the devil. They know they are working for money and fame.

I will tell you that many (or most) of all these beauty salons in town are owned by agents of the kingdom of darkness. Even those who are not direct or conscious agents have been demonized, in that their minds have been influenced or obsessed by the devil into doing that business, because the business glorifies the devil a lot.

When your business expands the works of the kingdom of darkness, are you not their agent? Whether or not you attend their night meetings, you are working for them. I know that, just as many Believers use those materials ignorantly, there are people who do the business, though they are not conscious or direct agents of the kingdom of darkness.

Yet, it doesn't change the fact that they are standing or working for the devil. Am I saying that women shouldn't take care of their hair? No, but they should do it in a Godly manner. Every sincere Christian lady or woman, who seeks to know, will be directed by the Holy Spirit on how to take care of her hair.

Therefore, if you take care of people's hair, as a Believer, you have to do it in a Godly manner. Any business that glorifies the devil and expands the kingdom of darkness, cannot be from God.

The beauty salons, the beauty stores, and the fashion centres, what do they stand for? The person that sales bleaching creams, and helps people to call God stupid for giving them the skin complexion they have, is he or she working for God or for satan? I will rather tell you the Truth and you hate me, than thwart the Word of God, and your blood will be on my head; after all, I am not interested in your sinful money!

If you are a tailor or a clothing designer/maker, what type of dresses and wears do you make for your customers/clients? We have demonic fashion designers also. They tell our good Christian ladies and women, "This style will not make you look 'sharp' and attractive." They will not use the word – seductive, because they are bent to deceive.

And before you know what is happening, you will see a Christian girl, lady, or woman wearing what will show us her armpits, her breasts, and her laps. Some demonic ladies will even carry those types of wears, and sit in front of the church congregation, so as to attempt to lead the man of God on the altar into lust and fornication, so that he will be reduced to an ordinary man, like the Philistines, with their Delilah, did to the 'powerful' Samson.

So, when you sell those marine weavons, demonic attachments, satanic nails, devilish cortex, bloody make-ups, and many other things in the group, are you a Christian, a Believer, or a Disciple? If you are a disciple, are you a disciple of satan or a Disciple of the Lord Jesus Christ? Who are you working for? What do you stand for?

Even those of you, who will make a long skirt, and divide (or, will I say, 'tear') that long skirt at the back, side, or front so that it reveals what a miniskirt or a short-skirt reveals, are you saying that you don't know what you are doing? If you say you did it to be able to walk freely, then why did you make a tight-fitting skirt in the first place? Others will cut their blouses or gowns to show us their back.

Get ready, for judgment is coming. I am not a prophet of doom, but a prophet of the Word of God; and I know that the Great Judge is ready to judge all unrighteousness! Therefore, count your soul more precious than your appearance now!

Those worldly and fashionable wedding gowns should be abolished for Believers and churches. Those wedding gowns are made to be glamorous, flamboyant, gorgeous, and for show and fashion. You may say that it is your day; but the Bible says, "Let your moderation be known unto all men. The Lord is at hand" (Phil. 4:5). Many people even go to the extent of making or using wedding gowns that reveal their sensitive parts.

Men wear (or make) normal wears or suits that they still wear even after the wedding ceremony. Therefore, the bride's wear or dress should be made to be normal and in such a way as to be something she can still wear at any other time after the wedding ceremony. It can be a gown or a skirt and blouse. Yes, make it to look good, but not something for fashion, show, or glamour.

Saying things like this may seem somehow, because my wife used wedding gown during our wedding. Even though the one she used covered her, yet, if I were to wed now, I cannot allow my wife to wear the conventional wedding gowns (even though now, weddings are done in many churches with those wedding gowns), because it does not reflect moderation, humility, Christ-likeness, and the Bible: it shows excesses for show.

But just because I didn't know the Truth at that time will not make me not to say the Truth when I know it. For instance, 'naturally', I myself hated (and I still hate) rings; but when I married, I loved (I think it was not just a liking) wearing wedding ring (maybe for the love of a husband for the wife). But I cannot wear a wedding ring again, because it is still a ring. Will I encourage wearing wedding rings because I loved or worn it?

Formerly, when people had good sense and judgment, the blouses of women were made in such a way that they didn't have buttons at the front, from their chest to their waist. But now, satanic fashion designers have designed what they call blouses for women which have spaced buttons from their chests downwards. And when they wear them, their breasts will push the material, so that someone can see their breasts from the spaces between the buttons.

The devil knew what he did in that demonic design. If their blouses are to be made that way, then they must have very well sealed zips, and not spaced buttons. When people listened to their consciences, men's shirts were made with spaced buttons, because men don't have breasts that will push open their chests. And don't wear those hanging blouses, which when you sit down or lift up your hands, your underwear will be exposed. Say "Amen!"

Men must button up their shirts (that is, they are not to leave their chests open). If you, as a woman, must wear a blouse with buttons, make sure it is not the kind that will reveal your breast or brassiere in-between the buttons. Zips are preferable to buttons for women's blouses; complete undivided blouses with neither zips nor buttons are best for women. Those short hanging jackets worldly women wear are satanic.

If many of our ladies and women will devote the energy they use to beautify themselves, to work on their spirit and soul, brother, many husbands will be running to their homes immediately they are through with their work and business. However, even in the homes of many Believers, the husbands prefer to stay away from home as much as possible.

When you talk to your husband as if he doesn't have authority over you, do you think that he will want to stay with you? This is one of the reasons why many unbelieving husbands go after strange women, because when they see the lady that will honour and respect them, the devil tells them, "Have you seen?"

And the Bible says, "Wives, likewise, be submissive to your own husbands, that even if some do not obey the Word, they, without a word, may be won by the conduct of their wives, when they observe your chaste conduct accompanied by fear" (1 Pet. 3:1-2).

On this issue of the dressing of the women, women should make their dresses – blouses, skirts, gowns, and wrappers – in such a way that they will cover their sensitive parts. When you dress, people shouldn't see your laps, breasts, and armpits. Make your skirts in such a way that even when you sit down, people shouldn't see your laps. If you use handkerchief to cover it when you sit down, are you hypocritical?

Your sensitive parts are for your husband; therefore reserve them for him, and not for us. When you keep on straightening your skirts or you use handkerchief to cover your laps as you are sitting down, why didn't you tell them to make it longer than it is, when they were making it? Or, are you deceiving yourself?

Use the blouses that were made with well-sealed zips. Condemn those blouses which, when you put them on, people, other than your husband, see your breasts in-between buttons; you understand? You are a Christian, and not an unbeliever! The neck of your blouse is to be in such a way that even when you bend down, no one will see your breast.

Don't wear body-hug dresses, because they reveal your body contours. Don't wear see-through dresses. What do I mean by see-through dresses? In physics, the scientists talk of transparent, translucent, and opaque materials. The translucent materials are semi-opaque and semi-transparent. The see-through dresses are the semi-covering and semi-uncovering dresses.

Many Believers wear short-skirts, and they 'think' that because the skirts are not miniskirts, then nothing is wrong with the skirts. A sincere, serious, and dedicated Christian whose mind is in Heaven (and whose eye has not been blinded by the devil) will not be comfortable wearing a short-skirt. A short skirt or gown is the one which when you sit down, somebody can see any part of your laps; while a miniskirt or mini-gown is the one which even when you are standing up, somebody can see your laps.

If, as a man, I open the back or front of my shirt the way some women open the back or front of their blouses and gowns, will you be happy? And if a man will not open his front or back, how much more the women!

Your armpits are not to be seen when you lift up your hands; therefore, the sleeves of your blouses and gowns must be made, both in length and in design, in such a way as to guard against this.

In your church, ministry, or fellowship, be mindful of the dressing and appearance of those who minister, speak, or appear before the crowd, especially those that appear before them often; because they, consciously or unconsciously, tell the rest of the people how they should dress and appear.

To this end, the pastor and minister should be mindful of how his wife dresses and appears, because many women, ladies, and girls in the church, ministry, or fellowship will likely learn from her. Many churches, ministries, and fellowships that dress and appear like the people of the world became that way because of the ministers' wives and other women leaders and ministers.

And don't even wear shorts or trousers inside your skirt or gown; use your appropriate underwears. Somebody may say that she will wear shorts to avoid being raped; but it is God Who keeps and protects you. By the way, even trousers will not stop being raped; but God will stop it. The person who can forcefully rape you can also pull the trousers; and at gunpoint, if you fear weapons instead of believing and trusting God, you yourself will pull the trousers out. But if you do the right thing, angels of God are there to intervene on your behalf. Also, don't use trousers for night-wears: don't allow the devil to deceive you.

Be careful of the pictures and signs that are drawn or imposed on your blouses, shirts, wears, and dresses. The devil puts satanic, demonic, devilish, and occult pictures and signs on some wears and dresses to entangle and enslave people. Those pictures and signs can attract and permit the presence of demons and their works.

Do not use Lycra material to make your dresses and clothes. Lycra material is a material that stretches, which is used for making tight-fitting clothes. This is because it tights your body and shows your body contours, thereby sending lustful messages and impulses to the opposite sex. God hates the use of it for dresses and clothes.

Do not send your children to any school where they are forced to wear sleeveless dresses and clothes as their school uniform: they will end up corrupting them. And the schools which use such school uniforms either have demonic targets from the leadership, have been deceived by the devil and his demons, or they have satanic workers/teachers (conscious or unconscious). Of course, this is not to say that all schools where they wear sleeved dresses and clothes are free from demonic works.

Men dress up to cover their chest and back; who then designed (or planned the design of) the open chest blouses or gowns that show women's breasts' cleavage and breasts, or the open back blouses or gowns that show their back? It could be no other beings/people than satan and his associates; they are the beings/people that stand against the Will of God and promote lust among men.

For those who say that they use pairs of trousers to guard against cold, the human race has been in existence for about six thousand years on the surface of this earth: Did people not keep themselves safe from cold from the beginning of the human race till about some decades ago when women started wearing trousers, which many of them hypocritically call slacks?

You, as a Christian lady, should appear natural. What do we men lose by appearing natural? You may say you want to attract people, but you are attracting men (whether or not they are Believers) who have not known the Truth, because those things get me annoyed, when I see them on the bodies of believing ladies and women. Therefore, all those lipsticks, cortexes, demonic/artificial nails, and paint or pencil will not be required.

Somebody asked me, saying, "Can I use brown powder since I use white powder?" One needs to wonder why some women want to look horrible the way they look. Why do people really want to paint themselves as if they are buildings that need to be painted and repainted? Many of those women seem not to know that their minds have been obsessed by demons, and they 'do not even know' what they are doing to themselves. I wonder why many husbands allow their wives to dress and appear the way they appear! Some men even tell their wives to look that horrible.

Well, as for the question of, "Can I use brown powder since I use white powder?" Why do you want to use the brown powder? The Bible says, "Moreover, when you fast, do not be like the hypocrites, with a sad countenance. For they disfigure their faces that they may appear to men to be fasting. Assuredly, I say to you, they have their reward. But you, when you fast, anoint your head and wash your face, so that you do not appear to men to be fasting, but to your Father Who is in the Secret Place; and your Father Who sees in secret will reward you openly" (Matt. 6:16-18).

Here Jesus Christ tells you to use ointment on your head and wash your face instead of disorganizing your head (hair), wearing sackcloth, and sitting on ashes, to appear to men to be fasting. But notice that the purpose for anointing your head (rubbing oil/ointment on your hair) and washing your face is for you to look normal, so that people will not know that you are fasting.

Of course, it is not compulsory that you anoint your head and wash your face whenever you fasting, because if you were to be in the desert, on the mountain, or in the room alone, where people will not see you, you may decide to neither anoint your head nor wash your face, at least for some time. However, the purpose of the anointing (rubbing) and washing is to appear normal.

So, whereas somebody may use white powder to remove or neutralize oil on his or her face, another person may just wipe his or her face with a handkerchief to remove the oil that might have been accumulated on his or her face, maybe due to heat. But why will you even paint/parch your face with white powder or brown powder? Do you want white or brown colour for your face and 'building'?

Therefore, apart from the brown powder issue, there is certainly a difference between using white powder to neutralize oil on your face and using white powder to paint your face. So, apart from using white powder to neutralize oil on your face, using white powder (maybe the medicated one) to stop or treat heat rashes on your body, or for any other good special case(s), do not even paint your face with white powder for beauty. Of course, this concerns both males and females.

Don't put your mind on costly or expensive things. Never be obsessed by them. Moderately priced and inexpensive clothing is good for the women. It helps to prevent pride. Don't pressurize your husband to buy expensive things for you; for it will not be to your advantage. If the man starts misbehaving and disobeying the Word of God in order to satisfy you, you will suffer it more.

Why? Because when someone starts stealing, lying, or cheating, the fellow can also start following strange women, since they are all from the same heart. Any person, who can be committing evil and hiding it from men, without fearing God Who sees all things, can do what you may not believe.

God said to Jacob, "Arise go up to Bethel and dwell there; and make an altar there to God, Who appeared to you when you fled from the face of Esau your brother." And Jacob said to his household and all who were with him, "Put away the foreign gods that are among you, purify yourselves, and change your garments. Then let us go up to Bethel...."

So they gave Jacob all the foreign gods which were in their hands, and the earrings which were in their ears; and Jacob hid (buried) them under the terebinth tree which was by Shechem. And they journeyed, and the Terror of God was upon the cities that were all around them, and they did not pursue the sons of Jacob (Gen. 35:1-5).

Earrings were among the things they purified themselves from to be clean before God. The Egyptians, Babylonians, Assyrians, Mesopotamians, and the other foreign and heathen nations were given to these things, just as the people of the world today. When you leave the world, you will also leave these things.

And piercing your ear to wear earrings is of the devil. Why do you pierce your ear? Are you a slave? If your ears were pierced by your parents, having repented from it, how can you wear earrings in it again? Where then is your repentance?

When God told Moses to tell the children of Israel to collect those things from the Egyptians, God wanted to plunder the Egyptians, because they made those things from gold and silver. And the Israelites, instead of keeping those things for the construction of the Ark of the Testimony and other things, they started with using them to construct a calf which they worshipped, and said that it was the calf that brought them out of Egypt (Exo. 32). God was very angry with them for that act; and had it not been that Moses interceded for them, He would have wiped them out!

People wear and use things that bring them into the bondage of the devil, even unknowingly. And God says that His people are destroyed for lack of knowledge (Hos. 4:6); and His people have gone into captivity, because they have no knowledge (Isa. 5:13). When you use the things that God has condemned, you are selling yourself to the devil, and he will oppress you. The devil, satan, is a master-strategist: he wants to have your spirit, soul, and body; and if he doesn't get this one, he will go for the other.

Earrings, bangles, rings, necklaces, and such things are not needed on your body by God. They promote the desire of the devil, which is ornamenting your body. Even wedding rings won't be necessary. Of course, you would have seen some who would even put an extra ring on top of the wedding ring to make it look more beautiful. Who even invented the wedding ring as a means of distinguishing the married from the unmarried? Get rid of wedding rings and engagement rings from your fingers, brothers and sisters! Your soul is much more precious than wedding rings and engagement rings.

Some people try to use Abraham (or his servant) to defend themselves in this issue; but they fail to know that Abraham didn't know everything at the same time. Before Jacob grew up and matured, having come from Isaac of Abraham (many years after Abraham), they would have known how God reacts to those things.

Remember that Abraham was a heathen and idol worshipper (from Ur of the Chaldeans – Babylonians) before he was called by God; and he had learned their ways. It still took some time to refine him. Abraham lied on two different occasions, because of fear (and Isaac also lied over his wife, because of fear). Does that make lying good, because Abraham lied?

If your dresses are worldly in appearance, condemn them, because of Jesus Christ and your soul. Don't be afraid, for God is able to provide you with new good dresses. Don't put your trust in man, no matter what he owns: put your trust in God, and His angels will bring all you need to you in due time.

The same things that were happening when God destroyed the whole earth with the Flood are happening now. The same things that the Israelites (God's people) did, for which God destroyed them in the wilderness, are happening today in many churches.

When God destroyed the world, they didn't carry arms for Him; they didn't shoot at Him with guns: they were disobedient to His Commands, and they lived to gratify the lusts of their eyes and the desires of their flesh.

And the same things that happened to the people of old, will happen to many (even Believers) in the Last Day, but in a different dimension – Hell Fire. The Church is giving the Lord Jesus Christ more 'headache' and trouble than the world! But just as the Jews didn't believe Prophet Jeremiah until they were engulfed in the disaster that God brought upon them, many will not believe this Message and Word until they will end in Hell Fire.

God is not from any nation, and He owns all nations. Though we know, from the Bible, that God has a special link with the nation of Israel, yet, He is not from Israel. Israel cannot dictate for Him; and He will not change His Standard because of Israel. God cannot change His Standard for anyone and for any church. No matter how anointed you are, no matter what you may have, all came from God.

Many people do the things they do, because they think that since people from this or that nation do the same things, they must be right; but this is not true in the ultimate sense. The thing that many people seem to fail to understand is that the devil is working in every nation of the earth.

No matter the nation you may come from, the devil had been working in your nation before you were born, and he will continue to work there. The devil has succeeded to work in many nations without being recognized.

There are many things that are being done in some nations of the world, which people don't see as having come from the devil. For instance, when a country legalizes abortion, whether or not they know it, the work of the devil is being fulfilled in their midst.

God hates abortion; for no one has right to take any other person's life. No matter the theory or proposition medical science may make to make abortion look good, they are just dancing to the tone of the devil's deception. Once the zygote has been formed, a human being has come.

Let us consider the issue of women liberation movements. Have you noticed the rate of divorce and juvenile delinquencies these days? These are the long-term effects of women liberation movements.

When women decide to abandon their basic responsibilities in pursuit of secondary issues, the devil is at work, whether they recognize it or not. Women have the responsibility to be helpers suitable to their husbands.

We will now consider the issue of whether it is good for women to put on trousers. One thing about dresses is that they are meant to cover the person putting them on, whether they are men or women.

Gowns, wrappers, skirts, blouses, trousers, shirts, etc, are to cover the person wearing them. I want you to know that over the years, in every continent (America, Europe, Africa, Asia, etc), there have been changes in the modes of their dressing.

However, any dressing or change in dressing that does not glorify God is satanic and demonic, no matter what any person may think or say, even though you may not have it in mind as you put them on. That is the Truth. The devil prefers to work under cover and without being noticed.

When women put on sleeveless blouses, mini-skirts, tight-fitting and partly transparent (revealing) dresses, they are glorifying satan, and helping him to fulfil his purpose, whether or not they know it.

As I said before, considering the biological features of women, women should not use pairs of trousers. Why? When a woman is matured sexually, one of the features that biologists tell us will be noticed in her is enlarged buttocks. Have you never noticed that trousers show their body contours for everybody to see? Trousers reveal their buttocks and laps seductively.

Now, don't say that you are going to allow your children wear pairs of trousers, and when they mature they will stop using them. If you train them up that way, when they are old, they will not depart from it (Prov. 22:6).

But seductive dresses or dressing seductively helps the devil spread his lust wave, and people get into the sins of lust, fornication, adultery, etc. Some will say that whoever wants to fall will fall; but you and I know that some things can make someone fall, when he wouldn't have fallen without them.

Let the Spirit of God lead you, and do not be led by your mind and thought. Trousers are neither an American culture nor a British culture. It started at a time, and got so much opposition there then; but over so many years later, the opposition has waned so much that some think it is their culture.

After all, was there anything like America until Amerigo sailed past the Atlantic Ocean and found the land which was later developed to be America? And it is Britain that developed and colonized America before they got their independence. And all countries and continents of the world will appear before God for judgment.

Know this once again: any dressing that helps the devil fulfil his will, plan, and purpose is from him. If you can't stop dressing this or that way because of Jesus Christ, can you lay down your life for Him? (Matt. 10:39). Don't you want to be worthy of Him?

Christians (both males and females) should avoid wearing jeans materials for some reasons. Jeans tight your body to show your body-contours. Jeans seem to have been made/designed by the devil to provoke rough, wild, and worldly feeling and lifestyle, as evident in the fact that you may see some of them as stone-wash jeans, jeans which look like they have been decolourized (or partly decolourized), perforated jeans with different kinds of openings, patched jeans with pieces of the material sewn on it, torn jeans proudly worn as style (whereas other clothing materials that are torn would make the same person feel ashamed), jeans trousers or shorts with rough cutting or design at the edges, etc.

If the physical appearance of many Believers are worldly, how much more the sins of spirit and soul (inward sins) that are hidden from us! If many Believers don't care about their worldly appearance, how much more do they care less concerning the hidden sins (inward sins) which we do not see!

God hates tribal marks and tattooing your body, as He said, "You shall not make any cuttings in your flesh for the dead, nor tattoo any marks on you: I am the Lord" (Lev. 19:28). No matter the kind of design or picture you tattoo yourself with, it is evil.

Funky (modern and fashionable) style of hair cut like what is called 'punk', 'afro-cut', etc must not find its place in you. Also, leave your hair the natural shape it has in haircut; and avoid carving it, for it gives it an unnatural or/and fashionable shape.

There are many reasons why Christians should not use weavons. Using weavons is like telling God that He is stupid and imperfect for giving you the kind of hair you have. It is like bleaching, which many do; they feel that God should have made them fair in complexion instead of dark. But on the Day of Judgment, you will find out that you tried to degrade God. Using relaxer and hair extensions for your hair or another person's hair is demonic and satanic in origin, and leads to Hell Fire.

The Word says, "For this reason God gave them up to vile passions. For even their women exchanged the natural use for what is against nature. Likewise also the men, leaving the natural use of the woman, burned in their lust for one another, men with men committing what is shameful, and receiving in themselves the penalty of their error which was due" (Rom. 1:26-27).

This place implies turning the nature to artificial/perversion in women/men. Turning the nature to artificial/perversion in women/men does not only apply to lesbianism and homosexualism. Of course, the Bible emphasized on homosexualism here; but on the side of the women, it says, "...women exchanged the natural use for what is against nature."

And you see the exchanging of the natural for what is against nature and God's Plan, Wisdom, and Ability in bleaching the skin, perfuming the body, painting the nails with cortex, fixing of artificial nails, frying and perming the hair, artificially relaxing and extending the hair, painting the face with lipstick and eye-pencil, dyeing the hair, fixing of eyelashes, using and wearing of weavons and attachments, tattooing the body, etc.

And, "The Wrath of God is revealed from Heaven against all ungodliness and unrighteousness of men, who suppress the Truth in unrighteousness, because what may be known of God is manifest in them, for God has shown it to them" (Rom. 1:18). You can see that God has given and shown you the reason why you shouldn't change His Handiwork; therefore, if you do, then you decided to corrupt yourself, turn yourself against God, suffer unnecessary things in this earth, and finally deprive yourself of Heaven!

God asked whether a leopard can change its spot, because He has made it that way (Jer. 13:23); and many human beings say, "God, we are wiser than You and leopards, and we know how to change our skin." The Ethiopians would have refused to change their skin in the old times; now many of them may do it because of science and technology.

It is like those who use high-heel shoes to increase their height, because they feel that they should be taller than they are. When Jesus Christ tells you not to worry about your height, because you can't add a cubit to it (Matt. 6:27), you say, "God, I know how to increase my not-good size in height."

Some use perfume to say, "Why must people not identify my scent? This natural neutral 'scent' is too boring!" Why do people try to bring themselves into different bondages? Others use breast-pads to make their breasts look big and seductive. When you see some others paint themselves with powder, you wonder why they want to look that way in the first place!

Many others say, "God, it is not now that I should have grey (gray) hair; I am still young." (Grey is British English, while gray is American English). And they end up dyeing their hair. Many spend hours designing themselves – time they should have used for Godly and spiritual things. The silver-haired head is a crown of glory, if it is found in the way of righteousness (Prov. 16:31). The glory of young men is their strength, and the splendour of old men is their grey head (Prov. 20:29). Silver-haired or grey head is the Handiwork of God!

Also, many of those weavons are real human hair which were cut and sold. How can you be wearing another person's hair as a Christian lady or woman? This is worldliness; this is satanic and demonic; sister, the ground you are treading on is dangerous.

Then, even though some of those weavons may be synthetic or artificial (which the first point still condemns), many of those weavons ladies use are manufactured in the water-kingdom of darkness and brought to this earth for sales to contaminate the people of the world.

The thing that some people don't know is that some companies which exist physically on this earth came from the dark kingdom of satan, especially the water-world of the devil. In fact, many things we see physically came from the dark kingdom. Even many legal and morally good things (like pre-fabricated food) we see are manufactured in the dark kingdom, some of which I wouldn't mention here.

This is why you need to pray over and sanctify the things that you use, especially edible things. But how will you want to sanctify the things that the Lord has rejected and condemned (like weavons, artificial nails, wet-lips, lipsticks, eyelashes, etc)? You are already offending God!

Everything is not demonic, don't misunderstand me; don't live in fear either, because greater is He that is in us than he that is in the world. The anointing breaks every yoke of the enemy. But many Christians create loopholes for the devil through sin, disobedience, and worldliness.

You need to be watchful and sober, because if you are not, the devil can lead you into sin and worldliness; and if the Lord Jesus Christ meets you in that state at His Coming, or you die in that state, you will miss Heaven and go to Hell.

But that is not God's Plan for you; and He did not bring you out of the world to condemn you later. Therefore, don't condemn yourself. You condemn yourself by despising His Word and the Promptings of His Spirit.

Many are busy 'binding and loosing' the devil while they are the ones that are inviting the devil. Preachers and ministers, many of you are busy saying you are destroying the works of the devil, while the devil is binding people comfortably through worldliness among Believers. May their blood not be on your hands because you refused to tell them the Truth!

Some say that it is not written in the Bible that you must not smoke. Okay, continue to destroy your body, which is the Temple of God (1 Cor. 3:16), until you hear, "Get behind Me, you who practice iniquity!" Cigarette is a destructive tool of satan, the devil. It is suicide in disguise.

Others say that it is alright to drink alcohol as far as you don't get drunk (or in small quantity). Firstly, assuming that the wine which Apostle Paul told Timothy to drink was not a totally non-alcoholic wine, little sense should have told you that if the Believers of the New Testament were drinking it in small quantity, Apostle Paul wouldn't have needed to tell Timothy to take small of it as medicine.

Even if you have stomach problem, do you now envy that archaic and unrefined medical practice when you have always wanted development and civilization, just because you want to satisfy your flesh? Will you have the boldness to defend yourself before God on the Judgment Day? Can you forsake alcohol for God and for your soul?

Secondly, according to the Dake's Annotated Reference Bible's explanation of 1 Tim. 5:23, "With two kinds of wine mentioned in the Scripture – one, unfermented new wine found in the cluster (Isa. 65:8), we can be assured that Timothy was not urged to take the intoxicating kind to strengthen him." Someone may ask, "If this is true, then why did he tell him to drink little of it?" First, you don't even have to drink non-alcoholic drink to excess.

Second, who knows whether they (Timothy was his disciple and associate) had altogether stopped drinking even non-alcoholic wine as a kind of self-denial, continuous partial fasting, or living the fasted life, even as John the Baptist did not eat and drink all kinds of even morally good food and drinks? Even now, many Believers and ministers decide to (or, are commanded by God) to stop or minimize the intake of certain kinds of food or/and drinks as a way of self-denial and living the fasted life.

The Bible says, "Who has woe? Who has sorrow? Who has contentions? Who has complaints? Who has wounds without cause? Who has redness of eyes? Those who linger long at the wine; those who go in search of mixed wine. Do not look on the wine when it is red, when it sparkles in the cup, when it swirls around smoothly; at the last it bites like a serpent, and stings like a viper. Your eyes will see strange things, and your heart will utter perverse things" (Prov. 23:29-33).

Here, the Bible says, "Do not look on the wine...." Can you take a small amount of what you are not supposed to look on to? That is to say, "Don't even desire any amount of wine or alcohol." Whether the wine contains 1% or 5% of alcohol, it is still alcohol and sinful. Can you allow small amount of alcohol to take you to Hell?

When a company that manufactures wine puts '5% alcohol' on the label of the wine, it shows that they know the difference between wine that is free from alcohol and the one with alcohol. And there was no alcoholic content in the wine that Jesus Christ made. No wonder the master of the feast said, "...You have kept the good wine until now!" (Jn 2:10). Jesus Christ made a good quality wine with a difference!

People used to abort unborn human beings in secret before; now satanic and demonic laws have empowered them. And subtly and craftily, the enemy (satan, the devil) has 'moralized' abortion in certain birth-control measures.

People used to smoke secretly before; now they are bold to smoke anyhow outside. Homosexuals and lesbians used to practice their wickedness in secret and darkness, being ashamed of it; now they even boast that they are homosexuals and lesbians. Boasting and waiting for damnation in Hell Fire!

The devil has penetrated and destroyed many people through films. Most of those films from Hollywood, Nollywood, and others promote the works of the devil. Even, many (or most) of the so-called Christian films still advertize and promote the works of the devil.

When films are promoting immorality, indecent dressing, vices, violence, hatred, and other demonic activities, do they promote God? Be careful with the type of film that you and your family watch! Many of those films are dedicated to the devil to serve his interest and increase sales; and so, playing them attracts the presence of demons into your house (and to the watchers). Watching of wrestling, karate, horror films, and many others are inspired by the devil.

So, you film director, producer, actor, or actress, whose interest are you serving? Who is inspiring you, and who are you working for? Sometimes, the devil will wittingly package some of the films in such a way that they look harmless; but ultimately, his interest is being promoted.

Just as many Believers and ministers preach and teach heresies and anti-Christ, anti-God, and unbiblical doctrines and practices, when half-baked and non-Biblically sound Believers direct and produce their so-called Christian films, they end up expanding false teachings and doctrines.

The Internet is a major way that the devil uses to enslave the children of men. Through the Internet, the devil has made many people to go into indecent dressing, lust, and sexual immorality. In Twitter, Facebook, Google, etc, you will see things that can lead you away from the Word of God, if you are not careful, disciplined, and determined.

There are many satanic, demonic, and occult websites in the Internet. Even many of those sites, blogs, and websites which were not opened by conscious agents of satan have things that can still make you to be corrupted and polluted if you are not careful. Many times, even when you are doing something else in the Internet, they will start flashing you with seductive pictures and worldly things.

You might have observed that many of the programmes, movies (films), music, and activities that are spread by televisions, digital satellite stations, cables networks, and radio stations are satanic and demonic in origin. Therefore, be careful of what you watch and ponder on, and what you allow your children and family to watch, listen to, and be exposed to.

Beware of the cartoons that you allow your children to watch, because many of those cartoons are demonic, and they are capturing souls for the devil. Evil spirits possess people when they watch some cartoons. Also, many of the video games that people play are demonic and satanic; and they get people who play them demonized. Horror films are from the devil, and they promote his plans and works.

These are apart from the time that people spend on these things and more, and the passion with which they pursue and get attached to them, thereby making them their gods. When you use the time you should use for God and His Things for activities that do not glory His Name, the Jealous God gets jealous and angry!

Change your name if it is satanic and demonic. Dissociate yourself from any satanic, demonic, and ungodly name. Don't you say that what you confess is what you possess? Why then do you want satanic, demonic, or negative confession on what you are called by? Do you think that God will like to call you by satanic or demonic names?

Concerning the covering of the hair, the Bible says, "Every man praying or prophesying, having his head covered dishonours his head. But every woman who prays or prophesies with her head uncovered dishonours her head, for that is one and the same as if her head were shaved. For if a woman is not covered, let her also be shorn. But if it is shameful for a woman to be shorn or shaved, let her be covered.

"For a man indeed ought not to cover his head, since he is the Image and Glory of God; but woman is the glory of man. For man is not from woman, but woman from man. Nor was man created for the woman, but woman for the man. For this reason the woman ought to have a symbol of authority on her head, because of the angels.

"...Judge among yourselves. Is it proper for a woman to pray to God with her head uncovered? Does not even nature itself teach you that if a man has long hair, it is a dishonour to him? But if a woman has long hair, it is a glory to her; for her hair is given to her for a covering. But if anyone seems to be contentious, we have no such custom, nor do the churches of God" (1 Cor. 11:4-16, New King James Version).

I want you to notice that it did not say that her 'long hair' is given to her for a covering, but her hair. I also want you to notice that this place is talking about covering the hair, and not about long or short hair. To convince you that it is speaking of covering or veiling your hair, the Bible says, "Every man praying or prophesying, having his head covered dishonours his head" (verse 4).

Covering the hair indicates using something (not your hair) to veil your hair. Forget about the distortion of the Bible: according to the Longman Dictionary of Contemporary English, 'veil' is a thin piece of material worn by women to cover their faces at formal occasions such as weddings or for religious reasons.

You can see that this portion of the Scripture is dealing with veiling yourself, as a woman, and not about long or short hair. Speaking of long or short hair, it says, "Does not even nature itself teach you that if a man has long hair, it is dishonour to him?" (verse 14). This is to say that, naturally, long hair doesn't befit a man.

Speaking on the being good if a woman has a natural long hair, it says, "But if a woman has long hair, it is a glory to her; for her hair is given to her for a covering" (verse 15). This is why I ponder on it when I see Christian women cut their hair as low as a man's hair (and I am talking of even outside the church building).

If a woman has to cut her hair as low as men's hair in any given society or nature of hair (because the nature or natural texture of the hair will affect the length), then she should also be ready to wear cap on it, because, naturally, it doesn't befit a woman, except that 'human civilization' and disregard for God-ordained procedures has gripped many. This is what these women liberation movements, which are inspired by satan, have caused over time: disregard for God-ordained authority and natural tendencies.

And know that it didn't say that the long attachment or weavon of the woman is given to her for a covering, because God didn't give any woman any attachment or weavon. Therefore the attachment or weavon on the head of the woman is no glory, but satanic and demonic bondage, whether or not she knows of it.

It says, "But if a woman has long hair…" and not, "When a woman has long hair…." So your hair may not be 'long' or very long, but should not be as short as men's hair in the race/nation you are from (I am not talking of mixed society: where the society is mixed, consisting of people from different nations and races, then use the shortness of men's hair from the same nation or race as you to ascertain the minimum length of your hair); but it is best long, as far as the being 'long' or very long is not achieved by perming or artificially relaxing your hair or with the use of attachments or weavon!

If you find it difficult to comb it or keep it neat, then shorten, reduce, or cut it, to the length that you can comb it well and keep it neat; but do not let it be as low as the general length of the hair of the men from the same race or nation as you, except you are going to wear cap or hair scarf on it as you go around.

Look at what verses 4 and 7 say: "Every man praying or prophesying, having his head covered dishonours his head. For a man indeed ought not to cover his head, since he is the Image and Glory of God; but woman is the glory of man." This is telling a man, who already has a short hair (or may decide to be shorn) to not cover his hair in the church. To be shorn is to shave someone's hair clean, as you would shear the skin of the sheep. Is this not clear enough that what the Bible is talking about here is covering the hair and not short or long hair?

And verses 5 and 6 say: "But every woman who prays or prophesies with her head uncovered dishonours her head, for that is one and the same as if her head were shaved. For if a woman is not covered, let her also be shorn. But if it is shameful for a woman to be shorn or shaved, let her be covered." And this place is saying that the woman whose hair is not covered (veiled) in the church is the same as being shorn (shaving her hair clean).

And verse 10 says that a woman should have a symbol of authority on her head because of the angels. That is either to teach the angels submission to God, or in order not to grieve the angels of God, who, normally, are present in any Believers' meeting; because angels don't like disorder and unrighteousness. Lucifer and his cohorts rebelled against God; they were angels, just like the present obedient angels. Genesis 24:65 says: "...So she took a veil and covered herself." Rebekah, whose hair was already long, took a veil to cover herself to show respect for Isaac.

The Greek word used in verses 6 and 7 of First Corinthians, chapter eleven, for covered and cover is 'katakalupto'. Katakalupto means veiled. It had been a custom for ages for women to be veiled. Only public prostitutes in the East went without veils. But those who want all they can do to avoid covering their hair use: "But if a woman has long hair, it is a glory to her; for her hair is given to her for a covering" (verse 15). They misapply this verse to do what they want to do.

For whoever may be contentious about these things, Apostle Paul wrote: "We have no such custom, nor do the churches of God" (verse 16). Could he be saying that there is no custom of covering hair when he took many verses to persuade the women to cover their hair? I don't believe so; rather, I believe that he is talking of the custom of the contentious person saying that it makes no difference if women cover their hair {or even try to convince people that covering of hair is not for Believers (those in the church, or their church)}.

Many people do not take time to consider some things about the design of many women dresses – gowns, blouses, and skirts. Consider how the design and making of even average unbelieving men are – how they do not expose their armpits, laps, and chests. Just take time to consider the length of the sleeves of their shirts (even their short-sleeved shirts) and that of their trousers; and I know that the men also want fresh air.

Compare it with how many women move around with gowns, blouses, and skirts that show people their armpits, laps, breasts, and shapes. Can you not detect that satan and mermaid spirits are at work in the lives of many women (even Believers) whether or not they are aware of it, as far as dressing is concerned? The devil wants to corrupt men and the human race; and one great weapon he uses is women and their dressing.

Please, if you are a Believer, when you go to buy an already-made dress, check the design and method of their making before buying them. And when you meet a dress designer and maker for your dresses, tell them how they should make your dresses. No wonder the world (which is ruled by satan) has decided to call them fashion designers, because many of them design what satan and demons inspire and tell them to design!

Just take time to consider how those satan-inspired fashion designers design and make women dresses! Some of them will make a long gown, but they will make its sleeves to be so short (and even sleeveless) so that the armpits will be the point of attraction and seduction.

Some other demons-prompted designers will make the blouse that has a good length of sleeve, but they will 'cut' the back or the front in such a way as to show their back, breasts, and breast cleavages; because what satan wants to seduce men through the blouse is her breasts and exposed body.

Others will make long skirts, but they will cut and divide the skirt at the back, by the side, or at the front, because the point of seduction is their laps. Then others will design and make short skirts and gowns which when the women wearing them sit down people will see their laps and even underwears, because that is the heart and desire of the devil.

And others will not care and make mini-skirts, so that even if they are standing, people will be seeing their laps and what they call long legs. Do you know that many women (even Believers) are serving the devil, even without their knowledge? And surely, serving the devil has rewards (or do I say punishments?).

I wonder why many women spend hours in making and dressing their hair with attachments, wool, and thread! This is the love of the world and idolatry in operation. Notice that the modern frying of hair and the use of attachment were not even in existence among the unbelieving Israelites and Jews of the days of the Early Church, and also among the Gentiles of the places where Paul ministered! Therefore they had no business writing about frying of hair and the use of attachments (they did not even know the possibility or the reality of people trying such abominations).

You can use map to check the places where Apostle Paul ministered in his first, second, and third missionary journeys to see whether the inhabitants of those places (except possible immigrants) have the kind of hair which those that fry their hair and use attachments to make their hair long use nowadays.

Yes, they wrote about braiding or plaiting, and also of jewellery, which existed in their days among the unbelievers and possibly among some Believers who had carried their worldly lifestyle of hair dressing into their Christian faith. And you can see what they wrote about braiding/plaiting the hair, use of jewels, and wearing of fashions and costly clothing and apparel (and women relationship with their husbands) in First Timothy 2:9-10 and First Peter 3:1-6.

When God created everything, He saw that all the things He created were good, that the Bible says, "Then God saw everything that He had made, and indeed it was very good" (Gen. 1:31). Who are you to challenge the Handiwork of God? Bleaching your skin, painting your face, perming your hair, wearing weavons, dyeing your hair, painting your nails, etc are ways of challenging God's Creative Ability.

Someone may say, "But Jesus Christ said that it is not what enters a man that defiles the man, but what comes out of the man" (Matt. 15:11). You have to understand well what He was saying. But if what goes into a man doesn't defile a man, why did Jesus Christ rebuke the church in Thyatira for allowing Jezebel to teach His Servants to eat things sacrificed to idols? (Rev. 2:20). And when there was a debate/argument on what the Gentile Christians should keep, why did the counsel at Jerusalem tell them to abstain from things polluted by idols, from strangled meat/animals, and from blood? (Acts 15:20).

Somebody may say that Apostle Paul said that idol is nothing, but fail to see that he said that if your brother will be offended, because you ate the meat sacrificed to idol, you are to avoid it (1 Cor. 8; Rom. 14). When somebody says that Jesus Christ said that not what enters a man defiles a man, but what comes out of the man, he doesn't even know that they were discussing about washing of the hands before eating.

By the way, does vomiting defile you before God, since it came out of you? And those who want to destroy themselves have used that excuse to drink alcohol and smoke cigarettes, destroying their bodies, which is for God and should be kept holy for our God. Think of it! If the Believers were already drinking alcohol by little measure, why will Apostle Paul tell Timothy to use little wine for his stomach's sake (as a kind of soothing medicine, in that their ancient and unrefined medical practice)?

A WORD IS ENOUGH FOR THE WISE! Shall we continue to sin that grace may increase? (Rom. 6:1) Is faith without works not dead? (Jas 2:17). What will make Jesus Christ to tell those that had prophesied, cast out demons, and done mighty works in His Name, that He never knew them? (Matt. 7:21-23). Surely, they had known Christ before. I am not reducing righteousness and holiness to physical things, physical appearance, and dress code alone? Why did the Word of God put the sin of the flesh first before sin of spirit in Second Corinthians 7:1?

Some people say that we are laying unnecessary burdens on people. Which burden (if it were even to be a burden, as you think) is greater than sacrificing small things for Jesus Christ and Heaven? If you can't deny yourself of small things, because of Heaven, can you lay down your life for Jesus Christ? He who loves his life more than Christ Jesus is not worthy of Him.

By the way, have you ever seen it in the Bible that Apostle Paul gave ordinances to New Testament Believers? He wrote, saying, "Now I praise you, brethren, that you remember me in all things and keep the traditions (ordinances, the King James Version) just as I delivered them to you" (1 Cor. 11:2). Was he putting burdens on them? Certainly the Corinthian church was a 'Gentile' church.

Apostle Paul wrote: "But beware lest somehow this liberty of yours become a stumbling block to those who are weak. And because of your knowledge shall the weak brother perish, for whom Christ died? But when you thus sin against the brethren, and wound their weak conscience, you sin against Christ. Therefore, if food makes my brother stumble, I will never again eat meat, lest I make my brother stumble" (1 Cor. 8:9-13).

Writing to the Galatians, he said, "For you, brethren, have been called to liberty; only do not use liberty as an opportunity for the flesh, but through love serve one another. And those that are Christ's have crucified the flesh with its passions and desires. If we live in the Spirit, let us also walk in the Spirit" (Gal. 5:13,24,25).

Jesus Christ rebuked the scribes and the Pharisees, not because they paid tithes (because God commanded them to pay tithes), but because they neglected justice, mercy, and faith, while paying tithes (Matt. 23:23). Will you cancel tithe (for example), because they neglected justice, mercy, and faith? Certainly, no! Or you will still be disobeying God.

In other words, because somebody can dress virtuously and Godly like a Christian and still be evil, immoral, and wicked on the inside, will not cancel the fact and Truth that a Christian is to dress and appear like a Christian. By that, I mean that Christians and Believers are to dress decently, Godly, and Biblically. Inside and outside, you are to be like Christ – Christian.

As a woman, it is either you decide to worship and serve God in Spirit and Truth, or you join the rest of the women and ladies who follow their minds instead of the Mind of God. Writing to the Corinthians, Apostle Paul said, "But I fear, lest somehow, as the serpent deceived Eve by his craftiness, so your minds may be corrupted…" (2 Cor. 11:3).

The devil deceived Eve at the Garden of Eden by craftiness, just as he has been deceiving many women and ladies today, especially in the areas of indecent dressing and worldliness. When God told Adam and Eve to avoid the fruit of the tree of knowledge of good and bad, telling them that they will die any day they eat from the fruit, satan came afterwards to tell Eve: "You will not surely die…" (Gen. 3:4).

But what happened when they ate the fruit? They died spiritually, being separated from the Life of God. Apart from the spiritual death, God had intended that they live forever; however, when they disobeyed God, they could now die physically after some years. Though you may not see the punishment for your disobedience now, if you don't repent and change, know that you can't enter into the Kingdom of Heaven. Do you want to end in Hell after speaking in tongues and carrying Bible?

The Bible says, "For you were bought at a price; therefore glorify God in your body and in your spirit, which are God's (1 Cor. 6:20). But if you are led by the Spirit, you are not under the

Law (Gal. 5:18). Both your body and your spirit are God's – belong to God – and you have to glorify God in both of them.

Furthermore, it is those who are led by the Spirit of God who are not under the Law. The essence of God making us to not be under the Law is because He expects us to be led by His Spirit. But if your flesh and desires still lead you, then you are not led by the Holy Spirit; and there is danger.

The Book of Romans says that those who are led by the Spirit of God are those who are the sons of God. You wash both the outside and the inside of your plates. Why do you think of the opposite concerning God and His people? Certainly, God wants both the inside and the outside of His people to be clean, purified, and holy.

Many people talk against many things in the name of Old Testament; but they will readily teach about blessings from the twenty-eighth chapter of the Book of Deuteronomy, and expound tithes and offerings from the third chapter of the Book of Malachi – both in the New Testament.

Let us know that we have not arrived in Heaven yet; therefore, we are to be careful of how we live our lives and of the utterances we make, including how we think and reason. Let us always be open to the Holy Spirit to direct and lead us all the days of our lives till we see the Face of Jesus Christ in Heaven.

(For an in-depth Scriptural study on this subject, refer to the book: Indecent Dressing and Outward Appearance by GODSWORD GODSWILL ONU)

ABOUT THE BOOK

The Bible says that the Lord reveals what He wants to do to His Servants, the prophets. God warns us ahead of time concerning His Plans and Purposes, and concerning the plans and purposes of the devil. Reading through the Bible you will see many things that the Lord warned us, ahead of time, will happen. And many of these things are happening now. He loves us so much, that He warned us ahead of time, so that when they happen, we will not be taken unawares. One of the things that the Lord warned us of, is that there will be increase of lawlessness or iniquity in the last days, which will lead to the love of many Believers growing cold. But He has told us that he that endures to the end that shall be saved. The Lord told us that false prophets, teachers, and ministers will abound. There will be wars, rumours of wars, pestilences, and earthquakes in various places. He also let us know that we will be persecuted, and warned us to be ready for His Coming.

ABOUT THE AUTHOR

Apostle Godsword is the President and Overseer of WHOLE LIFE SPIRIT-WORD MINISTRIES (a.k.a. HOLY GHOST AND GODSWORD CHRISTIAN NETWORK). Godsword, a Teaching Prophet and Evangelist, is a Minister of the Lord Jesus Christ who believes in the Demonstration of the Spirit and Power and takes delight in the Declaration and Teaching of the Word and Will of God.

Godsword Godswill Onu studied Building Construction in his First Degree, and later had Master of Urban and Regional Planning (MURP) from Abia State University, Uturu.

BOOKS BY APOSTLE GODSWORD

1. *75 Great Biblical and Spiritual Truths (As Inspired by the Holy Ghost)*
2. *Preparing for Our Maker (The Cry of the Spirit and the Lord's Witness)*
3. *Lessons from the Seven Churches*
4. *Vessels and Instruments of Honour and Dishonour*
5. *Divine Protection*
6. *The Power-filled Life*
7. *From Glory to Glory*
8. *Always and Without Ceasing*
9. *The Whole Life from God to Men*
10. *Right and Wrong Thinking, Belief, and Confession*
11. *He Came to Set You Free*
12. *A Better Covenant Based on Better Promises*
13. *Apostles, Prophets, Evangelists, Pastors, and Teachers*
14. *Being Strong in the Lord*
15. *Real Freedom and Gain*
16. *Faithfulness and Diligence in Stewardship*
17. *Heirs of God and Joint-heirs with Christ*
18. *Open and Closed Heavens and Doors*
19. *A Heaven to Gain, and a Hell to Avoid*
20. *The Anointing and Power of the Holy Spirit*
21. *The Glory, Presence, and Power of God*
22. *The Fulness of the Blessing of the Gospel*
23. *Prosperity and Success*
24. *Seducing Spirits and Doctrines of Demons*
25. *My God and Father*
26. *The Works of the Flesh and Youthful Lusts*
27. *The Spiritual Christian*
28. *The Commandments of the Lord and Master*
29. *The Total Man*
30. *The Virtuous Woman*
31. *Contending with the Forces of Darkness*
32. *Developing a Strong Relationship with God*
33. *Secrets to God's Miracle-working Power*
34. *Concerning the Roman Catholics*
35. *Ministers-Workers Training Manual*
36. *The Christian Virtues*
37. *The God-approved Minister*
38. *Taking It by Force*
39. *God's Generals*
40. *Blessings, Curses, and Spiritual Attacks*
41. *Pressing Towards the Mark*
42. *My Father's Business*
43. *Walking in the Anointing*
44. *The Weapons and Armour of Our Warfare*
45. *Tithes and Offerings*
46. *Greater Levels and Glory (An Annual Reading)*
47. *God is Not from Any Nation*
48. *The Power and Authority of the Believer*

49. Sin, Disobedience, and Rebellion
50. Wisdom, Knowledge, and Understanding
51. The Christian Marriage and Home
52. Patience, Endurance, and Longsuffering
53. Indecent Dressing and Outward Appearance
54. Keys to Financial Prosperity
55. Witnesses and Ministers of the Word
56. False Prophets, Teachers, and Ministers
57. I Give You Dominion
58. Making Your Calling and Election Sure
59. Prayer and Fasting
60. Christians, Disciples, and Followers
61. Understanding the Strategies of Your Enemy
62. The Fruit of the Spirit
63. Obedience, Holiness, and Righteousness
64. Excellence in Life and Godliness
65. Being Led by the Holy Spirit
66. Knowing and Following God's Will
67. Manifesting God's Glory
68. Confronting Your Confrontations
69. The Church of Jesus Christ
70. Power Over All Devils and Evil
71. The Power of Faith
72. Filled with the Fulness of God
73. The Man of God
74. Signs and Wonders
75. Pursue, Overtake, and Recover
76. More Than Conquerors
77. Redefining Christianity
78. Prosperity in Every Area
79. Godliness
80. Being an Example to the Believers
81. Diligently Obeying the Voice of God
82. A Crown of Righteousness
83. Evangelism by Power
84. The Fellowship of Other Believers
85. The Kingdom of Light and of God
86. Casting Out Devils
87. A Friend of God
88. Watchfulness, Vigilance, and Sobriety
89. Perfecting the Saints
90. Called, Chosen, Faithful, and Glorified
91. Acts and Signs of Believers
92. Secrets to Successful Ministry
93. Preaching and Teaching the Word
94. The Work and Ministry of the Holy Spirit
95. Demonstration of the Spirit and Power
96. The Ministry of Angels
97. Walking Worthy of God
98. The Qualities of a Christian

99. Running the Race
100. The End-time Realities
101. The Ministry Gifts
102. Soldiers of Christ
103. Government by the People of God
104. Jesus Christ Comes Very Soon
105. Being Fruitful and Productive
106. The Unstoppable Christian and Minister
107. The Gifts of the Holy Spirit
108. Perfect and Blameless
109. The Kingdom of Darkness and of Satan
110. Divine Health and Healing
111. Tests, Temptations, Trials, and Wilderness Experiences
112. The Power of Prayer
113. The Manifestation of the Sons of God
114. The Lord Jesus Christ
115. The Word of the Living God
116. Love
117. Earnestly Contending for the Faith
118. Becoming a Prayer-warrior
119. Revival
120. Partakers of the Divine Nature
121. Fasting, Discipline, and Self-control
122. The Gifts and the Calling of God
123. Testing and Proving All Things
124. Pulling Down Strongholds
125. Giving to God and to Men
126. The Unsearchable Riches of Christ
127. From Faith to Faith
128. The More Abundant Life
129. Being on Fire for God
130. Agents of the Kingdom of Darkness
131. The Power of Spoken Words
132. Arise and Shine
133. There is Power in Praise
134. The Promises of the Lord
135. Spiritual Hunger and Thirst
136. The Untouchable Christian
137. The Overcomer
138. Commissioned with Power
139. Our Lord and Master
140. God Cares for You
141. Worshipping in Spirit and in Truth
142. Operating in the Supernatural
143. Repentance and Restitution
144. Warnings from the Lord
145. Divine Direction and Strategy
146. Power Encounter
147. Pleasing God
148. The God that Answers by Fire

149. Serving God, Your Maker
150. Speaking in Tongues and the Gift of Prophecy
151. The Life and Ministry of Jesus Christ
152. Apostle Paul's Life and Ministry
153. Lessons from the Life of Moses
154. Abraham, the Father of Faith
155. David, the Man After God's Own Heart
156. Peter, the Leader of the Apostles
157. Joseph, the Dreamer
158. Joshua, the Finisher of Moses' Assignment
159. Samuel, the Prophet and Judge of Israel
160. Job, God's Man
161. Prophets Elijah and Elisha
162. Adam, the First Man, and Noah, God's Favourite
163. Isaac and Jacob, the Patriarchs of Israel
164. Aaron and Barnabas, the Helpers of the Men of God
165. Daniel, Shadrach, Meshach, and Abed-Nego
166. Sarah, Deborah, Esther, Ruth, and Mary Magdalene
167. Miriam, Martha, and Sapphira
168. Isaiah, Jeremiah, and Ezekiel, the Prophets
169. Saul, Solomon, and Asa, the Kings Who Disappointed God
170. Jehoshaphat, Hezekiah, and Josiah, the Kings Who Pleased God
171. Stephen, the Martyr, and Philip, the Evangelist
172. Ahab, Nebuchadnezzar, and Herod, the Wicked Rulers
173. Gideon, Jephthah, and Samson
174. Ezra and Nehemiah, the Men Who Feared God
175. The Apostolic Ministry
176. The Prophetic Ministry
177. The Evangelistic Ministry
178. The Pastoral Ministry
179. The Teaching Ministry
180. Knowing and Understanding God
181. The Extraordinary Life
182. The Pathway to Good Leadership
183. The Christian Youth
184. False Religions, Beliefs, and Teachings
185. Witches and Wizards
186. Foundations
187. The Anointed
188. Spiritual Authority
189. None of Those Diseases and Sicknesses
190. The Power of Temperaments and Emotions
191. The Christian Rituals of Water Baptism, the Lord's Supper, Laying on of Hands, Etc
192. Dignity and Integrity
193. Tempted and Tried by the Devil
194. The Deliverance Ministry
195. The Healing Ministry
196. The Prayer Ministry
197. The Events of the End of Ages and Eternity

198. *The Music Ministry*
199. *The Laws of God's Kingdom*
200. *You Can Pay the Price!*
201. *Missions and Missionaries*
202. *Exceedingly Abundant Grace*
203. *Keep on Doing Good*
204. *Islam and Muslims*
205. *Fear Not!*
206. *Laying Up Treasures in Heaven*
207. *You Are a Watchman*
208. *Fulfilment*
209. *You Are God's Battleaxe*
210. *The Name of the Lord*
211. *God Has the Final Say!*
212. *The Blood of Jesus Christ*
213. *Sunday School and Bible Study Manual*
214. *Altars, Spiritual Gates, and Covenants*
215. *Enduring to the End to Be Saved*
216. *Destroying the Works of the Destroyer*
217. *Visions and Dreams*
218. *The Pathway to Greatness*
219. *Should We Send Back to Sender?*
220. *Vows, Oaths, and Swearing*
221. *Comforting and Encouraging One Another*
222. *Do You Really Love God?*
223. *Backsliding and Falling Away*
224. *Why Bad Things Happen to Good People*
225. *Mastering and Defeating Weak Points*
226. *Conditions for Answered Prayers*
227. *Rejoice in the Lord Always!*
228. *Watch and Pray!*
229. *Waiting Upon the Lord*
230. *Looking Up Unto God!*
231. *The Spirit of Love, Mercy, and Grace*
232. *Orderliness*

Any of the titles (ebooks) can be bought/downloaded immediately. And the printed books, if it is not available at your local bookstore, can be ordered.

NEVER PIRATE ANY OF THE EBOOKS/BOOKS!

For enquiry, you may contact Apostle Godsword Godswill Onu, by calling or texting him on +2348030917546.

Printed in Germany
by Amazon Distribution
GmbH, Leipzig